A Thoughtful Profession

A Thoughtful Profession

The Early Years of the American Philosophical Association

JAMES CAMPBELL

OPEN COURT
Chicago and La Salle, Illinois

To order books from Open Court, call 1-800-815-2280
or visit www.opencourtbooks.com.

Open Court Publishing Company is a division of Carus Publishing Company.

© 2006 by Carus Publishing Company

First printing 2006

Printed and bound in the United States of America.

Buildings from the following college campuses are pictured: University of Virginia,
p. xii; Cornell University, p. 16; Yale University, p. 276.

Library of Congress Cataloging-in-Publication Data

Campbell, James, 1948-
  A thoughtful profession : the early years of the American Philosophical
Association / James Campbell.
     p. cm.
  Summary: "Chronicles the activities of the American philosophical
associations founded at the beginning of the twentieth century that merged
into the present American Philosophical Assocation in 1927. The field of
philosophy's development as a profession, its relation to domestic and
international politics, and the evolution of its ideas and ideals are discussed"—
Provided by publisher.
  Includes bibliographical references and index.
  ISBN-13: 978-0-8126-9602-8 (trade paper : alk. paper)
  ISBN-10: 0-8126-9602-6 (trade paper : alk. paper)
  1. American Philosophical Association—History—20th century.
  2. Philosophy, American—Societies, etc.—History—20th century.
  3. Philosophy—United States—Societies, etc.—History—20th century.
  I. Title.
     B11.C36 2006
     106'.073—dc22

                                                              2006023000

For Patrick J. Hill—
builder of community

Contents

Preface

*We operate in an environment in which philosophers
constitute an organized professional group. That organized
professional group did not exist one hundred years ago—it
is a modern development, the occurrence of which is itself
a major part of the history of philosophy in America.*

— Murray G. Murphey, "Toward an Historicist History
of American Philosophy"

What follows is a philosophical history of the American Philosophical
Association—or a professional history of philosophy in America—from the
end of the nineteenth century until the mid-1920s. As a philosophical history of the APA for the years in question, this volume considers the importance of four major philosophical movements: common-sensism, the
inherited philosophical stance that was virtually eliminated when philosophy teaching became an academic, rather than a pastoral, activity; idealism,
the powerful tide of systematic inquiry that expanded the area of the philosophical landscape and heightened the intellectual respectability of philosophical claims; pragmatism, the attempt to maintain the importance of
individuals and their lives in philosophical work and to connect up philosophical inquiries with those in psychology and the other areas of social
thought; and realism, the defense, in the face of the prior two movements,
of the pursuit of an uninfluenced and uninfluencible 'something' beyond
the range of human input, especially as it is found in mathematics and
logic. As a professional history of philosophy, it considers the ideas of the
major figures on the American philosophical scene, the nature and possibilities of philosophical progress, the place of philosophy in academe, the
aims of the association, the nature of higher education in America, the role
of intelligence and of intellectuals in society, World War I as a moral and
philosophical event, and so on.

This is one of many possible accounts of the history of the APA. Others have been written,[1] and I hope that still others will be. William James notes, in rejecting any attempt to tell a final story in metaphysics, that "[t]he word 'and' trails along after every sentence. Something always escapes. 'Ever not quite' has to be said of the best attempts made anywhere in the universe at attaining all-inclusiveness."[2] The same is at least as true when chronicling the progress of any human endeavor. No story of an event or a discovery, of a life or an institution, is the final one. "Something always escapes" to await a later chronicler.

This history that I have written avoids, I hope, two extremes. On the one hand, it is not simply an institutional history, as someone (or, more likely, a committee) might write to detail the corporate adventures of Proctor & Gamble or General Motors. Such a history of the APA would emphasize meeting locales and presidents, numbers of members and of papers read at meetings, the fiscal well-being of the association, and all the other practical business over the years. The APA's real 'business,' if that notion is not improper, is the development, care, and transmission of the philosophical ideas that are vital to the lives of the citizens in a democratic republic; and, in its history, the institutional aspects are but the framework. On the other hand, this is not simply a history of American philosophy or philosophy in America from late in the nineteenth century until the mid-1920s. Such a book could quite legitimately overlook all of the significant institutional developments, and their social context, that did not have a direct influence on the development of philosophical ideas.

Throughout the writing of this volume, my primary goal has been to help contemporary philosophers better understand the state of philosophy in America during the years that philosophy teaching was becoming a profession. A second intention of this study has been to enable other philosophers, less interested in the history of American philosophy than I am, to develop—through a better understanding of the history of the APA—an informed sense of the possible directions that the association might follow as it moves into the future.

There are many incomplete aspects to this study. This is perhaps appropriate for a history of an association that has never attained—although it has on a number of occasions pursued—unanimity of purpose. Individuals and themes approach and recede, often without full introductions or clear dispositions, as happens in institutional life where multiple levels of activ-

---

[1] Prior histories of this intellectual terrain include: Harry Norman Gardiner, "The First Twenty-Five Years of the APA"; Edward I. Pitts, "The Profession of Philosophy in America"; and Daniel J. Wilson, *Science, Community and the Transformation of American Philosophy, 1860–1930*. Full bibliographic information can be found in the list of works cited below.

[2] James, *Pluralistic Universe*, 145.

ity coexist at all times. Further, many of the notes contain comments with which I am not necessarily in agreement, but that add depth to the picture. Some of these loose ends I hope to tie down in future studies; all of them remain, of course, available to poachers.

This book owes its origins to the centennial efforts of the APA, especially to its History Committee—under the direction of Marcus G. Singer and, later, Andrew J. Reck—that offered me guidance and support as my efforts took shape. The National Office of the APA at the University of Delaware similarly offered me its support, and free access to its very modest historical archives. This material initially appeared in the form of a series of six talks that I offered at the various meetings of the APA throughout the country in 1998–2000. At no time has either the History Committee or the National Office attempted to influence either my interpretation or my presentation of the history of the early years of the APA.

While almost all of the material for this study comes from published sources, I gained access to some of it through the cooperation of a number of archives. My gratitude is due to the archivists and librarians at: the American Philosophical Society, the Boston Public Library, Columbia University, the University of Illinois, and Smith College. Permission to quote from archival materials was granted by the American Philosophical Society and Smith College, for which I am also grateful.

Portions of this study have previously appeared in *Teaching Philosophy* and *The Transactions of the Charles S. Peirce Society*. I am grateful to the editors of those journals both for initially publishing the essays and for consenting to their reworking here.

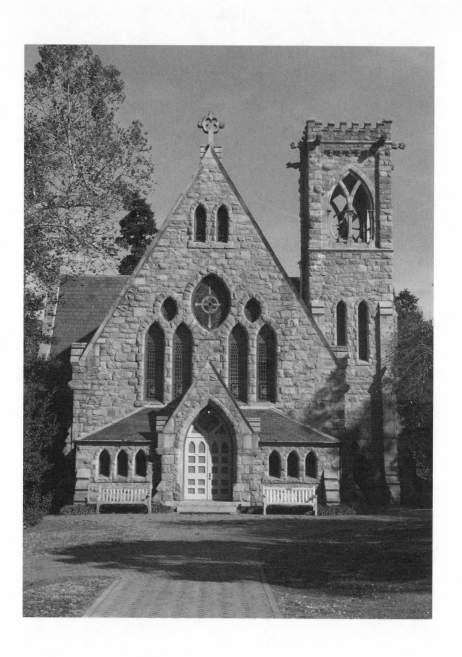

1

What Philosophy in America
Had Been

Humans like simple histories; and philosophers, being humans, like them too. Unfortunately, simple histories are of little use in understanding who we are or where we come from. The history of American philosophy is, in particular, no simple story, although we often see it presented as such. When we look at what Harvey Gates Townsend in 1934 calls "the sprawling largeness of present philosophical discussions," we tend—as he did—to think that there is more clarity to be found in what he calls "the smallness of the past."[1] To do so, however, is to forget that what might appear as "smallness" from our temporal distance has always been a "sprawling largeness" to its contemporaries. The history of American philosophy was never a simple story; it is made simple only by our lack of knowledge or interest or sympathy.

Still, if the past is to be understood at all, if its "sprawling largeness" is ever to be brought under intellectual control, history's complexity must be simplified and shaped into a coherent story. A particular time frame must be chosen and certain important themes emphasized. As to the former, to understand the situation of American philosophy and higher education at the beginning of the twentieth century, it will be necessary to go back a bit further. We need not go back much further, however, if we can trust the view often expressed at the time that higher education in English-speaking America had changed more in the last few decades than it had over all the years since its start in 1636. As to the latter, the story involves two central themes, the system of the 'old-time' colleges that had come to dominate higher education and the philosophical program known as 'common-sense' realism.

---

[1] Townsend, *Philosophical Ideas*, iii. (Full bibliographical information can be found in the list of works cited below.)

The purpose of this chapter and the next is to portray what it was like to be a philosopher and philosophy teacher in the years leading up to the founding of the Western Philosophical Association in 1900 and the American Philosophical Association in 1901. My emphasis in this chapter will be upon the inherited meaning of philosophy and the role that it had played in American culture and higher education. In the second chapter I will consider those factors that were changing philosophy's meaning and role.

Scottish common-sense realism originated in the work of Thomas Reid, Dugald Stewart, William Hamilton, and others who, although they are largely forgotten now, created a powerful philosophical perspective that was primary in the United States for most of the nineteenth century. The common-sense philosophers were empirically inclined thinkers who recognized in the work of John Locke the roots of serious problems. While these philosophers believed that it was possible to learn from his respect for experience and his principles of inquiry, they also believed that his starting point ultimately forced the abandonment of the causal order of nature and other aspects of our common-sense world. As Edward H. Madden writes:

> Locke's premise is that the only things of which we are directly aware are our own ideas, impressions, sensations, phenomena, or whatever else the alleged non-physical entity of direct awareness insisted upon might be called. Once granted this premise, the slippery slope from Locke to Berkeley to Hume's scepticism is inevitable. Since no sensation can in principle in any way resemble an object, Locke's representative realism is untenable and we are left with the equally untenable alternatives: Berkeley's subjective idealism . . . or Hume's scepticism . . .

For common sense, our world is not one of epistemological guarantees; but, by and large, our knowledge is secure. Epistemology is the study of what we can know, not the vestibule to skepticism. Common-sensism realizes that the many problems that can be uncovered in the work of Locke— for example, solid tables that dissolve into primary and secondary qualities and the difficulties of perspectival error—need not lead us to skepticism. There is a world independent of us, and it contains the furniture of our experiences. When the conditions are right, there is real knowledge; and we can learn what the 'right' conditions are by comparing multiple experiences. General skepticism does not arise because of the orderliness and continuity of our ongoing world, a world that was founded ultimately upon theological guarantees. Given this practical tone, it should be no surprise that of greatest interest to those who adopted common-sensism seems to have been its rejection of moral skepticism.[2]

---

[2] Madden, "Common Sense School," 447; cf. "Metaphilosophy of Commonsense"; Johnston, introduction to *Selections from the Scottish Philosophy*; Marsden, *Soul of the*

The most important representative of common-sense realism in our time frame was James McCosh, who came from Belfast to assume the presidency of Princeton in 1868. He begins his two-volume 1887 study, *Realistic Philosophy*, with three fundamental claims. First, he tells us that for realism "there are real things" and we can "know them." Hume, he writes, began "with mere impressions or ideas, and thereby, of purpose, landed us in scepticism or what would now be called agnosticism . . ." Kant, on the other hand, started "with phenomena, in the sense of appearances, and tried from these to reach things, but utterly failed to extract reality from what had no reality." Both of these approaches are necessarily futile. "If we are ever to get hold of reality, we must seize it at once." This is what common-sensism does. "Realism holds that the mind perceives matter." As a result, he continues, "[w]e have no need to resort to such theories as those of intermediate ideas or occasional causes coming between the perceiving mind and the perceived object." Such approaches are twice flawed, "brought in to remove supposed difficulties which do not exist, and have only introduced real difficulties." McCosh's second realistic claim is that "we have an immediate knowledge of self in a particular state." This does not mean, he writes, that "we know Self apart from a mode of self . . ." Rather, we know the self in action: "under a certain sensation, or . . . remembering, or thinking, or deciding, . . . in joy or in sorrow." Further, he writes, realism recognizes that "in Memory we know things as having been before us in time past, and do thus know Time as mixed up with the event in time from which it can be separated by an easy process of abstraction." His third claim is that realism maintains that "[w]e know certain voluntary acts as being Morally Good or Evil, say as being just or unjust, benevolent or cruel, candid or deceitful." In other words, mind "perceives benevolence, and perceives it to be good, as clearly as the eye perceives objects to be extended." The goal of common-sensism is, for McCosh, to develop a set of certain truths based upon a series of tests— self-evidence, necessity, and universality—that will enable us to resist the philosophical and religious dangers of skepticism and idealism.[3]

McCosh believed that common-sensism had indeed attained this goal. As he writes in 1875, "Scottish philosophy . . . has by patience and shrewdness succeeded is establishing a body of fundamental truth, which can never be shaken, but which shall stand as a bulwark in philosophy, morals, and theology, as long as time endures." Some twenty years later, in 1894,

---

American University, 90–93; Meyer, *Instructed Conscience*, 35–42; Riley, *American Philosophy*, 475–79.

[3] McCosh, *Realistic Philosophy*, 1:5–7; cf. 34–36; *First and Fundamental Truths*, 16–18; "Scottish Philosophy," 329–31; Flower and Murphey, *History of Philosophy in America*, 1:208–15.

Granville Stanley Hall discussed what he took to be the meaning of common-sensism. While not favorably inclined toward its truth claims, he writes that the success of common-sensism was quite understandable in the American context:

> As Berkeley's problem widened into Hume's scepticism and that went on to Kant and heroic age of German philosophy, American professors drew back. The Scotch philosophy represented by Reid, Stewart, Brown, and Hamilton, opened a far safer way. The "common sense," which was its watchword, contained an immediate conviction of right and wrong, of the reality of the external world, freedom, etc., about which there was no need or warrant for debate or doubt, while its discussion of association, desire, will, and feeling, was lucidity itself, and fitted our practical country and had a wider vogue here than in Scotland itself . . . It has no quarrel with religion, is not unsettling, is full of stimulus to the young, and opens but does not close the mind against future growth.

We can surely understand why a largely frontier society would develop a strong affinity for a philosophy that offered clear and quick answers to questions of knowledge and conduct, even if it did so by ceding much of its philosophical responsibility to theological control. Central to common-sensism was the belief that Protestant Christianity was correct, and that its Bible was correct, and that whatever was true about the world—that is, whatever science might discover—would ultimately have to agree with the Scriptures. Consequently, educators could concern themselves more with the development of their charges into Christian gentlemen, who could defend their faith if challenged, than with the production of intellectuals and scholars who would seek to uncover the new. The negative aspects of the common-sense approach became especially true after the publication of *The Origin of Species* in 1859.[4]

The standard view of later commentators has been that the orthodoxy of Scottish common-sense realism is of little interest for understanding the developing history of American philosophy. The general reasons offered for this position are two. First, as we have just seen, the *content* of this common-sense realism was viewed as compromised: instead of doing 'real' philosophy, these philosophers were offering a kind of apologetics for religious and political conservatism.[5] Second, the *locus* of the philosophizing

---

[4] McCosh, *Scottish Philosophy*, 11; Hall, "On the History," 158. Cf. Elizabeth Flower and Murray G. Murphey: "Convinced that conflict between true science and true theology was impossible, the Scots were at once fearlessly empirical and naively sure that the results of such empiricism would always turn out to support Protestant theology" (*History of Philosophy in America*, 1:xvii; cf. Townsend, *Philosophical Ideas*, 75).

[5] John Dewey writes that, even at his reasonably liberal University of Vermont, "the

was isolated from the broader life of the community. In the college setting, philosophy became an academic subject, something smoothed out so as to be teachable to the young and uninterested. Morris Raphael Cohen addresses both of these themes in 1921, writing that common-sense realism "did not depart widely from the popular views as to the nature of the material world, the soul, and God." Rather than being intellectually vigorous, it avoided "subtle arguments" and appealed to "established beliefs." As a result, common-sensism "could easily be reconciled with the most literal interpretation of the Bible and could thus be used as a club against freethinkers." Similarly, he notes that it was very effective in structuring the recitations of "adolescent minds" because it "eliminated all disturbing doubts by direct appeal to the testimony of consciousness, and readily settled all questions by elevating disputed opinions to indubitable principles." Cohen summarizes his interpretation of common-sensism as follows: "To the modern reader it is all an arid desert of commonplace opinion covered with the dust of pedantic language."[6]

Another commentator who offers this standard view is Herbert Wallace Schneider. He introduces his discussion of common-sense realism in 1946 as follows: "To recognize wormy knowledge when one sees it is not difficult, but to explain critically what causes philosophy to putrify and why it continues to exist in a decayed state is a difficult and disagreeable task, for it is not easy to define the life of an idea and it is not pleasant to look for signs of life among skeletons." Sometime in the nineteenth century, he continues, "philosophy lost its living connections with the general culture of the American people and became a technical discipline in academic curricula." Whereas philosophers in the eighteenth century had been "investigators (either natural or moral)," in the nineteenth century they became "professors of philosophy." By this term, Schneider means classroom teachers whose "ambition was to be orthodox, to teach the truth, i.e., to instruct their students in correct doctrine by relying on the best authors, by using systematic texts, and by inventing precise terminologies." In 1952, Joseph Leon Blau offers a third example of the standard interpretation of common-sense realism, with an emphasis on its role in the classroom. He writes that systematic instruction

> requires that in addition to concern for system there must be concern for teaching. The materials had to be organized and reduced to teachable form.

---

teaching of philosophy had become more restrained in tone, more influenced by the still dominant Scottish school. Its professor, Mr. H. A. P. Torrey . . . said: 'Undoubtedly pantheism is the most satisfactory form of metaphysics intellectually, but it goes counter to religious faith'" ("From Absolutism to Experimentalism," 14).

   [6] Cohen, "Later Philosophy," 229.

Textbooks of philosophy were produced in great numbers . . . These textbooks were responsible for a major change in the perspective of the study of philosophy. Under their sway, philosophy was considered as a body of material to be learned by the students and recited to the teachers . . . there were "truths" to be presented and illustrated, not the search for and love of wisdom . . . Before this time, philosophy had been a search for wisdom, not a subject matter; it was a method of approach to problems, not a study of conclusions.

Philosophy as it was practiced in these colleges was not the living activity of speculating minds addressing new issues. If we want philosophically interesting materials, we will need to look elsewhere.[7]

The standard history of American academic philosophy suggests that for most of the nineteenth century interesting philosophical work was taking place independently of the colleges. Blau, for example, writes that philosophy in America "has grown as much outside of academic circles as it has within the colleges and universities."[8] Particularly with regard to the years within our present focus, and especially if we follow the accounts of those who lived through these years, we get the impression of an academic wasteland surrounded by a series of intellectual high points, all of which were outside of academe. At a distance from the prying eyes of the college guardians who would safeguard the intellectual and religious orthodoxy of the young men of the community, it was possible for freethinkers to gather into groups and to speculate in ways that were more 'romantic' and 'idealistic.' The names of these philosophical movements are familiar; and they represent the enduring material of American philosophy until perhaps the 1890s. There was Transcendentalism, the glorious flowering of New England. There was the Platonist movement in Illinois. There were Hegelians throughout the Midwest, with centers in Cincinnati and St. Louis. The latter location was the home of William Torrey Harris's seminal organ of philosophical exploration, *The Journal of Speculative Philosophy* (1867–93). There was the later amalgam of Transcendentalism and Hegelian thought at the Concord School of Philosophy (1879–88). There was Thomas Davidson and the Glenmore School. There was the Ethical Culture Movement. And, of course, there was the Metaphysical Club of Chauncey Wright, Charles Sanders Peirce, William James, and others in Cambridge. Each of these centers of philosophical inquiry,

---

[7] Schneider, *History of American Philosophy*, 195–96; Blau, *Men and Movements*, 80–81. Cf. Isaac Woodbridge Riley: "not only was the philosophy of reality convenient, compact and teachable, appealing to a common sense of which every youngster had some spark, but it was also an eminently safe philosophy which kept undergraduates locked in so many intellectual dormitories, safe from the dark speculations of materialism or the beguiling allurements of idealism" (*American Philosophy*, 477).

[8] Blau, *Men and Movements*, v.

although often disparaged as 'amateur' endeavors, provided evidence that, for many, the academic philosophy of the time could not adequately speak to all of the elements of American culture.[9]

It remains possible, of course, to reconsider the blanket condemnation of common-sensism contained in the 'standard view' that we have been surveying; and, when we recall that the philosophical figures upon whom we are to focus reacted to it in an almost uniformly negative fashion, we must at least recognize the importance of its influence. Here we have the help of a number of commentators who work outside of the inherited view. Some of these individuals are interested primarily in historical accuracy. In any consideration of the history of American philosophy, they remind us, the main philosophical movement for a century cannot be overlooked— even if that line of inquiry appears to later chroniclers to have been a 'dead end.' To fail to recognize this is to fail to understand the difference between real history and popular fiction. A more philosophically sympathetic reading of common-sensism suggests that, once we place ourselves in the situation of its practitioners and address their problems with the tools available to them, we will recognize in its workings a series of interesting and creative solutions. We may thus uncover, perhaps, valuable possibilities not found elsewhere. A still more sympathetic reading finds actual value in the work of the early common-sense realists, emphasizing their turning from the primacy of revelation in Calvinism to the modified humanism of 'mental' philosophy.[10] Whether we need to go this far is a matter for another time, however; and my emphasis on the centrality of common-sensism is primarily based on a recognition of its historical importance in the American college.

The institution that lent itself to the propagation of this common-sense philosophy was the 'old-time' college of nineteenth-century America. Of

---

[9] For material on these movements, readers may consult, in addition to the studies by Blau, Flower and Murphey, Riley, Schneider, and Townsend already mentioned: Anderson, *Platonism in the Midwest*; Easton, *Hegel's First American Followers*; Harmon, *Social Philosophy*; Pochman, *German Culture in America*; and Wiener, *Evolution and the Founders of Pragmatism*.

[10] Cf. Flower and Murphey: "this realism is now uniformly regarded as a wasteland of secondhand ideas servicing orthodox Calvinism . . . far from being a drag on the American Enlightenment, Common Sense Realism was a part of it. It was integral to that astonishing burst of intellectual energy that began in Scotland in the early eighteenth century and extended well into the nineteenth . . . The 'Wasteland' criticisms . . . [i]n part . . . are a justified reaction to the stereotyped picture of the movement given by some of the tag-end epigoni of Scottish Realism itself, above all—whatever else his virtues—by James McCosh, the immensely influential president of Princeton who made himself the official biographer of the movement" (*History of Philosophy in America*, 1: 203–5; cf. Ahlstrom, "Scottish Philosophy and American Theology"; Duncan, "Eighteenth-Century Scottish Philosophy"; Haldane, "American Philosophy"; Kuklick, *Churchmen and Philosophers*).

course, there was no such single entity as *the* old-time college: even before
the Civil War, there were all sorts of differences among the two hundred
or so colleges then existing, and each was evolving in response to different
factors and according to a different rate of change.[11] Still, the simplifica-
tion is a useful one if used with care. It is thus safe to say that such institutions were religious in their orientation—not seminaries, of course—but
institutions that emphasized religion and morals. Noah Porter, for example, writes in 1870 that "the American Colleges should have a positively
religious and Christian character . . . a religious college will, in the long
run, if all else is equal, do more for science and culture than the college
which sets aside or makes little of religious influence and of Christian
truth."[12] It is also safe to say that the overall aim of the old-time college
was to ensure the supply of leaders for the future well-being of society. The
specific goal was to prepare young men for careers in the ministry, law, and
medicine.[13] The schools were quite small, and admission was based on
adequate preparation for the inherited curriculum. These colleges offered
their students the classics and mathematics and bits of science; but the
imparting of academic knowledge was not always the main interest. Nor
should the instructor concern himself much with the discovery of new
knowledge. Only rarely, writes Franklin Carter in 1881, is "the progress of
truth . . . sacrificed by the teacher's laborious occupation to the training of
the immature . . ." In most cases, fulfilling his primary classroom duty
keeps that teacher "from the pride of learning, that too often results in the
mere discoverer of truth, left alone to develop his own powers and to
delight in his own progress."[14] The focus in the college was on developing the students' mental discipline by memorizing and recitation.

Underlying this emphasis upon mental discipline was an understanding
of psychology that divided human mental powers into a set of 'faculties'
that could be developed by deliberate effort. As D. H. Meyer writes, "The
various faculties of mind, grouped under reason, the emotions, and will,
were thought to be, like muscles, susceptible of improvement through
exercise."[15] McCosh, for example, writes that educating the faculties

---

[11] Cf. Blau, introduction to Wayland, *Elements of Moral Science*, ix–xii.

[12] Porter, *American Colleges*, 208, 224.

[13] Cf. James Burrill Angell: "formerly few went to college except those intended for one
of the three professions,—law, medicine, or the ministry. But now [1890] men looking to
every pursuit wisely take the college course" ("Religious Life," 370).

[14] Carter, *College as Distinguished from the University*, 19; cf. Hofstadter, *Age of the
College*, 226–32; Metzger, *Age of the University*, 277–83; George P. Schmidt, "Intellectual
Crosscurrents," 47–48.

[15] Meyer, *Instructed Conscience*, 66–67. Cf. Alexander Meiklejohn: "the theory of mental training is a 'gymnastic' theory of mind. It is a notion drawn from analogy with the body.
Just as the arm may, by exercise, develop strength which may then be used for many purposes,

"should be one of the aims, one of the main aims, of education." These faculties, he continues, "are in the first instance mere capacities with a tendency to act. They are in infants in the form of a seed, or germ, or norm, and need to be cherished in order to grow and to be useful." Trying to determine the exact number of these faculties need not detain us. McCosh notes, for example, "*It is difficult to form a classification of the faculties which deserves to be regarded as complete,*" and he offers a "provisional division" that yields six: the cognitive (sense perception, self-consciousness), the representative (retention, association), the comparative (identity, space, time, causation), conscience, the emotions, and the will.[16] The important point is that the job of the old-time college was to develop these inchoate faculties to their full potential through discipline. One of the most explicit defenses of mental discipline was offered by McCosh in his inaugural address at Princeton in 1868, in which he asserts: "I do hold it to be the highest end of the University to *educate*; that is, draw out and improve the faculties which God has given." To fulfill this sacred duty, the college

> should seek specially to stimulate, and strengthen by exercising, the intellectual powers; such as the generalizing or classifying, by which we arrange the things that present themselves into groups, ordinate and co-ordinate; and the abstracting, analyzing capacities by which we reduce the complexities that meet us to a few comprehensible and manageable elements; and the reasoning faculty by which we rise from the known and the present to the unknown and remote.

Only secondary to this "highest end" of education is the transmission of knowledge. "Under this, it should be the aim of a University to impart knowledge," McCosh continues, "I say *under this*, in order to impose the proper limit on the principle held by so many in the present day, that a college should give itself mainly . . . to practical knowledge . . . the various branches of physics, or . . . of natural science."[17] Porter also emphasizes the broad value of disciplinary training. "The discipline which is required

---

such as throwing a ball, wielding a pen, holding a plow, so the mind and its various faculties may, by proper training, be increased in power, which may then be expended wherever demand may call . . . the mind has many faculties, each doing its own part of the mental toil, each of these may be strengthened thru exercise . . ." ("Is Mental Training a Myth?" 128).

[16] McCosh, *Psychology*, 16, 13, 15. Cf. George Trumbull Ladd: "To speak of mental faculties . . . is, at bottom, a rather mythological way of saying: I know (by memory and self-consciousness) that my mental life assumes a variety of recurrent forms, more or less like or unlike to each other; and I know (by inference from observed physical signs) that the mental life of others assumes a similar variety of the same recurrent forms" (*Psychology*, 50).

[17] McCosh, *American Universities*, 6–8; cf. Kolesnik, *Mental Discipline*, 89–112; Veysey, *Emergence of the American University*, 21–56.

for the higher education is not a simple gymnastic to the intellect, it is not the training of the curious philologist, or the sharp logician," he writes. Rather, "it is a liberalizing discipline which prepares for culture and thought, and which gradually lifts the mind from the hard and dry paradigms of the pedagogue, and the enforced syntax of the class-room, to the comparative judgment and the aesthetic culture of the philosopher and critic."[18] Education in the old-time college was thus a process of inculcation through memorization and recitation of the central cultural values of the community, with religious and moral values being primary.[19] As such, a general education in the liberal arts with a strong moral component seemed appropriate.

The curriculum of the old-time college can be considered in a series of snapshots given by former students. In 1903, Nicholas Murray Butler, who graduated from Columbia in 1882 and became its president twenty years later, reports that the college was designed to continue the work of the high school. "The college course, properly so called," he writes, consisted centrally of "Latin, Greek, and mathematics, some English literature and rhetoric, a little logic, a little political economy, a little moral philosophy, and, usually, a little mental philosophy or metaphysics." Other offerings included chemistry and "a combination of mechanics and physics called natural philosophy." History, Butler reports, "unless it was ancient history, played a small part, and the modern European languages were rarely included." In another report offered in 1930, George Herbert Palmer writes of his matriculation at Harvard in 1860:

> Nearly all its studies were prescribed, and these were chiefly Greek, Latin, and Mathematics. There was one course in Modern History, one in Philosophy, a half course in Economics. There was no English Literature, but in the Sophomore year three hours a week were required in Anglo-Saxon. A feeble course or two in Modern Languages was allowed to those who wished it. There were two or three courses in Natural Science, taught without laboratory work.

Palmer further notes, "All courses were taught from textbooks and by recitations"; and, perhaps in defense of what he recognized was a very bad situation, he remarks that the curriculum at Harvard "was no worse than

---

[18] Porter, *American Colleges*, 46–47. Cf. James McCosh: "Having seen that there are *a priori* truths in mathematics, the mind will be better prepared to admit that there are eternal and unchangeable principles lying at the basis of morality and religion . . ." (*American Universities*, 20).

[19] Cf. Franklin Carter: "exercises . . . [are] . . . not merely a means of mental training but of moral development. The habit of monotonous obedience and the acceptation of uniform limitations are two of life's most valuable lessons" (*College as Distinguished from the University*, 20–21).

in other colleges . . ." In a third account, James Hayden Tufts looks back in 1930 on his undergraduate study at Amherst from 1880–84. He writes that while the curriculum "had been partially liberalized by the introduction of a considerable number of elective courses," still "the spirit of the college remained much as it had been in the days of its founders, sixty years earlier." This meant that the young scholars "studied the Classics, mathematics, the basal natural sciences, the modern languages and literatures," and in their senior year "all students had the course in philosophy." Tufts further notes that "the outstanding feature of the college, as I now picture its atmosphere and its influence, was the religious seriousness."[20]

The faculty of the old-time college was small, often five or six for a student body of one hundred or so, and the few instructors were generalists. Each faculty member possessed more than a casual familiarity with all of the material taught in the college: he had studied all of it himself a few years earlier.[21] In most cases, a casual understanding of the material was all that was necessary. As Richard J. Storr writes:

> the customary method of instruction [was] by recitation . . . drill . . . A college with a prescribed course taught by recitation did not need a great variety of specialists, who, after receiving the Bachelor's degree, had studied systematically for academic careers . . . The typical campus figure was the general scholar with a B.A. degree and, perhaps, some theological training. He might possess wisdom as well as scholarship, ripened during many hours of midnight work; but the student could not assume that the professor was prepared to offer advanced courses.[22]

In our attempts to understand the old-time college, recognizing its need for having 'safe' instructors is just as important as noting its low level of scholarship.[23] Colleges, ever mindful of their social role, routinely hired as their presidents ministers who were to guide the intellectual and religious

---

[20] Butler, "American College," 12; Palmer, introduction to *Contemporary American Philosophy*, 20; Tufts, "What I Believe," 336.

[21] Cf. Carl Lotus Becker: "College faculties were composed, with some notable exceptions, of men who were entirely competent to teach by this [rote] method, since they had suffered an extremely competent training in it" (*Cornell University*, 17).

[22] Storr, *Beginnings of Graduate Education*, 3–4. Cf. David Starr Jordan: "A candidate for a chair in an Illinois college demanded of the Board of Trustees that he must be allowed some time for study. He was not elected; for the Board said that they wanted no man who had to study his lessons. They wanted a professor who knew already all that he had to teach" (*Trend of the American University*, 18–19).

[23] Cf. Rand B. Evans: "The professor, particularly the professor who taught moral philosophy, had to be 'safe,' holding to the orthodox tenets of the trustees, one who could present the facts of moral philosophy without the danger of leading students to irreligion or scepticism. The Scottish philosophy, with its appeal to common sense, was quite amenable to this new orthodox fervor, since its concepts avoided the skeptical pitfall of an unrestrained Locke, Berkeley, or Hume" ("Origins of American Academic Psychology," 36).

life of the institution. Part of this guidance involved the hiring and over-sight of the instructors.[24] Another part involved teaching the senior course in moral philosophy.

The moral philosophy course—often an array of courses that more or less filled out the senior year's studies—was understood as having a job to do in this conception of education: to demonstrate the unity of truth and to put the final touches on the education of the Christian gentleman. As Tufts indicated, philosophy was usually a subject taught to all students in their senior year. Of course, he did not need to remind his 1930 audience of the fact that this philosophy course was almost always offered by the col-lege president—himself almost always a clergyman—in a fashion more dogmatic than philosophical, to insure the inculcation of the proper inter-pretation of the material.[25] As George P. Schmidt writes in 1936, "The loosely organized moral philosophy course, with its core of ethics and its smattering of logic and literary criticism, of political, economic, and psy-chological data, mostly derived from the old Aristotelian categories, offered limitless opportunities to the ingenious teacher."[26] This introduc-tory examination of philosophical themes under the protective constraints of common-sense realism was, except for the very few students who went on to study in a theological school or in Europe, just about the only explic-itly philosophical content they would encounter in their academic careers.[27] Douglas Sloan writes, "The foremost task of the moral philoso-pher was to demonstrate to his students that humans are fundamentally moral creatures and that man's ethical striving is undergirded and sus-

---

[24] Cf. Charles William Eliot: "The most important function of the President is that of advising the Corporation concerning appointments, particularly about appointments of young men who have not had time and opportunity to approve themselves to the public. It is in discharging this duty that the President holds the future of the University in his hands. He cannot do it well unless he have insight, unless he be able to recognize, at times beneath some crusts, the real gentleman and the natural teacher" (*Educational Reform*, 35–36; cf. "American Education since the Civil War," 4–5; George P. Schmidt, *Old Time College President*, 184–225; Reuben, *Making of the Modern University*, 157, 201).

[25] Cf. George Stuart Fullerton: "what has traditionally been regarded as the most digni-fied of the sciences could best be taught by the man who held the most dignified position in the college. It is thus that one might set a redheaded man to teaching the theory of colors, or a tall man, long division. But a little thought makes it evident that the practice . . . is by no means so senseless as it appears . . . it does not seem absurd that the president of a college is made the custodian of the morals and of the religious and philosophical opinions of the stu-dent" ("Aim of Philosophy Teaching," 19–20).

[26] George P. Schmidt, "Intellectual Crosscurrents," 49–50; cf. *Old Time College President*, 108–45; Kuklick, *Churchmen and Philosophers*, 128–45.

[27] Cf. George M. Marsden: "the most formidable intellectual strongholds of the day were theological seminaries. These schools were in the forefront of American professional educa-tion and offered about the only American opportunity for anything resembling graduate edu-cation" (*Soul of the American University*, 79).

tained by a moral universe." Philosophy in the old-time college was thus a religious, rather than an intellectual, undertaking.

> The task was nothing less than to show that religion, science, and the human mind all, if rightly understood, revealed and contributed to the highest values of the individual and of society . . . Within the college itself moral philosophy was important as more than merely another single course. Moral philosophy carried the task of preserving unity in the college curriculum and, thereby, of ensuring the existence of a unified and intelligible universe of discourse.

As Meyer further notes, "The senior-year course in moral philosophy, joining education, inspiration, and exhortation . . . was intended to produce not the analytical mind but the committed intellect, the pious heart, and the dedicated will."[28]

From among the numerous descriptions of these senior philosophy courses, we can consider a pair of accounts. The first was offered in 1930 by John Dewey, who discussed the "senior-year course" at the University of Vermont in the late 1870s. "This course was regarded as a kind of intellectual coping to the structure erected in earlier years, or, at least, as an insertion of the key-stone of the arch." He continues that its content was far-ranging, including "courses in political economy, international law, history of civilization (Guizot), psychology, ethics, philosophy of religion (Butler's *Analogy*), logic, etc., not history of philosophy, save incidentally." Dewey's senior-year course of study with the president thus filled his senior year with work in many areas, some of which were to emerge as the social sciences. The important point of this course in moral philosophy was, he reports, that "after three years of somewhat specialized study in language and sciences, the last year was reserved for an introduction into serious intellectual topics of wide and deep significance—an introduction into the world of ideas." A parallel account of the final year of college study was offered in 1897 by Andrew Campbell Armstrong:

> After the student had been trained in the time-honored classics and mathematics, after he had learned his modicum of rhetoric and history and natural science and the rest, there remained the "higher branches," which were held not only to train him in scholarship but to fit him for practical life. Political science would make him a good citizen; the evidences of Christianity would ground his religious faith. Between the two and merging into the latter came his [more narrowly] philosophical instruction: in the elements of deductive logic very probably, and the elements of introspective psychology (often termed mental science or mental philosophy), and the elements of ethics, based

---

[28] Sloan, "Teaching of Ethics," 194–95; Meyer, *Instructed Conscience*, 4; cf. xi, 63–64; Daniel J. Wilson, *Science, Community*, 13–14.

perhaps on a psychological study of the conscience and including a considerable amount of applied morals as well as ethical theory. In addition to these
courses one in natural theology was favorite and common, forming in many
cases an introduction to the "evidences" or a part of a single course with them;
and, in connection with the work in "mental philosophy," or as an independent course when the department began to broaden and advance, some discussion of the history of philosophy was given . . .

Beyond this, however, the philosophy course in the old-time college was
unlikely to go.[29]

It should be obvious from these accounts that, whatever the value of
this senior-year course (or set of courses) in philosophical themes, it seldom represented philosophical inquiry in any rich sense. Rather, it was an
attempt to present to the students a unifying picture, tinctured by religion,
that would defend the Scriptural vision of reality from any potential challenges lurking elsewhere in their education or in their future experience.
Edward I. Pitts notes that there was little "explicit philosophical content
approached critically." While at a few colleges "the moral philosophy
course approached being a philosophy course in this sense"—that is, a critical course—he suggests that in most colleges "it was probably a highly
eccentric course in Christian dogmatics mixed with a dose of whatever
social and psychological, political and economic prejudices the college
president carried." Still, he maintains that, excluding any earlier courses in
logic and rhetoric, the senior-year course in moral philosophy "was the
most philosophical curricular aspect of the American college of the
time."[30] The educational ambivalence to which Pitts points is heightened
when we recognize that this philosophical component also represented the
initial inroad of social science into the curriculum, a point that remains
true even if the nature of the educational climate and the role of the individuals involved determined that the function of social science remain
almost exclusively conservative. Most important from the perspective of
our inquiry, however, is the fact that compared to what philosophical
inquiry might be doing for these students the senior-year course left much
to be desired.

It was becoming clear to many individuals that philosophy had a
greater potential than this senior-year course could satisfy. One of the earliest and sharpest critics was Hall. In January of 1879, he reported on his
recent examination of the catalogues of "nearly 300 non-Catholic colleges
in the United States." In the course of his report, Hall confirms much of

---

[29] Dewey, "From Absolutism to Experimentalism," 13; Armstrong, "Philosophy in
American Colleges," 11; cf. Reuben, *Making of the Modern University*, 3, 22–23; Daniel J.
Wilson, *Science, Community*, 2–3.

[30] Pitts, "Profession of Philosophy," 59–60.

what we have seen. "In nearly all these institutions," he notes, "certain studies, aesthetical, logical, historical, most commonly ethical, most rarely psychological, are roughly classed as philosophy and taught during the last year almost invariably by the president." Further, his evaluation of this philosophical work is almost uniformly grim. In most of these colleges, he writes, "the instruction given in philosophy is rudimentary and mediaeval . . . Many teachers of philosophy have no training in their department save such as has been obtained in theological seminaries, and their pupils are made far more familiar with the points of difference in the theology of Parks, Fairchilds, Hodges, and the like, than with Plato, Leibnitz or Kant." In Hall's account, not all is complete darkness; he notes, for example, that there are a few American colleges or universities "where metaphysical thought is entirely freed from reference to theological formulae." In the vast majority of cases, however, "while slight differences among the philosophical *idola* of orthodoxy are thus disproportionately magnified, all these institutions unite in impressing upon their students the lesson that there is an abyss of scepticism and materialism into which, as the greatest of all intellectual disasters, those who cease to believe in the Scriptures as interpreted according to the canons of orthodox criticism, are sure to be plunged." In consequence, he continues, "[t]he mere brute force of unreasoned individual conviction . . . has long been one of the stumbling-blocks in the way of philosophy in America." In line with the criticisms of Hall, there was a growing feeling that philosophy could contribute more to the academic life of the colleges, and to the education of students, if it were freed from its restraints. George Albert Coe writes in 1892 that a number of factors, including the nature and aims of the old-time college and "the traditional notion that the chair of 'mental and moral philosophy' is a natural appendage of the office of president, and that the chief qualifications for this office have been clerical ordination and financial and executive ability" have contributed to produce "the dreary fudge that has been handed down under the name of philosophy."[31]

---

[31] Hall, "Philosophy in the United States," 89–92; Coe, "Philosophy in American Colleges," 282–83.

2

What Philosophy in America Was Becoming

Transitions are always difficult to map. Social processes do not exist in isolation, and their changes have neither distinct boundaries nor temporal limits. Our task is somewhat simplified, however, because we are considering the transition in American educational history from the old-time college to the university primarily from the perspective of the discipline of philosophy. So far, we have been focusing upon the nature and role of philosophy in America as it was developing toward the end of the nineteenth century, with an emphasis upon its continuities with the past. In the face of a series of challenges, however, the old-time college was to evolve into something like the university with which we are more familiar, and the philosophy it housed was to change.

In 1897, Andrew Campbell Armstrong writes of the institutional change that had taken place in the colleges since the Civil War:

> think of . . . the introduction of the elective system, the development of "university work," including as a chief factor the addition of research to instruction, the broadening of the field on both instruction and inquiry, the correlation of the college downward with the secondary schools and upward with the professional schools . . . the striking advance of a whole group of subjects—as the increased importance of the natural sciences in the curriculum . . . and the prominence claimed and received by the historical, economic, and social sciences . . .

As to when these changes had occurred, Armstrong suggests a loose chronology. "Probably the early [eighteen-] seventies may be accepted as marking the beginning of the movement," he writes, "the line of progress being taken up by the various institutions as their needs or opportunities or general pedagogical advance led them toward it." This means that in some of the "stronger universities," and even in some other institutions,

17

this change began almost immediately after Appomattox. For the large majority, however, the great institutional change did not come "before the eighties; and many are still engaged in their endeavors to advance."[1] This account gives us a sense of the complexity of the process of educational change. There was no sharp or quick break between the old-time college and the new university. Rather, there was an ongoing process of shifts and modifications and adaptations, of advances and reversals, that eventuated in a new understanding of the nature and possibilities of higher education.

As Charles William Eliot writes of the "new education" in 1869, "[n]o thoughtful American" could fail to think about the nature of the education that was then needed. "He will not believe that the same methods which trained some boys well for the life of fifty or one hundred years ago are applicable to his son . . ."[2] For simplicity's sake, we can bundle the causal factors into three interrelated groupings that emphasize respectively the content, the breadth and the depth of American higher education. The first was the impact of contemporary science and technology on American thinking. The second was the increasing democratizing of American higher education. The third factor was the impact of the German system of higher education. As a result of these three factors, higher education in America was fundamentally changed; and the practice of academic philosophy was changed with it.

While the challenge of scientific and technological learning to the traditional classical curriculum began before the Civil War, with such institutions as West Point and Annapolis, Rensselaer and Norwich, the creation of institutions of 'engineering' studies that paralleled the four-year college began in earnest after the War. Here a brief listing would include: the Massachusetts Institute of Technology, Worcester Polytechnic Institute, and the Stevens, Drexel, Rice, Carnegie, and California Institutes of Technology. In addition to these institutions dedicated to the study of science and technology, the pre-War period also witnessed the establishment of parallel courses of study within some of the existing institutions of higher learning. Among them were the Lawrence Scientific School at Harvard, the Sheffield Scientific School at Yale, the Chandler Scientific School at Dartmouth, and the Columbia School of Mines. After the War, many more existing schools joined the new institutes of technology in teaching this scientific material to the American students. At either of these

---

[1] Armstrong, "Philosophy in American Colleges," 10, 14.

[2] Eliot, "New Education," 203–4. As has already become apparent, the story that I am telling in this volume is largely a male story. For some accounts of women's education in America, see: Boas, *Women's Education Begins*; Newcomer, *Century of Higher Education for American Women*; Solomon, *In the Company of Educated Women*; Thomas, "Education of Women"; Woody, *History of Women's Education*; and Rogers, "Before the APA."

sorts of institutions, Charles Franklin Thwing writes, "[m]en who rebelled against an education of the linguistic and philosophic type have willingly given themselves to the education of the laboratory." Philosophers are already familiar with the remarkable turnaround in the academic career of one Charles Sanders Peirce, who went from being a mediocre student at Harvard College (BA, 1859) to a *summa cum laude* graduate of the Lawrence Scientific School four years later. The difference perhaps was, as another graduate of the Scientific School writes, that its use of the laboratory method taught the students "how to use their material rather than to memorize text-books."[3]

In addition to this introduction of new material into the curriculum of higher education, the scientific challenge also involved changes in the mood of the college. No longer simply a place to learn the inherited truths of the past, the college became a place of inquiry. In 1914, James Hayden Tufts displays this shift as follows:

> whether the scholarship of earlier days be considered as vocational or as liberalizing in its end, it had one preeminent characteristic. The scholar was the man of learning and culture. He knew many things and knew them exactly. He made no blunders in accent or quantity. He never confused gerund and gerundive . . . this conception of scholarship . . . suggested a world complete rather than a world in the making. It suited admirably a theology of eternal and changeless decrees; it suited a morality of immutable laws discovered by innate ideas or intuitive reason . . .

Now, however, he continues, "[i]nstead of the ideal of learning has been set the ideal of investigation and reconstruction." This new way of thinking about the nature and evaluation of evidence, and the purposes of higher education, emerged with the acceptance of a Darwinian world in which humans are natural, problem-solving creatures who use their intelligence to address the problems of living. On the fiftieth anniversary of the publication of *The Origin of Species* in 1859, John Dewey writes of the abandonment of "the assumption of the superiority of the fixed and final"; and, with regard to Darwin, he notes that his influence upon philosophy "resides in his having conquered the phenomena of life for the principle of transition, and thereby freed the new logic for application to mind and morals and life."[4] In hindsight, of course, we recognize that there has been no decisive victory of transition over fixity. Still, the vastly expanded role of science and technology in higher education has transformed both the curriculum and the world.

---

[3] Thwing, *History of Higher Education*, 424; Sharples, "Some Reminiscences," 539.

[4] Tufts, *Selected Writings*, 168–70; Dewey, "Influence of Darwinism on Philosophy," 3, 7–8.

The related democratic challenge countered the elitism of the old-time college and broadened the demographic base of American higher education. Laurence R. Veysey writes, "The college, with its classical course of training, had hitherto been a means of confirming one's respectable place in society."[5] No longer was this to be true as other pursuits and professions entered the curriculum. The democratic challenge to the old-time college might be seen to have begun with the passage of the Morrill Act in 1862. This act, named for U.S. Senator Justin Smith Morrill of Vermont, allocated money from the sale of public lands in the West for funding a nationwide string of 'land-grant' colleges with an agricultural and mechanical and technical focus. In some states, this money was allocated to previously existing institutions, like the Michigan State Agricultural College or the Maryland Agricultural College; in other states, the Act led to the funding of completely new institutions like the Kansas State Agricultural College and the Iowa State Agricultural College.[6] Once in operation, these institutions helped to advance the shift of higher education from the intellectual and cultural toward practical uses, and opened up the schools to a larger segment of society.[7] The democratic challenge might also be seen as having begun earlier in the Midwest, in colleges like Oberlin and Antioch where women and minorities were given fuller access to higher education. Either way, over time the college became a more democratic institution, one that a wider sweep of potential students and their parents could envision as a possible and sensible preparation for living.

The most important of the three interrelated challenges for our consideration of the birth and development of philosophy in America was the German challenge. It was primary because it contained an alternative model for organizing higher education, one that emphasized intellectual depth and rigor.[8] In marked contrast with the old-time college, the Germanic institution of higher education was seen by its champions in America to be a center of research and progress, with high standards of professorial expertise and student scholarship. The professors were part of a professionalized class based in hard-won knowledge, and they were free to investigate and teach what they found compelling (*Lehrfreiheit*); the students were presumed adults who were free to follow inquiries into what-

---

[5] Veysey, *Emergence of the American University*, 4.

[6] Cf. Geiger, "Rise and Fall of Useful Knowledge," 163.

[7] For discussions of the import of the Morrill Act, see: Becker, *Cornell University*, 23–42; Earle Dudley Ross, *Democracy's College*.

[8] Cf. Nicholas Murray Butler: "Just as the historic American college traces its origin in direct line to Oxford and Cambridge and their influence, so the new American university represents, to a remarkable degree, the influence and authority of the academic tradition of Heidelberg and Göttingen, of Leipsic and Berlin" ("Relation of the German Universities," ix; cf. Cohen, "Later Philosophy," 227–28).

ever area of study they chose, with whichever professors at whatever universities would welcome them (*Lernfreiheit*). In the German academy, theology had its place; but it wielded nothing like the power it had in the old-time American college. In Germany, which Hopkins President Daniel Coit Gilman called "the land of universities,"[9] *Wissenschaft* [science] reigned supreme. The changes that this vision of German higher education brought to America reflected these points, and they can be considered in order.

Professionalization is a fact in current American academia that is often seen as primarily negative: narrowly trained faculty members with narrow areas of interest whose commitment to instruction, especially at the undergraduate level, ranks far behind their commitment to research.[10] As we can easily recognize from our consideration of the old-time college, however, the professionalization of American higher education included much that was positive. Some of the mixed aspects of academic professionalism are contained in the following description. Using the development of Harvard as his model, Bruce Kuklick discusses the professionalization of philosophy in terms of five aspects:

> first, the disappearance of the amateur philosopher, the thinker with no institutional affiliation; second, the hiving-off of various areas of study from what was known as philosophy in the 1860s; third, the beginning of a discipline of philosophy, a limited field of knowledge in the university distinguished by special techniques and by an accepted set of doctrines; fourth, the concomitant growth of departmentalism, defining disciplinary integrity by the number of positions in a given field that the university would finance; and fifth, the training and placing of teachers in this field by an intensified apprenticeship leading to the doctorate and appointment as a college professor.[11]

As an example of how this professionalization was to affect career choices of the young men at institutions like Harvard by the end of the century, we can consider how different was George Herbert Palmer's pursuit of a

---

[9] Gilman, *University Problems*, 11. Cf. Charles Sanders Peirce: "The German universities have been the light of the whole world . . ." (*Collected Papers*, 5.583).

[10] This theme will return in chapter 16.

[11] Kuklick, *Rise of American Philosophy*, xxii. Cf. Bernard Barber: "Professional behavior may be defined in terms of four essential attributes: a high degree of generalized and systematic knowledge; primary orientation to the community interest rather than to individual self-interest; a high degree of self-control of behavior through codes of ethics internalized in the process of work socialization and through voluntary associations organized and operated by the work specialists themselves; and a system of rewards (monetary and honorary) that is primarily a set of symbols of work achievement and thus ends in themselves, not means to some end of individual self-interest" ("Some Problems," 18; cf. Daniel J. Wilson, "Professionalization," 53–54).

teaching position in higher education around 1870. Palmer's intention was
to begin by "treating my subject [philosophy] as final and then looking for
a college where it might be taught . . ." He was counseled by one of his
former professors at Harvard, however, to "turn the matter round. Choose
a first-class college and teach whatever they would accept. If I had power,
it would be discovered and I should ultimately be in the place that fitted
me . . . three days later I received from President Eliot an appointment in
Greek."[12] Palmer accepted this offer and eventually worked his way into a
position teaching philosophy. Very soon, however, this old method of seeking a philosophical career would prove useless.

Professionalization meant the increasing recognition that the job of
professor in a college or university was a unique one that required certain
special qualities and a specialized preparation.[13] One of the earliest formulations of this recognition comes from President James Burrill Angell of
Michigan who wrote in 1871 that only recently had it become clear that
"teaching in the college or university is a special profession, in which as a
rule a man can no more attain high usefulness without natural aptitude and
appropriate training than he can in any of the other learned professions."
No longer was college teaching a transitional or second career; no longer
was it 'easy.' Angell continues, "A man may have eminent success as a
lawyer or a clergyman or a literary writer or even as a school-teacher, and
may yet prove a very indifferent professor."[14] The reason is contained in
Tufts's distinction between "the man of learning and culture" and the new
professor interested in "investigation and reconstruction." As the recognition that college teaching was a unique profession grew, the nature of hiring changed from a process based upon personal character or social success
to one based upon learning, and the ability to communicate that learning,
in narrow areas of expertise. Disciplines were developing as new 'expert'
areas, and the qualifications to teach in these areas in the new academic
environment were changing as well.

The rise of electives in undergraduate education is the counterpoint to
faculty professionalization. Electives were made possible by the increasingly specialized training of faculty members; they were made necessary by
the ongoing development of faculty research. Eliot of Harvard is often

---

[12] Palmer, introduction to *Contemporary American Philosophy*, 27; cf. 39.

[13] The term 'professor' itself continued to have a wider life. As Logan Wilson writes in
1942, "a professor in this country may be many things besides a member of a college or university faculty. He may be a secondary school teacher, an instructor in a barbering college or
a business school, a quack 'psychologist,' a circus barker, or even a piano player in a house of
prostitution" (*Academic Man*, 4n.; cf. Mencken, *American Language*, 272–73; *American
Language—Supplement I*, 529–31).

[14] James Burrill Angell, *Selected Addresses*, 16.

credited with inventing the elective system, but his own account points to its roots further back in Harvard's past. In his "Inaugural Address" in 1869, he reminds his audience of how things had been before electives. "Only a few years ago, all students who graduated at this College passed through one uniform curriculum," and each one "studied the same subjects in the same proportions, without regard to his natural bent or preference." Things had already changed at Harvard; but "[t]his system is still the prevailing system among American colleges, and finds vigorous defenders." As the great champion of the elective system, Eliot was not one of them. He was particularly concerned that the students take responsibility for the direction of their own education. As he notes, "the young man of nineteen or twenty ought to know what he likes best and is most fit for." Moreover, he maintains, the youth who is studying what he finds interesting is a better student. The elective system, he continues, both "relieves the professor and the ardent disciple of the presence of a body of students who are compelled to an unwelcome task," and at the same time "enlarges instruction by substituting many and various lessons given to small, lively classes, for a few lessons many times repeated to different sections of a numerous class." The electoral system thus has benefits both for the individual student and for the college. By its advancement of "variety, not uniformity, of intellectual product, which is needful," the elective system also benefits the society in general. Eliot finally announces his intention "to establish, improve, and extend the elective system."[15] As must be obvious from this discussion, he had a conception of education that was in stark contrast with that of the old-time college. In this new educational world, students had to use their new freedom to make choices that would affect the directions of their lives. Their expectations of the courses changed as well: no longer was the focus upon mastering the content of a textbook but rather upon mastering the topic; the aim was to keep moving forward, not to memorize. And, ahead for the students remained the increasing possibility of graduate study.

Among the contemporary objections to the elective system was its presumed excess of freedom. Abbott Lawrence Lowell, who in 1909 was to succeed Eliot as president of Harvard and rein in electives with a system of concentration and distribution, wrote in 1887 that the average student was not prepared to make all the choices that the elective system required: "As well might one imagine that a sick man in an apothecary's shop would be moved to choose the medicine he required from the appearance of the bottles on the shelf." Perhaps the most thorough repudiation of the elective

---

[15] Eliot, *Educational Reform*, 11–14; cf. Brubacher and Rudy, *Higher Education in Transition*, 96–115; Robinson, "Elective System Historically Considered"; West, "American College," 4–21.

system was offered by James McCosh in 1885. It was based in the faculty psychology that we considered in chapter 1:

> Education is essentially the training of the mind . . . the drawing forth of the faculties which God has given us . . . The powers of the mind are numerous and varied, the senses, the memory, the fancy, judgment, reasoning, conscience, the feelings, the will; the mathematical, the metaphysical, the mechanical, the poetical, the prosaic (quite as useful as any); and all these should be cultivated, the studies necessary to do so should be provided, and the student required so far to attend to them, that the young man by exercise may know what powers he has and the mental frame be fully developed.

This sort of mental discipline is impossible in a system that allows college students to determine their intellectual direction based upon their current wants. The young simply do not know what to choose. Many of them will simply select "easy subjects . . . which are not fitted to enlarge or refine the mind, to produce scholars, or to send forth the great body of the students as educated gentlemen." Even if the majority were not to choose the classes "which will cost them least study" or the professors "who give them the highest grades with the least labor," far too many will still make serious mistakes in their choices. For example, McCosh discusses the student who elects to avoid the difficulties of Greek but later finds himself intellectually crippled when "a voice, as it were, from God, calls him to preach the gospel of salvation."[16]

In areas beyond this vocational question, toward the end of the nineteenth century theology was losing its central position in American higher education. The attractions of the intellectual life were replacing the comforts of piety. For some, the move away from theology was an advance. Josiah Royce, for example, writes in 1900 that "the strongest of the denominational Colleges, once established, have very generally tended . . . to outgrow the narrower ideals of their original founders." The reason that he sees for this process is that the growing college "tends, in the long run, to humanise the asperities with which the earlier history of its special sect may have been associated, rather than to lose sight of its academic ideals in its task of defending a single group of dogmas."[17] For Royce, then, there is a certain naturalness to the diminishing of religious control over higher

---

[16] Lowell, *At War with Academic Traditions*, 4; McCosh, *New Departure*, 8–9, 4–5, 18. Cf. Frank Thilly: "The weakness of the free elective system is that it is not a system at all; there is no guiding principle or purpose to it; it is clay in the potter's hands, and the underclassman at least is not much of a potter" ("Modern University Problems," 9; cf. Peabody et al., "Elective System").

[17] Royce, "Recent University Movement," 135; cf. Santayana, "Spirit and Ideals of Harvard University," 314; Veysey, *Emergence of the American University*, 203–12.

education. From another point of view, however, this shift in focus in higher education represented a declension. No longer was the purpose of education to inculcate the proper *Weltanschauung* into students and thereby to rightly place the coping on the education of the Christian gentlemen. Now, professional academics, philosophers included, each presented their own path to uncovering the meaning of human existence and students were able to follow the one that seemed most compelling; and, in this marketplace of ideas, the theological perspective—imposing as it did limits and demands, and crippled in its common-sense rejection of science—proved less attractive than other alternatives. Or, to phrase this point in a more Emersonian tone, faculty and students became more able to define their lives free from the general denominational control of institutions of higher education.

Into this theological void rushed the various emerging perspectives. Our focus is on the philosophical; and, if philosophy were to have any hope of replacing theology as the central academic discipline, it would have to articulate a new content, a new area of expertise, that was just as vital to the meaning of human existence as theology had been. In its quest for its own domain, philosophy did not need to move far from its prior one of systematizer of knowledge. Holmes Dysinger of Carthage College in Illinois wrote in 1893 that philosophy's "office is, partly at least, to systematize and explain all the principles of the particular sciences. This gives the unity so desirable in a course of study, and so essential to the thoroughly-trained mind . . . The unity of all being is the ultimate problem of philosophy." Lest this synoptic vision seem like some misguided voice from the wilderness, consider the position of two figures who were central to the later developments in philosophy. In 1895, James Edwin Creighton describes philosophy as the synthesizer of knowledge. He writes that, beyond the separate accounts that the special sciences offer of fields of inquiry, "it is still legitimate to ask as philosophy does, What is the nature of the world as a whole?" He believes that an adequate answer cannot come through simply adding up the reports of the various sciences; philosophy must "evaluate, harmonize, and reconstruct into a coherent whole . . . the reports of the world presented by all special inquiries into the nature of the external world and of man." At this point, Creighton waxes idealistic to explain the nature of the relation of philosophy and the special sciences. "All the objective sciences," he writes, "abstract from the nature of the knowing mind, and deal with the world as something that exists on its own account quite independently of any consciousness of it." His position, on the contrary, is that "in seeking for an intellectual and coherent conception of the world, philosophical reflection must restore the abstraction made by the objective sciences, and reconstruct and unify the results of the latter in the light of some consistent theory, regarding the relation of the external world to the knowing consciousness."[18]

A second description of the nature of philosophy is offered by William Pepperell Montague, who was an opponent of such idealistic thinking but a defender of a synthesizing role for philosophy. He wrote in 1910 that philosophy "may be defined as the attempt to formulate a coherent theory of the world as a whole in distinction from the attempt on the part of each science to explain some particular phase of the world." Thus, for Montague, "the relation of philosophy to the sciences is analogous to the relation of biology to botany and zoology. It is 'the science of sciences.'" Rather than focusing on small points in the sciences, philosophy explores fundamental issues, especially those that occur between and among the sciences. "Philosophy aims, in short, to give a bird's-eye view of the field of knowledge and to interpret reflectively the bearing of that knowledge upon human life and human conduct," he writes. "This relation of philosophy to the sciences could be represented diagrammatically by a wheel, each spoke of which stood for a branch of science while the hub symbolized the central position of philosophy." In this way, he suggests, each particular science began "as a more or less undifferentiated phase of philosophy," and grew independent as it developed "a body of specific laws that could be extended and verified apart from any view of the general nature of things." Such a perspective, while clearly distinct from the theological, is not necessarily opposed to it. Philosophy could be offering another interpretation that ran parallel to the theological. Montague, however, emphasizes the opposition between philosophy and theology. "In our colleges today there are many young men and women who have been brought up in the unquestioning acceptance of certain theological views which seem to be in direct contradiction with what they will be taught in their courses in geology and biology," he writes. The resulting intellectual crisis could leave them "[w]ith no basis for distinguishing the essential from the unessential, the ethics of the New Testament from the physics of the Old"; but philosophy can help "to guide them thru this crisis by helping them to adapt to the new teaching their standards of conduct and of life." Philosophy, the quest for "the life of reason," can perform its social function if it continues to strive to readjust "the spiritual ideals of the race to the scientific knowledge of the day."[19]

Many of the philosophers themselves tell personal stories of a conflict between theology and philosophy, between religion and science, in their

---

[18] Dysinger, "Philosophy in the College Curriculum," 16; Creighton, "Study of Philosophy," 31–32; cf. Armstrong, "Philosophy in American Colleges," 14–15.

[19] Montague, "Philosophy in the College Course," 489–90, 492.

own development. In these accounts, the professorship and the ministry vie for control until at some point the value of intellectual inquiry forced the choice of the lectern over the pulpit. One example of this conflict can be found in this report of the philosopher/psychologist, Charles Augustus Strong, who wrote in 1930: "In correcting the proofs of my father's work on theology I was so repelled by the unnaturalness of the suppositions which theologians made in order to reconcile the conflicting stories in the Gospels, that the foundations of my belief in Christianity began to crumble and I could not become a minister myself as I had intended." Other accounts come quickly to mind; but they are perhaps best summarized by Max Carl Otto, who in his 1931 review of *Contemporary American Philosophy* describes the general process of philosophy's replacement of religion. "Speaking generally" of these authors, he writes, "philosophy is not a first love." Rather, these individuals turned to philosophy "on a rebound from an ill-starred wooing of religion." He continues, "If these thirty-four [philosophers] are fairly representative—and they probably are—then a surprisingly large proportion of those who occupy chairs of philosophy in our country either were, or intended to be, preachers before they became teachers." They changed their minds, as their individual accounts illustrate, when the intellectual inadequacies of theology fell victim to philosophical inquiry.[20]

Now that almost all of the relevant pieces have been introduced, it is time to begin to consider the nature and role of the new university. It is within this university that the new conception of education that had been developing was able to flourish. The new university was a place of research and discovery, where 'learning' meant not recitation and drill of age-old knowledge, but explorations of the unfamiliar. This novelty was most pronounced in the creation of a kind of institution of higher learning that was completely new to America: the research universities like Johns Hopkins (1876), Clark (1889), Stanford (1891) and the University of Chicago (1892). Josiah Royce, who earned one of the first doctorates from Hopkins, described it as follows in 1890: "The Johns Hopkins University was the first academic institution to announce that its principal purpose would be the training of advanced students, who already held Bachelor's degree, or some equivalent degree, and their preparation for higher work

---

[20] Strong, "Nature and Mind," 313; Otto, review of *Contemporary American Philosophy*, 231. Cf. Montague's account of his conflict: "Church services in the early morning with my mother gave me a poignant sense of the beauty of the Christian doctrine. Sunday-school and the atmosphere of a small New England community gave me an equally poignant sense of the falsity and incredible ugliness of the authoritarian and ascetic aspects of that same doctrine . . . Love and enthusiasm for one half of the Church, righteous hate and contempt for the other, are sternly called for" ("Confessions of an Animistic Materialist," 135–36).

in research and in teaching."[21] Of course, many of the more established institutions of higher education also took part in this process of academic growth. At Harvard, for example, Elliot—a chemist—became president in 1869, and began to rebuild the school in the image of a new university.

A number of questions emerge at this point. One is the general question of the quality of the five hundred or so institutions of higher education that existed in America around the turn of the twentieth century. M. Carey Thomas, the president of Bryn Mawr, suggests in 1904 that there was little official oversight or control: "in most states the name of college, or preferably that of university, and the power to confer degrees are granted to any institution whatsoever without regard to endowment, scientific equipment, scholarly qualifications of the faculty or adequate preparation of the students."[22] There were, in other words, institutions of both high and low quality. A second question considers whether any of these institutions would qualify as a 'university.' Twelve years earlier, one foreign visitor, James Bryce, indicated that somewhere between eight and twelve universities existed, defining 'university' as "a place where teaching of a high order, teaching which puts a man abreast of the fullest and most exact knowledge of the time, is given in a range of subjects covering all the great departments of intellectual life . . ." About the same time, another visitor, Herman von Holst, emphasizing that a university must have the four faculties of theology, law, medicine, and philosophy and perform no college-level work, asserts that in America there were none.[23] This disagreement leads us to a third question of whether there was a line that distinguished the college from the university. While the concepts were and remain vague, the term 'university' was increasingly used to describe the new institution that housed the former 'college' and its growing clutch of graduate and professional schools. This change in nomenclature did not represent agreement on the part of all the institutions, nor was it fully understood as it was taking place. Numerous contemporary commentators even suggested, as did Edward Delavan Perry in 1904, that "[t]he names 'university' and 'college,' as used in the official titles of institutions, are absolutely worthless as indications of the character of these institutions." Not all saw this lack of precision as a problem, however; for some, it was an advantage. John Merle Coulter, for example, writes in that same year, "The imperceptible gradation from college to university that characterizes the American system of higher education is not a thing that can be abolished or that ought to be

---

[21] Royce, "Recent University Movement," 144.

[22] Thomas, "Education of Women," 11–12n. Cf. Laurence R. Veysey: "Of the five hundred institutions of higher learning in the United States in 1903, a majority may not even have deserved the title of 'college'" (*Emergence of the American University*, 359).

[23] Bryce, *American Commonwealth*, 2:545; cf. Holst, "Need of Universities," 113.

abolished . . ." For others, this lack of precision demonstrated a guarded hope in future possibilities.[24]

Philosophers also offered numerous formulations at the time of the ideal meanings of the two terms. An examination of a number of these suggests that the 'college' was an educational setting that the grown boy entered at about the age of eighteen and from which he emerged four years later as a man. In 1903, President Nicholas Murray Butler of Columbia described the ideal of the college as follows: "That ideal was to train men roundly, thoroly, and well for manly and worthy living. Their spirits were to be furnished, not their pockets filled, by a course of study and training which fell just at the right period of their lives, and by close and intimate association with others having aims similar to their own."[25] The college had been designed to perform this task of maturation and enculturation; and, for the most part, it performed this task well. Increasingly, however, a new task had been added on and this was one that the college could not perform. The task of the university was to offer the students more: a chance to develop their abilities beyond the general and the inherited, a chance to grow along with one of the emerging disciplines. In 1895, Butler had defined a 'university' as: "any institution where students, *adequately trained by previous study of the liberal arts and sciences*, are led into special fields of learning and research by teachers of higher excellence and originality; and where, by the agency of libraries, museums, laboratories, and publications, knowledge is conserved, advanced, and disseminated . . ." Such institutions of higher education would build upon the general education of the college to produce the needed experts. "What science and practical life alike need is not narrow men," he continues, "but broad men sharpened to a point. To train such is the highest function of the American university . . ."[26]

A similar understanding of the university was offered a few years later by Granville Stanley Hall, who wrote in 1899 that "[a] college is for general, the university for special, culture." The former is designed to develop "a wide basis of training and information," while the latter brings this base to "a definite apex." In other words, "[o]ne makes broad men, the other

---

[24] Edward Delavan Perry, "American University," 4; Coulter, "Contribution of Germany," 348. Cf. Samuel Paul Capen: "The name 'university,' as applied to American establishments for higher education before the 1880's, represented a prophecy and a hope—sometimes, perhaps, a delusion" ("Dual Obligation," 57).

[25] Butler, "American College," 13. Cf. William James: "The best claim that a college education can possibly make on your respect, the best thing it can aspire to accomplish for you, is this: that it should *help you to know a good man when you see him*" ("Social Value of the College-Bred," 106; cf. Jordan, "University-Building," 330–31).

[26] Butler, "Relation of the German Universities," xiv, xxxi.

sharpens them to a point." Hall believes that this takes place when each institution is faithful to its proper role in higher education. "The college digests and impresses second-hand knowledge as highly vitalized as good pedagogy can make it, while the university, as one of its choicest functions, creates new knowledge by research and discovery." Finally, we can consider the position of Royce. In 1891, he writes that the college had "as its chosen office the training of individual minds," whereas "[t]he modern University has as its highest business, to which all else is subordinate, the organization and the advance of Learning." For the university, the task is "to train . . . the mind of the nation, that concrete social mind whereof we are all ministers and instruments." As such, he continues, its "daily business" is "the creation and the advance of learning, as the means whereby the national mind can be trained."[27] In the new university, the creation of new knowledge and the development of the creators of this new knowledge were to go hand in hand.

If we view the elective system as increasing the range of university offerings, then we must see graduate study as increasing their fineness. Clearly, the most obvious difference for the individuals, who as students or as professors were filling the new universities in the late nineteenth and early twentieth centuries, was the emergence of graduate education in areas other than theology. In 1899, President Angell of Michigan wrote:

> One of the most striking and encouraging facts in the growth of the new university is the rapid development of the graduate school. Yale College established such a department in 1847 . . . now every important university has a well-organized graduate department, with a considerable company of zealous students who are pushing their work far beyond the frontier of the undergraduate department . . . In these are some learned, conscientious, and inspiring professors who impart as good instruction as can be obtained in any European university. The fact that most of them are handicapped by the necessity of giving instruction to undergraduates, of course, seriously interferes with the attainment of the best results.

We can see in Angell's suggestion that professors were being held back by the needs of undergraduate instruction the extent of a shift that, while very good for graduate students and professors, was less good for undergraduates. The general impression of this shift in institutional emphasis, however, was positive. As William Rainey Harper of the University of Chicago noted in 1903: "The professor of former times had little or no opportu-

---

[27] Hall, "Decennial Address," 53–54; Royce, "Present Ideals," 387–88. Cf. George Stuart Fullerton: "University instruction aims to produce, not an educated man, but a well equipped specialist" ("Aim of Philosophy Teaching," 8; cf. Thilly, "What Is a University?" 500.)

nity for any work aside from his teaching . . . the spirit of research, once hardly recognized in our higher educational work, is now the controlling spirit; and opportunities for its cultivation wait on every side."[28]

Nine years earlier, Hall had emphasized the liberation that professors experienced in graduate-level teaching. "To be thus emancipated from routine teaching, marks, examinations, and other forms of tuition-earning," he wrote, "and to be left with ample opportunity to do his best work, was a boon as new as it will forever be welcome to every professor who has ability and inclination for higher scientific work . . ." In 1899, he spoke lovingly of "the higher plane of purely graduate work." As regards the benefits to the graduate students, the future professors of philosophy, he describes the period of doctoral education as transformative. "In beginning more or less independent research . . . our best college graduates are often in a sense suddenly reduced back to infancy and need constant individual help to go alone." This situation does not last long, however, and "[h]aving once discovered a fact or made ever so small an original contribution and had the baptism of printer's ink, the novitiate is henceforth a changed man." The graduate student "has tasted a free and creative activity which puts him on his mettle like the first taste of blood to a young tiger."[29] While some may have doubted the value of all this research,[30] Hall himself maintains in 1894 that the researcher benefits immeasurably from undertaking it. "The weakest thesis, which generally makes a tiny contribution to the sum of knowledge," he writes, still "puts the author— as every man of modern culture must be once in his life—beyond authority, books, custom, tradition, or habit, where he can take a fresh, independent look at reality." Such an individual "ceases to be a passive recipient, escapes the insidious self-indulgence of knowing merely, and

---

[28] James Burrill Angell, *Selected Addresses*, 148–49; William Rainey Harper, *Trend in Higher Education*, 152. Cf. Edward Delavan Perry: "The American university professor is rarely able to devote himself exclusively to advanced scientific work with well-prepared students, but must, in most cases, carry on a good deal of mere class work as well, which cannot but prove detrimental to the progress of his researches . . . Each university aims to cover the entire field of instruction; the result is that the professors, who are . . . almost always college instructors as well, are cruelly overburdened with teaching and administrative duties, with the inevitable result that few of them can carry on much research" ("American University," 11, 58).

[29] Hall, "American Universities," 153; "Decennial Address," 49; "Philosophy," 180–82.

[30] Cf. David Starr Jordan: although "original research is the loftiest function of the university . . . [m]uch of the so-called research even in Germany is unworthy of the name of science. Its subject matter is not extension of human experience, but an addition to human pedantry. To count the twists and turns of literary eccentricity may have no more intellectual significance than to count the dead leaves in the forest . . . Of a thousand doctor's theses each year scarcely a dozen contain a real addition to knowledge" ("University-Building," 336, 335).

does or produces something, acts from scientific insight, critical testing, personal conviction."[31]

Although it may have slipped from the foreground of my presentation of late, we have been considering the third of the challenges to the old-time college system. In addition to the challenge of scientific and techno-logical learning and the democratic challenge of practical education for the broader populace, the American schools (whether called 'colleges' or 'uni-versities') faced a third, the Germanic, challenge, responding to which made them more secular and more professional. Perhaps at this point, the *Germanic* elements of this challenge should be made more explicit. The challenge was Germanic because Germany's system of higher education was *gemütlich* to foreign students, welcoming them for a year or more of graduate study, often culminating in a Ph.D.[32] From a trickle in the early years of the nineteenth century,[33] and in increasing numbers through the century, Americans went to Germany for graduate study. As Joseph Leon Blau reports in 1952, "By the end of the century it was rare to find a teacher of philosophy in the major colleges who had not studied in Germany."[34] While even a short list of such figures would include such non-rarities as: Dewey, George Trumbull Ladd, Hartley Burr Alexander, Arthur Oncken Lovejoy, Evander Bradley McGilvary, and Alexander Thomas Ormond, Blau in general is right. One of the most enthusiastic of these *deutsche Studenten* was Royce, who discussed in 1900 the impact of study in Germany on those whom he described as "some of our most ambitious and studious young men." What they found in the German uni-versity—"its freedom, its erudition, its specialism, and its ideality"—influ-enced them deeply. "From Germany our returning students brought back ideals of University life and of higher scholarly research, which in the end were extremely potent factors in academic reform." Nine years earlier, Royce had noted that "the rapidly growing interest in higher learning among our academic youth found vent in a positively passionate enthusi-asm for the methods and the opportunities of the German Universities." He presents his own German study in 1875–1876 as follows:

> in those days there was a generation that dreamed of nothing but the German University . . . German scholarship was our master and our guide . . . A little

---

[31] Hall, "Research," 566; cf. "Scholarships, Fellowships," 454.

[32] For discussions of the attractiveness of the German system of higher education, see: Herbst, *German Historical School*, 1–22; Thwing, *American and the German University*, 40–77; Veysey, *Emergence of the American University*, 125–33.

[33] Cf. Herbert Wallace Schneider: "Even before the Civil War it had become fashionable for American professors with scholarly ambitions to spend at least a year in German universi-ties, and after the war this fashion spread rapidly" (*History of American Philosophy*, 376).

[34] Blau, *Men and Movements*, 189.

GERMAN UNIVERSITY STUDIES OF SOME PROMINENT
AMERICAN PHILOSOPHERS

*Felix Adler	Berlin/*Heidelberg (1870–73)
Andrew Campbell Armstrong	Berlin (1885–86)
Charles Montague Bakewell	Berlin (1894)
James Edwin Creighton	Berlin/Leipzig (1889–90)
Walter Goodnow Everett	Berlin/Strassburg (1895)
Harry Norman Gardiner	Göttingen/Leipzig/Heidelberg (1882–84)
John Grier Hibben	Berlin (1882–83)
Albert Ross Hill	Heidelberg/Berlin (1893–94)
William Ernest Hocking	Berlin/Göttingen/Heidelberg (1902–03)
Alfred Henry Lloyd	Göttingen/Berlin/Heidelberg (1889–91)
Rupert Clendon Lodge	Marburg/Berlin (1911–14)
George Herbert Mead	Leipzig/Berlin (1888–91)
Max Carl Otto	Heidelberg (1909–10)
George Thomas White Patrick	Leipzig (1894)
Josiah Royce	Leipzig/Göttingen (1875–76)
Edward Leroy Schaub	Berlin (1910–11)
*Frank Chapman Sharp	*Berlin (1888–92)
*Guy Allan Tawney	*Leipzig (1894–96)
*Frank Thilly	Berlin/*Heidelberg (1887–91)
*James Hayden Tufts	Berlin/*Freiburg (1891–92)
*Wilbur Marshall Urban	Jena/Munich/Graz/*Leipzig (1895–97)
Norman Wilde	Berlin (1891–93)
Frederick J. E. Woodbridge	Berlin (1893–94)

(The asterisk indicates a German Ph.D.)

Sources:
Richard D. Hull, ed., *Presidential Addresses of the APA*, I–III;
Adams and Montague, eds., *Contemporary American Philosophy*.

---

travel and expense, a little necessary pains with the language—and then the American student found himself able to come into immediate contact, as it were, with the great minds of the German world of scholarship. Lotze, or Helmholtz, or Mommsen, was his master . . . there was little in the freedom of the German University to remind him of the old and narrow "disciplinary" ideals of his home.

The effect of German study was transformative, Royce continues, "one returned an idealist, devoted for the time to pure learning for learning's sake, determined to contribute his *Scherflein* [little bit] to the massive store of human knowledge, burning for a chance to help build the American University."[35] In the century between 1815 and 1914, perhaps as many as ten thousand Americans went to Germany to study, and many returned home certified as "Doktor." While there were some critics,[36] almost all the Americans who studied there came away with a great respect for the German system of *Lehrfreiheit* and *Lernfreiheit*; for the seminars, laboratories, and specialized publications; for the deep commitment of each individual to *ein besonderes Fach* [a special area of expertise]; and, in general, to an understanding of education far different from the one under which they had suffered as American undergraduates.

The fact that so many American philosophers studied in Germany would have been nothing more than an interesting statistical aberration had they not returned ready to embody this new understanding of the nature and possibilities of scholarship. As Blau writes, "It could scarcely be expected that when they returned they would teach their students the old Scottish orthodoxy in which they no longer rested. They expounded an idealistic philosophy not so much as a support for traditional religion, but as a spiritual substitute for it." These German-trained scholars returned to America with a conception of education as the uncovering of new knowledge; and they saw their role in the university to be revealing more and more about the nature of existence and, in what the Germans called the *Geisteswissenschaften*, about the nature of our social existence. Fulfilling this function meant the 'scientific' study of economics, sociology, psychology, and of course philosophy, especially philosophy of an idealistic sort. As Herbert Wallace Schneider writes, "The passage from orthodoxy to idealism was an almost invisible transition, but its total effect was startling . . ." In particular, in the new university philosophy becomes "a reflective, systematic enterprise." He continues:

> "Philosophy," during the last quarter of the nineteenth century, became the name of an independent department in the faculties of our standard colleges and

---

[35] Royce, "Recent University Movement," 139; "Present Ideals," 382–83.

[36] Cf. James McCosh: "The American youth of the present day [1887] who wishes to carry on research goes for a year or more to a German university. In particular, those of a metaphysical taste do not feel that they have enough to satisfy them at home, and they betake themselves to Berlin or Leipsic to get a full supply of the food for which they crave. On entering the lecture-rooms there they find certain formidable distinctions proceeded on without being explained . . . As they go on they find themselves in a labyrinth, with no clew to bring them out into the open air and light . . . Some of them remain for a time in Germany, caught in the toils of the profound systems, and then return . . . to expound them in formidable language to students who wonder and admire, but are not sure whether the tenets taught are as true as they as sublime" (*Realistic Philosophy*, 1:16; 2:30; cf. Hall, *Aspects of German Culture*, 114–20; Baldwin, *Between Two Wars*, 1:35–36; *American Neutrality*, 58–60).

universities . . . it was clearly a significant change in the curriculum, and this change in philosophy's academic status was not without its more general cultural implications. Philosophical thinking and writing became professionalized, and as a result American *systems* of philosophy began to be produced.

This professionalized understanding of the nature of philosophy, divorced from its collegiate ministerial function, Schneider notes further, "was itself a German importation"; and it was no accident "that German schools of idealism were the first to gain systematic expression in American life."[37]

Even before this transformation was complete, we can see—at least in outline—the system of higher education in which we operate; and, while we may be justified in our preference for the present over the prior system, we do not want to overlook the fact that there were serious costs involved in this transformation. Some of the more obvious ones are that research does not necessarily connect up with good teaching or rational learning, that the fragmentation of the curriculum can allow for the awarding of degrees based upon accumulating sufficient credit hours even though an 'education' has not been attained, and that philosophy freed of any social guidance severely narrowed its focus. In its initial stages, however, I suspect that we can barely imagine what the feeling of liberation was like. Philosophy changed from a form of indoctrination, however willingly accepted, into the pathway into wisdom, from a kind of Christian apologetics into an open-ended inquiry into the meaning of existence, life, and morality. And, even if we cannot fully imagine what this liberation was like, we surely recognize the emergence of the golden age of American philosophy as its result.

In these first two chapters, we have been considering what it was like to be a philosophy teacher during the transitional period about a century ago. The list of specific changes that we have considered is fairly brief; but the resultant shift is almost total. With a new conception of education and a new interpretation of the task of philosophy, a new understanding of the philosophy professor was required as well. No longer could the professor function as a defender of faith or an expounder of Truth. The new philosopher had to be a leader of inquiries and a publicizer of results. This shift was made obvious when certified (often German-certified) philosophy Ph.D.s replaced theology graduates and ministers in the philosophy classroom. The period between the time when almost no one had a Ph.D.

---

[37] Blau, *Men and Movements,* 189; Schneider, *History of American Philosophy,* 375. Cf. Walter P. Metzger: "A small contingent of Americans who had studied at German universities came home to insist that power was better exercised over subjects than over subject schoolboys, that a contribution to philology was far more significant than a contribution to student manners, that the whole emphasis of the college should be shifted from discipline to scholarship" (*Age of the University,* 310).

REPRESENTATIVE AMERICAN ACADEMIC PUBLICATIONS, WITH FOUNDING DATES

American Journal of Mathematics (1878)
American Journal of Philology (1880)
Science (1883)
Publications of the Modern Language Association (1884)
Quarterly Journal of Economics (1886)
Political Science Quarterly (1886)
American Journal of Psychology (1887)
American Anthropologist (1888)
Annals of the American Academy of Political and Social Science (1890)
Monist (1890)
International Journal of Ethics (1890)
Educational Review (1891)
Pedagogical Seminary (1891)
Philosophical Review (1892)
Journal of Political Economy (1892)
Psychological Review (1894)
Psychological Index (1894)
Psychological Monographs (1895)
American Journal of Sociology (1895)
American Historical Review (1895)
Journal of Philosophy, Psychology, and Scientific Methods (1904)
Psychological Bulletin (1904)

Sources:
Roger L. Geiger, *To Advance Knowledge*, 23–24;
Bernard Berelson, *Graduate Education in the United States*, 15;
L. L. Bernard and J. S. Bernard, "A Century of Progress in the Social Sciences," 502.

---

to when almost everyone did was very brief. Royce, Harvard's first Ph.D. philosopher, did not arrived until 1882; but he wrote in 1900 that "the Ph.D. degree is already generally recognised as a pre-requisite to any appointment as a College Teacher . . . smaller, local Colleges, denominational or otherwise, are ambitious to follow the course of progress, and to maintain their local prestige."[38] The doctorate, moreover, was more than a license to teach: it was a certificate that the prospective philosophy

---

[38] Royce, "Recent University Movement," 146.

instructor was well, if narrowly, trained and ready to undertake independent work in the now specializing and restricted field of academic philosophy. These new philosophers functioned in independent departments of philosophy (that often included the subdiscipline of psychology), constructing curricula and fashioning courses with some semblance of academic freedom. They were making real gains in their research, creating a body of philosophical work that remains central to our study even now. These new philosophers also set their own standards for success, publishing in the recognized organs of philosophy that were being founded at the time: *The Monist* (1890), *The International Journal of Ethics* (1890), *The Philosophical Review* (1892), and *The Journal of Philosophy, Psychology, and Scientific Methods* (1904). And, of course, these philosophers were banding together into societies—the American Psychological Association (1892), the Western Philosophical Association (1900), and the American Philosophical Association (1901)—to consolidate their academic positions and advance their philosophical work. Telling the stories of the emergence of psychology and of the founding of these societies will take up the next two chapters.

WILLIAM JAMES

Philosophical Portrait Series, Open Court Publishing Company, Chicago

3

Philosophy and Psychology

We have been considering the changes that resulted in the emergence of the new American university. This new educational institution provided the home for a new kind of professor, one with a deeper mastery of the philosophical literature and with professional interests broader than the old-time college classroom. We now turn to consider more carefully the content of this expertise, focusing on developments in the history of philosophy in America from roughly 1890 to 1905. Primary among these developments were the emergence of, and the later divergence between, the disciplines of philosophy and psychology, and the reinforcement of this separation through the establishment of the American Psychological Association in 1892, the Western Philosophical Association in 1900, and the American Philosophical Association in 1901. The evolving relationship of philosophy and psychology is the subject of this chapter.

Central to these developments was the redefining of 'psychology' and, to a lesser extent, 'philosophy.' To a contemporary audience, talk of the overlapping disciplines of psychology and philosophy would probably be seen as the mistake of an uninformed undergraduate. Despite philosophy's continuing focus on the workings of the mind and psychology's lingering interest in consciousness, the vast preponderance of work in either discipline has at present little to do with work in the other. From an historical perspective, however, we get a far different story of the relationship of philosophy and psychology. Consider, for example, the following list of significant psychology textbooks written by individuals whose work legitimately encompassed both philosophy and psychology: John Dewey, *Psychology* (1887); George Trumbull Ladd, *Elements of Physiological Psychology* (1887); William James, *The Principles of Psychology* (1890); Mary Whiton Calkins, *Introduction to Psychology* (1901); and Josiah Royce, *Outlines of Psychology* (1903). Or consider the presidents of one of the relevant academic associations. In the first decade of its existence, from 1892–1901, before there were any philosophical associations, the American Psychological Association (AΨA) elected from its membership to be president such philosophical luminaries—and later presidents of the American Philosophical Association (APA)—as Ladd, James, Hugo Münsterberg, Dewey, and Royce.[1] Other AΨA presidents from this first decade who were at the time seen as major philosophers included Granville Stanley Hall, George Stuart Fullerton, and James Mark Baldwin. What we might now see as two separate careers did not seem distinct at the time because the memberships of these associations largely overlapped.[2] By and large, all of these individuals, and the vast majority of philosophers and psychologists active at the time in America, shared the same roots in post-Kantian idealism of one sort or other and had used this background to break free from the tradition of what had been called 'mental philosophy.'

In 1903, Edward Franklin Buchner, a member of both the APA and the AΨA, offered the following account of the prior twenty-five years of American psychology. From our perspective, the most interesting aspect of his account is its similarity to the history of philosophy from the same period that we considered in chapter 1. Buchner writes that earlier

> psychology in America, borrowing heavily from British and German sources, predominated in the theological turn given to its speculative type. Universal hypotheses concerning the soul were turned to account chiefly by the theologians. Religious interests profoundly stirred our colonial forefathers in both a philosophical and an academic sense . . . Education and psychology became closely related very early in American development . . . Psychology was taught in the higher schools then existing,—not by psychologists,—but by pastors . . . Men spoke unblushingly of "the soul." And they meant by it the same thing in their theology as in their philosophy. The object of study flourished under the somewhat dubious terms of "mental philosophy" and "moral philosophy." Psychological knowledge, as this has since become distinctly recognized, occupied but a small, unnamed portion of the entire field of philosophy . . . Another

---

[1] In its second decade, from 1902–1911, the AΨA chose as president only three individuals who also served as presidents of the APA or the Western Philosophical Association (WPA): James (again), Walter Bowers Pillsbury, and Calkins.

[2] The membership list of the AΨA of 1902 lists 127 names. The corresponding membership list of the APA lists 98 names, and the membership list of the WPA lists 53 names. Two persons are listed as belonging to all three associations. One person is listed as belonging to both philosophical associations. Five persons are listed as belonging to the AΨA and the WPA, and 57 others are listed as belonging to the AΨA and the APA. Combining these membership lists we get: 64 individuals who were members of both a philosophical association and the psychological association, or 43 percent of the APA/WPA and 50 percent of the AΨA.

striking feature of this early type of American psychology is the fact that its books were written by men who were primarily theologians and educators, authors whose profession combined in one person the functions of the chair of mental and moral philosophy and the president of the college, and of a preacher.[3]

Thus, whether the story was told from the standpoint of philosophy or psychology, the moral was the same: significant academic work was hamstrung by the theological domination of what passed for serious intellectual inquiry in the colleges. With the birth of the modern university, however, the power of the new academic disciplines—philosophy or psychology— was released to address their nontheological problems. Contemporary psychologists told the same story of overcoming the restraints of theology that philosophers told.

Another aspect of the story of the liberation of philosophy and psychology, however, is that psychology felt itself to be trapped in a status inferior to philosophy and still wanting a full liberation. In other words, as the profession of philosophy was emerging from its preprofessional background, it was at the same time feeling the initial stages of the separation of its psychological component. Sheldon M. Stern discusses this time of dual emergence at Harvard. He writes that "[b]etween 1860 and the inauguration of President Eliot in 1869, psychology was treated as a minor aspect of the study of logic and metaphysics." Francis Bowen was responsible for what philosophy was taught; but only in the early 1870s "did Bowen introduce into the Department of Philosophy Harvard's first well-structured course in the philosophy of mind." The psychological value of this course, however, was modest: "That the study of mind was, and must remain, outside the area of scientific inquiry was the real theme of Bowen's course." The arrival of William James tilted this unstable situation towards naturalism, and attempts to understand the mind were brought within scientific inquiry. Stern continues:

> Although James had begun teaching at Harvard as an instructor in anatomy and physiology as early as 1872, he did not initiate the new psychology until the academic year 1875-76 . . . James's approach to man was biological rather than metaphysical, theological, or logical. His epistemology was natural experience. James shifted the view of human psychology from subjective introspection to controlled experimentation; he was not reluctant to identify man with the material world.[4]

---

[3] Buchner, "Quarter Century of Psychology," 667–668; cf. Baldwin, "Psychology Past and Present," 364–66.

[4] Stern, "William James," 177–78, 180–81; cf. Jastrow, "Reconstruction of Psychology," 170; Leary, "Telling Likely Stories," 317–18.

This shift in focus from metaphysics to biology made possible an academic discipline of psychology; but it was a clear shift only in hindsight. For those philosophers and psychologists, and philosopher/psychologists, who were attempting to develop their areas of interest into academically respectable disciplines, there were still many questions to be answered.

One of these questions dealt with the relation between the two disciplines. Here, the philosophers and the philosopher/psychologists suggested that philosophy dealt with more general or more foundational topics than the (other) sciences. Psychology was thus characterized as an inferior line of inquiry, at least in the minds of those for whom metaphysics remained a valid study. We can consider a few examples, beginning with Ladd, the president of the AΨA for 1893, who writes in 1896:

> The different positive sciences [e.g., psychology], as forms of *science*, possess a particular degree and kind of certainty. But they all involve a host of presuppositions,—of unverified conceptions, postulated entities and relations of entities, assumed modes of the being and behavior of things. Upon the basis of these presuppositions they move onward toward the discovery of further empirical truths . . . But philosophy, with its claim to investigate the grounds of all reason, and the universal forms and laws of being, holds out the hope of a more nearly absolute certainty of knowledge.

In a similar fashion, Calkins, the 1905 president of the AΨA, distinguishes philosophy and psychology by their range of vision. "Philosophy is the attempted study of the self-dependent whole of reality, or of partial realities as related to this fundamental work," she writes in 1901, whereas a science like psychology, on the contrary, is "a systematic study of facts or phenomena; that is, of limited or partial realities, as related to each other without reference to a more fundamental reality." Philosophy alone considers the problems of "ultimate reality" and studies "the ultimate nature" of the phenomena of science. Thus, for Calkins, philosophy "seeks not only to relate each phenomenon with every other, but to fit it into a complete scheme of reality." A third version of this distinction is offered by George Holmes Howison in 1902, who writes that "[t]he man of science . . . confessedly deals with phenomena only, with reality that is only derivative and relative; the philosopher hopes, on the contrary, to deal with absolute reality." Science, as a narrow undertaking, considers only "particular aspects or portions of the eternal Whole—that portion, especially, which is known as the phenomenal, the temporal, the changeable; not the changeless, the eternal, as such." Philosophy, on the contrary, he continues, "always views the Whole, or at least has it in its scope." Finally, we can consider the relation of philosophy and psychology as offered by Frank Thilly in 1902:

> The different sciences dealing with different sets of facts may find ultimates capable of accounting for their facts respectively, but only by ignoring other

facts. They give us, as it were, cross-sections of reality while we wish to get a comprehensive view of the whole . . . Will the psychologist, who deals with states of mind or consciousness, be able to account for the existence of these from the physicist's principles, atoms and motions? A science is needed that will consciously and methodically aim to bring order into this chaos, that will consider *all* the facts, and, if possible, *unify* these facts. It will subject the principles offered by the various sciences to the most critical examination, compare them with one another, point out their inconsistencies where such exist, it will in short, rectify, harmonize and if possible *unify* results.

This science, of course, is philosophy, the more general or more fundamental means for understanding existence and experience as a whole.[5]

Behind these elaborations of the relation between philosophy and psychology there is a definition of psychology as an empirical, if limited, study of the workings of the mind. Needless to say, this study had very fuzzy boundaries. To get a better sense of the uncertainties with which these individuals were dealing, we can consider a few of their working definitions of psychology, taking special note of how they dealt with the issue of the relationship between 'metaphysics' and 'science.' James, in *The Principles of Psychology*, makes explicit an interest in both aspects: "Psychology is the Science of Mental Life, both of its phenomena and of their conditions." The phenomena are, of course, the thoughts and feelings that constitute our mental lives; the conditions, the functionings of the human organism. In the preface, he writes of his intention to work as a natural scientist and to steer clear of metaphysical questions. "Every natural science assumes certain data uncritically, and declines to challenge the elements between which its own 'laws' obtain, and from which its own deductions are carried on." In the case of psychology, "the science of finite individual minds," these assumptions are three: "(1) *thoughts and feelings*, and (2) *a physical world* in time and space with which they coexist and which (3) *they know*." He continues that, while these data can be discussed, "the discussion of them (as of other elements) is called metaphysics and falls outside the province of this book." James thus commits himself to the position that psychology can only go so far "as a natural science. If she goes farther she becomes metaphysical."[6]

---

5 Ladd, *Introduction to Philosophy*, 57–58; Calkins, *Introduction to Psychology*, 4–5; Howison, "Philosophy and Science," 130, 157; Thilly, "What Is Philosophy?" 515–16. Cf. Ralph Barton Perry: "The scientist proper . . . is not troubled by the supposed paradoxes of space and time, or by such problems as the nature of causality, the unity of the world, and the meaning of truth. He moves, in short, within intellectual limits which he does not question, and of which he may even be unconscious. But the scientist is also a man, and hence may readily become a philosopher as well" (*Present Philosophical Tendencies*, 45–46).

6 James, *Principles of Psychology*, 1:15, 6. Cf. George Stuart Fullerton: "the psychologist . . . must be scientific rather than metaphysical, accepting without question the assumptions

James's Harvard colleague, Royce, offers a similar definition in his *Outlines of Psychology*: psychology is "the doctrine which attempts to describe our mental life, and, as far as possible, to discover its conditions and its laws." Lest the introduction of the notion of 'laws' lead to misunderstanding, he remarks further that the psychologist is "concerned solely with certain problems of the natural history of mind; metaphysical issues are here not at all in question." While he seems interested in separating off metaphysical issues from psychology, Royce's desire to carve "a sharp difference between the business of the student of philosophy and that of the psychologist" had not been present in Dewey's *Psychology*. There, Dewey attempts to present an analysis that would be—just as Royce intended— "scientific and up to the times, free from metaphysics" and at the same time would function as "an introduction to philosophy in general . . ." Whatever the uncertainties and imprecisions among these attempts to delimit the boundaries of psychology, we still find Dewey defining psychology in such a way as to incorporate both the biological and something more 'metaphysical': "Psychology is the science of the reproduction of some universal content or existence, whether of knowledge or of action, in the form of individual, unsharable consciousness."[7]

There were many other similar attempts to define psychology. In his *Elements of Physiological Psychology*, Ladd writes that it is no longer possible to use "the most common definition of psychology, up to the present time . . . as 'the science of the human soul'" for the simple reason that such a definition implies "that it is the business of psychology itself to demonstrate the existence of a particular entity called 'the soul' . . ."[8] Such a demonstration has not happened and cannot be assumed as part of the task of any psychology hoping to be scientific. His "definition, or rather description" of psychology is "that science which has for its primary subject of investigation all the phenomena of human consciousness, or of the sentient life of man." What makes this metaphysically oriented focus in any way novel is that, for Ladd, psychology uses biological advances to do its job better. As he writes, physiological psychology

> partakes of the nature and methods of two sciences that differ widely from each other. One is a science which involves introspection; for it is only by the method of introspection that the real and present facts of human consciousness

---

upon which the natural sciences rest, and investigating the phenomena of mind much as they investigate material phenomena" ("Psychological Standpoint," 115).

[7] Royce, *Outlines of Psychology*, 1, vi; Dewey, *Psychology*, 4, 11.

[8] Ladd, *Elements of Physiological Psychology*, 1. Cf. James McCosh: "Psychology is the science of the soul . . . By soul is meant that self of which every one is conscious" (*Psychology*, 1).

can be reached. The other is a physical science, and involves external observation to determine the external facts of the structure, development, and functions of a physiological mechanism.

He is unwilling to give up this dual emphasis. He writes, for example, that "[i]n studying the higher mental phenomena, physiological psychology is obliged almost wholly to adopt, as the only direct path open, the *non*-physiological method." He thus maintains his regard for the prior metaphysical approach even when he champions the adoption of biological methods whenever possible. As Ladd continues, "whatever may be said in disparagement of the 'old psychology,' it cannot fitly be denied that it has most thoroughly and subtly analyzed the phenomena of judgment, memory, and choice, as these phenomena appear connected with each other in the flowing current of our conscious life." Psychology's task, emerging and still somewhat confused, was to make scientific our knowledge of the self by bringing together the results of metaphysics and biology. Or, as Baldwin writes in the preface to his *Dictionary of Philosophy and Psychology* in 1901, "Psychology is the half-way house between biology with the whole range of the objective sciences, on the one hand, and the moral sciences with philosophy, on the other hand."[9]

It is common at present to discuss the emergence of this biological psychology as the 'birth' of the discipline of psychology; but, at the time, it was seen as the 'new' psychology, implying that there must have been some sort of psychology previously. Of this latter opinion was Gardner Murphy, who writes in 1930, "Psychology, in the sense of reflection upon the nature and activities of the mind, is a very ancient discipline, one which reached great heights in ancient Greece and has continued (in intimate relation with philosophy) with every phase of European civilization." The great changes occurred during the nineteenth century, he continues, when "this literary and philosophic psychology" was remade "chiefly as a result of the progress of biology, from which both concepts and methods were freely borrowed."[10] While some were willing to look back as far as Aristotle or Locke, the more common position—one that emphasized the novelty of the 'new' psychology—suggested that it began in the mid-nineteenth century. For example, in 1903 Buchner places the birth of the new 'sci-

---

[9] Ladd, *Elements of Physiological Psychology*, 3, 6, 533–34; Baldwin, *Dictionary of Philosophy and Psychology*, 1:x.

[10] Gardner Murphy, *Historical Introduction to Modern Psychology*, xiii. Cf. James McKeen Cattell: "The history of psychology here prior to 1880 could be set forth as briefly as the alleged chapter on snakes in the natural history of Iceland—'There are no snakes in Iceland.' The eminence of the theologian Jonathan Edwards is witness to the lack of any psychologist. We had only text-books by college presidents setting forth Scottish realism" ("Advance of Psychology," 536; cf. "Psychology in America," 12–13; Stern, "William James," 177).

ence' of psychology in Germany a half century earlier. "Lotze's 'Medicinische Psychologie' appeared in 1852, and that year must be regarded as the beginning of the new psychological calendar," he writes. "Some twenty years later Wundt's 'Grundzüge der Physiologische Psychologie' appeared (1874), and about a quarter of a century passed before the first distinct experimental institute for the psychologist had its beginning in Leipzig (1878)." Buchner continues that these developments signaled the emergence of a new kind of psychology that, when it fully understood itself, would not accept oversight from philosophy. "The world-old veneration for Reality, Being, Becoming, the Absolute," he writes, "slowly gave way before a growing regard for the *facts in* consciousness and for the *facts about* consciousness."[11]

While the philosopher/psychologists attempted to maintain one foot in metaphysics and the other in biology, there were many psychologists who believed that, if psychology was to progress to the status of a science, it would have to leave behind its philosophical past. In Baldwin's *Dictionary*, Edward Bradford Titchener defines "the new Psychology" as "Modern psychology, in its experimental and physiological aspects; scientific as opposed to philosophical psychology." With this dividing line in place, other possible distinctions were of lesser importance. He continues, "while individual authors may, for pedagogical purposes, classify and distinguish the new psychology, experimental psychology, physiological psychology, psychophysics, psychophysiology, &c., there is really no sharp line of demarcation to be drawn."[12] The line between philosophical psychology and scientific psychology remained important for Titchener and others; and in spite of the following remark by James, drawing this line does represent a fundamental change. In his *Talks to Teachers* of 1899, James, perhaps facetiously, remarks: "in my humble opinion there *is* no 'new psychology' worthy of the name. There is nothing but the old psychology which began in Locke's time, plus a little physiology of the brain and senses and theory of evolution, and a few refinements of introspective detail . . ."[13] I can only suggest that he was trying to put his audience of

---

[11] Buchner, "Ten Years of American Psychology," 193; "Quarter Century of Psychology in America," 669; cf. Hall, *Founders of Modern Psychology*, 65–121, 311–45; Gardner Murphy, *Historical Introduction to Modern Psychology*, 156–87.

[12] Titchener, "Psychology (the new)," 391; "Psychology (physiological)," 390. Cf. Titchener: "Until very recently, psychology was not a science at all, but a branch of philosophy. Now that her independence is established, psychology naturally tends to emphasize the breach between herself and the philosophical disciplines. Philosophy, on the other hand, unwilling to recognize the independence of a revolted subject, insists that psychology runs into danger as soon as ever she rejects metaphysical guidance. There is truth in both attitudes" ("Psychology," sixth page).

[13] James, *Talks to Teachers on Psychology*, 15.

school teachers at ease, because these few changes *are* what makes the 'new' psychology new. They are what takes psychology out of the realm of metaphysics and places it within the realm of biology.

To get a slightly different interpretation of the new psychology, we can examine it from a later perspective. Edwin G. Boring notes in 1929 the fundamental aspects of the developing American psychology: "By 1900 the characteristics of American psychology were well defined. It inherited its physical body from German experimentalism, but it got its mind from Darwin. American psychology was to deal with mind in use." We can explore these aspects in turn. At times the emphasis of the new psychology was primarily upon the shift that occurred with the adoption of experimental methods. In the late 1890s, Edward Wheeler Scripture, for example, notes simply: "By the 'old psychology' I mean psychology before the introduction of experiment and measurement." For him, while observation is necessary for successful scientific practice, it is not sufficient: "Sitting at home in the arm chair is very pleasant but it is not the way to do business, and consequently psychology has been going backward." The method of scientific experimentation has given us "our electric cars and lights, our bridges and tall buildings, our steam-power and factories"; and our failure to adopt this method in psychology has forestalled progress. "It is to the lack of experiment that we must attribute the medieval condition of the mental sciences." Scripture continues:

> The new psychology is entitled to its special adjective because it employs a method new in the history of psychology, although not new in the history of science . . . The old psychologist, like Locke, Hamilton, and many of the present day, sits at his desk and writes volumes of vague observation, endless speculation, and flimsy guesswork. The psychologist of the new dispensation must see every statement proven by experiment and measurement before he will commit himself in regard to it . . . The difference between the old and the new is not one of material; the subject is the same for both, namely, the facts of mind. The difference lies in the carefulness with which the information in regard to the phenomena is obtained. Instead of careless observation and guesswork the utmost care and self-sacrificing labor are expended in the laboratory in order to obtain single facts.

The result of the adoption of these methods was the generation of vast amounts of new data about reaction times, color perception, taste and smell and balance, and so forth. "The development of a science consists in the development of its means of extending and improving its method of observation," he writes. Science came to psychology with the introduction of systematized "experimental and clinical methods," a change that the physical sciences had undergone long before, but that had occurred in psychology "only a few decades ago." Psychology thus was able to become a science only when it rose above its prior satisfaction with feelings and impressions and sought hard data. "Qualitative experiments are necessary for preliminary investigations," he admits, "but they are inexcusable where quantitative ones can be made . . . the scientist may never rest satisfied with them, but should regard them only as stepping-stones for future progress."[14]

Some of this data gathering went beyond the more peripheral workings of the body and focused upon the brain. As James writes, "a certain amount of brain-physiology must be presupposed or included in Psychology." Baldwin echoes this position in 1894 when he points to the Germans' interest in the workings of the brain. They asked the questions, "how can psychology be a science when one of the evident conditions of the flow of mental states, of their integrity and their trustworthiness, the brain, is left quite out of account? What is the law of connection of mind and brain?" This "law" was beginning to be uncovered by experimentation. Further, Baldwin writes, these experiments were grounded in a pair of physiological assumptions. "The first of these assumptions is this: that our mental life is always and everywhere accompanied by a process of nervous change . . . The second assumption is based upon the first, viz., that this connection between mind and body is uniform." He continues that, while the work has been difficult, the value of this experimental approach to the understanding of consciousness has been proven: "philosophy has in the present half-century thrown open her doors to the entrance of critical and empirical methods, and . . . the results already accruing are evidence of the bigness of her future harvest."[15]

In discussing the fundamental nature of the 'new' psychology, we also find at times an emphasis upon the evolutionary, or 'genetic,' attempts to understand consciousness. Psychological studies were attempting to connect up humans with their animal cousins as developing, evolutionary beings. Baldwin writes, for example, that under the genetic point of view "[t]he mind is looked upon as having grown to be what it is, both as respects the growth of the man from the child, and as respects the place of man in the scale of conscious existences." Central to this Darwinian approach was the understanding of the human as a functionally organized being. He continues, "The old conception of 'faculties' made the different phases of mental process in large measure distinct from one another." Memory and thought and imagination were each faculties, powers of the

---

[14] Boring, *History of Experimental Psychology*, 494; Scripture, *New Psychology*, 452; *Thinking, Feeling, Doing*, 24–25, 282–83; *New Psychology*, 1, 72–73; cf. "Methods of Laboratory Mind-Study"; Nichols, "Psychological Laboratory at Harvard."

[15] James, *Principles of Psychology*, 1:18; Baldwin, "Psychology Past and Present," 366, 375, 373.

mind. The new functional understanding, however, asks "how the mind as a whole acts, and how this one form of activity adapts itself to the different elements of material which it finds available . . . the process in consciousness is one; and it is a psycho-physical process as well." This understanding of the self as a functionally-organized being was, of course, central to the message of James, who used as one of the working hypotheses of his *Principles* the assumption that "*no actions but such as are done for an end, and show a choice of means, can be called indubitable expressions of Mind.*"[16]

We are all familiar with the role that James played in the growth of the new psychology, both in America and elsewhere. It is usual to emphasize the publication of *The Principles of Psychology* in 1890 as the watershed. James McKeen Cattell, for example, writes in 1917 that its publication "was a declaration of independence, defining the boundary lines of a new science with unapproachable genius." *The Principles* had been a dozen years in preparation, and many of its chapters had been published previously; but, when it appeared as a volume, its impact was overwhelming. As early as 1894, Baldwin called *The Principles* "a *vade mecum* to psychological inquirers."[17] It was this volume that finally demonstrated to the philosophy and psychology audience that the new psychology encompassed a body of material that the average philosopher was not prepared to teach. As James had written to President Eliot of Harvard in late 1889, "Psychology is rapidly differentiating itself from the main body of Philosophy, as a body of doctrine needing men specially trained."[18] Thus, the new, scientific psychology was finally recognized as distinct from the older, philosophical psychology; and work in one of these disciplines, as distinct from work in the other.

While we need to recognize the importance of James as a supporter and a publicist of the new psychology, we also need to realize that, from an institutional perspective, it is equally important to consider the role played by Hall. He earned a divinity degree at Union Theological Seminary and taught at Antioch before enrolling for doctoral study with James at Harvard. He finished in 1878, writing a psychological dissertation on the perception of space—Harvard's first doctorate in philosophy and America's first in psychology.[19] Hall followed this degree with two years of

---

[16] Baldwin, "Psychology Past and Present," 368; James, *Principles of Psychology*, 1:23.

[17] Cattell, "Our Psychological Association and Research," 276; Baldwin, "Psychology Past and Present," 386; cf. Daniel J. Wilson, *Science, Community*, 87–99.

[18] James to Eliot, 20 October 1889, *Correspondence*, 6:538. Cf. Edward Wheeler Scripture: "As long as psychology was an arm-chair science, anybody could teach it; to-day no one but a carefully trained man can do so" (*Thinking, Feeling, Doing*, 295; cf. Baldwin, "Psychology Past and Present," 386).

[19] Hall's dissertation was published in 1878 as "The Muscular Perception of Space." Cf. Dorothy Ross, *G. Stanley Hall*, 62–80.

postdoctoral study in Germany: in Berlin (1878–79), and in Leipzig with Wilhelm Wundt (1879–80). He taught psychology at Johns Hopkins beginning in 1882, winning in 1884 the position for which he, George Sylvester Morris, and Charles Sanders Peirce had competed.[20] In 1883, he set up what may have been America's first psychological laboratory.[21] He was professor of psychology at Hopkins from 1884 to 1888, where he founded *The American Journal of Psychology* in 1887. Hall left Baltimore for the presidency of the newly founded Clark University in 1888. Later he was, as we shall see in chapter 4, the founder and first president of the AΨA.

In the lead editorial in the first issue of *The American Journal of Psychology*, Hall writes: "The object of this Journal is to record the psychological work of a scientific, as distinct from a speculative character, which has been so widely scattered as to be largely inaccessible save to a very few, and often to be overlooked by them." He notes that the journal was especially interested in *"[o]riginal contributions of a scientific character"*:

> These will consist partly of experimental investigations on the functions of the senses and brain, physiological time, psycho-physic law, images and their association, volition, innervation, etc.; and partly of inductive studies of instinct in animals, psychogenesis in children, and the large fields of morbid and anthropological psychology, not excluding hypnotism, methods of research which will receive special attention; and lastly, the finer anatomy of the sense-organs and the central nervous system, including the latest technical methods, and embryological, comparative and experimental studies of both neurological structure and function.

Such contributions, supplemented by digests, reviews, and notes, would carry forward "the main objective" of the journal, which was "to record the progress of scientific psychology . . ."[22]

---

[20] Cf. Michael M. Sokal: "Daniel Coit Gilman . . . preferred Hall's laboratory-based psychology to George Sylvester Morris's Idealism and Charles Sanders Peirce's marital uncertainties . . . He also appreciated Hall's interest in child study and pedagogy, in part because he could cite its implied practicality, and (especially) Hall's status as an ordained Congregational minister, to defend the university against charges of religious irregularity" ("Origins and Early Years," 113; cf. Hall, *Life and Confessions of a Psychologist*, 225–26).

[21] The question of whether James or Hall established the first psychology laboratory in America resembles James's question of whether the man went *"round the squirrel."* James clearly had something, while less than a research facility, at Harvard in the mid-1870s for doing work related to his physiology lectures. Whether it should be counted as a psychology laboratory depends on what we *"practically mean"* by the term (*Pragmatism*, 27). For more on this question, see: Hall, "Editorial [on Experimental Psychology in America]," 4; James, "Experimental Psychology in America"; Cattell, "Advance of Psychology," 536–37; Boring, *History of Experimental Psychology*, 493–97, 506–7; Robert S. Harper, "Laboratory of William James"; Dorothy Ross, *G. Stanley Hall*, 154, 246; Stern, "William James," 184–85, 214.

[22] Hall, "Editorial Note," 3–4.

Hall's various connections made him a central figure in the progress of the new psychology, a position that he cherished. He writes in 1894 of the range of work in which the new psychology is engaged. It is that area

> which studies the body as well as the mind; which experiments on the senses, memory, association, attention, etc., in the laboratory; that utilizes nature's cruel experiments by laborious and systematic observations upon the insane, blind, deaf, idiots, paupers, and criminals; that explores the laws and nature of growth in childhood, animal instinct, savage customs and beliefs; that has already shed so much light upon the nature and growth of volition and motor powers, and is now approaching the awful mysteries of feeling and the religious life . . .[23]

Hall was himself particularly interested in advancing the experimental aspects of the new psychology, although he found in them the means to accomplish psychology's prior tasks. He writes in 1901, for example, that laboratory "instruments and methods have taught us a sharpness and refinement of introspection and self-knowledge which make these methods almost comparable with a microscope for the soul." He discusses the workings of the brain in a similar fashion. "The brain," he writes, "is the mouthpiece of God, or the absolute in the world, and is perhaps the most highly organized of all substances, anatomical or chemical . . ." This focus upon the gross physiology of the brain led the new psychology to perform experiments on the relationship of the mind and the brain. In one such experiment, "[a] man lies exactly balanced on knife edges, so that he oscillates freely or in equilibrium." When asked to think about a problem that requires "mental effort," the result is that "the blood is so drawn to the brain that it tips the end of the balance on which his head rests downward and lifts his feet in the air just in proportion to the effort he makes." We can see the same combination of metaphysical and biological interests in Hall's discussion of the skin. "The skin is the boundary between the self and the external world," he writes. "The retina, the ear, and all the other senses are infolded skin, and thus touch is the mother-sense of all the rest. We have now applied electricity, heat, and cold, and have an elaborate method of studying the many dermal senses."[24] By expanding our knowledge of the workings of the body in these ways, he believed that the new psychology was coming closer to answering the questions with which psychology had long struggled.

The growing academic disciplines of philosophy and psychology were coexisting, but in tension. For some, as we have seen, the meaning of these

---

[23] Hall, "Universities," 300; cf. "On the History," 160–61.
[24] Hall, "New Psychology," 731, 730, 727; cf. "Psychological Progress," 21–24.

recent developments was the birth, or at least the liberation, of an independent new discipline of psychology. In 1903 Buchner writes, for example:

> In the past psychology was given a small corner in a philosophical system. The approach to a knowledge of mind lay through the fields of abstract conceptions, of which those presumed to fit such an entity had to be analyzed and adjusted to other abstractions before a discussion of subjective experience could be entered upon. *Then* one's psychology grew out of, and was dependent upon, his philosophy. *Now* one's philosophy depends upon his psychology, upon his recognition of the psychological facts of experience and his methods of interpreting them.[25]

Others, for example, Jacob Gould Schurman, the founding editor of *The Philosophical Review*, saw these developments somewhat differently. In his "Prefatory Note" in its first issue in 1892, he announces, "The scope of the REVIEW will be as wide as Philosophy, in its broadest sense." To him, this range incorporated the historic branches of philosophy: "Psychology, Logic, Ethics, Aesthetics, Philosophy of Education, Philosophy of Religion, Metaphysics, Philosophy of Nature, and Epistemology." He admits that psychology, "by enlarging its field of observation and improving its methods of investigation, has within the last decade probably outstripped every other province of human knowledge in the rate of its growth." Such progress for one philosophical discipline should not lead to the fragmentation of philosophy—he anticipated similar growth spurts by logic and ethics—because ultimately philosophy "is and must be directed upon nothing short of the whole of existence." Schurman thus explained the need for the "general philosophical magazine" that he was inaugurating.[26] Still, the tension increased over the next decade or so and ended only with the recognition of the divergence of two disciplines with the founding of distinct professional associations.

---

[25] Buchner, "Quarter Century of Psychology," 674; cf. Daniel J. Wilson, *Science, Community*, 76–77, 112–13, 116.

[26] Schurman, "Prefatory Note," 6–7. Cf. the similar statement in the premier issue of *The Journal of Philosophy, Psychology, and Scientific Methods* on 7 January 1904: "It is a matter of importance at the present time that the relations between philosophy and psychology should remain intimate, and that the fundamental methods and concepts of the special sciences, now receiving attention on all sides, should be kept in touch with philosophy in its historic development" (*Journal of Philosophy* 1:27)

JAMES EDWIN CREIGHTON

4

Founding of the Academic Associations

Academic associations are strange social institutions. While they often deal with issues that are of supreme importance to their members, they seldom manage to achieve even modest fiscal well-being. Although they frequently require large amounts of effort from their members, they seldom seem to achieve their intended goals. And, in spite of the fact that from the inside their work appears vital, few outsiders know much about what they are doing or often of their existence. Academic associations do, however, serve as powerful forces for the self-definition of their disciplines.

The tension just considered between philosophy and psychology that was leading to their separation was increased with the founding of the American Psychological Association (AΨA) in 1892. The background is offered by Edward Franklin Buchner in 1903:

> In the hope of conserving the great gains which had been made for the science [of psychology], and with the desire of having an exchange where psychological efforts might be pooled and where a more personal and direct mode of checking off results might be available than through the existing channels of publication, President [Granville Stanley] Hall [of Clark University] nursed the idea of a society of psychologists, and took counsel by pen and by mouth with many workers in this field. Everybody consulted was in sympathy with the idea, and wanted to become a member of whatever organization might be effected, pledging his hearty cooperation. Fortified and clarified by these preliminaries, including a conference of some length with Professor [George Trumbull] Ladd, he issued a letter of invitation to more than a score of psychologists to meet at Clark University, on July 8, 1892. A company of men gathered at the appointed time and place, and the preliminary meeting was held, six papers being presented and discussed, and plans projected for a permanent organization.[1]

---

[1] Buchner, "Ten Years of American Psychology," 197; cf. Sokal, "Origins and Early Years," 113–14.

Directing this planning was a committee of seven renowned psychologists: Hall, Ladd, George Stuart Fullerton, James Jastrow, William James, James McKeen Cattell, and James Mark Baldwin. They represented, respectively, the premier North American psychology programs of the day: Clark, Yale, Pennsylvania, Wisconsin, Harvard, Columbia, and Toronto. The proceedings of this meeting report that the thirty-one "original members" of the AΨA were the twenty-six psychologists "who were either present at this meeting or sent letters of approval and accepted membership" and five additional individuals who were elected to membership at this meeting.[2]

Fullerton had invited the association to meet later that year at Pennsylvania; and the first annual meeting of the AΨA took place in Philadelphia on 27–28 December 1892. At this meeting, Hall read his presidential address, "History and Prospects of Experimental Psychology in America," in which he presented his understanding of the course of American psychology from Jonathan Edwards to his day, with an account of the various investigations that had been taking place in recent years.[3] The other papers—almost all of which were 'experimental' in nature— explored such topics as: observational errors, pain, and reaction times. Hugo Münsterberg, recently arrived from Freiburg to take over the psychology laboratory at Harvard, discussed problems of experimental psychology with a special emphasis upon resisting the temptation to focus upon measurement without thinking sufficiently about what the measurements mean. His simple formulation was that contemporary psychological practice was "rich in decimals but poor in ideas." If psychology was to further its advance, he continues, it would be necessary to place more emphasis "not upon the precise instruments, but upon the right questions," an emphasis that requires that psychology recognize the importance of the contribution of philosophy to its central aim of improved "self-observation." Also at this first meeting, the association adopted, in lieu of a constitution, a series of interim "regulations" to bring some organization to its collective actions.[4]

---

[2] American Psychological Association, *Proceedings*, 2. Cf. James McKeen Cattell: "There were no women among the 31 original members of the American Psychological Association; two, Professor Calkins and Mrs. Ladd-Franklin, were elected at the second meeting. In 1917 there were 39 women, 13 per cent of the number" ("Psychology in America," 28).

[3] Hall's paper, which was to be part of a larger study of American psychology, was never published (cf. Hilgard, *American Psychology in Historical Perspective*, 20). Some of Hall's themes are presumably replicated in his 1893 address, "Psychological Progress."

[4] American Psychological Association, *Proceedings*, 3–13. A constitution—written by James, Cattell, and Baldwin—that emphasized that the objective of the association was "the advancement of Psychology as a science" was adopted at the third meeting (*Psychological Review*, 2:150–51; cf. *Proceedings*, 29; Sokal, "Origins and Early Years," 114–15).

The AΨA met for the second time at Columbia on 27–28 December 1893. In his presidential address, published under the title "President's Address before the New York Meeting of the American Psychological Association," Ladd considered three large questions. The first was the proper methods for psychology. Here he indicates the necessity to characterize both laboratory experimentation and introspective studies as legitimately scientific. The second question that Ladd examined was the relation of psychology and philosophy. Although he notes that, as we have seen in chapter 3, there are many who would attempt to divorce the two disciplines, he maintains that it is ultimately impossible. As he writes, "the relation of psychology, as a science, to the philosophy of mind, and through it to all philosophy, is so intimate and binding that not one of the larger psychological problems can be thoroughly discussed without leading up to some great debate in the field of philosophy." Thus, while the association was "formed in the interests of a science of psychology" and could not be expected "to occupy its time and energies largely in the discussion of philosophical problems," still the psychologists should "add the philosophical spirit to our scientific intent" and be "tolerant and generous toward the various possible expressions of philosophical views." Ladd's third topic was the relation between the efforts of psychology and "the practical welfare of mankind"; and he advocates further practical work, especially in pedagogy, neurology, and jurisprudence.[5]

The third meeting of the AΨA took place at Princeton in December 1894. James read as his presidential address a highly philosophical paper, "The Knowing of Things Together," in which he explores the question of our ability to experience both a gathering of friends and a party, a number of stars and a constellation. "In a glass of lemonade we can taste both the lemon and the sugar at once." His desire was to understand how this happens. "Common sense simply says the mind 'brings the things together,' and common psychology says the 'ideas' of the various things 'combine,' and at most will admit that the occasions on which ideas combine may be made the subject of inquiry," he notes. "But to formulate the phenomenon of knowing things together thus simply as a combining of ideas, is already to foist in a theory about the phenomenon." James questions this assumed associationism, emphasizing that a careful consideration of the phenomena of experience reveals that each phenomenon "offers itself, in the first instance, as that of *knowing things together*; and it is in those terms that its solution must, in the first instance at least, be sought." After a brief examination of "two ways of knowing things, knowing them immediately or intuitively, and knowing them conceptually or representatively," and

---

[5] Ladd, "President's Address," 17–18.

suggesting that in the former kind of knowing the "*mental content and object*" are "*identical,*" he finally rejects the associationist assumption and the transcendentalist project designed to repair it. He maintains further than within even "the minimal pulse of experience" there is felt change. For example, "[t]he smallest effective pulse of consciousness, whatever else it may be consciousness of, is also consciousness of passing time."[6] While James admits that he has offered no complete solution to the problem of the knowing of things together—and that no adequate anti-associationist position had as yet been offered—he is confident of the starting point: the full undifferentiated experience.

The early presidential addresses demonstrate the continuing unsettled relation between philosophy and psychology.[7] The rest of the programs reflected this confusion between science and speculation as well. For some, this meant that the AΨA was slow in its development into a 'true' psychological organization. Cattell offers such a critical stance in 1929. He notes that of the thirty-one original members of the association, "[t]he majority were not primarily psychologists." In fact, he continues, perhaps "only four or five of the number were then actively engaged in psychological research and so continued." Psychology itself "was entangled with philosophy and parasitic on other sciences." Over the years, however, psychology had become less 'philosophical,' less interested in taking what he saw as shortcuts to speculative generalizations, and more willing to do the painstaking research necessary to true psychological advance. Cattell continues that while "[t]heories assumed to explain the way people learn may be more interesting than crude facts," all too often these philosophical theories "are likely to become beds of Procrustes into which observations are fitted." The search for regularity and law in psychology cannot hope to achieve any "simple equation," since people do not learn "everything in the same way . . ." Psychologists must forego any hopes of simple results: "we are concerned with the real world in which we live; it is not the scientific man but the philosopher who hopes to see from his armchair a vision of monism seated in the lap of the absolute."[8]

---

[6] James, "Knowing of Things Together," 71–77.

[7] Cf. Edward Franklin Buchner: "The borderland between the scientific and the speculative interests has not only been wandered over, but there have been technical discussions of the latter. This appears unquestionably in such themes as [James's] 'The Knowing of Things Together' [1894], [Fullerton's] 'The Self in Its Function as Knower' [1896], [Royce's] 'Recent Logical Inquiries and their Psychological Bearings' [1901]. Six presidents dwelt upon the relation between psychology and philosophy, some at length, but all approvingly, including one who has stood most stoutly and clearly for the development of exact, quantitative results in the laboratory" ("Ten Years of American Psychology," 202).

[8] Cattell, "Psychology in America," 22, 30; cf. Boring, *History of Experimental Psychology*, 520–21.

This was Cattell's more settled position in 1929; but we can get a better picture of the initial years of the association if we compare this later evaluation with one that he offered thirty-five years earlier. In his AΨA presidential address at the fourth meeting in 1895, he had been more appreciative of the contribution of philosophy and the need for the cooperation of the disciplines.

> Psychology has long been and properly remains the gateway to architectonic philosophy. It may be that experiment cannot answer the final questions of philosophy, but the worldview of each of us depends increasingly on what the natural and exact sciences contribute to it. The white light of philosophy can only result from the proper commingling of the colors of the sciences. Systems of philosophy, elaborated prior to the development of modern science or without regard to this, may receive our admiration as poetry, but they cannot claim our adherence as truth . . . Epistemology, ethics, logic and aesthetics are regarded as philosophic disciplines, but they rest increasingly on psychology . . . The twilight of philosophy can be changed to a dawn only by the light of science, and psychology can contribute more light than any other science.[9]

Over the years, this understanding of psychology as a prolegomenon to philosophy had been replaced, in Cattell's mind at least, with an understanding of psychology that valued it instead of philosophy.

In agreement with the earlier Cattell, however, there were many other philosopher/psychologists who saw philosophy as the central academic discipline. While psychology might focus upon the experimental and the 'scientific' and avoid the speculative and the 'metaphysical,' still philosophy could defend the importance of its broader inquiries into consciousness and truth and meaning. Andrew Campbell Armstrong, for example, wrote in 1897 of the essential role of philosophy. For him, the growth in psychology meant eventual greater growth for philosophy, because we will still need philosophy to explain the meaning of what psychology had discovered. "After detailed [laboratory] inquiries, after systematic discussions, the inevitable philosophical questions are forcing their way to the front," he writes. "American scholars have joined heartily in the world-movement that has made psychology a science in its beginnings and its empirical development," and they are now beginning to recognize "the metaphysical issues which the science involves and are commencing to face them with earnestness and success."[10]

---

[9] Cattell, "Address of the President," 148.

[10] Armstrong, "Philosophy in American Colleges," 16. Cf. Frank Thilly: "before the division of labor, the kingdom of knowledge formed an undivided whole, and philosophy was monarch of all she surveyed . . . in our day all that has changed . . . Philosophy, the sometime queen, has become a dowager; her children have deserted her . . . The only members of the

As the first decade of the AΨA drew to a close at the end of the nine-teenth century, the relationship between the two disciplines remained unset-tled; and, even with no agreement on precise definitions of philosophy and psychology, the two disciplines continued slowly but surely to drift apart. While the AΨA grew in size and in prominence over the decade from 1892–1901, psychology as an emerging discipline was itself drifting away from its philosophical parent. As a result, the meetings of the association became more and more disjointed. Buchner categorized the 283 papers read during the first decade of the meetings of the AΨA as: "eighty-six items of an experimental character, thirty-four philosophical, twenty-eight on appa-ratus, twenty-five theoretical, twenty-five genetic, twenty-three descriptive, twenty physical and physiological, twelve historical, twelve pedagogical, seven comparative, seven miscellaneous" and four discussions with natural-ists. He notes further that a few of the meetings "have been markedly philo-sophical," and over the years there had emerged a "philosophy group."[11] The 'philosophy group' to which Buchner is referring began at the fourth meeting in 1895. The proceedings note, "Between the morning and the afternoon sessions on Saturday an informal meeting of those interested in the formation of a Philosophical Society, or the organization of a Philosophical section within the Psychological Association, was held, and at the afternoon meeting the matter was brought before the Association and by vote referred to the Council with full power to act" (S 3:124).[12] The decision that the council made for the next meeting was apparently to bun-dle the philosophically oriented papers into a single session, separated from the "scientific" papers (ΨR 4:107; S 5:207, 210–11). At the business session of the fifth meeting in December 1896, Lightner Witmer proposed that future AΨA programs contain "only such papers and contributions . . . as are psychological in subject matter," that the association form "an American Philosophical or Metaphysical Association," and that it elect to AΨA mem-bership only individuals who had made "contributions to psychology" (ΨR 4:109). These proposals were referred to the Council.

---

original household left are psychology, logic, aesthetics, epistemology, and metaphysics, a pal-try remnant of a once brilliant and numerous crew . . . And now the demand is frequently heard that psychology too cut loose from her old-fashioned sisters, and set up an establish-ment of her own or go to live with the natural sciences . . . The proposed separation, how-ever, would, in my opinion, be beneficial neither to philosophy nor to psychology itself. The affiliation is to the advantage of both parties" ("Psychology, Natural Science, and Philosophy," 130–31; cf. Armstrong, "Philosophy in the United States," 9–10).

[11] Buchner, "Ten Years of American Psychology," 201; Cf. Cattell, "Psychology in America," 24–25.

[12] The following set of abbreviations has been used: AJΨ: *American Journal of Psychology*; JP: *Journal of Philosophy*; PR: *Philosophical Review*; S: *Science*, new series; ΨB: *Psychological Bulletin*; ΨR: *Psychological Review*.

An unsigned note in the *American Journal of Psychology* had earlier in 1896 commented about the lack of experimental papers at the recent meetings of the AΨA, noting, "The retirement of the experimentalists,— emphasized further by the proposal to devote a certain amount of time at each meeting to philosophical inquiries,—cannot but be regretted" (AJΨ 7:448). Still, at the sixth meeting in 1897 there was again a special session for papers "of a strictly philosophical character." There was also, apparently for the first time at AΨA meetings, the separation of the audience into concurrent sessions for the "discussion of physical and mental tests" and "the reading of psychological papers" (ΨR 5:145). At the business session of the seventh meeting in 1898, the AΨA voted, at the proposal of Edmund Clarke Sanford, to consider the creation of a "philosophical section," to organize future meetings so as "to gather together philosophical papers as far as practicable into the programme of one session," and to survey the membership about the entire philosophical question (ΨR 6:147–48). In response to these developments, Charles M. Bliss maintained that these changes would be "unwise at the present time." Among the reasons that he offered was his belief that, while at AΨA meetings "philosophical papers never called forth as much interest as the scientific," still "our best psychologists are among our best philosophers, and their withdrawal from even a part of the meetings of the Association would be a serious loss." For him, "the greatest need of psychology at present is more of sound philosophy, and the greatest need of philosophy more of sound psychology. Closer union is more to be desired than further separation."[13] Bliss's view seems, however, to have been in the minority among AΨA members.

From the philosophical side, the history of this increasing separation is told a bit differently. Harry Norman Gardiner, for example, writes in 1926:

> The American Psychological Association, while defining its object as "the advancement of psychology as a science," and declaring eligible for membership "those who are engaged in this work," nevertheless admitted to membership a goodly number of teachers of psychology who, though keenly interested in watching the developments of the science, could hardly be regarded as engaged in promoting them. Some of the philosophically minded of these members took occasion of the meetings of the Association to offer papers on subjects in which they were more particularly interested, and these papers were accepted and sometimes formed a not inconsiderable portion of the programme.[14]

We can consider the exact numbers of papers as the two emerging disciplines moved toward their eventual divergence. For example, at the eighth

---

[13] Bliss, "Proposed Changes," 237–38.
[14] Gardiner, "First Twenty-Five Years of the APA," 145.

meeting in 1899, in addition to John Dewey's educationally oriented presidential address, "Psychology and Social Practice," seventeen 'philosophical' papers were read out of a total of forty-four. Among them were: Mary Whiton Calkins, "Elements of Consciousness"; James Edwin Creighton, "Methodology and Truth"; John Grier Hibben, "Practical Procedure in Inference"; Joseph Alexander Leighton, "Metaphysical Method"; and Alexander Meiklejohn, "The Concept of Substance" (ΨR 7:127–54). At the beginning of this meeting, "the association met as a whole, and papers of interest to both philosophers and psychologists were presented"; but later on the association "divided into two sections: Section A (Experimental) and Section B (Philosophical)" (PR 9:237). One report on this meeting notes: "The plan of meeting in two sections (an experimental and a philosophical), tried for the first time at this meeting, worked satisfactorily, though many members would have been glad to have been present in both sections at the same time" (AJΨ 11:280). At the ninth meeting of the AΨA in 1900, eleven 'philosophical' papers were read out of a total of twenty-four. Among them were: William Caldwell, "Professor Ladd's Theory of Reality"; Grace Neal Dolson, "Nietzsche"; F. C. French, "The Doctrine of Twofold Truth"; Fullerton, "The Kantian Doctrine of Space"; and Christine Ladd-Franklin, "Reduction to Absurdity of the Ordinary Treatment of the Syllogism" (ΨR 8:158–82). Again "parallel sections" were adopted (PR 10:111) so that "the Philosophical Section of the Association" met in large part separately (S 13:213).

Gardiner continues that this state of affairs "was satisfactory neither to the philosophers nor to psychologists." Each side recognized that the two groups were drifting apart. "The philosophers were fully aware of the anomalies of a situation in which their claims were allowed only on sufferance; the psychologists were disposed to regard these claims as an impertinence and to resent the intrusion of the philosophical camel into the psychological tent." The situation was felt to be increasingly problematic from each side. "Two ways only seemed open to regularize the procedure," he continues, "either a separate Philosophical Association should be formed, or the Psychological Association should be so reorganized as to include a philosophical section." The AΨA seemed unable, however, to adopt the latter course of action. Still, as Gardiner notes, "The tolerated arrangement spoken of might have continued indefinitely had not the philosophers taken matters into their own hands, and by founding an independent society ended a situation that was becoming intolerable."[15] The philosophers, in fact, founded *two* such societies.

---

[15] Gardiner, "First Twenty-Five Years of the APA," 146–47. At the transitional tenth meeting of the AΨA, in December 1901–January 1902, 'philosophical' papers still made up about 40 percent of the total; but at the eleventh meeting, in December 1902–January 1903, 'philosophical' papers represented only about 20 percent of the total.

SOME ACADEMIC ASSOCIATIONS, WITH FOUNDING DATES

American Philological Society (1869)
American Chemical Society (1876)
Modern Language Association (1883)
American Historical Association (1884)
American Economic Association (1885)
American Mathematical Society (1888)
Geological Society of America (1888)
American Psychological Association (1892)
American Physical Society (1899)
Western Philosophical Association (1900)
American Philosophical Association (1901)
American Anthropological Association (1902)
American Political Science Association (1903)
Southern Society for Philosophy and Psychology (1904)
American Sociological Society (1905)

Sources:
Roger L. Geiger, *To Advance Knowledge*, 23–24;
Bernard Berelson, *Graduate Education in the United States*, 15;
Frederic Austin Ogg, *Research in the Humanities and Social Sciences*, 3n;
Caroline Winterer, *The Culture of Classicism*, 155.

Thus it was that in the first dozen years after the founding of the AΨA in 1892, various developments led to the founding of two explicitly philosophical societies—the Western Philosophical Association and the American Philosophical Association—and of another society—the Southern Society for Philosophy and Psychology—that was (and remains) dedicated to advancing both disciplines. We can begin with the earliest, the Western Philosophical Association (WPA). Frank Thilly, who was teaching at Missouri, had been working for the establishment of some sort of philosophical association for a number of years; and, in conjunction with Olin Templin of Kansas, Albert Ross Hill of Nebraska, and Cleland Boyd McAfee of Park College, he finally succeeded in January 1900. In the March 1900 issue of *The Philosophical Review*, there appears a brief announcement that begins as follows: "A number of teachers and students of philosophy in the West met at Kansas City on January 1, 1900 and organized the Western Philosophical Association. The aim of this society is 'to stimulate an interest in philosophy in all its branches, and to encourage original investigation.' All advanced students of philosophy are eligible for membership." The particular geographical focus of this Western association was to be from the Mississippi to the Rocky Mountains. Approximately thirty members were in attendance at this meeting, representing institutions of higher learning from Minnesota, Missouri, Kansas, Iowa, South Dakota, Colorado, and Nebraska. Among the other items of business settled in Kansas City was the choosing of officers for the upcoming year. The five officers selected were: Thilly, president; Templin, vice-president; Hill, secretary-treasurer; and McAfee and George Thomas White Patrick of Iowa as the remaining members of the executive committee. The announcement concluded: "The first regular meeting of the Association will be held at Lincoln, Nebraska, during the Christmas vacation of 1900" (PR 9:237).

This first meeting of the WPA occurred as announced at Nebraska, on 1–2 January 1901. Thilly, a member of the AΨA and the driving force behind the founding of the WPA, offered his presidential address, "The Theory of Interaction." This paper did not touch upon the issues of the nature of philosophical or psychological associations or the professionalization of academia. It was rather a discussion of parallelism in the philosophy of mind. He notes the importance of the mind-body issue since the work of Descartes and the recent popularity of "parallelism, the theory which denies that there can be a causal relation between the mental and physical realms." He himself favors the theory of interaction, which maintains "that states of consciousness are causes of changes in the physical world, and physical occurrences the causes of changes in consciousness." The bulk of Thilly's address was designed to demonstrate that interaction is not impossible, and he closes with a kind of common-sense assertion that a state of consciousness "is a cause in the sense of being an element without which another element called a physical occurrence cannot take place" even if "we do not know *how* a state of consciousness can be the cause of a physical change."[16] The proceedings contain the abstracts of a number of philosophical and psychological papers on such topics as the will, early Greek philosophy, imitation, and the psychology of profanity. Included among the business matters at the meeting was the announcement that "[t]he constitution, which had served as working basis for the first year, was adopted by the association, with an additional clause providing for changes by a two-thirds vote of the members present at any annual meeting." (Unfortunately, this constitution was never published, and all copies appear to have been lost.) The proceedings also list forty-six "charter" members of the association, almost all of whom had university or college affiliations (PR 10:162, 173–74).

The organization of the American Philosophical Association (APA) presents a history similar to that of the WPA. In particular, both were

---

[16] Thilly, "Theory of Interaction," 124, 137.

related if only negatively to the AΨA. Gardiner writes, "The American Philosophical Association, founded in 1901, is, historically, an offshoot from the American Psychological Association founded ten years earlier. Thus in the case of the two Associations we have a reversal of the historical order of development of their respective disciplines."[17] He also recounts the events that led up to the founding of the APA. "The initiation was taken by the Cornell group, headed by Professor Creighton," he writes. "Sometime in the Fall of 1901 there was a gathering at James Seth's rooms in Ithaca, as I have lately been informed by President Hibben [of Princeton], at which the suggestion of an independent organization was discussed and as a result of which Hibben started the call for an official meeting in New York." Those taking part in this meeting were Creighton, Seth, David Irons, Hibben, and Thilly.[18] "Professor Thilly, then at the University of Missouri, was the President of the Western Philosophical Association, which had been founded the year before, and it is probable that this fact exerted a stimulating influence on the decision."[19] The initiative for establishing a philosophical society was carried forward later that fall in New York City. Gardiner describes this organizational meeting as follows:

The meeting in New York at which the American Philosophical Association was founded was held on November 2, 1901, following an informal luncheon at the Murray Hill Hotel. The meeting was attended by representatives from Brown, Columbia, Cornell, Princeton, Wesleyan, and Yale Universities and Bryn Mawr, Hobart and Smith Colleges. The names of these founders it may be of interest to record; they were [Walter Goodnow] Everett and Meiklejohn (Brown), [Herbert G.] Lord (Columbia), Creighton (Cornell), Hibben (Princeton), Armstrong (Wesleyan), [George M.] Duncan (Yale), Irons (Bryn Mawr), Leighton (Hobart), and Gardiner and [Ralph Barton] Perry (Smith).[20] Many letters favorable to the formation of the society were received from other teachers of philosophy who had been invited, but were unable to be present.[21] It was decided that the society should be called the American Philosophical

---

[17] Gardiner, "First Twenty-Five Years of the APA," 145.

[18] Of this quintet, all but Seth were members of the AΨA—and Seth was a former member.

[19] Gardiner, "First Twenty-Five Years of the APA," 147. Creighton had been at the first meeting of the WPA in January 1901. The unsigned record in *Science* lists his presentation as "'Some Philosophical Problems of the Present Time'—An informal address by J. E. Creighton, Professor of Logic and Metaphysics, Cornell University, and editor of the *Philosophical Review*" (S 13:394).

[20] Gardiner's draft also lists E. Hershey Sneath (Yale) as being present at this meeting (Black Notebook, 1).

[21] Gardiner's draft lists the following sample of absent supporters: Josiah Royce, George Santayana, and Dickinson Sergeant Miller (Harvard), Fullerton (Pennsylvania), Caldwell (Northwestern), and J. G. Russell (Williams) (ibid.).

Association, and that the first meeting should be held during the following [1902] Easter vacation.[22]

From among their number, three officers were chosen—Creighton as president, Alexander Thomas Ormond of Princeton (who had not been able to attend the New York City meeting) as vice-president, and Gardiner as secretary-treasurer—and four others—Armstrong, Duncan, Everett, and Hibben—joined them on an executive committee "to invite others to membership, to draw up a constitution and to arrange for the first meeting" (S 15:583; cf. PR 11:264). The executive committee met immediately after this organizational meeting adjourned and "slightly revised" the list of individuals who would be invited to join the association. Further, "[t]he question of inviting women to membership was left to be decided by the Association."[23]

Before turning to efforts to recruit members, I would like to consider the name of this new association. Following upon the WPA, it might have seemed that the obvious choice of a name should have been the 'Eastern Philosophical Association.' This name was rejected, however, for two reasons. The first was that the founders of the APA did not envision it as a 'regional' association; the second, the strong connotation of 'Eastern' philosophy with theosophy and the occult.[24] The name chosen for itself by the APA did lead to some trouble, however, and I will divert the chronological flow a bit to deal with it here. The problem was that the name APA resembled quite closely the name of the American Philosophical Society (APS), the society founded by Benjamin Franklin in 1743 in Philadelphia for promoting useful knowledge. This similarity quickly came to the notice of some members of the APS; and, on 7 April 1902, its president, General Isaac Jones Wistar, wrote to Creighton to call his attention to "the apparent confusion between our corporate name and that recently selected by your Association . . ." While recognizing that the name APA "was in no wise intended as trespass upon us," Wistar still requested that the APA "give a renewed and generous reconsideration to the subject of your official or corporate name." He was sure that "your wide learning and fertility of thought will enable you—if so disposed—to select a name which might equally accomplish your purpose without even the appearance of trespass upon us." Creighton responded that, although he was by this time no longer APA president, he regretted any potential harm to the APS "which has had such a long and honorable history." Still, he maintained

---

[22] Gardiner, "First Twenty-Five Years of the APA," 147–48.

[23] Gardiner's Black Notebook, 3.

[24] See, for example, Gardiner to Hugo Münsterberg, 23 November 1901 (Münsterberg Papers).

that, because "the general character and aims of the two Associations are so different," no confusion is "likely to arise." He continued that he would forward Wistar's letter to APA secretary Gardiner for consideration by the executive committee. While he indicated that that committee would no doubt consider the matter "in the same friendly and generous spirit which manifests itself in your letter, and with a due respect for the historic rights of your Society," he did not hold out any false hope. Creighton maintained that the name APA "seems to describe—as words are used at present—the character of our organization, and serves to mark out our place among other similar bodies, such as The American Psychological Association, The American Philological Association, etc." and he closes with the assertion that "in a sense there was no other name possible."[25] In an internal memo of 14 April 1902, Wistar noted that "our position in the matter should be insisted upon even to legal resort—if necessary . . ."; and at the APS meeting of 18 April 1902 the membership stood behind its president and directed him to "take such further measures as he may deem advisable for the protection of its interests . . ."[26] The controversy continued with a small flurry of additional letters over the next year or so. In these, the APS mentioned some actual confusions—like misdirected letters from abroad and journal announcements that had scrambled the names—and the APA minimized any possible future confusions.[27] A century later occasional confusions still occur.

To return now to the task of recruiting members for the APA, we find Gardiner himself heading up the operation. He reports that on 12 November 1901, ten days after the organizational meeting, "a circular letter was sent to college and university teachers of philosophy, and to a few others, informing them of the steps already taken and inviting them to join the Association . . ."[28] The text of this printed recruitment letter ran as follows:

Dear Sir:—

At a meeting held in New York on the second of November and attended by representatives of the philosophical departments in Brown, Columbia, Cornell, Princeton, Wesleyan and Yale universities and Bryn Mawr, Hobard and Smith colleges, it was decided to form an association to

<hr />

[25] Wistar to Creighton, 7 April 1902; Creighton to Wistar, 9 April 1902 (APS Archives).

[26] Wistar to APS secretaries, 14 April 1902; APS Minute Book, 18 April 1902, 655 (APS Archives).

[27] Wistar to Gardiner, 1 December 1902; Gardiner to Wistar, 2 December 1902; Gardiner to Wistar, 8 December 1902; Edgar F. Smith to Josiah Royce, 12 December 1903 (APS Archives); cf. Gardiner, "First Twenty-Five Years of the APA," 150.

[28] Gardiner, "First Twenty-Five Years of the APA," 148.

be called the American Philosophical Association. Many letters favorable to the establishment of such a society were received from teachers of philosophy in other institutions who were unable to be present. The Association was temporarily organized by the election of Prof. J. E. Creighton (Cornell) as President, Prof. A. T. Ormond (Princeton) as Vice-President, Prof. H. N. Gardiner (Smith) as Secretary and Treasurer, and of an Executive Committee consisting of Prof. A. C. Armstrong, Jr. (Wesleyan), Prof. W. G. Everett (Brown), Prof. G. M. Duncan (Yale), Prof. J. G. Hibben (Princeton) and the officers mentioned. This Committee was empowered to invite to membership in the Association such persons as seemed to them eligible, a tentative list of names having been presented at the meeting. Acting on their instructions, I have the honor to inform you that you are hereby invited to membership and co-operation in the Association, of which invitation I shall be happy to receive your acceptance. It was thought that at present the membership fee should be small, a merely nominal sum, sufficient to meet current expenses. A Constitution is to be submitted at the first regular meeting, which will be held in New York during the Easter recess at a time to be more precisely determined on later.

Kindly reply as soon as may be convenient, to

Yours very truly,

/s/ H. N. Gardiner
Secretary.

While it is possible that any number of prospective members were reluctant to join such an association,[29] Gardiner records that only one negative response to the invitation was received. It came from James, who replied to Gardiner on the back of the invitation:

Dear Gardiner,

I am still pretty poorly & can't "jine" anything—but, apart from that, I don't foresee much good from a philosophical Society. Philosophical discussion proper only succeeds between intimates who have learned how

---

[29] Dewey expressed his reservations to Cattell—both were former presidents of the AΨA—in late 1901 as follows: "I have a circular from Gardiner about an American Philosophical Association. You must know more about this thing than I do. I do not think I care about joining if it is going to detract from the interests of the Psychological Association. It would seem to me much better to provide for a separate meeting of the philosophical section of the old association, if it is desirable to have an additional meeting at Easter time" (Dewey to Cattell, 19 November 1901—*Correspondence of John Dewey*, # 00794). In any case, Dewey was one of the charter members of the APA.

to converse by months of weary trials & failure. The philosoph[er] is a lone beast dwelling in his individual burrow.—Count me *out!* . . .[30]

From James's response, it appears that there was a significant difference between his approaches to the disciplines of psychology and philosophy. He was, as we have seen, one of the founders of the AΨA in 1892; and, although he missed its first meeting in 1892, he was an active participant at the 1893 meeting and was elected its third president for 1894. (He would later serve as AΨA president again in 1904.) We can only guess that, for James, psychology benefits from the sort of interaction and cooperation that a professional association facilitates, whereas philosophy is for the most part the work of 'lone beasts.' In any case, he later relented and joined the APA, becoming its sixth president in 1906.

To return to the narrative, *The Philosophical Review* reports in its issue of March, 1902: "The American Philosophical Association will hold its first annual meeting March 31st to April 2d, at Columbia University" (PR 11:216). Gardiner records that: "The membership of the Association, including those who had joined by invitation and the thirty-one elected at the first meeting, numbered ninety-eight. It was noted that these should be recorded as charter members. Forty were in attendance."[31] The forty members present adopted a constitution that delineated its purpose as "the promotion of the interests of philosophy in all its branches, and more particularly the encouragement of original work among the members of the Association." In Article II, membership procedures were specified. Articles III and IV discuss the offices and their duties. The president, vice-president, and secretary-treasurer were all established as annual offices, with an executive committee consisting of those three and four others, elected in pairs for staggered two-year terms. Among the duties of the executive committee were those of nominating officers, recommending new members, and organizing the annual meetings. "The Executive Committee shall arrange the Programme, and direct all other arrangements for the meetings; in particular, they shall have the power to determine what papers shall be read at the meetings." Article V describes the procedures for amendments. In addition to this constitutional business, the newly founded association took up the issue of its relationship with the previously established WPA: "The relation of the Association to the Western Philosophical Association was referred to the Executive

---

[30] James to Gardiner, 14 November 1901 (*Correspondence*, 9:558). It is due to the efficiency of James's response that we know the text of the invitation letter. It was saved by Gardiner, apparently for its *James value* rather than its *APA value* (Gardiner Papers, College Archives, Smith College).

[31] Gardiner, "First Twenty-Five Years of the APA," 149.

Committee to confer with the Executive Committee of the latter Association and to report at the next meeting." This hint at unification was only the first of many such announcements over the next few decades, as we shall see in chapter 14. It was also arranged at the first meeting that *The Philosophical Review* would publish the proceedings of the meetings (PR 11:264–66).

The proceedings of this initial meeting of the APA contain abstracts of the sixteen papers presented. Among them we find a few papers of a 'psychological' slant—on the philosophy of mind, individuation, and functionalism—but the vast majority of the papers dealt with more narrow 'philosophical' issues. There were discussions of such figures as Aristotle, Kant, and Thomas Hill Green. There were papers on logic, on ethics, on aesthetics, and on the philosophy of religion (PR 11:267–83).[32] The most interesting paper, for our purposes, was the presidential address, in which Creighton offered his thoughts on the purposes of the newly founded association. Setting aside minor aims like the intention "to renew old friendships and to form new ones," he focuses upon what he takes to be the central purpose of the association and its likely effects on the future of philosophy in America. Creighton writes, it is "in promoting and facilitating the interchange of ideas between the philosophical workers of the present day, who are scattered throughout this part of the country, that the Association will find its main function." Although almost all of those "philosophical workers" had careers teaching philosophy in colleges and universities, he rejected an interest on the part of the association in teaching, which he disparages as "*die zeitraubende und kraftabsorbirende academische Lehrthätigkeit*" ["the time-stealing and strength-sapping academic busy-work"]. Along this line, he continues:

> it would be a mistake to make the discussion of methods of teaching philosophy a coordinate purpose, or even to introduce papers on this subject into the programme of the meetings. Even if the membership of the Association were composed wholly of teachers of philosophy, which will never, I hope, be the case, the meetings should not, it seems to me, be occupied with the consideration of such secondary and subordinate topics . . . the discussion of methods of teaching philosophy is in itself rather a stupid way of wasting time . . . even in our capacity as teachers it is courage and inspiration to attack problems for ourselves, to go to first-hand sources and so actually discover by our own efforts what we teach to students, that is the one thing needful . . . it will be an advantage in every way for the members of this Association to forget, so far as possible, their profession during the days of meeting, and to

---

[32] Gardiner reports that a few of the scheduled papers were omitted because their authors were absent, and another was "read by title"—i.e., not read—because of a lack of time (Black Notebook, 5).

come together simply as human beings interested in philosophical investigation and scholarship.[33]

The focus of the APA, Creighton maintains, should be different. "The main purpose which we *should* conscientiously set before us," he tells the membership, "is to promote and encourage original investigation and publication." He continues that by adopting such criteria as "setting a high standard, and demanding that the papers presented shall represent the best work and most original thought of those who offer them, by keeping before us as the main purpose of the organization the advancement of philosophy," the APA can do a great deal "both to inspire and direct original work." He especially emphasizes its important role as "agent in creating the atmosphere and furthering the spirit which are essential to scholarly research." This scholarly research includes, of course, work in the history of philosophy. "In philosophy, it is perhaps more essential than in any other field of inquiry that one should build upon the work of one's predecessors," he writes; good historical work "makes possible a more adequate comprehension of the genesis and meaning of our own problems." The focus of the APA is thus to be upon the creation of original work; the advancement of philosophy is to be through scholarly research.[34]

Creighton maintained that a philosophical association that managed to advance philosophy in this way would go a long way toward redressing the current "standing of philosophy in the learned world as a specialized subject of inquiry." He continues that "philosophy does not enjoy the general recognition, even among educated men, that is accorded to many of the other sciences, nor is the philosophical teacher and writer universally conceded to be a specially trained scholar whose opinions in his own field are as much entitled to respect as those of the physicist or biologist in his special domain." Philosophy was still understood by too many as being what it had been: the religiously oriented capstone on the education of a Christian gentleman. Because philosophy—in the consciousness of its external evaluators at least—was still an activity of amateurs rather than of professionals, its "scientific status as a real and independent subject of

---

[33] Creighton, "Purposes of a Philosophical Association," 220, 224, 231–32. Cf. Bruce Wilshire: "Teaching a secondary and subordinate topic for a philosopher! This foretells the course of professional philosophy in this century. Removed is the only sure foundation that philosophy ever had: the cooperative effort of young and old, person to person, to orient ourselves in the world, make some sense of life, and to live sanely" (*Moral Collapse of the University*, 118; cf. Pitts, "Profession of Philosophy," 139–40). While Creighton did not want to mix teaching and the APA, he was not uninterested in philosophy teaching in general. See, for example, his "Discussion" of "Aim of Philosophy Teaching in American Colleges."

[34] Creighton, "Purposes of a Philosophical Association," 230–31, 222.

investigation is tacitly or explicitly denied." Thus, part of the problem of
philosophy's low status was the result of its prior role as "handmaid to theology." In this "subordinate and ancillary position which it so long occupied in this country," he continues, philosophy too often degenerated
"into empty logomachies and lifeless definitions and justly becomes a
byword and reproach among real thinkers."[35]

Turning from this historical factor, Creighton placed at least some of
the blame for philosophy's continuing low status at the feet of his contemporaries. He offers "two indictments" of present philosophers for philosophy's failure to "occupy the place in public esteem which properly
belongs to it . . ." First, he notes that "as a class" philosophers do not display "the same zeal in original investigation, or the same scholarly devotion to their subject that is exhibited by many other groups of scientific
workers," and as a result "outsiders are not quite convinced that philosophers are in earnest, or that they believe in the seriousness of their own
work." Creighton's second, and principal, point is that "the educated outsider withholds his recognition from philosophy, because he believes that
it has been barren of real results." He notes that it is necessary that philosophy, "like the other sciences, minister to human life"; but up to that
time philosophy had failed to convince the public "that their results are
capable of becoming vital and directing influences in the spiritual life of the
individual and of society at the present day." While this problem was serious, he was certain that he had the answer in the establishment of the APA.
If philosophers wanted to achieve the respect and status that had been
achieved by the *other* scientists, then they would need to cooperate like
other scientists. "The most striking characteristic of all modern scientific
work is found in the fact that it is the result of conscious cooperation
between a number of individuals," he continues, "the necessities of cooperation and mutual help in scientific work were more or less completely
realized at an early date." In field after field we find "the effort of the individual to free himself from the idols of the cave, by appealing to the reason of his fellows to confirm or correct his own subjective opinions." The
realization on the part of the other sciences "of the necessity of a more
extended as well as a more systematic and intimate comparison of views
among workers in the same field" led to the creation of the many academic associations that were an earmark of the current age. *Pace* James,
Creighton believed that even among philosophers this recognition had
arisen. While he admits that "[p]hilosophers have been slower than their
fellow workers in inaugurating any movement to secure this end," he
maintains that with the establishment of the APA there would be the pos-

---

[35] Ibid., 232–33.

sibility of greater personal interaction and of more sustained public and cooperative work.[36]

Creighton's call for an interactive and cooperative society to advance the work, and eventually the status, of philosophy reflected his own idealistic perspective, one that emphasized the partiality of individual consciousness and the possibility of redemption in the group. He writes that "the insufficiency of the isolated individual and the consequent necessity of cooperation have not been so clearly realized by philosophers as by workers in almost every other department of knowledge." Moreover, this has been so even though "philosophy, of all species of scientific inquiry, is that which demands, in order to be fruitfully prosecuted, the closest and most intimate intellectual relations between a number of minds." Our methods as we attempt to recognize the meaning of experience must be inductive and cooperative. Philosophy's "starting point and basis must be the facts of experience." Creighton continues that "the data of the philosopher are so complex and many-sided that, working by himself, he is certain to fail to take account or properly estimate some facts of importance . . . no single individual can look, as it were, in all directions at once." The philosopher, therefore, stands in "constant need of criticism, of supplementation, and of having objections forced upon his attention"; and this need is best met through personal interaction with other philosophers. As he puts it, "when objections and opposing views are backed by the immediate presence of one's neighbor, they cannot easily be ignored." This kind of cooperative interaction was what the APA would be able to provide.[37]

A second idealistic theme in Creighton's presidential address—a theme that we have seen before and that will continue to be important throughout the early years of the APA—is the necessity that our advancing society adopt the synoptic vision of philosophy before it can hope to understand the meaning of the findings of the other sciences. In other words, it is necessary to interpret, philosophically, the results with which the special sciences present us. "Facts in the form in which they are delivered to him by the naturalist, have in themselves no special significance for the philosopher," he continues. "Nor can he use them as the foundation stones of his system." The philosopher must approach the facts, "from his own standpoint, he must read them in the light of his own concepts, and cannot accept a formulation of them which is confessedly one-sided and abstract like that of natural science." This means that "philosophy, to be philosophy at all, has to *humanize* its facts, that is, to look at them from the standpoint of complete and self-conscious human experience, for it is only from

---

[36] Ibid., 233–34, 221–22.
[37] Ibid., 224, 226–27.

this standpoint that a meaning for them can be found." The philosopher, although a scientist, is "essentially a humanist rather than a naturalist," and philosophy's "closest affiliations" are to be found with those sciences "that deal with the products of man's thought and purposive activity."[38] As we continue, we will see that philosophy's relationship with science will occupy much of the efforts of the APA as it move into the future.

Before I conclude this chapter, two tasks remain. One is to introduce at least some critical thoughts about the founding of the philosophical associations that we have been examining. The other is to examine, however briefly, one more such association. The fourth of the academic societies in the present story is the Southern Society for Philosophy and Psychology (SSPP). It was founded by Buchner, then a member of the APA and the AΨΨA, who had, after a number of years of teaching, become professor of philosophy and education at Alabama. He found the academic situation there to be far worse than at other institutions where he had taught; and he believed that an academic association would do much to overcome isolation and inadequate facilities. Early in 1904, he began by writing to such well-regarded philosophers and psychologists as: James, Cattell, Ladd, Fullerton, Gardiner, Baldwin, Thilly, Henry Rutgers Marshall, Livingston Farrard, James Rowland Angell, William A. Hammond, and Henry Heath Bawden seeking "advice as to the inauguration of such an organization, and as to its affiliation with the national societies." Based on their favorable responses, a preliminary meeting was held in Atlanta in February 1904, at which Baldwin, of Johns Hopkins, was elected president, and Buchner secretary-treasurer. The first annual meeting of SSPP began with papers and official business on 27 December 1904 at Hopkins, and ended the next day at Pennsylvania in conjunction with the joint meeting of the AΨA and the APA. This society was, and to this day remains, committed to the creation of a social place in which philosophy and psychology can offer mutual nourishment to each other.[39]

My final theme in this chapter will be to hint at the nature of some of the criticisms to which the philosophical associations that we have been considering have been subjected. Creighton's emphasis upon the need for philosophy to address its problem of low social status brings up the question of the motivation of philosophers in their establishment of the WPA and the APA. One interpretation, with which my presentation has been infused, is that these philosophers were addressing the great disparity between the respect and hope that they had for their discipline and the lack

---

[38] Ibid., 237.
[39] Miner, "Twenty-Fifth Anniversary," 2–3; cf. Buchner, "Work of the Southern Society"; Pate, "Southern Society."

of any comparable status in the eyes of so many others, both inside and outside of academia. Inspired by the possibilities of the new university situation, in which philosophy had broken free of past theological restraints and liberated itself to address philosophical problems of contemporary import, the creation of the philosophical associations to foster this work was a significant step forward. There are, of course, other possible interpretations. The most clearly articulated is that of Daniel J. Wilson, who writes:

> both the Western and the American Philosophical associations rose out of a twin desire to prevent further splintering of new disciplines from philosophy and to provide a professional framework and common forum in which the increasingly specialized philosophers could cooperate to mutual benefit. Unlike the newer disciplines of economics, sociology, political science, and psychology, which were formed by breaking away from nineteenth-century moral philosophy, academic philosophy professionalized in response to these challenges to its traditional domain. Whereas for the other disciplines professionalization represented progress and the achievement of an independent intellectual and institutional identity, philosophic professionalization was defensive—an attempt to prevent further defections from the traditional preserve of moral philosophy by making philosophy itself more specialized, more scientific, and more professional.[40]

We should keep this interpretation in mind as we proceed through the first few decades of the associations' histories; but, so far, it seems to be an a priori application of the thesis about academic status insecurity that we have known since C. Wright Mills.[41] Rather than focusing on seeing these associating philosophers as individuals who were attempting to defend their eroding academic turf, it seems to me more valuable to see them as attempting to carry the emerging profession of philosophy forward to fulfill its inchoate potential.

---

[40] Wilson, *Science, Community*, 124; cf. 5, 99, 110; "Professionalization," 54.
[41] C. Wright Mills, *Sociology and Pragmatism*.

HARRY NORMAN GARDINER

Photo courtesy of Smith College Archives, Smith College.
Photograph by Randall, New Haven, CT.

5

The Activities of the Philosophical
Associations

The actions of those philosophers who formed the WPA and the APA demonstrated many virtues; but conspicuously absent from the set was leaving a good historical trail to follow. Caught up, perhaps, in the shaping of these nascent associations, they did very little to document and preserve their actions. As a result, I have been able to uncover very little of the relevant correspondence and few of the scattered programs and drafts that once existed (and may yet be found). Still, studying the proceedings and accounts of the meetings that were published and carefully integrating the wider philosophical and historical literature tell us much about the nature of American philosophy and the lives of the associations in the years leading up to World War I. In this chapter, we will be examining some aspects of the activities of the philosophical associations, beginning with the second meetings of the WPA and the APA.[1]

The WPA met first, as we have seen, at Nebraska on 1–2 January 1901. The second meeting was announced for Iowa City; but it took place instead at Chicago, on 31 December 1901–1 January 1902. This schedule change was effected so that the association might meet together with the AΨA (of which Josiah Royce was then president). The WPA program contained five sessions: "two general, one experimental [i.e., psychological], and two philosophical . . ." (PR 11:152). Beginning with its third meeting, which was on 10–11 April 1903 at Iowa, the WPA's familiar Spring meeting time was adopted. At this meeting, the usual array of philosophical and psychological papers was presented; and Frederick J. E. Woodbridge offered as his presidential address "The

---

[1] A complete listing of the meetings of these associations through 1930—along with information on the meetings of the AΨA, the SSPP, and the Pacific Division of the APA—is offered in an appendix after chapter 16.

Problem of Metaphysics." In it, he calls upon the assembled philosophers to resist the contemporary temptation to overvalue the importance of science in philosophical work. He believes, on the contrary, that it is necessary for metaphysics "to free itself from science on the one hand and from religion on the other." In particular, he is concerned to maintain a distinction between science and metaphysics. In his words: "There is scientific knowledge and there is metaphysical knowledge, and these two are widely different. They involve different tasks and different problems. Science asks for the laws of existence and discovers them by experiment. Metaphysics asks for the nature of reality and discovers it by definition." Among the particular metaphysical categories that Woodbridge recommends for careful study were individuality, continuity, purpose, potentiality, and chance.[2] In the business session, a change of name of the association—another step in the decades-long process of unification—was proposed. "A suggestion [to] change the name of the society to 'American Philosophical Association: North Central Section,' in case a corresponding change is made in the name of the present American Philosophical Association . . ." was referred favorably to the executive committee (PR 12:537). The fourth meeting of the WPA took place at Missouri on 1–2 April 1904. Seventeen members were in attendance. As reported by the secretary-treasurer, Arthur Oncken Lovejoy, the proceedings note that at the business meeting, "the question of affiliation with The American Philosophical Association was again brought up, but after some discussion was laid on the table" (PR 13:529). In a less formal account, he is a bit more forthcoming. "The question of a change of name and affiliation with the eastern society was laid upon the table," Lovejoy writes, "in the failure of the American Philosophical Association to take any definite action upon the matter at its last [i.e., third] meeting" (JP 1:270). The WPA's fifth meeting was held at Nebraska on 21–22 April 1905.

After its initial meeting in New York City in the spring of 1902, the APA met for the second time in 1902 that December, at the Columbian (i.e., George Washington) University in Washington, DC. This meeting was held in conjunction with the American Association for the Advancement of Science and the AΨA. In his presidential address, "Philosophy and Its Correlations," Alexander Thomas Ormond holds philosophy partly responsible for its current academic insecurity and recommends that philosophers vindicate their efforts by adopting a distinct point-of-view, method, and criterion of validity. To do so would enable philosophy to clarify its uncertain relation to science. For him, it is important to recognize that "while the sciences and philosophy represent two

---

[2] Woodbridge, "Problem of Metaphysics," 370–71.

ways of dealing with the world that are really different, and either of which may be adopted to the exclusion of the other, yet, from the standpoint of a broader concept of relation, they form complementary parts of any scheme of world-interpretation that would lay claim to completeness." With this fuller vision in mind, Ormond maintains that "the aim of the philosopher is not immediately practical" but emphasizes that humans need to "rise above the level of their every-day demand for utilities."[3] At this meeting, there was also some discussion of the relationship with the WPA, both in terms of a common name and joint meetings (PR 12:164). The third meeting of the APA took place at Princeton in December 1903. Princeton's president, Woodrow Wilson, addressed the association and there was a response by APA president Royce. Again, the question of the relationship with the WPA was considered; but no action was taken (PR 13:176–77).[4]

The APA met next at Pennsylvania in December 1904, in part with the AΨA and the newly founded SSPP. In his presidential address, George Trumbull Ladd considered "The Mission of Philosophy," one that "never has been, nor is now, otherwise than very imperfectly and temporarily fulfilled." His explanation for this situation removes all sense of failure. Philosophy requires "a progressive realization." This means that the task of philosophy is never to be completely accomplished: "the critical and reflective thinking of mankind . . . is always in a process of evolution . . . Each day and generation inherits from that [philosophical] past; but each day and generation must have its very own philosophy." He continues that it is "no light and easy task . . . [t]o bring science, morality, religion, and art, into each other's more intimate presence, to bid them keep peace with one another by showing them that they are all parts of one great truth . . ."[5] There is a slightly melancholy tone to this address, perhaps influenced by Ladd's impending forced retirement[6]; but his belief in the value of the mission of philosophy, a belief that he hoped the other members of the APA

---

[3] Ormond, "Philosophy and Its Correlations," 124, 126.

[4] Cf. Harry Norman Gardiner: "With reference to the action of the Association last year looking to a closer affiliation with the Western Philosophical Association, it was voted on recommendation of the Executive Committee that the subject of a change of name be left in abeyance till a joint meeting is arranged with the Western Association and that the latter be invited to meet with us next year. (This recommendation was made on account of the question raised by the American Philosophical *Society* as to our name and the question in our Association as to the best form of friendly affiliation with the Western Association)" (Black Notebook, 22).

[5] Ladd, "Mission of Philosophy," 126–27, 137.

[6] Ladd had been told by Yale president Arthur Twining Hadley on 17 May 1904 that "after July 31, 1905, your services as professor will no longer be required" (Eugene S. Mills, *George Trumbull Ladd*, 201).

shared, was unbent. Among the new members elected at this meeting were George Santayana and William James, the current president of the AΨA who was to be elected APA president the next year (PR 14:167). The fifth meeting of the APA was held in the new Emerson Hall at Harvard in December 1905, again in part with the AΨA (PR 15:157).

My suspicion is that a continuation of this sort of running catalogue of events, while significant in themselves, would quickly become dreary. Rather than continue, I will shift from this litany to a consideration of themes that were important in the early years of the associations. The six that I have chosen are: the history of American philosophy, the teaching of philosophy, leadership issues, membership matters, pieties, and academic freedom.[7]

From almost its earliest days, there was some interest shown by the APA in the thought of earlier American philosophers.[8] At the third meeting, for example, which was at Princeton, Ormond, himself from Princeton, read a paper on Jonathan Edwards, who had died in 1758, soon after taking over the presidency of Princeton (PR 13:183–84). The following year, Isaac Woodbridge Riley, a Yale Ph.D. then teaching at the University of New Brunswick, read a paper entitled "Deism in America" that focused on philosophical figures at Yale: Samuel Johnson, Thomas Clap, and president Ezra Stiles (PR 14:184–85). Riley, who became the main figure in this modest movement to reclaim the history of American philosophy, then moved to Johns Hopkins for a three-year position as a research fellow where he continued his work on American figures. At the fifth meeting of the APA in 1905, he read a paper entitled "The Influence of American Political Theories on the Conception of the Absolute" that considered such thinkers as Ethan Allen and Emerson (PR 15:160–61). The next year, Riley read a paper on the American materialist, Cadwallader Colden of King's College (i.e., Columbia) (PR 16:62).[9]

---

[7] The now-vital function of providing a centralized employment service for philosophers does not seem to have emerged until much later. At the APA's 1930 meeting, the establishment of an "Appointments Bureau" was rejected (cf. PR 39:199; 40:176).

[8] In the WPA, such interest seems to have been more modest and related to the history of American philosophy in the West: e.g., its 1909 meeting in St. Louis explored the St. Louis Movement and the influence of Hegel.

[9] Riley continued to read papers on the history of American philosophy at later APA meetings. At the thirteenth meeting, he read a paper on the new realism (PR 23:193–94); at the sixteenth meeting, on French philosophy in America (PR 26:200–201; JP 14:202–3); and at the seventeenth meeting, on "Early Free Thinking Societies in America" (PR 27:178–80). He was also active at meetings of the AΨA. For example, at its fourteenth meeting that met together with the APA at Harvard he read "Early American Psychology," a discussion of Colden, Jefferson and Joseph Buchanan (ΨB 3:75); and, at its next meeting that also met with the APA at Columbia, he offered to read "Benjamin Rush, M.D., on Mental Diseases" but was unable because of time restraints (ΨB 4:220–21).

At the seventh meeting of the APA in 1907, this interest in the history of American philosophy took a turn toward reprinting texts. In the proceedings, we read the following: "Upon motion the President [Harry Norman Gardiner] was instructed to appoint a committee of three (including the chairman) to consider the advisability of undertaking the publication of certain works of early American philosophers, and to present a report at the next meeting. Professors Gardiner, Royce, and Dr. I. W. Riley were named as members of the Committee" (PR 17:168). The report that this committee offered at the next meeting, when filtered through the amendment process, was adopted as recommending the following: (1) that the APA cooperate with Columbia to republish Samuel Johnson's *Elements of Philosophy*, (2) that the APA work with other institutions to foster the republication of other similar works by early American philosophers; (3) that the committee prepare "a complete bibliography of (early) American philosophy"; and (4) that the committee be given a budget of $75 to accomplish these tasks. The committee of Gardiner, Royce and Riley—who was now at Vassar—was renewed, with permission to increase the size of the committee if necessary (PR 18:165). At the APA's 1910 meeting, the committee, now called the Committee on Early American Philosophers, reported that: the Columbia University Press was to reprint Johnson's *Elements of Philosophy*, edited by Woodbridge; that the Princeton University Press was to reprint John Witherspoon's *Lectures on Moral Philosophy*, edited by Varnum Lansing Collins; and that the University of Pennsylvania Press was to republish Benjamin Rush's *Medical Inquiries and Observations upon the Diseases of the Mind*. The committee also reported that three other volumes were in earlier stages of planning: *Selections from Thomas Jefferson* (University of Virginia Press); *Selections from Jonathan Edwards* (Yale University Press); and *The Dudleian Lectures* (Harvard University Press). Further, the committee reported that its bibliography had reached 1,200 titles and that it had spent $48.50 of its allocated $75 (PR 20:174).

At the eleventh meeting of the APA, the Committee on Early American Philosophers reported that their work was continuing; and, at this meeting, Riley read a paper on early evolutionary thought in America (PR 21:191, 206–7). The next year, the Committee reported that the Yale University Press would publish *Selections from Jonathan Edwards*, edited by Williston Walker. Further, it announced that the cost of republishing the Rush volume, *Diseases of the Mind*,[10] had been one-third pledged, and that a similar amount had been pledged for the proposed Jefferson volume, which had been endorsed by Princeton president Woodrow Wilson. The

---

[10] Here referred to as "*Diseases of the Blind*" (PR 22:168).

committee also reported that, of the three previously announced titles, the Johnson volume was nearing publication and the Witherspoon volume had already appeared from Princeton (PR 22:167–68).

The 1912 reprint of Witherspoon's *Lectures on Moral Philosophy* contains the following unsigned statement as a "Prefatory Note":

> As this book is the first of a proposed series of reprints of works of early American philosophers, a word may be said as to the general plan of which it forms a part.
>
> Projected by the American Philosophical Association, the series is to be published under the Association's auspices by the institutions with which the authors of the works chosen were more particularly affiliated. Thus, this volume bears the imprint of the Princeton University Press; and it is hoped to issue in due course, at Columbia University President Johnson's "Elements of Philosophy", at Harvard University the Dudleian "Lectures on Natural Religion", at Yale University selections from the philosophical writings of the elder Jonathan Edwards, and elsewhere other works of similar character, representative of the deeper currents of American thinking in the early period. Much of this thinking is at least respectable, and some of it significant and important; but knowledge and appreciation of it seem at the present day to be remarkably lacking. The aim then of this series is to develop a consciousness of the historical background of our native American philosophy, especially among those who, as teachers and students of philosophy, are heirs to the tradition, and therefore should also be its keepers.[11]

Despite this semiofficial APA pledge to be the "keepers" of the tradition of American philosophy, in fact the Witherspoon volume was the only one to ever appear. The committee continued in existence over the next decade or so; but it seems to have accomplished little or nothing. Moreover, there was no public accounting of what had transpired to cancel the publication of the five scheduled volumes and to end any further publication plans. Neither was any mention later made of the bibliography of early American philosophical writings that had by 1912 reached approximately 2,000 titles (PR 22:167–68). At the meeting in 1916, the committee—now described as the "Committee on American Philosophy"—was reformulated. Gardiner resigned as chair, Royce had died, and Riley was placed in charge (PR 26:197). Although it continued to be listed in the proceedings as one of the "special" committees as late as 1922 (PR 32:200), as of the 1923 meeting mention of the committee is omitted (PR 33:173), presumably indicating that it had been disbanded.[12]

---

[11] "Prefatory Note" to Witherspoon, *Lectures on Moral Philosophy*, v.

[12] Perhaps indicating a shift in interest away from the history of American philosophy, work on *Contemporary American Philosophy* began at the APA meeting in 1924. This project is discussed in chapter 14.

In spite of the suggestion of the first APA president, James Edwin Creighton, that the association not involve itself with matters pedagogical,[13] there was from the earliest years an interest in teaching in both of the associations.[14] At the second meeting of the WPA, for example, a few months before Creighton gave his warning in early 1902, John H. MacCracken, the president of Westminster College in Missouri, discussed the purposes of philosophy in the college curriculum and the approach to teaching that is most likely to attain them. He notes that the aim of mental discipline is most likely to be reached through logic, psychology and ethics; and the aim of familiarization with culture, through the history of philosophy. The further aim of leading "the student to philosophize, to raise the ultimate questions, and thus to enter upon the noblest activity of his manhood," he continues, will only be attained by courses in metaphysics that he thought were being crowded out by introduction to philosophy courses. These, he thought, were all too often mistaken attempts "to furnish an encyclopaedia of philosophy" that run "the risk of disgusting the student with philosophy" because they present it "in its driest possible form." As MacCracken formulates this point: "There is as much difference between such a bare outline of philosophical problems, and the works of a philosopher like Descartes or Locke, as between a brief history of the world and a good historical novel" (PR 11:167).

At the second meeting of the APA, there was also a session of particular interest to philosophers as teachers. In this session, Royce and Dickinson Sergeant Miller of Harvard, Francis L. Patton, the president of Princeton, and William Torrey Harris of the U.S. Bureau of Education discussed the approach of philosophy teachers toward religion. Royce, for example, notes that, while "Religion . . . is the most important business of the human being," it is "among the worst managed of humanity's undertakings." The greatest contribution that the philosophy teacher can offer to improve religion, he continues, would be to bring "(a) clearness of thought about religious issues, and (b) a judicial spirit in the comparison, the historical estimate, and the formation of religious opinions." He also recommends that "the philosophical teacher . . . conscientiously avoid all connection with any sect or form of the visible church" (PR 12:172–73).[15]

---

[13] This theme was considered in chapter 4 .

[14] I have published an earlier version of this section and related issues under the title "The Ambivalence toward Teaching in the Early Years of the American Philosophical Association."

[15] In the published version of this paper, Royce writes: "The philosopher . . . gains by an avoidance of relation to the visible church, just as a judge gains by declining to be a party man. To the invisible church the philosopher, if loyal to his task, inevitably belongs, whatever be his opinions. And it is to the invisible church of all the faithful his loyalty is due" ("What Should Be the Attitude?" 285).

Returning to the WPA, we can survey briefly the sessions on philosophy teaching over the first decade or so. At its fifth meeting in 1905, Albert Ross Hill offered as his presidential address "Psychology and Education" (JP 2:377).[16] In 1907, two papers related to teaching were read: James Hayden Tufts, "Garman as a Teacher"; and James Rowland Angell, "The Teaching of Psychology" (JP 4:515–16). In the former, Tufts discusses the work of the recently deceased Charles Edward Garman of Amherst, focusing on his pragmatic conception of philosophy and his method of using little pamphlets that he printed himself to help bring contemporary issues into the classroom.[17] At the WPA's tenth meeting in 1910, there was a trio of papers of importance to philosophy teachers, especially those concerned with introductory-level teaching. Edgar Lenderson Hinman discusses what he took to be the three main aims of an introductory philosophy courses: (1) to display "the unity of human culture" and offer "a breadth of vision and of sympathies much needed in our time"; (2) to train students "to the spirit of critical and fundamental thinking"; and (3) to give "an ordered survey of the system of the sciences" to help students integrate broad cultural ideas with "the present state of speculation in natural science." Jay William Hudson discusses an introductory course that emphasized historical events and institutions rather than the more familiar approach. This view could still manage to reach issues of "the true, the real, and the right," he maintains, and it would have the added advantage of not losing student interest. As he notes: "In themselves, the metaphysical problems are not likely to heighten the pulse of the average sophomore. But the conditions are changed when problems are made to emerge from absorbing social conflicts and compelling natural crises." In the third paper, Bernard Capen Ewer offers a naturalistic approach to introductory philosophy, one that avoided the metaphysical emphases of the "ordinary" course and explored "the popular writings of eminent scientists," attempting to uncover "the numerous metaphysical assumptions and problems involved, and thus gradually leading up to the fundamental questions of ethics and religion" (JP 7:426–28).[18]

This discussion of the introductory course apparently struck a sympathetic chord within the membership of the WPA, because at the next meeting Ewer reported on the work that had been undertaken by a Committee on the "Introduction to Philosophy" that had presumably been formed the year before. The committee, consisting of Hudson, Hinman, and

---

[16] The paper was never printed; but it has been reconstructed by Richard T. Hull. See: *Presidential Addresses of the APA*, 1:ix–x, 135–44.

[17] Cf. Tufts, "Garman as a Teacher," 263–67.

[18] The first two papers were later published. See: Hinman, "Aims of an Introductory Course"; and Hudson, "Introduction to Philosophy."

Ewer, had mailed a questionnaire to fifty teachers of philosophy about such topics as favored methods, texts, and so on, and received thirty-four responses. Ewer offered the following as the committee's preliminary findings: "The text preferred by a majority [of professors] is that of Paulsen"[19]; there are some doubts among philosophy teachers about the utility of the course, but "most regard it as a systematic statement of philosophical problems, and rely mainly on the history of philosophy for material"; and finally, in the introductory course as it is most frequently taught, "there is a comparative neglect of the synthesizing functions of philosophy as applied to the special sciences" (JP 8:235). The full report, based upon thirty-five responses to the fifty questionnaires, appeared in early 1912. In it, Hudson, the committee's chair, describes in greater detail the specifics of the responses and suggests the importance of information-gathering if individual instructors are to have the benefit of "the reflective experience of numbers of teachers." While admitting that this particular survey was "more or less off-hand," he still defends its general accuracy and its overall impression that in successful philosophy teaching the philosophical problems must "emerge from . . . the student's point of view" and the students must not see philosophy as "a thing of futility, an empty speculation."[20] Despite this successful beginning, however, no further accounts of the activities of this committee were recorded.

When the WPA met in Chicago in 1912, the overall theme was ethics; and much of the time was devoted to the problems of teaching ethics, especially as related to the first course. One of the speakers was again Hudson, and he emphasized the important role that ethics plays in a system of education for democracy. A second speaker, Frank Chapman Sharp, maintained that, because of its importance "for the guidance of life," the introductory course in ethics should be free from prerequisites and limited to one semester so that it would be "accessible to the largest possible number of students." He also recommended that the normal "pouring-in method" of familiarizing students with the history of ethics be replaced with "the method of discovery, in which the members of the class are given problems to work out," thus treating society as "an ethical laboratory." A more traditional emphasis was offered by Gregory D. Walcott, who defended the importance of teaching the history of ethics. He also stressed the need to inform students in the introductory ethics class about such topics as the proper method of ethics, the field of ethics as distinct from sociology, the different planes of ethical living, criteria of moral progress, and the ideal and its realization. Tufts helped out with the discussion of

---

[19] The text in question was Friedrich Paulsen's *Einleitung in die Philosophie*, the third edition of which had been translated by Frank Thilly as *Introduction to Philosophy*.

[20] Hudson, "Aims and Methods," 29, 38.

teaching, and Ewer proposed a course that would familiarize beginning undergraduates with the ethical ideals of college life (JP 9:351–53).

Back East, a modest level of interest in the teaching of philosophy continued. At the seventh meeting of the APA in 1907, a paper by Brother Chrysostom (Joseph J. Conlen[21]), "The Teaching of the History of Philosophy," was scheduled but bumped from the program—"read by title"—because of a lack of time (PR 17:172); and the next year Frances H. Rousmaniere considered replacing Mill's methods in introductory logic with a method she saw as more in conformity with scientific practice (PR 18:167; JP 6:45). At the 1912 meeting, George Clarke Cox of Dartmouth reported on his recent experiences with replacing his "old methods" for teaching ethics—"teaching men ethics rather than to be ethical"—with a case-study method that attempts to engage students in what becomes "not a study of human opinions but of human conduct" (PR 22:179–80). In December 1915 Ewer read a paper entitled "Hindrances to the Teaching of Philosophy." In this paper, he considered the difficulties presented by the artificial classroom situation, the limitations on thought imposed by (ecclesiastical) authorities, and the mechanistic assumptions of a generally 'scientific' atmosphere to teaching philosophy that aims at "guiding human life and . . . synthesizing facts and principles of science in a unitary view of the universe" (PR 25:172). In spite of these occasional papers, however, the interest of the APA in matters of pedagogy remained modest. At the 1917 meeting, for example, the Committee on Discussion declared its willingness that the association "consider from time to time the pedagogical aspects" of philosophy, as long as this interest "be kept decidedly subordinate" to interests in "philosophical scholarship" and "the promotion of philosophical inquiry" (PR 27:166). And, perhaps as a further indication of the increasing research orientation of academic philosophy, and the consequent loss of interest in the role of philosophy teacher, we can consider the fact that the initial choice for the discussion session for the 1920 meeting was "Aims and Methods in Teaching Philosophy" (PR 29:157). When this discussion was later announced, however, the theme had been modified to "The Role of the Philosopher in Modern Life, with Reference Both to Teaching and Research" (JP 17:688).[22]

Turning now to issues of leadership, we note that from its inception the APA was directed by an executive committee.[23] This seven-member committee, composed of Creighton (president), Ormond (vice-president),

---

[21] Schneider, "Philosophy," 541.

[22] The discussion sessions will be considered in chapter 10.

[23] While the WPA began with an executive committee of five members, the records that I have uncovered are too sketchy too allow much comment upon the development of its leadership arrangements.

Gardiner (secretary-treasurer), Andrew Campbell Armstrong, George M. Duncan, Walter Goodnow Everett, and John Grier Hibben was, as we saw in chapter 4, appointed at the organizing meeting on 2 November 1901 and charged "to invite such persons as they deemed eligible to join the Association, to draft a Constitution, and to arrange for a meeting for the reading of papers and the transaction of business, to be held in New York some time during the Easter holidays" (PR 11:264). The original constitution of the APA was adopted during the business session of the first meeting on 31 March 1902. According to this document, the direction of the APA was to continue under the leadership of a seven-member executive committee composed of the three officers and two pairs of members chosen for two-year terms of service. The ongoing responsibilities of the members of the executive committee required them to nominate officers and other members of the executive committee,[24] decide the time and place of the annual meeting if this had not been determined at the business session of the prior meeting,[25] and arrange the program, including deciding what papers would be read. Among the other duties acquired by the committee was the ongoing effort to effect an integration between the APA and the WPA (PR 11:264–66). The executive committee for the year leading up to the APA's second meeting consisted of: Ormond (president), Alexander Meiklejohn (vice-president), Gardiner (secretary-treasurer), Armstrong and Hibben, with William Caldwell and David Irons replacing Duncan and Everett (PR 11:266).

Over the first few decades the leadership system of the APA was modified only slightly. At the seventeenth meeting in 1917, the executive committee proposed that it be increased in size to nine members: the three officers and three pairs of three-year members, with a pair of these at-large members being elected each year (PR 27:165). This amendment was passed at the 1918 meeting (PR 28:181). At that same meeting another amendment was proposed by the committee that would specify the secretary-treasurer's term as three years in length (PR 28:178). This amendment was approved at the 1919 meeting (PR 29:156). At the latter meeting, the committee again recommended an expansion of its number to include a tenth member: the past president (PR 29:156). The next year, this amendment to Article III was adopted as follows: "There shall be an Executive Committee composed by ten members, and the retiring president shall be *ex officio* member for one year" (PR 30:195).

---

[24] Article III of the constitution allowed any member of the association to present other names in nomination with the second of two other members.

[25] This seems to have been the case at least half of the time in the early years, largely because the APA was interested in coordinating joint meetings with other associations.

Apparent dissatisfaction with this top-down leadership began to emerge after World War I. One instance of this occurred at the APA's 1920 meeting, when it was moved and voted that the executive committee develop "a plan for nominating and electing officers by mail" (PR 30:195) rather than at the business meeting. At the following meeting, in a seemingly reluctant response to this directive, "the Executive Committee presented the following formula: that officers of the Association be nominated and elected by mail, according to a procedure to be determined by the Executive Committee. The Committee recommended the rejection of the formula, which recommendation was accepted" by the members present (PR 31:165–66). Another modest revolt surfaced at the twenty-third meeting in December 1923, when contrary to past practice the 'official' candidate for president was not simply voted in by acclamation: "The Executive Committee presented nominations for President, and a ballot was taken, as a result of which Dr. Alexander Meiklejohn was declared elected. This election was made unanimous" (PR 33:172). This appears to be the first time that a ballot was necessary, although Clarence Irving Lewis, the secretary of the APA, makes no mention of the source of the other candidate(s)—from within the executive committee or from the floor—or the name(s) of the vanquished.

Perhaps as a continuation of this modest democratic movement, at the 1924 meeting Morris Raphael Cohen proposed a constitutional amendment that a three-member nominating committee be established with the members serving staggered three-year terms (PR 34:165–66).[26] The next year, the proceedings contain the following: "The amendment to the Constitution, providing for a Nominating Committee, notice of which was given by Professor Cohen at the preceding annual meeting, was brought up. Owing to the absence of Professor Cohen, it was voted that this be laid on the table for further consideration" (PR 35:163). Cohen's amendment was adopted at the 1926 meeting, with former presidents John Dewey, Gardiner, and Charles Montague Bakewell being elected to serve for one, two, and three years respectively (PR 36:62). At the next meeting this amendment was superseded in a form that did not necessarily lead to further democratization when it was mandated that only former divisional presidents would serve on the committee: "There shall be a nominating committee of three to nominate officers for the Association [i.e., the Eastern Division]. It shall consist of former presidents in order of their seniority. The senior member, Chairman, shall each year retire to be replaced on the committee by the next in order of seniority" (PR 37:163).

---

[26] Article V of the constitution reads: "Amendments to this Constitution, which must be submitted in writing, may be made by a vote of two thirds of the members present at any meeting subsequent to that at which such amendments have been proposed" (PR 11:265).

The APA was organized, as we saw in chapter 4, with the objective of "the promotion of the interests of philosophy in all its branches, and more particularly the encouragement of original work among the members of the Association." Access to membership in the APA was placed temporarily in the hands of the executive committee, which was instructed to invite "such persons as they deemed eligible" to join. Article II of the constitution adopted at the first meeting formalized procedures for membership. It reads as follows: "1. Candidates for Membership must be proposed by two members of the Association and recommended by the Executive Committee before their names are voted upon by the Association. 2. There shall be an Annual Fee of one dollar, failure in payment of which for three consecutive years shall *ipso facto* cause membership to cease" (PR 11:264). At the APA's first meeting, the sixty-seven individuals who had joined at the invitation of the founding executive committee and the thirty-one elected at that meeting were made "charter members" of the association. Of these ninety-eight charter members, at least eight were women (PR 11:266, 283–86).[27]

The membership arrangements remained unchanged for a decade. At the eleventh meeting in 1911, the executive committee proposed two constitutional amendments. The first was the addition of a class of "associate" members to the current class of "regular" members. (These associate members were to have "all the privileges of the Association except voice and vote in its meetings.") In the course of this addition of a membership category, the criteria for regular membership were to be narrowed (or at least made more explicit). The proposed change read: "Election to active membership shall be limited to persons professionally engaged in the teaching or study of Philosophy whose academic rank is above that of assistant, and to such other persons as in the opinion of the Executive Committee shall have published contributions of substantial value to Philosophy." According to the proposal of the executive committee, all current members (as of 1 January 1913) were to be considered "active" members. The second of the proposed changes was that the annual dues for such associate members were to be $3 (PR 21:190–91). In accord with Article V of the constitution, these proposed amendments were approved by a two-thirds vote of the members present at the 1912 meeting, although the exclusionary clause—"whose academic rank is above that of assistant"—was not part of the final version of the amendment (PR 22:166).[28]

---

[27] There may have been more women—some members used only their initials. The eight were: Mary Whiton Calkins, Anna A. Cutler, Grace Neal Dolson, Christine Ladd-Franklin, Clara M. Hitchcock, Vida F. Moore, Ellen Bliss Talbot, and Margaret Floy Washburn.

[28] At the APA's 1920 meeting, it was voted that the executive committee should consider the issue of electing "corresponding" members (PR 30:195). This question was tabled at the 1921 meeting (PR 31:165).

As far as can be determined from the proceedings, election to membership in the APA was virtually automatic, as long as the proposed member was approved by the executive committee. There is no way of knowing, of course, what might have happened behind the scenes to prevent potential candidates from being voted upon by the membership (or even if any potential candidate was ever spurned). The only recorded instance of a candidate being publicly rejected by the membership in the early years was at the APA's 1919 meeting. At this meeting, although the membership voted to admit seventeen regular members and two associate members, it also decided not to approve the nomination of one candidate. "It was moved and carried that the application of George Johnson, Ph.D., Lincoln University, be laid over for one year, pending investigation of the standing of Lincoln University" (PR 29:156–57). Johnson's candidacy was reconsidered in 1920, and he was admitted to membership (PR 30:194).[29] As late as the APA's twenty-fifth meeting in December 1925, in the fashion that had continued since the founding of the association, candidates for membership were still being nominated by two members, approved by the executive committee and voted on by the membership. At that meeting twenty-five new members, including Brand Blanshard and Alfred North Whitehead, were approved; the list of members included in the proceedings for that meeting contains 291 regular (or "active") members—including at least twenty-seven women[30]—and five associate members (PR 35:159–71).

As we have seen in chapter 4, the WPA was founded in Kansas City on 1 January 1900 "to stimulate an interest in philosophy in all its branches, and to encourage original investigation." In a formulation that perhaps worked more democratically than with the APA, membership was to be open to "all advanced students of philosophy." The unpublished constitution contained as one of its articles a clause "providing for changes by a two-thirds vote of the members present at any annual meeting." (As we have just seen, the APA constitution required a one-year waiting period for

---

[29] Johnson, who had earned a theological degree from the Princeton seminary and a philosophy doctorate in 1911 from Pennsylvania with a dissertation on Nicomachus of Gerasa, was a professor of theology and philosophy at the historically Black institution near Philadelphia.

[30] These women were: Frances B. Blanshard, Gertrude C. Bussey, *Mary Whiton Calkins, Mary S. Case, Mary E. Clark, Lucy S. Crawford, *Anna A. Cutler, *Grace Neal Dolson, Savilla A. Elkus, Eleanor A. McG. Gamble, Katherine E. Gilbert, Georgia E. Harkness, Marjorie S. Harris, *Clara M. Hitchcock, Ethel P. Howes, *Christine Ladd-Franklin, Grace A. de Laguna, Margaret W. Landes, Ethel G. Muir, Elizabeth V. Nagy, Helen Huss Parkhurst, Ethel E. Sabin-Smith, Edna A. Shearer, Marie Colins Swabey, *Ellen Bliss Talbot, Matilda Castro Tufts, and Ethel M. Kitch Yeaton. (The asterisk indicates twenty-five-year members.)

constitutional changes.) On presumably constitutional grounds, officers were elected: president, vice-president, secretary-treasurer, and three members of the executive committee. There were forty-six charter members of the WPA, of whom at least two were women (PR 10:162–74).[31] At its second meeting, thirteen new members were elected according to whatever constitutional procedures were in effect. Additionally, "the Executive Committee was authorized to add to the list of members during the ensuing year the names of such persons of recognized standing in philosophy as might express a desire to become members" (PR 11:152). At its next meeting in 1903, "[t]he report of Executive Committee in regard to the election of new members, under special provision made at the last meeting, was accepted and approved. This extends membership to include practically all the men actively interested in philosophy in the North Central States" (PR 12:537). At the WPA's ninth meeting, a recommendation "[t]hat non-payment for three years shall automatically cancel membership" was passed (JP 6:403). When the WPA met in 1918, procedures were taken to attempt to enforce the decision from nine years earlier: "Action was taken whereby, beginning in 1919, membership in the association lapses automatically whenever the regular dues are unpaid for a period of three years" (JP 15:519). While the practice of listing WPA members in the annual proceedings had been abandoned after the fourth meeting, there is a listing of 139 members for 1927—including at least six women—one of whom was an honorary member.[32]

Another of the important matters of business at the annual meetings was the effort to memorialize the deaths of its more distinguished members.[33] Each of the associations was at the time made up of a small group of philosophers who were part of a close web of relationships of mentors and students, colleagues and former colleagues. In such a communal situation, the deceased were not names in a journal or faces in a crowded ballroom, but also friends (or rivals) whose passing would make a difference. The first APA memorial[34] was prepared by two idealists, Royce and Bakewell, to commemorate the death of William Torrey Harris (1835–1909), a member of the APA and retired U.S. Commissioner of Education. Harris, the founder of *The Journal of Speculative Philosophy* and a central figure in both

---

[31] Alice Hamlin Hinman and Louise M. Hannum.

[32] These women were: Mary Hegeler Carus (honorary member), Lois Shepherd Green, Winifred Hyde, Mabel C. Kemmerer, Zora Schaupp, and Ella H. Stokes. For the circumstances of Mrs. Carus's election to honorary membership, see chapter 14.

[33] At its 1909 meeting the APA had appropriated 100 marks "as a contribution to the Fichte Memorial at Berlin" (PR 19:169).

[34] No memorials appeared in the proceedings of the early years of the WPA. It is not clear why.

the St. Louis movement and the Concord Summer School of Philosophy, was remembered as "a welcome and kindly presence" at earlier APA meetings.[35] Harris, they continued, "shared the belief that it was the destiny of philosophy to guide and, in its own way and time, to transform all human life, educational, political, social, religious." Further, he "helped to win serious recognition for philosophy, and to free it from its bondage to some of the more deadening of its older associations in our American life . . . We all work to-day the better and the more effectively because of what he did to make our own life-work possible" (PR 20:175–78).

The second APA commemoration was for its sixth president, William James, who died in Chocorua, New Hampshire, on 26 August 1910. At its 1910 meeting, a committee consisting of Dewey, Ormond, and Ralph Barton Perry "was requested to present at the next annual meeting a memorial on the death of Professor William James" (PR 20:174). In this memorial, read by Dewey the next year, James was praised for the quality of his work in the areas of psychology, religion, and pragmatism: "To few men and probably to no other American has it been given to be a leader in three distinctive directions." Turning to the personal, the memorialists noted that it was both impossible and unnecessary to indicate to the APA audience "that fullness of being which overflowed at every point of his life . . ." What they could try to do was much more modest: "We can but record our sense of what we, as a guild of philosophers, owe to him. As has been noted over and over again, all the world esteems philosophy more highly because William James practised it" (PR 21:192–96).

Charles Sanders Peirce died in Milford, Pennsylvania, on 19 April 1914. At the APA's 1915 meeting in Philadelphia, in December of the following year, Josiah Royce "was requested to present a minute on the death of Mr. C. S. Pearce" (PR 25:169).[36] Peirce, of course, was never a member of the association and he had died before the *prior* meeting; but there was still a mystique about this founding pragmatist, and Royce, who was at the time working with Peirce's manuscripts at Harvard, was the obvious choice to memorialize him. There is no published record of what he said, although presumably his remarks are related to his 1916 essay, "Charles Sanders Peirce."[37] Before the association met again, Royce himself would be dead.

At the APA's sixteenth meeting the deaths of two former presidents were memorialized. One was Ormond, the association's second president, who had spent the bulk of his teaching years at Princeton. In his memory,

---

[35] Harris had appeared on the APA's second through fifth programs, 1902–05.

[36] Misspellings of Peirce's name were common at the time. In the JP account, he is listed as "C. H. Peirce" (JP 13:102).

[37] This essay, edited by W. Fergus Kernan, is derived from Royce's remarks about Peirce at Harvard in March of 1915 (cf. Kernan, "The Peirce Manuscripts and Josiah Royce").

Creighton read remarks that he had prepared in cooperation with Wilbur Marshall Urban and R. B. C. Johnson. These remarks placed Ormond as a student of James McCosh at Princeton, and described him as "[i]n spirit, though not in literal doctrine" a follower of that formidable Scot. Ormond, Creighton continues, "was a man who had seen the divine vision and who, through the transparent simplicity and lovableness of his life, gave to all those associated with him in the search for truth an example which can never be forgotten . . . He believed that philosophy is not primarily a doctrine, but a life, and throughout all his teaching his students felt the vitality of the process by which he sought to make his theories expressions of living experience" (PR 26:191).

The other memorial at this meeting was for Royce, who died on 14 September 1916. He had been feted in celebration of his sixtieth birthday at the meeting before. At that meeting in Philadelphia, there were two sessions exploring Royce's thought, as well as a celebratory dinner. The sessions contained papers by: Bakewell, Richard Clarke Cabot, Mary Whiton Calkins, Dewey, H. H. Horne, George Holmes Howison, Wilmon Henry Sheldon, E. E. Southard, and Edward Gleason Spaulding. The discussion of these papers sparked a number of responses from Royce, including the following one recorded by Theodore de Laguna. In reply to Horne's paper on his philosophy of education, Royce said that "in attempting to formulate his educational views he had always been embarrassed by an internal conflict of tendencies. On the one hand he felt himself a rebel, a natural-born dissenter, always prompt to challenge an accepted standard; while on the other hand he recognized that salvation for the individual lies in union with the community." On the evening of 29 December 1915, there was a dinner at the Walton Hotel at which APA president Armstrong read from among the telegrams and letters that had been received from Royce's supporters. "Then Professor Royce spoke . . . It was a retrospect of his spiritual life . . . his introduction to the 'majesty of the community' . . . LeConte . . . Germany . . . Lotze . . . he owed far more to Peirce than to Hegel . . . his own incapacity for most forms of social life . . . the company of his graduate students . . . the love of logic . . . the European war" (JP 13:98–102). The papers were later published, together with ten other papers—by: George Plimpton Adams, B. W. Bacon, William Adams Brown, Cohen, Lawrence J. Henderson, William Ernest Hocking, Lewis, Alfred Henry Lloyd, Jacob Loewenberg, and Edgar A. Singer—a bibliography by Benjamin Rand, a prefatory note by Creighton, and the "Words of Professor Royce at the Walton Hotel in Philadelphia, December 29, 1915" in a special edition of the *The Philosophical Review* (PR 25:229–522).

At the 1916 meeting, Bakewell read a memorial for Royce that he had prepared with the assistance of Hibben, Wendell T. Bush, and Frank Thilly. Royce was described as a "small, quaint, lovable figure . . . [a] loyal servant

of truth," who played a role of vital importance to the fledgling philosophical profession by being "one of the first thinkers in America to devote
himself whole-heartedly to the problems of speculative philosophy in
entire freedom from the associations and prepossessions of theological tradition." They also pointed to "his concern to find in the world of the
absolute elbow room for the individual, to show that the finite and temporal are not by this idealism shorn of the meaning they actually possess in
concrete experience." They also praised Royce for his "ever-increasing tendency to express the nature of reality in terms of purpose, and thus a tendency to bring together the theoretical and the practical, and in the end to
make the practical itself the source of theoretical vision." In addition, in
the proceedings of the meeting we also read the following: "A committee
with Professor Urban as chairman was appointed by the president, on the
recommendation of the Executive Committee, to prepare a minute on the
death of Professor Münsterberg" (PR 26:191–95), who had dropped dead
in his classroom less than two weeks earlier on 16 December 1916. By the
time that the APA met again in 1917, America was at war with the Central
Powers; and no mention was made in the proceedings of any memorial to
Germany's staunchest philosophical champion.

At the APA's nineteenth meeting in 1919 a resolution, the author of
which is not named, was adopted to memorialize the death of Paul Carus
of La Salle, Illinois. Carus, a publisher rather than a university teacher, had
earned a Ph.D. in Germany before he immigrated to the United States.
Carus had been elected to membership in 1903. The association expressed
its sense of loss and sympathy for the family of this pioneering figure,
whom it described as "a man of fine comradeship, and of wise and catholic
idealism . . . whose devotion to the cause of Philosophy, through his own
work as editor and author and through his encouragement of the work of
others, has been of high value to philosophic learning" (PR 29:156).[38]

Turning finally to academic freedom, in the proceedings of the APA's
thirteenth meeting in 1913 we find the following:

> Secretary's Report of the Joint Meeting of the American Philosophical
> Association and the American Psychological Association, Held at New
> Haven, December 31, 1913.

> The meeting of the two societies was called to hear the report of the
> committee appointed to ascertain the facts regarding the resignation of
> Professor Mecklin from the faculty of Lafayette College. Professor H. C.
> Warren presided. Professor W. V. Bingham was appointed secretary. The
> report of the committee was presented by its chairman, Professor A. O.

---

[38] The establishment of the Carus Lectures is discussed in chapter 14.

Lovejoy.

On motion of Professor Spaulding it was voted that the report be accepted and printed at the expense of the two societies and that copies be sent to all members of these associations, to the editors of scientific journals who may care to publish the report, and to such other persons as the executive committee of the associations in conjunction with the members of the committee may designate.

On motion of Professor Overstreet the associations adopted a cordial vote of thanks to the committee for the completion of a piece of work which stands so finely for the honor and dignity of the teaching profession.

W. V. Bingham,
Secretary. (PR 23:178)

To get some sense of what this Mecklin case was, we must turn to the report itself, which appeared in *The Journal of Philosophy* immediately after the account of the meeting. In this "Report of the Committee of Inquiry of the American Philosophical Association and the American Psychological Association," we find the story of John Moffatt Mecklin—an ordained Presbyterian minister and a Leipzig Ph.D., and a member of both associations—who was forced to resign from his position at Lafayette under questionable circumstances. The Committee—comprised of Lovejoy, Creighton, Hocking, Evander Bradley McGilvary, Walter Taylor Marvin, George Herbert Mead, and Howard C. Warren—had been empowered by the presidents of the two associations to attempt to uncover the facts behind the case (JP 11:81).

Up to that point, some information had become public. Mecklin's resignation from his position as professor of mental and moral philosophy at Lafayette at the end of the 1912–1913 academic year "because his teaching was regarded as not in accord with the standards of the Presbyterian Church" had been reported in August 1913 (JP 10:504). Soon after, however, Mecklin described that report as "somewhat misleading" and noted that the issue was "one of text-books and teaching methods, not of attacks upon church standards." He explained that authorities at the college had objected to his use of such texts as Angell's *Psychology*, Dewey and Tufts's *Ethics*, William McDougall's *Introduction to Social Psychology*, and Edward Scribner Ames's *The Psychology of Religious Experience*, "on the ground that the functional and genetic method employed in them is opposed to the traditions of the college and subversive of the faith and morals of the students." He pointed out in his response that such texts and methods were used without complaint at other Presbyterian colleges. The problem at Lafayette, as he saw it, was that "a well-meaning, but misguided loyalty to outworn theological beliefs" has taken precedence over "approved scientific methods and well-attested facts." Thus, he presented himself as being "a menace" not to Presbyterianism generally but only to "the particular type of Presbyterianism" that then dominated Lafayette.[39]

The APA/AΨA report begins by listing a series of issues that the committee wanted to investigate: whether Mecklin's resignation was given under compulsion; whether the cause was the college president's objection to his philosophy teachings; whether the exact problem with these teachings had ever been made clear to him; and whether his resignation might result in damage to his professional reputation. Overall, the committee was interested in determining whether "the procedure used in bringing about his separation from the Lafayette College faculty was of a somewhat summary and peculiar character." The committee began its work with a letter to President Ethelbert Dudley Warfield of Lafayette on 12 November 1913 that explained the interests of the two associations in events in the teaching profession and in the impact of "doctrinal restrictions" on philosophy and psychology teachers "in the principal American institutions of learning." The letter ended with a series of eight questions that attempted to explore the circumstances of Mecklin's resignation and the credal requirements for professors at Lafayette. Warfield did not respond to this letter; and, when a copy of it was sent, he answered in a letter cosigned by two Lafayette trustees. In their response, they asserted in very general terms the necessity for the professor of mental and moral philosophy to uphold the college's tradition of providing "a foundation for conservative Christian thought and character" and that in this regard his teaching had been found wanting. Lovejoy, operating under time constraints to gather information for the impending meeting, replied on 19 December 1913, again asking specifically what Mecklin's harmful teachings were, what explicit or implicit doctrinal requirements for professors of philosophy and psychology existed at the college, and whether any such doctrinal requirements might conflict with article VIII of the college's charter that states that there shall be no religious tests at

---

[39] Mecklin, "Letter from Professor Mecklin," 559–60. As Mecklin later writes, "I quietly ignored all the old musty texts my predecessors had used and . . . I adopted what is called the 'case method' and made the students gather together all the facts of their own individual experience in the field of morals and apply to them the pragmatic test . . . The president . . . was scandalized beyond words, and . . . claimed that I was undermining all standards of morals and was a menace to campus life" (*My Quest for Freedom*, 148). Readers of Mecklin's 1913 essay, "The Problem of Christian Ethics," can determine the extent of his heterodoxy for themselves.

Lafayette.[40] In the final piece of correspondence between the college and the committee, Warfield replied on 26 December 1913, offering none of the requested information and asserting "the impropriety of my discussing with your committee questions affecting the college or its members" (PR 11:67–72).

The report then continues with the committee's conclusions offered under three general headings. Its first issue was whether there had been known limits on the teaching of philosophy and psychology professors at Lafayette. In general, the committee writes, "American colleges and universities fall into two classes: those in which freedom of inquiry, of belief, and of teaching is, if not absolutely unrestricted, at least subject to limitations so few and so remote as to give practically no occasion for differences of opinion; and those which are frankly instruments of denominational or political propaganda." While the committee passed on the question of determining the value of each kind of institutions, it notes that it was concerned to determine if one of the latter sort is pretending to be one of the former. With regards to this question, the committee reports finding contradictory evidence with regard to Lafayette: at one and the same time "[i]t is committed to no specific creed; it is committed only to the principles of 'evangelical Christianity'; and it is committed to the principles of the Presbyterian Church." While assuming that the third is the accurate position, the committee asserts only that such confusions should not be allowed to continue: "the committee can not but think it highly undesirable that in any college a question of such importance should be left open too such divergent official answers . . ." (JP 11:73–74).

The committee's second issue was to determine the circumstances of Mecklin's dismissal/resignation. Here the committee notes, "No connected and altogether definite statement seems ever to have been formulated of the specific points in Professor Mecklin's teaching to which objection was made, or the manner in which these were held to conflict with Presbyterian principles." Further, the committee notes that he was at the time an ordained Presbyterian minister who frequently preached within the Synod of Pennsylvania. While the committee was willing to speculate somewhat as to possible reasons—dissatisfaction with his examinations or his choice of text-books, the fact that he held an endowed chair that might carry special limitations, and so on—it maintained that the procedures followed in this case were unacceptable: "It is the position of the committee

---

[40] Article VIII of the college charter reads as follows: "That persons of every religious denomination shall be capable of being elected trustees, nor shall any person, either as principal, professor, tutor or pupil be refused admittance into said college, or denied any of the privileges, immunities or advantages thereof for or on account of his sentiments in matters of religion" (Skillman, *Biography of a College*, 2:307).

that in no institution, of whatever type, should a professor be compelled to relinquish his position for doctrinal reasons, except upon definite charges, communicated to him in writing and laid, with the supporting evidence, before the entire board of trustees and the faculty . . ." (JP 11:75–76).

The third major conclusion of the committee concerned the response of the administration of the college toward the committee's inquiry, which it describes as "a courteous declination to give these associations the definite information asked for." Here, Lovejoy and the rest of the committee assert the right of the professoriate and the public to know what transpires in this and similar cases, and to be informed about the general situation of higher education:

> We believe it to be the right of the general body of professors of philosophy and psychology to know definitely the conditions of the tenure of any professorship in their subject; and also their right, and that of the public to which colleges look for support, to understand unequivocally what measure of freedom of teaching is guaranteed in any college, and to be informed as to the essential details of any case in which credal restrictions, other than those to which the college officially stands committed, are publicly declared by responsible persons to have been imposed (JP 11:79–81).

Mecklin, of course, was not returned to his chair at Lafayette—he went on to have a distinguished career at Pittsburgh and Dartmouth—but President Warfield was himself soon dismissed from the college.[41]

In the proceedings of the APA's fourteenth meeting, held in December 1914 at Chicago, there is no further mention of the Mecklin case. The following, however, does appear: "The members of the Philosophical Associations had been invited to express opinions on the organization of the Society of American Professors. Great interest was manifested in the undertaking, together with a cordial approval of its purpose" (JP 12:107). The American Association of University Professors was founded on 1 January 1915 in New York City, with Dewey as president and Lovejoy as secretary.[42] At the APA's 1915 meeting, a special APA committee on academic freedom and tenure was established, consisting of Dewey, Lovejoy and Hocking, with the intention of making it permanent at the next meeting (PR 25:169). This committee was charged "to investigate cases of alleged arbitrary dismissal" (JP 13:102). At the next meeting of the APA, Dewey "reported that during the year no cases had been brought to the committee's attention" (PR 26:195).

---

[41] Cf. Skillman, *Biography of a College*, 2:198–204.

[42] Cf. Lovejoy, "Organization of the AAUP"; Dewey, "Introductory Address to the AAUP"; "Annual Address of the President to the AAUP"; Metzger, *Age of the University*, 468–95; Pollitt and Kurland, "Entering the Academic Freedom Arena."

JOSIAH ROYCE

Department of Special Collections, Charles E. Young Research Library, UCLA

6

Idealism, Pragmatism, and Realism

In his 1926 retrospective of the first twenty-five years of the APA, Harry Norman Gardiner writes:

> It would be interesting, were there time, to speak of the various incidental activities of the Association carried on through special committees, such as the diligent, but unsuccessful, committee on early American philosophy and the Committee on International Cooperation, through which, since the War, the Association has given practical expression of its sympathies by grants and gifts of American philosophical literature to impoverished institutions and individuals abroad. Mention might also be made of the donation of a hundred marks to the Fichte Memorial in Berlin in 1909, and of $200 for the sustaining of the *International Journal of Ethics* in 1916.

Some of these "incidental activities" we have already considered; others will be considered in later chapters. Gardiner wraps up this particular theme by pointing to what he considers to be the central work of the APA: "the main thing, of course, that concerns us in this retrospect of twenty-five years is the work proper of the Association as exhibited in the papers read and discussed at our meetings."[1]

This emphasis upon the primacy of the papers is, of course, not just the theme of Gardiner's retrospective. It can be seen as far back as James Edwin Creighton's initial vision of the APA, discussed in chapter 4, for "promoting and facilitating the interchange of ideas" and "demanding that the papers presented shall represent the best work and most original thought of those who offer them." Before we attempt a survey of the

---

[1] Gardiner, "First Twenty-Five Years of the APA," 156–57. The $200 subvention of the *International Journal of Ethics* was paid and reported in 1917 (PR 27:165).

papers read at the meetings, however, it would seem advisable to spend some time reminding ourselves of the general shape of American philosophy at the birth of the philosophical associations and of its major developments during the pre-War years, considering in turn idealism, pragmatism, and realism. These three terms represent, as we shall see, central ways of carrying out the philosophers' task of understanding and explaining the human journey. Each approach reflects an understanding of the meaning of existence; each offers an interpretation of the nature and power of knowledge. And each approach views the other approaches as sadly inadequate.

In the course of our consideration of idealism, pragmatism, and realism, it is necessary to keep in mind the imprecision of these labels, especially when they are applied by individual philosophers to the perspectives of others. Charles Montague Bakewell wisely writes in 1910 that "if a man under stress of circumstances reluctantly gives himself a label in order to mark in a general way certain broad characteristics of his position, he himself always makes many saving mental reservations." So, should Bakewell characterize himself as an idealist, he would implicitly include numerous distinctions between his form of idealism and other versions, as well as whatever similarities exist between his idealism and certain aspects of pragmatism and realism. When applied to others, however, such characterizations are more crude. When a philosopher "gives a label to another," Bakewell continues, "it generally stands for something much more rigorously definite, and there is usually something invidious in the characterization." In a similar fashion, Creighton notes in 1917 how criticism "from other schools has served to unite under a common flag philosophical thinkers who are by no means at one either in their presuppositions and method, or in the general character of their results."[2] Keeping the limitations of philosophical labels in mind, we can proceed, beginning with idealism.

Despite James McCosh's 1887 pronouncement that "[i]dealism has no place in philosophy any more than it has in science," it was and remained a powerful force in both. Idealism, the *Weltanschauung* of completeness and integration and system—the philosophical perspective that Otto F. Kraushaar praised for "its passionate search for wholeness and spiritual security"—was especially important in the face of the unsettling wave of naturalism that was washing over intellectual and cultural life during the period. For Joseph Leon Blau, idealism was the attempt to find some reality behind the flux of experience. He writes that for the idealist,

---

[2] Bakewell, "Problem of Transcendence," 118n; Creighton, "Two Types of Idealism," 514.

what men experience, the constant flux of becoming, the confusion of sensation, instability, and change, is not really existence, not Reality. These are but
appearance, the shadow of the real. A knowledge of Reality can not be derived
from consideration of its counterpart in experience. Our only instrument for
gaining a knowledge of Reality is the mind, man's spiritual part, for Reality is
spiritual in its fundamental character. The real universe is rational; it has an
orderly, stable, permanent nature. Ultimately, in the real universe, existence,
meaning, truth, and value are one. To the idealist, Reality is intelligible and
valuable through and through, and it is man's system of meanings and man's
system of values with which Reality in imbued.[3]

While for some, like Blau, idealism's search for hidden meaning was an
essential part of philosophy's task of understanding Reality, for others idealism functioned as a means for avoiding reality. May Brodbeck, for example, writes that the philosophers who replaced the minister-presidents late
in the nineteenth century were still "primarily concerned with problems
arising out of the attempt to justify the ways of God to man," and the
means that they used was absolute idealism, "the last, boldest, and most
grandiose systematic defense of God, immortality, and eternal values."
For her, the function of idealism was reactionary: it was a philosophy that
would "counteract the corrosive influence of mechanistic science by providing a foundation for belief in things of the spirit, in the fundamental
intelligibility of the universe, and in the validity of a universal moral
code." Such a philosophy had become attractive when the growing role
of science in society and higher education had overwhelmed the potential
defenses of common-sensism. Increasingly, Brodbeck continues, the scientific view of the universe "as a meaningless clash of atoms in the void
seemed to lead inevitably to what was felt to be a dangerous and demor-
alizing ethical relativism." In response to this relativism, the idealists set
out to prove "the universal necessity of religious and moral truths" based
upon "a speculative theory of reality which, at one stroke, provided the
intelligibility the scientific view lacked and 'proved' the universal necessity
of moral laws."[4]

Brodbeck's interpretation of idealism, while one-sided, is not false.
Idealism was the philosophy that challenged the materialistic claims of late

---

[3] McCosh, *Realistic Philosophy*, 1:14; Kraushaar, "Introduction [to Josiah Royce]," 181;
Blau, *Men and Movements*, 188.

[4] Brodbeck, "Philosophy in America," 4–7. Cf. Arthur Oncken Lovejoy: "I am . . . not
unaware how strong and natural are the religious motives which make for this sort of metaphysics. It is a very soothing and comforting self-contradiction . . ." ("Temporalistic
Realism," 90; cf. Cohen, "Later Philosophy," 231; Holt, *Concept of Consciousness*, ix–x;
Reuben, *Making of the Modern University*, 92–93; Turner, "Secularization and Sacralization,"
81–82).

nineteenth-century science. It was also, however, the philosophy that had overcome the bifurcation between the spiritual and the intellectual that was present in the common-sense realism of the American colleges. This bifurcation was what John Dewey was referring to when he wrote, "My earlier philosophic study had been an intellectual gymnastic" and "Hegel's synthesis . . . was . . . a liberation." Idealism satisfied "a demand for unification" in his life and thought; it overcame "divisions and separations"; it cured "an inward laceration."[5] Frank Thilly offers a slightly different formulation: "What is common to the representatives of this school is the emphasis they place upon the organic conception of mind and knowledge in opposition to the atomistic treatment characteristic of English associationism; their repudiation of mechanism as a universal theory; and their view that the world of experience constitutes the subject-matter of philosophy."[6] This world of experience, interpreted as idealists were wont to do, made the efforts of the special sciences dependent upon a philosophical overview; and idealism was the perspective that was able to carry philosophy safely into the developing university as the science of sciences.[7] Idealism moreover was the philosophical perspective that could connect American philosophers with academic life in their beloved Germany.

At times, as in this 1906 passage from Alexander Thomas Ormond, the completeness that idealism sought was primarily intellectual in nature. "The true antidote" for "specialism" and the loss of faith in "the unity of truth" is only to be found "in a discipline whose special business it shall be to investigate the grounds and principles of the whole body of truth with a view to its unity and meaning as a whole," he writes. "To this discipline we apply the old name, philosophy, and we . . . claim for it the old function of unification and the old interest in the whole upon which the exercise of this function proceeded." At other times, this completeness was more moral. George Herbert Palmer, for example, writes in 1930 that "[i]n reality, a single person is a contradiction in terms . . . a person is an individual being plus his relations, and these relations are what constitute him to be what he is." In his own particular case, he wonders, "What would I be if I were not

---

5 Dewey, "From Absolutism to Experimentalism," 19. Cf. Gustavus Watts Cunningham: "From Hegel himself I caught a glimpse of the synthesis I had long desired—a synthesis through which reality was brought to thought, and will and feeling were linked with reason" ("Search for System," 256).

6 Thilly, *History of Philosophy*, 549.

7 Cf. George H. Sabine: "idealism felt itself to be in possession of a single principle which enabled it to evaluate the conclusions of the special sciences, to view them all as contributing to a total understanding of man and nature . . . Consequently the correlation of the separate results and points of view of scientific investigation was an integral part of the claim of idealism to be an all-inclusive philosophical system" ("Philosophical and Scientific Specialization," 19; cf. Arthur Edward Murphy, "Situation in American Philosophy," 44–47).

an American, if I were not a Harvard man, if I had not had the friends I have had, or read the books I have read? . . . Such relations are not external, like those of space and time. They are constitutive."[8]

Whether primarily an intellectual or a moral perspective, whether ultimately a positive or a negative factor, the role that the various strands of post-Kantian idealism played in the history of American philosophy probably cannot be overestimated. Idealism's dominance on the American philosophical scene during the crucial period of academic growth between 1875 and 1910 is echoed by any number of studies. William Pepperell Montague, for example, writes in the late 1930s that at the end of the prior century, while empirical approaches to philosophy were suffering, "Idealism, both epistemological and ontological, was everywhere rampant." Earlier, Ralph Barton Perry had noted that "European and American Philosophy, as I saw it at the close of the nineteenth century, was a dispute between the extravagant claims of the party of science (naturalism) and the equally extravagant claims of that post-Kantian idealistic philosophy, which, invigorated by its transplantation from Germany to a foreign soil, had become the bulwark of English-speaking Protestant piety." Earlier still, in 1914, Thilly had written in his *History of Philosophy*: "The idealistic philosophy, partly through the mediation of English Neo-Hegelianism, and partly through a direct study of German thought, has also won a large following in the United States, counting many professors of philosophy in the universities among its adherents, with Josiah Royce at their head."[9]

In his 1892 volume, *The Spirit of Modern Philosophy*, Royce maintains that "the world in space and time, the world of causes and effects, the world of matter and of finite mind, whereof we know so little and long to know so much, is a very subordinate part of reality." At the same time, he also maintains that "there is absolutely nothing, not even the immediate facts of our sense at this moment, so clear, so certain, as the existence and the unity of that infinite conscious Self of whom we have now heard so much." The connection between these two statements can be found in this

---

[8] Ormond, *Concepts of Philosophy*, 3–4; Palmer, introduction to *Contemporary American Philosophy*, 35.

[9] Montague, *Ways of Things*, 231; Ralph Barton Perry, "Realism in Retrospect," 189; Thilly, *History of Philosophy*, 549. Cf. Arthur Oncken Lovejoy: "The metaphysics of the philosophical teachers whose influence was dominant in most of the American universities thirty-five years ago [c. 1895] had one common and fundamental premise which was supposed to be established beyond the possibility of reasonable doubt; to question it was simply to betray one's want of a genuine initiation into philosophy. It was the proposition that, in Bradley's words, 'to be real, or even barely to exist, is to fall within sentience; sentient experience, in short, is reality, and what is not this is not real'" ("Temporalistic Realism," 85; cf. Arthur Edward Murphy, "Philosophical Scholarship," 173–76).

idealist's further belief that the world "extends infinitely beyond our private consciousness, because it is the world of an universal mind." The "universal mind" or "infinite conscious Self" is the guarantee of the ultimate meaningfulness of human existence. "Absolutely the *only* thing sure from the first about this world," he writes, "is that it is intelligent, rational, orderly, essentially comprehensible, so that all its problems are somewhere solved, all its darkest mysteries are known to the supreme Self." Royce later notes that "especially in recent American thought, idealistic tendencies are prominent," and that this idealism was "not a new and foreign feature grafted on to the life of the country by the Transcendentalists, or by their most recent successors amongst technical philosophers." On the contrary, it is his position that despite its surface intellectually, "idealism goes, side by side with interest in material prosperity, throughout the whole of our natural life, is present and prominent in all the phases of our civilization, appears amongst us in evil as well as in good forms, and is responsible for very much in our national life besides philosophy."[10]

Whether we focus on Royce as the central figure in late nineteenth-century American idealism,[11] or Palmer, or Creighton, or George Holmes Howison, or Mary Whiton Calkins, or someone else, or no one in particular, it remains critical that we recognize the powerful position of this tradition as the philosophical associations were coming into existence. As the WPA and APA were being founded, however, idealism's hold as the dominant American philosophy was slipping. This overall decline was taking place despite the obvious facts that so many of the early presidents of the associations—Thilly, Creighton, Ormond, Royce, George Trumbull Ladd, Albert Ross Hill, Hugo Münsterberg, Bakewell, and Calkins—were themselves idealists and that many other members were still so inclined. In the

---

[10] Royce, *Spirit of Modern Philosophy*, 344–45, 380; introduction to *La Philosophie en Amérique*, xii, xiv.

[11] Cf. George Herbert Mead: "We wished to be free to follow our individual thinking and feeling into an intelligent and sympathetic world without having to bow before incomprehensible dogma or to anticipate the shipwreck of our individual ends and values. We wanted full intellectual freedom and yet the conservation of the values for which had stood Church, State, Science, and Art. We came out of a narrow Scottish intuitional philosophy, that crystalized problems into dogmas, and paralyzed thought; out of a puritan conception of life that standardized conduct by self-denials both passional and economic, and yet found in the business and social success which the community approved a sort of guarantee of rightness with God and His universe. Emerson had represented for us a mood rather than a method, and only irritated our thirst for a doctrine which would let us think without barriers and still do God's service in a world of moral order . . . Professor Royce opened up the realm of romantic idealism. What had been barriers of thought became but hazards in the game. Contradictions, instead of marking the no thoroughfares of reflection, became the guide posts toward higher levels of reality" ("Josiah Royce," 168–69; cf. Kraushaar, "Introduction [to Josiah Royce]," 199; Palmer, "Josiah Royce," 7–8).

climate of the new university, along with the creation of the new profession of philosopher as distinct from the minister-president of the college, a complex three-way struggle developed over the meaning of philosophy itself; and idealism slipped from prominence. In the words of Montague, "the epistemological controversy was triangular: Idealism, Pragmatism, Realism—each one against the other two." He delineates what this controversy meant from the realistic standpoint:

> the idealists were right in holding to the ordinary concept of truth as something absolute and not relative to finite minds, but wrong in their insistence that facts exist ultimately only as items of a single, all-embracing experience; while, on the other hand, the pragmatists were right in holding to a pluralistic world of facts, but wrong in supposing that truths about those facts were relative to and dependent upon the changing and conflicting experiences of verification.

In a similar fashion, Perry notes that both realism and pragmatism "reject absolute idealism, but while one [realism] rejects this doctrine on the score of its idealism, the other [pragmatism] rejects it on the score of its absolutism."[12] Before idealism declined, however, it flourished for a glorious moment; and, more importantly for us, idealism played a central role in the creation of a philosophical discipline in America, and hence in the creation of the philosophical associations.

Morris Raphael Cohen writes that pragmatism grew amidst "the American worship of visibly practical results . . ." Any philosophical perspective that evolved within this environment had to reflect its pressures. "In a country where so many great deeds in the conquest of nature are still to be performed," he continues, "the practical man's contempt for the contemplative and the visionary is re-enforced by the traditional American puritanic horror of idle play and of that which is uselessly ornamental." Cohen is largely correct, although we must be careful not to interpret pragmatism in a narrowly practical fashion. As Addison Webster Moore notes, pragmatism "does not call upon the scientist to turn out every week a new flying machine or a new breakfast food." The 'results' that the pragmatist wants may be slow in coming and they may require much careful interpretation. Moore continues that pragmatism "has nothing but approval for the investigator who shuts himself up with his 'biophors,' his 'ions' and 'electrons,' provided only he *finally* emerge with *some* connection established between these 'idols of the den' and the problems of life and death, of growth and decay, and of social interaction."[13] Pragmatism

---

[12] Montague, *Ways of Things*, 244; Ralph Barton Perry, "Realism in Retrospect," 190; cf. Brodbeck, "Philosophy in America," 11, 61; Blau, *Men and Movements*, 283.

[13] Cohen, *American Thought*, 291; Addison Webster Moore, *Pragmatism and Its Critics*, 10.

emphasizes that the human being is an embodied creature, rooted in the complexities of our natural situation, and that human consciousness and self-consciousness serve us as a means to understand and control our natural situation. It also maintains that the natural world is a place of openness and possibility where we can use our tentative webs of knowledge, without foundation or finality, to help meliorate our existence. And pragmatism emphasizes as well the communal context that makes this improved knowledge and action possible. Philosophy's job to address our problems of living—whether the metaphysical ones that tormented William James, or the scientific ones that challenged Charles Sanders Peirce, or the social ones that invigorated Dewey—and to be ever vigilant in challenging the purely intellectual solutions to which philosophers too often acquiesce.[14]

A quick survey of the early history of pragmatism would consider such high points as: the Metaphysical Club of Cambridge in the early 1870s; a long period of latency that included Peirce's essays in *The Journal of Speculative Philosophy* and *Popular Science Monthly*; James's 1897 volume, *The Will to Believe and Other Essays in Popular Philosophy*, followed by his address, "Philosophical Conceptions and Practical Results," at the University of California in 1898; the development of the Chicago School from 1894 through at least the publication of the cooperative volume, *Studies in Logical Theory*, in 1903 and Dewey's departure in 1904; the publication of James's *Pragmatism* in 1907, and *The Meaning of Truth* in 1909; and the appearance of *Creative Intelligence: Essays in the Pragmatic Attitude* in 1917.[15]

This brief listing of pragmatic high points leaves out much that is of importance to understanding this diverse and growing perspective. It should suggest, however, that pragmatism offered no finely honed and unified philosophical position; and, although individuals like Arthur Oncken Lovejoy might have registered dismay,[16] none should have been expected. As Frederick J. E. Woodbridge writes in his review of *Pragmatism*, "there is as yet no precise general agreement as to just what pragmatism is. Indeed, those who call themselves pragmatists and those who are called so by others exhibit often such marked differences in their individual thinking that one is not always sure who the genuine pragmatists are." He concludes that any attempt to decide what the movement means has to be

---

[14] Cf. Horace Standish Thayer, *Meaning and Action*, 419–47; McDermott, *Streams of Experience*; Campbell, *Community Reconstructs*.

[15] Cf. Dewey, "Development of American Pragmatism"; Fisch, *Peirce, Semeiotic, and Pragmatism*, 114–36, 283–304; Madden, *Chauncey Wright*; Wiener, *Evolution and the Founders of Pragmatism*; Rucker, *Chicago Pragmatists*.

[16] Cf. Lovejoy, "Thirteen Pragmatisms."

"tentative and subject to revision." His own tentative analysis indicates his belief that "[w]hatever else pragmatism may be, I think it is now generally admitted that it is, first, a method of conducting inquiry and of defining the meaning of ideas; and, secondly, a philosophy of the relation between facts and ideas." Beginning with the former aspect, he notes the similarity between pragmatism and the method of experimental investigation. Pragmatism, he writes, "points out that fruitful inquiry into any subject proceeds by discovering what our ideas about that subject lead us to expect and then by discovering whether these expectations can be fulfilled." Turning to the latter aspect, Woodbridge suggests that "pragmatism marks a rather important departure from the main trend of modern philosophy" when, instead of maintaining that facts and ideas inhabit "distinct and exclusive orders of existence," it presents them as "modifying each other" and emphasizes their relation to situations of doubt and hesitation and inquiry. As he writes, "That there should be ideas in a given situation is proof that the situation is incomplete, that it lacks the facts to which the ideas refer."[17]

Further, Woodbridge points to pragmatism's rejection of idealism. The pragmatists, he writes, "have shown that no philosophical theory is necessarily true because it has been logically deduced from accepted premises, and that, consequently, any attempt to confine our view of the world and our outlook upon life within the narrow limits of a philosophical system perfected out of the deductions we can make from what we already know, is an abuse of intelligence." Later on, Montague suggests a difference between James's and Dewey's anti-idealism: "Though the pragmatism of James and the instrumentalism of Dewey were alike in opposing the monism and intellectualism of the dominant forms of idealism . . . it was the metaphysical and psychological faults of those doctrines that aroused James to revolt, while for Dewey it was rather the sociological and methodical weaknesses of idealism that merited attack." Thus it was that James strove to establish metaphysical pluralism and Dewey was attracted to education and social questions.[18]

---

[17] Woodbridge, "Pragmatism and Education," 227–28, 233. In a later piece, Woodbridge noted that discussions of pragmatism had been sidetracked into considerations of the question of truth. The promise of pragmatism of helping to clarify our ideas, he writes, "was speedily put into a position of minor importance" when pragmatism became "a controversy about the nature of truth. Instead of encouraging analyses of the meaning of terms and ideas in the contexts wherein they occur, it encouraged a debate about the foundations of belief and the criteria of truth and falsity. How can we determine when our ideas are true, became a more important question than how can we determine what they mean" ("Promise of Pragmatism," 541–42; cf. 552).

[18] Woodbridge, "Pragmatism and Education," 232–33; Montague, *Ways of Things*, 232–33; cf. Thilly, *History of Philosophy*, 567.

Whether we focus on Peirce as the central figure of pragmatism,[19] or on James, or on Dewey, or on James Hayden Tufts or George Herbert Mead, or on someone else, or on no one in particular, it is important to recognize the role that pragmatism played both as a challenge to idealism and as a modest brake on the rush to professionalization. Ultimately, however, while pragmatism stirred up a great deal of discussion in the broader press, and caused some fundamental changes in other disciplines, there was clearly less ongoing interest in it at the meetings of the associations than in either idealism or realism. Arthur Edward Murphy notes in 1945, "The great influence of this philosophy in allied and related fields has not been matched by an equally general acceptance in philosophy itself." He attributes this failing primarily to "the continuing stubborn concern of most professional philosophers with just those hard and technical problems from which the instrumentalist theory of meaning was supposed to have emancipated their subject." While it is surely question-begging on Murphy's part to maintain that these technical problems "are just the issues that men have always had to deal with when they tried to solve their problems *philosophically*," or that "the pragmatists, in their zeal to get on with good works, have by-passed these problems, when their job as philosophers was to solve them,"[20] he is surely correct that professional philosophers have continued to puzzle over these problems. For pragmatism, however, with its fundamental inclination toward the practical possibilities of creative intelligence, professional success in philosophy remained elusive and secondary.

The same cannot be said for realism. This philosophical perspective avoided the broader religious and social aspects of idealism and pragmatism by focusing on narrowly professional questions of knowledge. Moreover, in opposition to both idealism and pragmatism, the realists challenged any suggestion that the objects of experience were not existences prior to and independent of that experience[21]; and, while relying to

---

[19] The choice of Peirce would be anachronistic. As John Henry Muirhead felt it necessary to write in 1931: "When the history of American philosophy in the nineteenth century comes to be written in greater detail than hitherto, the important place of Charles S. Peirce as a pathfinder in every one of the many fields that his work touched will have to receive fuller recognition than has as yet been accorded to it" (*Platonic Tradition*, 326). To survey Peirce's relative anonymity prior to the digestion of the eight volumes of his *Collected Papers*, see: *Philosophical Review: Index to Volumes I–XXXV*, 37–38, 81–82, 124; *Journal of Philosophy: Fifty-Year Index, 1904–1953*, 76–77, 264.

[20] Arthur Edward Murphy, "Situation in American Philosophy," 51–52; cf. Brodbeck, "Philosophy in America," 65–67.

[21] Cf. Frank Thilly: "In accordance with what it believes to be the spirit of the scientific method, this school rejects the idealistic theory of knowledge that relations are internal or organic, and conceives them as not affecting the nature of the things or terms related, that is,

a great extent on the direct or natural realism of common sense, these new philosophers shared none of the earlier realists' interest in matters theological. Some early moments of this renewed realism can be seen in James's essays "The Function of Cognition" (1885) and "Does 'Consciousness' Exist?" (1904), and in his various attacks on Royce and Bradley,[22] and in Montague's and Perry's 1902 reviews of Royce's two-volume work, *The World and the Individual.*[23] Montague notes in his review that Royce "attempts to force upon the realist the strange conclusion that such independence as is implied by and indicative of the numerical separateness of the object and idea carries with it a total inability of these two to interact, or to correspond, or to be in any way related." In his review, Perry defends the belief that reality is "a *datum, a somewhat that is given independently of whatever ideas may be formed about it.* According to the realist, the real has a *locus,* a *habitat,* whether or no within some individual experience." The realist distinguishes things and thoughts about them. "They are two orders, not necessarily two kinds; for the thing may be a thought," he continues. "But in every case the thing of the first order is indifferent, as far as its being is concerned, to the thought of the second order; which may reveal, but does not constitute or create its object."[24]

In opposition to the subjectivism that it finds in idealism and pragmatism, realism maintains that the objects of knowledge are independent of our knowledge of them. As Perry writes, "The realist believes that relations are external to the terms which they unite"; and, because such relations are external, we can learn a great deal about the objects of an experience

---

as external . . . The school, therefore, emphasizes analysis,—the very method of knowledge which Hegel and his followers, no less than pragmatists and intuitionists, had repudiated as an inadequate instrument of truth . . . This philosophy is also realistic in the sense of considering existence as not depending upon knowledge" (*History of Philosophy,* 580–81).

[22] Cf. James, *Meaning of Truth,* 13–32; *Essays in Radical Empiricism,* 3–19; *Pluralistic Universe.* May Brodbeck writes that James was "godfather to two quite disparate movements in American philosophy . . . James's 1904 essay 'Does Consciousness Exist?' . . . marks the beginning of systematically developed realism in America, though realistic articles, including some by the many-faceted James himself, had appeared even earlier" ("Philosophy in America," 13, 63; cf. Blau, *Men and Movements,* 275).

[23] Cf. George Holmes Howison: "*The World and the Individual* . . . has logically annulled Realism by reducing it to the unavoidable and ruinous shuttling from materialism to agnosticism, from agnosticism to materialism, ever back and forth . . ." ("Josiah Royce," 238–39).

[24] Montague, "Professor Royce's Refutation of Realism," 55; Ralph Barton Perry, "Prof. Royce's Refutation of Realism and Pluralism," 450–51. Montague later wrote, "*Realism is the doctrine that the same objects that are known by some one may continue to exist when they are not known by any one,* or that they may pass in and out of the cognitive relation without prejudice to their reality, or that the existence of a thing is not correlated with, or dependent upon, the fact that somebody experiences it, perceives it, conceives it, is conscious of it, or in any way aware of it" ("May a Realist Be a Pragmatist?" 460).

through the process of careful analysis that he characterizes as "only another name for a careful and discriminating examination of things." All of these realists further maintain the presentational belief that our experiences are of the things of nature and not just of our ideas or representations of the things of nature. The question of what our ideas are led realists to a number of different answers. One was the Jamesian answer of Perry, who writes that "ideas are only things in a certain relation; or, things, in respect of being known, are ideas." There was more agreement among realists on the need to focus on issues of epistemology. Perry, for example, writes, "The crucial problem for contemporary philosophy is the problem of knowledge . . . Epistemology is the bitter substance of every sugar-coated philosophical pill."[25] This realism grew continually, both as a philosophical perspective and as a component of the meetings of the associations, and it must be recognized as the primary perspective in American philosophy after about 1910. While much of the interest in the realistic movement was directed at untangling the complexities of the perspective, more important were its desire to develop a 'scientific' philosophy that used as its models mathematics and physics, and its fascination with 'the problem of knowledge' as the central issue in philosophy. Realism and its descendants have both directed and benefited from the nature and the increasing professionalization of academic philosophizing and have remained dominant in American academia, in one form or another, ever since.[26]

As with idealism and pragmatism, realism was not a unified or settled project. It developed in several directions over the early years of the associations, the first of which called itself "new" realism. A good entryway into this perspective is "The Program and First Platform of Six Realists" that was published in mid-1910. In that manifesto, the authors—Edwin Bissell Holt, Walter Taylor Marvin, Montague, Perry, Walter B. Pitkin, and Edward Gleason Spaulding—proposed a way for philosophy to finally progress. They maintained that disagreements, while due in part "to the subject-matter of philosophy," are due "chiefly to the lack of precision and uniformity in the use of words and to the lack of deliberate cooperation in research." Because of these failings, work in philosophy, unlike work in sci-

---

[25] Ralph Barton Perry, *Present Conflict of Ideals*, 373; *Present Philosophical Tendencies*, 308, 272; *Present Conflict of Ideals*, 6.

[26] Cf. Arthur Edward Murphy: The realists "proposed to base their thinking on knowledge of the real world as it exists in its own right and independently of men's ideas, wishes, or imaginings about it. Their chief opponents, therefore, were those idealists and pragmatists who had reduced knowledge to a mere construction of thought, whether Absolute or instrumental . . . Since such inquiries require professional skill and training and have usually a technical language of their own it is not to be expected that philosophy, thus pursued, will be everybody's business" ("Philosophical Scholarship," 190–91).

ences like physics and chemistry, seems to be "mere opinion." Further, "through the appearance of many figurative or loose expressions in the writings of isolated theorists, the impression is given that philosophical problems and their solutions are essentially personal." To rectify this situation, they called for "cooperation, common terminology, and a working agreement as to fundamental presuppositions . . ." The sort of cooperation that these six authors had in mind was to include three stages: (1) "a statement of fundamental principles and doctrines"; (2) the application of these principles and doctrines to "a program of constructive work"; and (3) a resultant "system of axioms, methods, hypotheses, and facts" that are acceptable as a whole "at least [to] those investigators." The six had engaged in this process of cooperation; and they presented, after their manifesto, a set of six statements about the nature of realism, hoping that they had thereby advanced philosophy. They anticipated further cooperative activities in their overall attempt to make philosophical practice more like that of the sciences. "By conferring on other topics, by interchange of ideas, and by systematic criticism of one another's phraseology, methods, and hypotheses," they continue, "we hope to develop a common technique, a common terminology, and so finally a common doctrine which will enjoy some measure of that authority which the natural sciences possess." They also hoped that their cooperative efforts might serve as a model for other philosophers "to form small cooperative groups with similar aims."[27]

This manifesto, and the subsequent volume by the six, *The New Realism: Co-operative Studies in Philosophy* of 1912, led to a flood of responses, pro and con.[28] When the dust had settled, both Montague and Perry saw the meaning of realism to be found most clearly in its oppositions. The new realism was first of all explicitly anti-idealistic. Montague writes that idealism was "not just a falsity to be neglected, but a positive menace debauching the minds of the youths who studied it." Because idealism saw it as self-evident that "the relation of the knower to the object

---

[27] Holt et al., "Program and First Platform," 393–94. Cf. May Brodbeck: The new realism "was, just as its proponents insisted, a return to the natural or naive realism of the man in the street to whom the world is as it appears to be, who believes that we perceive things as they really are . . . it seems perfectly commonsensical to say that we know the physical world as it really is by direct awareness, an immediate apprehension of the object. Unfortunately, it is too pat. A moment's thought reveals that common sense is fraught with perplexities. *With these perplexities all analytical philosophy begins*" ("Philosophy in America," 62, 64; cf. Blau, *Men and Movements*, 274–93; Cohen, "New Realism"; Schneider, *History of American Philosophy*, 509–16; Werkmeister, *History of Philosophical Ideas*, 369–436).

[28] Cf. Joseph Leon Blau: "Philosophic journals between 1910 and 1925 are filled with polemical articles dealing with one or another aspect of realism; these may be consulted profitably only by the most dogged of students" (*Men and Movements*, 377; cf. Victor E. Harlow, *A Bibliography and Genetic Study of American Realism*, 53).

known is an 'internal relation,' that is, a relation such that the terms related are dependent upon the existence of the relation," and thus that "no object can exist apart from consciousness or experience," it must assume "an infinite and absolute experience" upon which finite experience depends. As he puts it, "The second postulate of Absolutism is thus made necessary to repair the havoc wrought by the first postulate of Subjectivism." Perry finds in this absolutism the shadow of religion. As he writes, "Idealism is a form of spiritualism in which man, the finite individual, is regarded as a microcosmic representation of God, the Absolute Individual."[29] In addition to this anti-idealism, the new realism also demonstrated a rejection of pragmatism. Montague notes two major flaws. The first was methodological, having to do with difficulties interpreting of its practicalist criterion of truth. In particular, he complains that "[t]here are many false beliefs that have worked well over long periods of time for many people, and, again, there are many true propositions that can bring despair and even paralysis of action to some of the persons who believe them." The second and more serious flaw of pragmatism was that it demonstrated epistemological relativism. Pragmatism, Montague writes, "makes truth a psychological affair and, as such, an affair of individual experience and relative to each individual who has the experience"; but, in reality, "[t]he truth (or falsity) of a proposition *antedates* the process by which it is verified (or refuted)." Perry's criticism is, if anything, stronger: "Pragmatism is reactionary and dangerous in so far as it coordinates and equalizes verification by perception and consistency with verification by sentiment and subsequential utility."[30]

The diversity of emphases among the six new realists that gave the movement much of its original breadth also made it unstable.[31] Moreover, new realism also was ultimately unable to overcome the seemingly necessary concomitant of all presentationalism: the problem of error and illusion. If experience is the monistic apprehension of the objects of nature, then it must be accurate; at the same time, sticks do not bend in water and train tracks do not meet.[32] As discussions continued, a second, explicitly

---

[29] Montague, "Confessions of an Animistic Materialist," 143; *Ways of Things*, 240; Ralph Barton Perry, *Present Philosophical Tendencies*, 113.

[30] Montague, *Ways of Things*, 241–42; Ralph Barton Perry, *Present Philosophical Tendencies*, 213.

[31] Cf. Joseph Leon Blau: "The area of agreement among the new realists was small. They expressed complete agreement on two working procedures, and agreement with reservations on three principles of the theory of knowledge" (*Men and Movements*, 276; Harlow, *Bibliography and Genetic Study*, 68–69).

[32] Cf. Thomas English Hill: "The most often cited objection to the epistemological monism of the new realists remains one of the most powerful, namely, that the theory cannot be reconciled with certain facts concerning error and illusion. In dreams and hallucinations

dualistic movement emerged within realism, calling itself "critical" realism. It evolved out of a 1916 volume by Roy Wood Sellars entitled *Critical Realism*[33] and a discussion session at the APA's 1916 meeting that was organized around the theme of the 'mental' or 'psychical' and the 'physical.'[34] After a number of years of correspondence among the principals, a cooperative volume, *Essays in Critical Realism: A Co-operative Study of the Problem of Knowledge*, appeared in 1920. Its seven authors were Durant Drake, Lovejoy, James Bissett Pratt, Arthur Kenyon Rogers, George Santayana, Sellars, and Charles Augustus Strong.[35] In 1930, Drake offered his sense of how this critical movement differed from the prior one. He writes that new realism "had attempted to reduce the cognitive relation to two categories, the knower (or organism) and the object known." The problem with this was that "any cognitive experience may conceivably be hallucinatory; the awareness of physical objects is not, in itself, evidence that such objects *exist*." He indicates that for critical realists three categories are necessary to describe the cognitive situation adequately: "the knower (or self, or organism), the object of knowledge (which, in the case of knowledge of an existent, has its own independent existence), and the datum of experience, that of which we are aware." Sometimes, when our knowledge is accurate, "the datum is identical with the object of knowledge"; at other times, it is not. But whether knowledge *is* accurate and literal is a matter for inquiry in each case. Drake concludes, however, that the inquiries that are necessary in particular cases to determine if our knowledge is accurate are ruled out in advance by the assumptions of new realism that the cognitive relation contains only the

---

we seem to see what is not occurring at all. In illusions and double vision we see things differently from the way they are" (*Contemporary Theories of Knowledge*, 123; cf. Brodbeck, "Philosophy in America," 64–65; Blanshard, "Speculative Thinkers," 1289–90).

[33] Cf. Roy Wood Sellars: "I was unable to accept a return to naive, presentational, realism . . . I sought to move between presentationalism and representationalism . . . the new realists believed that some form of presentationalism, alone, was tenable. They were convinced that representationalism had long been shown to be a blind alley . . . But is there not a possibility between presentationalism and representationalism?" (*Reflections*, 44, 59–60).

[34] This session will be considered in chapter 8.

[35] The unsigned preface to this volume notes: "The present volume was projected in December 1916, and the work upon it has been carried forward since then by conferences and correspondence . . . The doctrine here defended, while definitely realistic, is distinctly different from the 'new' realism of the American group . . . Our realism is not a physically monistic realism, or a merely logical realism, and escapes the many difficulties which have prevented the general acceptance of the 'new' realism . . . To find an adjective that should connote the essential features of our brand of realism seemed chimerical, and we have contented ourselves with the vague, but accurate, phrase *critical realism*" (*Essays in Critical Realism*, v–vi; cf. Blanshard, "Speculative Thinkers," 1290; Blau, *Men and Movements*, 280–83, 293–302; Werkmeister, *History of Philosophical Ideas*, 437–518).

knower and the object known.[36] While this suggestion of critical realism did not lead to universal acceptance among philosophers, the focus upon issues of knowledge did become primary. Professional philosophers focused on the quest for certainty and truth, for the most part leaving aside issues of beauty and justice.

Critical realism, like new realism before it, was not a unified movement; and the cooperative study that marked its birth also foretold its dissolution. As I have suggested previously, however, there may be no great problem in the fact that philosophers seldom attain or maintain agreement. Simplifying labels, such as idealist or pragmatist or realist, can obscure many real differences among thinkers—but not all, and not forever. Moreover, these three labels do not adequately encompass all of the possibilities of work in American philosophy in the early twentieth-century. Still, a reemphasis on them has served, I hope, as a useful preparation for the next chapter, where we will focus on the papers that were read at the meetings of the associations.

[36] Drake, "Philosophy of a Meliorist," 284.

MORRIS R. COHEN

Image courtesy of Special Collections Research Center, Morris Library,
Southern Illinois University Carbondale

7

The "Work Proper" of
the Associations

Harry Norman Gardiner writes, as we saw in chapter 6, that "the work proper" of the APA is "the papers read and discussed at our meetings." Like many other academic associations, the philosophers assembled and presented to each other papers that represented their ideas on issues of mutual concern. In the discussions that followed, the philosophers disputed each others' claims and refined their own views on the topics under consideration. In form, the meetings of the associations corresponded more or less to what James Edwin Creighton had called for in his presidential address discussed in chapter 4: "promoting and facilitating the interchange of ideas between the philosophical workers of the present day."

The focus of the most significant portion of these APA papers, and of those at the WPA, over the early years was the trio of perspectives that we have just considered. Explicit work on the issues of idealism, pragmatism, and realism began with the beginning of the associations. Edgar Lenderson Hinman spoke on "The Primacy of Will" at the first meeting of the WPA in January 1901 (PR 10:167–69). At its second meeting later that year, Frederick J. E. Woodbridge considered "The Idealism of Spinoza" (PR 11:154–55). In March 1902, the first meeting of the APA included William Caldwell's "Some Recent Criticisms of the Philosophy of T.H. Green" and Joseph Alexander Leighton's "On the Study of Individuality" (PR 11:268–69, 277–78). When the APA met for a second time later that year, Caldwell considered a volume of essays entitled *Personal Idealism*, edited by Henry Sturt (PR 12:182). A few months later, at the WPA's third meeting in April 1903, Arthur Oncken Lovejoy offered a critique of Royce's *The World and the Individual* that presented these volumes as "an epoch in the working out of idealistic monism" that not only "shows the complete development of the doctrine" but also shows "its complete breakdown" by demonstrating "the inherently self-contradictory character" of idealistic monism (PR 12:545). At the APA's third meeting in December 1903, there were two major idealistic counterattacks on pragmatism. The first was the presidential address of Josiah Royce, "The Eternal and the Practical." In this paper, he grants that truth has a pragmatic component: "knowledge is action . . . the judgment which I now make is a present reaction to a present empirically given situation, a reaction expressing my need to get control over the situation . . . the world of truth is not now a finished world and is now in the act of making." His rejection of pragmatism, in what he calls its extreme or "pure" form, however, is based upon his claim that "one of the things that I seek, when I judge, is to express something that shall have some value as a standard. A judgment . . . not only says: 'I believe;' it says: 'This is to be believed.'" Royce's analysis of the rational import of judgment leads him through a consideration of the opinions of companions ultimately to the all-embracing perspective of the absolute, the need for which, he maintains, is "one of the deepest of all our practical needs."[1] The anonymous account of this meeting reports that, in his criticism, Royce aimed "to show, with his characteristic felicity and skill, the impossibility of a pure pragmatism and its need of supplementation from the philosophy of absolutism." This talk was followed by "a smoker at the Princeton Inn and an informal discussion in which the members from Chicago were invited to take special part" (JP 1:16).

Also on the program at the APA's 1903 meeting was a paper by Creighton entitled "Purpose as a Logical Category." In this paper, Creighton considered what he took to be the strongest reasons for and against "the position that thought is instrumental or teleological in character and subordinate to the purposes of practical life." Among the former, he mentions the utility of knowledge, the relationship of free will and action, and the support that this position receives "from biological analogies and from the general theory of evolution . . . ." Among the objections to pragmatism, he lists the ambiguous use of "practical purpose" to refer to the solution of both practical and theoretical problems, its subjectivism and relativism, a dualism between reflective thought and its antecedent experience, its inability to unify experience, and "the fact that the position presupposes as its indispensable background a logical and ontological system very different from that to which it explicitly appeals." Creighton's overall conclusion was thus, similar to Royce's, the general idealistic one that "pragmatism is only possible *within* the logical and ontological position that it supposes itself able to supersede" (PR 13:181; JP 1:17).

---

[1] Royce, "The Eternal and the Practical," 117, 125, 131–32, 142. This address also contains a joint idealist/pragmatist attack on realism (Ibid., 122–25).

At the APA's 1904 meeting, in the place of contemporary emphases, there were a number of papers in remembrance of Immanuel Kant's death on 12 February 1804 read in a joint meeting with the newly founded SSPP. Royce spoke on Kant's mathematics. Edward Franklin Buchner read a paper entitled "Kant's Attitude towards Idealism and Realism."[2] Caldwell spoke about Kant's ethics; James Hayden Tufts, about his aesthetics. Kant's religious thought was addressed by George William Knox, who spoke about his influence on theology. A further paper, on Kant and Aquinas, by Brother Chrysostom was omitted due to time constraints (PR 14:171–76). In summarizing the import of this session, Gardiner wrote: "in the opinion of the most careful students, Kant is neither to be ignored, nor belittled, nor 'outflanked,' nor, on the other hand, to be unduly exalted, but to be critically studied . . . he still counts, if not as the paramount, at least as one of the most potent influences in the philosophical thinking of our time" (S 21:98).[3]

In December 1905 the APA met, in part with the AΨA, in the newly opened Emerson Hall at Harvard University; and interest in the relationship between philosophy and psychology was primary. John Dewey read as his presidential address, "Beliefs and Realities."[4] In matters more closely related to our themes, Creighton again attacked pragmatism in a paper entitled "Experience and Thought" that developed the idealistic critique that full meaning cannot be found in any particular situation. "Thought always has," he writes, "in addition to the specific problem with which it is occupied at any particular time, a more general and ultimate end, the realization and maintenance of a rational life." It is only in connection with this larger end "that the particular problems and acts of thinking get their significance." Only because of this broader ordering of life, "when experience is regarded as the development of a single principle which maintains itself in and through its differentiations," is it proper to consider the parts of experience "as 'functions' or 'in functional relation' at all" (PR 15:165–66). Thus, Creighton concludes, "completely to get rid of dualism, and to attain to a truly functional standpoint, it is necessary to regard knowledge as the process through which a subject expresses and realizes a rational life" (JP 3:73–74). There were also a few other relevant papers at the 1905 meeting. In a paper entitled "Evolution and the Absolute," for example, Henry Heath Bawden attempted to give "a functional interpretation" of the absolute. Woodbridge offered a paper

---

[2] This paper had been bumped from the APA's second meeting (PR 12:167).

[3] At the WPA's fifth meeting in April 1905, "there was a general discussion on 'The Present Estimate of Kant's Place in the History of Theoretical Philosophy,' led by Professor A. O. Lovejoy . . ." (JP 2:252).

[4] Dewey's presidential address was published as "Beliefs and Existences."

entitled "Consciousness and Evolution" that emphasized that "[t]o regard consciousness as an outcome of evolutionary processes involves a radical transformation of many of the fundamental problems of modern philosophy . . ." A third paper, "Pure Science and Pragmatism," by Edward Gleason Spaulding offers a critique of "theoretical" pragmatism in the light of scientific practice (PR 15:166–70).

At the 1906 meeting of the WPA, there was a joint session with the North Central Section of the AΨA on "Recent Arguments for Realism, with especial reference to the Relations of Realism and Pragmatism." The proceedings report, "For this discussion a special bibliography of recent papers on the subject had been prepared and sent to members in advance of the meeting." Henry Walgrave Stuart began the discussion with a paper that supported pragmatism against realism. He notes that "[o]ne of the principal motives of realism is, apparently, a dread of solipsism" that it finds permeating idealism. Still, realists profess what he sees as "two incompatible principles: (1) In the knowing experience the object known is immediately present without the intervention of any mental image, and (2) knowledge is an awareness of a simultaneously existent real object." Pragmatism is better than realism here because it rejects the latter's representationalism "and thereby avoids the danger of being cut off, like realism and idealism, from any possibility of distinguishing truth from error in detail . . ." In conclusion, he maintains that "[p]ragmatism takes it as a matter of course that experiences empirically occur, and fixes its attention on the problem of determining the logical and ethical significance of these. Realism and idealism in the end succeed in saying no more than that experiences actually do occur—they can not account for these empirical qualities." Boyd Henry Bode followed with a second, if guarded, defense of pragmatism. He writes that it acts as a mediator between two forms of realism: one in which "the object [of knowing] is a modification of the conscious state itself," that is "acquaintance with," and another in which the object is not a modification, namely "knowledge about." According to pragmatism, realism treats the object of knowledge "as a ready-made datum"; but what is necessary is to "distinguish between pure experience and consciousness." When this pragmatic distinction is made, we are able to assert that "objects are experienced directly, since they are synonymous with pure experience, and . . . consciousness is reducible to one form, since it consists of relational elements." Bode continues, however, that ultimately the pragmatic analysis of consciousness fails and that dualism must be retained. In a third paper, Stephen S. Colvin criticized pragmatism for being insufficiently realistic. "The pragmatist," he writes, "nowhere finds room for a pointing to an extraexperiential reality." The essence of realism, for him, is "the belief that with every noetic state there is something that exists independent of this state, which is extramental and to which the noetic state points . . ." The pragmatist, on the other hand, "makes pure experience a reality independent of the noetic state, and conditioning it. Here he has reached a realistic basis, but without warrant. From experience as we know it we can never arrive at pure experience." Thus, "pragmatism has failed to recognize the transcending element in the noetic psychosis, and it must share the fate of all philosophies that regard merely the flow of experience and ignore the realistic attitude of knowing." Pragmatism is, in other words, "essentially idealistic" (JP 3:318–21).

At the APA's sixth meeting William James read his presidential address, "The Energies of Men," a pragmatic consideration of the reserves of human power that can become available in times of crisis. "The human individual lives usually far within his limits," he writes, "he possesses powers of various sorts which he habitually fails to use." In the course of normal quotidian living, "[h]e energizes below his maximum, and he behaves below his optimum."[5] James's point is that if we knew better what was possible, we would expect more of ourselves and would strive to figure out how we could attain this higher level of existence. At the same meeting, Charles Montague Bakewell read a defense of idealism entitled "The Ugly Infinite and the Good-For-Nothing Absolute." This somewhat fanciful title refers to opponents' terms for the essential elements of what he takes to be the central antinomy of philosophy. By "the antinomy of the infinite and the absolute," he means the opposition between "the boundless . . . 'the ever-not quite' . . . which is implied in empiricism, as the idealist views it; and . . . the fixed and definite and final . . . which is the flaw in idealism as viewed by empiricism." In hopes of settling this opposition in the idealists' favor, Bakewell writes that at least a dynamic understanding of the Absolute is useful for interpreting experience because it does not imply omniscience. Rather, it moves "by definite and sure steps into a world of meaning where nothing is ever lost," and where progress means that "a less complete view can once for all be set aside in favor of a more complete . . ." (PR 16:57–59).

At the 1907 meeting of the APA, there was a strong focus upon the meaning of truth. Gardiner offered as his presidential address "The Problem of Truth." He notes that the aim of his paper is "to set forth simply and clearly some of the more general considerations that ought, in my judgment, to be kept in mind when this subject is under debate." Among these considerations are that "our concern is with the truth of propositions," that "every proposition, whatever its range or comprehension, expresses and embodies a single, even if complex, truth," and that "the truth of any proposition must be judged with reference to its own unique

---

[5] James, "Energies of Men," 144.

meaning and intent." With these points in mind, he turns to what he sees as "the essential problems" of truth: "(1) What do we mean by calling any proposition true? and (2) How do we know that it is really true?" In attempting to answer these questions, he introduced themes from James's recently published *Pragmatism*; and he concludes his address by considering three pragmatic claims. The first—that the test of truth is "serviceableness in use"—seems to Gardiner acceptable. He is more doubtful about pragmatism's second claim. Rather than agreeing that only verifiable propositions are true, he wonders "why may there not be truths forever incapable of being thought, acknowledged, or validated by any human individual?" Finally, he rejects what he sees as the third claim of pragmatism—that "truth lives and has its being in a process of development," that "it is something made . . . an event that happens"—maintaining that "the proposition, if true, bears, as such, a purely logical relation to the fact that it is true of, and that this relation is not a process or event, like the cognitive process though which it gets into our minds . . ."[6]

Gardiner's presidential address served as a prelude to a discussion session on "The Meaning and Criterion of Truth" that included contributions by James, Creighton, Bakewell, John Grier Hibben, and Charles Augustus Strong. James begins with the familiar statement: "My account of truth is realistic, and follows the epistemological dualism of common sense . . . This notion of a reality independent of either one of us, taken from ordinary social experience, lies at the base of the pragmatist definition of truth. With some such reality any statement, to be accounted 'true,' must 'agree.'" The point at issue, between pragmatism and its critics, as he sees it, is what is meant by 'agreement.' For pragmatism, agreement means "certain actual or potential 'workings'": "these workings are indispensable to constitute the notion of what 'true' means as applied to a statement . . . Our critics nevertheless call the workings inessential, and consider that statements are, as it were, *born* true . . ." (PR 17:180–81).[7]

Creighton responded, in accordance with his previously seen idealism, that "[a] philosophical account of the nature of truth is possible only in the light of a general theory regarding the nature of experience." He thus maintains that pragmatism's "account of truth in 'practical' terms . . . has been definitely refuted . . . " Still, he is willing to find some value in pragmatism. As he writes, "it is possible to regard the pragmatic movement as a protest against abstraction, the besetting sin of philosophical constructions." Bakewell, also an idealist, maintains that when individuals seek

---

[6] Gardiner, "Problem of Truth," 113–15, 117, 131–33. James had offered his pragmatism lectures at the Lowell Institute in Boston in November-December 1906, and at Columbia in January 1907. James's volume *Pragmatism* was published in June 1907.

[7] Cf. James, *Meaning of Truth*, 117–19.

truth, they are trying not to solve problems but "to read the momentary fact of experience as it comes along in its absolutely total experiential setting, such a setting being the one in which no item of possible or actual experience is left out. The implication is that each particular object of experience has its definite place in that complete context, which is commonly referred to as the realm of experience." He further suggests that "[t]he impossibility of defining truth in terms of the verifying process" is clear when the temporal considerations are included. The pragmatists "are then forced to admit that 'when new experiences lead to retrospective judgments, using the past tense, what these judgments utter *was* true, even though no past thinker had been led there.'" The fourth speaker, Hibben, similarly attacked the pragmatic notion of truth, maintaining that it was "obviously inadequate" for three reasons. First, "[i]t is inadequate as a working hypothesis" because what is really useful is itself often disguised by the "expedient" and the apparently useful. Second, the pragmatic notion of truth is "inadequate because we instinctively subordinate its testing principle to higher considerations" like "order, coherence, universality, and necessity." Here, he seems to be offering the idealistic point that our conscious life is not a collection of particular experiences, but rather "a system of coordinately related parts . . ." Third, the pragmatic notion of truth is inadequate because it overestimates the creative function of human thought and action. "It is only in a very restricted sense," he writes, "that we can be said to make truth." Finally, Strong, who saw himself in agreement with James's epistemological realism and his rejection of absolute idealism, criticized James from what he believes is James's "own point of view" for failing to adequately connect cognitions and objects. Strong's point was that there are many relations between cognitions and objects that exist prior to the potential consequences. "Truth, then, is antecedent to the consequences, and does not consist in them" (PR 17:181–86).

At this same meeting of the APA, there was also a series of additional papers on themes related to our general interests. Gustavus Watts Cunningham defended the Hegelian concept of absolute knowledge, and Edmund Howard Hollands supported objective idealism against developing realistic trends that reject the representational theory of knowledge. Norman Kemp Smith discussed Bergsonian realism as a means to overcome subjectivity. Finally, in "An Introductory Statement of Realism," Bernard Capen Ewer maintains, "(1) that consciousness is directly aware of external things, (2) that it has internal qualitative differentiations of which it is also conscious, and (3) that these characters appear in varying degrees of relative prominence in actual experience" (PR 17:169–79).

At the APA's meeting in 1908, Hugo Münsterberg offered his presidential address, "The Problem of Beauty," in which he calls for a redirection of inquiries in aesthetics away from psychological approaches that yield theories of art that are "fundamentally not different from the psychological explanation of the enjoyment of fruit and coffee and candy." What is necessary, he writes, is an understanding of aesthetics that is built upon the idealistic recognition that beauty "comes to me as an ought to which I submit, that it comes as a perfection which belongs to the truest meaning of the world and which cannot be otherwise." The art object is "an impression which comes to me as a meaning, as a manifoldness of energies, of suggestions, of demands." Such an idealistic aesthetics would have little interest in "the pleasant feelings which beauty awakens," and would ultimately attempt "[t]o recognize beauty and truth and morality and religion in their eternal meaning as the deeds of our over-personal will . . ."[8]

In other papers at this meeting, the epistemological focus continued. Ewer returned to defend dualistic realism from charges that it leads to spatial and temporal paradoxes like "how 'what is evidently one reality could be in two places at once, both in outer space and in a person's mind.'" He believes that such apparent paradoxes "are not sustained by reflection as permanent theoretic inconsistencies" because there is no claim that "the same object is found 'in two places at once.'" Ernest Albee presented a defense of idealism that finds its value in its ability to "express adequately the various forms of interdependence within experience." William Pepperell Montague's paper, "The True, the Good, and the Beautiful, from a Pragmatic Standpoint," suggested that such values are "radically distinct from one another" when considered "in terms of the process of adaptation of an organism to its environment." Thus, it would seem that "the pragmatic method yields a conclusion at variance with that pragmatic doctrine which treats the true as a form of the good." In another attack on absolutism, Addison Webster Moore emphasized the importance of "evolutionism" as a challenge to "completionism" in such areas as metaphysics, logic, biology, and ethics. Evolution, he maintains, makes progress possible and responsibility necessary because it requires "that the agent participate in the construction of the ideal which he is to help execute." Additionally, J. H. Hume discussed the importance of pragmatism for the history of philosophy as "a continuation and extension of Empiricism" that is in fact "reconstructing empiricism so as to approach more closely to objective idealism" (PR 18:169–77).

There was also an organized discussion of realism and idealism at this meeting, with Royce, Dewey, Woodbridge, Bakewell, and Kemp Smith participating. In his report on the session, Harold Chapman Brown indicates that Royce began by stating "his well-known form of idealism": "The

---

[8] Münsterberg, "Problem of Beauty," 125–26, 128, 144.

real world is nothing but the true interpretation of the surroundings in which I find myself. To reject idealism is to declare that your world is interpreted in a way which is not an interpretation . . . human experience is only an ideal construction . . . The essence of idealism is to hold that the world is real only as an interpretation of experience" (JP 6:47). Next, Dewey offered a genetic account of the bifurcation of realism—"the function and role of observation, description, definition and classification"—and idealism—"the function of reflection, interpretation, reorganization of facts through the projection of ideas and hypotheses"—in conditions present at the origin of modern thought that liberated the power of ideas in "protest and rebellion against acceptance of the given and customary order . . ." He maintained further that recognizing the origin of this bifurcation should lead to its abandonment, so that eventually "the absolutistic opposition of realism and idealism will become an historic episode." Woodbridge suggested that idealists emphasize the reflective character of consciousness, whereas a realistic theory of consciousness is based upon "the study of the structure and functions of the sense organs and nervous system" in which "the nervous system secures to the organism individuality and unity of life in spite of very great diversity of stimuli and of environment." Bakewell began with the attempt to overcome what he saw as some subjectivist "misunderstandings" of idealism which, if unchallenged, would make idealism seem like "a form of madness." Then he attempted to draw out the common opposition of idealism and realism to subjectivism. In the position that he favored, "concrete or objective idealism," he maintains that ideas play their proper role: "The common motive underlying the efforts of science and philosophy alike is the desire in and through individual experience to reach universal experience." Finally, Kemp Smith supported a nonobjective type of realism that would emphasize the following two points: (1) objectivity requires "the irreducible minimum" of a distinction "between process of apprehension and object apprehended . . . "; and (2) "the relation of mind and body is the crucial problem through the treatment of which our theories . . . can best be tested by the relevant facts" (PR 18:182–86).

In April 1909, the WPA met in St. Louis for what its secretary, John Elof Boodin, describes as "the semi-centennial of philosophy in the west"; and, as might be expected, the theme of idealism saturated the program. George Rowland Dodson offered an interpretation of the success of the St. Louis Hegelian Movement as being due partly to its ability to satisfy the religious need for a supra-natural life and the intellectual need for a meaningful system. Its success was due mostly, however, to its ability "to meet opposing interests and reconcile them" in the political and educational realms. The program also contained a series of papers on general Hegelian themes. One was Henry Wilkes Wright's discussion of the moral significance of the dialectic as a means of overcoming hedonism and rationalism in a synthesis in which "the strength of present impulse is converted into a means to the attainment of the larger ends and ideals of reason." Jay William Hudson, whose interest in matters pedagogical we considered in chapter 5, suggests the efficacy of using Hegel's *Phenomenology of Spirit* for "introducing students to philosophy." The rationale offered for this unorthodox suggestion is that "Hegel's procedure rightly introduces all philosophies as solutions of problems which have first been actively realized as such by the reader . . ."[9] Tufts discussed some of the social aspects of Hegelianism and defended the adoption of the social perspective which, if shifted away from Hegel's focus on the monarch and toward experts in their roles as mediators in industrial, sanitary, social, and educational areas, would be advance the common good. Finally, W. M. Bryant offered a paper entitled "The Religious Trend of Hegelianism" that explored the belief in continued progress in rationality as a fundamentally religious belief. In other papers related to our general theme at this meeting, Boodin proposed, in "Realism and Idealism, a Discussion of Terms," the view that idealism is properly opposed to materialism (as in classical metaphysics) and realism to solipsism; Ewer discussed three versions of contemporary realism and their religious implications: new realism, "pragmatic realism," and traditional natural realism; and Emil C. Wilm supported Friedrich Schiller as a thinker whose position on the universal and particular is "falsely construed by Hegel into a metaphysical theory of the identity of the ideal and the real" (JP 6:403–11).

In his report on the 1909 meeting of the APA, Walter B. Pitkin notes that a number of papers "pitted realist against idealist in a series of encounters lacking nothing of briskness." He continues that the most remarkable aspect of the meeting was "the invisibility of pragmatist badges and the almost unbroken silence on those topics pragmatic with which reading-room gossip has identified the new movement." Pragmatism had not disappeared, however, it had merely been transformed.

> In reality . . . it had vanished only from the surface of events; its "isms" had evaporated, along with looser first generalities from its nascent stage, but its

---

[9] In the published version of this talk, Hudson compares Hegel's biography of the *Weltgeist*—"the story of the self as it proceeds on its way through the typical dialectical stages through which ordinary knowledge passes to philosophical insight"—to "an introduction to philosophy intended for every man, which is itself the story of the phases through which, indeed, Everyman passes in achieving philosophy." Thus while it would be "preposterous" to propose the *Phenomenology* as an introductory textbook, Hudson maintains that Hegel's "conception" is a good one for introductory philosophy courses and that "somebody ought to write an introduction in which some of its main suggestions are materially realized" ("Hegel's Conception," 347, 353).

spirit lived at a deeper level in the arguments of the realists. Their reiterated insistence upon the necessity of facing concrete situations and solving them on the basis of consciously accepted, definite, well-narrowed presuppositions was but the practising, rather than the preaching of pragmatism (JP 7:38).

It was at this meeting that Ralph Barton Perry read his paper, "The Ego-Centric Predicament," a paper that contains what I believe was the first gratuitous use of symbolic formulae at the APA. In this attack on idealists like Francis Herbert Bradley, John McTaggart, Ellis McTaggart, Royce, and Mary Whiton Calkins, Perry maintains that "*ontological idealism* is best expressed by the proposition: Everything (T) is defined by the complex, I know T." After generalizing the "I" to *ego* or "E" and liberalizing the "know" to "any form of consciousness that relates to an object ... to thinking, remembering, willing, perceiving, or desiring" or "R^c," he rephrases his definition of ontological idealism as "(E) R^c (T) defines (T)." Further recognizing the particular significance to idealism of the knowledge relation—that "the relationship R^c (E) is indispensable to T"—he wonders how such a claim is to be tested: "One must attempt to discover the precise nature of the modification of T by R^c (E); but one promptly encounters the fact that R^c (E) can not be eliminated from one's field of study, because 'I study,' 'I eliminate,' 'I think,' 'I observe,' 'I investigate,' etc., are all cases of R^c (E). In short, R^c (E) is peculiarly ubiquitous." Perry's point is thus that we cannot discover how a T is modified by the relationship R^c (E) by studying instances of the T outside of this relationship. More significantly, we should not make too much—as idealists are wont to do—of the fact that all known objects are in a relationship of being known. As he writes, this fact "is not an argument, but a methodological predicament."[10]

In a paper entitled "The Nature of Truth" read at the tenth meeting of the WPA in March 1910, Boodin attempted to move discussion beyond the function of truth that pragmatism emphasizes. In particular, he asserted the necessity of presupposing a series of four laws "as the conditions without which thinking is impossible." He explains these laws as follows: (1) the law of consistency, that incorporates the traditional laws of identity, contradiction, and excluded middle; (2) the law of totality, that

---

[10] Ralph Barton Perry, "Ego-Centric Predicament," 5–8; cf. JP 7:41. I suggest that these symbolic formulae were 'gratuitous' because Perry himself was quite able to present his ideas without them. See, for example, his 1912 formulation: "A body must be *perceived* in order to be known, and an implication must be *thought* in order to be known; but there is no more reason or sense in asserting the knowing to be necessary to the being, in the one case than in the other" (*Present Philosophical Tendencies*, 160; cf. "Realism in Retrospect," 192–93; Calkins, "Unjustified Claims for Neo-Realism," 54; Pratt, "Professor Perry's Proof of Realism," 575–76).

"the various kinds or attributes of reality must make such a difference to each other as to cohere in a system, if we are to have truth"; (3) the law of subject-object, that "within the universe of thought the subject-object relationship . . . is insuperable"; and (4) the law of finitude, that "the universe as the object of thought must have finite characteristics or relations" (JP 7:421–22).

At the APA's tenth meeting later that year, the presidential address presented by Bakewell was entitled "The Problem of Transcendence." In it, he defends the general idealist perspective from a series of charges: that it fails to respect ordinary experience, that it fails to respect the temporal character of experience, and especially that it "attempts to round up all facts of experience as belonging to one systematic whole which is so closely interlocked that every item of experience is once for all fixed in precisely the place which the unity of the whole order demanded." His "recognition of the transcendent" renders the familiar idealistic Absolute both useless and unnecessary; and he proposes an understanding of idealism that is pluralistic rather than monistic. Instead of one "absolute consciousness," Bakewell maintains, "there are many centers of conscious experience, egos if you will, each leading its own life, determined by its own ideals, yet making itself effective in a common order of experience and doing this by building up jointly with other intelligent agents a common world of ever increasing richness and complexity."[11]

The main interest at the APA's tenth meeting, however, was related to "The Program and First Platform of Six Realists" that, as we saw in chapter 6, had been published in July of 1910. Consideration of this theme began with a paper by Dickinson Sergeant Miller entitled "An Examination of Four Realistic Theories of Perception." In this paper, he criticized the four understandings that he found present in current realistic formulations—"the picture theory, the window theory, the doorway theory, and the sunshine theory"—although he "expressed himself in sympathy with the platform idea." Then there was a pre-organized two-part discussion session of the platform led by Dewey and Perry (standing in for Pitkin). For his part, Dewey presented himself not as "an out-and-out opponent of neo-realism" but as a methodological critic who rejected the claims of at least some of the new realists to have "reached conclusions about *existence* by developing purely *conceptual* implications." The remarks of Perry, and of the members of the audience who spoke, touched upon the various relevant themes in realism, pragmatism, and idealism (JP 7:92–96). Later papers at the meeting included Calkins's "Contemporary Criticism of Idealism," Montague's "The New

---

[11] Bakewell, "Problem of Transcendence," 117–18, 133–34.

Realism and the Old," and Theodore de Laguna's "The Externality of Relations" (PR 20:181–85).

At the APA's next meeting in 1911, the examination of aspects of the new realism continued. Durant Drake, in a paper entitled "What Kind of Realism?" maintained that "[a]n epistemologically monistic realism can not give us a single homogeneous order of objects," but that "the form of realism which accepts epistemological dualism can put all facts into one natural order, and is therefore in so far more plausible" (PR 21:196; JP 9:101). Creighton, in a paper entitled "The Determination of the Real," defended the view that "[p]hilosophy is not concerned to demonstrate the existence of a real world, or even to assign logical reasons for our belief in reality. Its genuine problem is to determine the nature of the real." In another paper, "Dogmatism versus Criticism," Walter Taylor Marvin suggested that "[f]or the idealist, epistemology is the fundamental science," whereas "for the realist, it is simply one of the special sciences and is not fundamental." Thus, the meaning of his title is that philosophy ought to abandon a critical stance that calls knowledge into question and adopt the approach of science that has a 'dogmatic' belief in our knowledge of the world. As he writes, "The most *certain* body of knowledge in our possession to-day is that of the exact and physical sciences and the most *certain* basis for metaphysics is the principles, postulates and all presuppositions of these sciences" (PR 21:197–99).

At the twelfth meeting of the WPA, Moore read his presidential address, "Bergson and Pragmatism." In this paper, he sharply contrasts Bergson's instrumentalism and anti-intellectualism with that of pragmatism and suggests that the greatest similarity between the two philosophies is to be found in their common evolutionism.[12] Also, Bode read a paper entitled "The Paradoxes of Pragmatism" that attempted to make it more acceptable by freeing it from misunderstandings. "Once we give up the attempt to cut off the past from the present and to make of knowing a process in which things are passively registered," he writes, "the pragmatic explanation becomes straightforward and natural." In a related paper, Günther Jacoby presented "the well-known German pragmatism" of Ernst Mach, Wilhelm Jerusalem, Georg Simmel, Richard Avenarius, Wilhelm Ostwald, and Hans Vaihinger as a forerunner of the contemporary American movement. He also maintained that American pragmatism was mistakenly viewed in Germany "as a kind of utilitarianism" (JP 9:355–57).

The next year, at the thirteenth meeting of the WPA, the majority of the papers read on the first day "bore more or less directly upon the subject of Objectivity or the Criterion of Truth, and led up to a prolonged

---

[12] Addison Webster Moore, "Bergson and Pragmatism," 397.

discussion in the afternoon, in which the standpoints of realism, idealism, and pragmatism were represented." One of these was Edward Leroy Schaub's paper, "Subjectivism and the Doctrine of Coherence" that criticized Bradley, McTaggart, and Green for subjectivism. W. L. Raub offered a paper entitled "The Bent Stick" in which he maintained that "[e]pistemology . . . must recognize that the senses do not deceive . . . The bent stick is a perceptual fact, while the straight stick that appears to bend is conceptual, a construction of thought." Evander Bradley McGilvary's paper, "The Realistic Criterion of Truth," defended the view that "in science and in common life the ordinary test of truth is found in the experience of something that points indubitably to the existence of something not experienced." For him, this is the criterion of truth—that is, what "produces conviction"—and we ought not bother asking the question "What ought to be the criterion of truth?" Henry W. Wright then offered a paper entitled "Voluntarism and the Criterion of Truth." In it, he discusses volition as "an agency of organization whose aim is to increase the unity and coherence of personal life under the actual conditions of human existence." Because this end of self-organizing operates through three coordinated activities—thought, action, and feeling—there are actually three effective criteria of truth: "intellectual consistency, technical efficiency, and emotional harmony." Moore then attacked Montague's claim "that 'true and false' are attributes of the *objects*, not of the *act* of 'belief or judgment'" in a paper entitled "Objectivity and Truth and Error." And, in the final paper related to our themes, "Reality and the New Realism," Horace Meyer Kallen examined the meaning of Spaulding's and Edwin Bissell Holt's views on the nature of secondary qualities (JP 10:319–25). At the APA's thirteenth meeting in December 1913, the focus was upon value and psychology, with only a modest interest in the issues of realism. However, Isaac Woodbridge Riley—in a rare nonhistorical presentation—considered "Some Aspects of the New Realism." He presented the movement as, on the one hand, "a reaction against the old idealisms with their emphasis on the abstract, the a priori," and, on the other, "a return to the richness of reality, the direct awareness of the external world" (PR 23:193–94). At the following meetings, these discussions continued; and after 1916, as we have seen in chapter 6, a second realist movement emerged, calling itself critical realism.

This survey of the relationship among idealism, pragmatism, and realism in American philosophy and at the associations could continue; but by now its general shape should be clear, and its later development is familiar to us all. Idealism has been removed from the core of the profession's concerns; pragmatism made a brief transit through the center of philosophic discussion and has since continued to operate on the fringes. Realism in one form or another—with its hopes to develop a 'scientific' philosophy that could finally settle 'the problem of knowledge' and put philosophy on the track of professional progress—was becoming the central approach of academic philosophers. Not all members of the associations were sanguine about the direction of philosophical work, however; and Morris Raphael Cohen presented a paper at the APA's 1909 meeting—published, ironically, in *The Journal of Philosophy* immediately after the platform of the new realists—that expresses his concern. The paper, entitled "The Conception of Philosophy in Recent Discussion," begins in a Comtean vein: "One might roughly divide the history of modern American philosophy into three periods, the theologic, the metaphysical, and the scientific. The first of these periods might be dated from the beginning of the *Journal of Speculative Philosophy* [1867], the second from the beginning of the *Philosophical Review* [1892], and the third from the *Journal of Philosophy, Psychology, and Scientific Methods* [1904]." The change from one of these periods to the next represents, he continues, a "shifting of the center of gravity of philosophic discussion." Beginning with *The Journal of Speculative Philosophy* that flourished during the heyday of the St. Louis Movement, there was a conception of philosophy that reflected the perspective of its leaders, William Torrey Harris and Hans Conrad Brockmeyer, who were "not academic or professional teachers of philosophy, but rather . . . practical men who believed they had found their superior point of view, fruitful insight into the fields of religion, art, history, education, and even practical politics." This perspective was superseded by the ascendancy of the metaphysical understanding of philosophy as reflected in *The Philosophical Review*. With its founding, Cohen writes, "the control of philosophy passed into the hands of a number of college professors, most of whom had been taught in Germany." For them, philosophy was not a practical activity but something more 'scientific': "Philosophy was thus conceived as an architectonic science, criticizing the assumptions of the special sciences, and supplementing the latter by building up their results into a complete *Weltanschauung*." This period ended around the turn of the century with the publication of Royce's *The World and the Individual* and James Ward's *Naturalism and Agnosticism*. The scientific period of American philosophy, reflected in *The Journal of Philosophy*, represented yet another shift, a shift that he describes as "on one hand, to give up the old idea of philosophy as a critique of the special sciences, and, on the other, to make philosophic discussion itself scientific, *i.e.*, to narrow it down to certain definite and decidable issues."[13]

---

[13] Cohen, "Conception of Philosophy," 401–2. Cf. Frederick J. E. Woodbridge: "I modestly shrink from a calling that imposes upon me the necessity of completing the fragmentary work of the physicist, the chemist, and the biologist, or of instructing these men in the basal principles of their respective sciences" ("Problem of Metaphysics," 370).

Such a 'scientific' conception of philosophy was not for everyone—certainly not for Cohen—and he describes even James's *Pragmatism* as having a negative impact. "To those who come to philosophy for the relief of a certain cosmic anguish, who are troubled by old-fashioned doubts about the meaning of life and destiny, who can not see whether there is or is not a divided government of the world in which we find ourselves, Professor James does not seem to offer any new or direct answer." On the contrary, he writes, the volume "simply raised a highly technical issue: How is truth to be defined?" In fact, neither pragmatism nor realism have had a positive effect on the role of philosophy in society, Cohen continues, and "the effect of the current reduction of philosophy to a purely formal discipline, viz., epistemology, can not be said to have as yet increased vital interest in philosophy." Idealism, though weakened, still offers an alternative. "It is only a confirmed idealist like Royce or Münsterberg that can still find his philosophy in such intimate contact with the content of life that he has to overstep the bounds of his particular academic function."[14]

Cohen's causal explanation for this shift is not directed towards the journals that have only reflected it, but towards the changing contexts of philosophizing. He writes especially of the shift from the 'metaphysical' to the 'scientific' conception of philosophy as being related to "the conditions of university teaching, for nearly all of our philosophers are now professional teachers." In this context, teaching has changed:

> the conditions of university teaching require a far higher degree of specialization on the part of pupils and teachers than the old college did. The old college teacher—of whom the late Professor [Charles Edward] Garman was a striking example—had to teach the whole field of philosophy, and could not, therefore, avoid bringing his subject into intimate relation with the various branches of science and life. The university teacher of logic, psychology, metaphysics, or even of ethics, as a rule feels no responsibility for the student's total view of the universe . . . the old idea of philosophy as a kind of universal knowledge, so vigorously maintained by [Friedrich] Paulsen, no longer finds any adherents.

In particular, these university teachers of philosophy with their new scientific approach to philosophy have an academic discipline to advance and make as respectable as physics or biology; and they thus find it necessary

---

[14] Cohen, "Conception of Philosophy," 403–4. Cohen continues: "If any one is inclined to minimize the extent to which the historical and wider conception of philosophy has been superseded by this narrow conception, let him reflect on the fate of Professor Ormond's recent volume, the 'Concepts of Philosophy.' This important book, the result of a whole lifetime of reflection covering the whole field of philosophy, has scarcely caused a ripple of the philosophic waters, and to many of our younger philosophers it appeared simply as a survival from a past which philosophy has rightly outlived" (ibid., 403).

to deny any personal element in their philosophizing. "The idea that philosophy may not be a science is so repugnant to professional philosophic teachers," he writes, "that it seems almost futile to maintain such a thesis."[15]

Such philosophers, however, are acting blithely in the face of philosophy's experience "that in spite of 2500 years of warfare, in spite of the fact that all methods have been tried . . . there is still a complete absence of any consensus" on what philosophy is. Philosophy remains a personal, human activity: "There is no such thing as a definite philosophy which can be taught impersonally." Rather than any sort of consensus, Cohen sees "only philosophies of different schools, and the choice between them is largely a matter of vital or temperamental preference." For him in consequence, this quest for philosophic consensus—and its resultant philosophic discord—is harmful. He writes, "It has generally been assumed that of two opposing systems of philosophy, *e.g.*, realism and idealism, only one *can* be true and one *must* be false; and so philosophers have been hopelessly divided on the question, which is the true one." He believe, however, that it is important to ask the question: "Can not two pictures of the same object both be true, in spite of radical differences?" Cohen emphasizes that no particular philosopher's picture of the world is "one in which every stroke is necessitated by pure logic." On the contrary, "[a] creative element is surely present in all great systems, and it does not seem possible that all sympathy or fundamental attitudes of will can be entirely eliminated from any human philosophy." To admit this is only to admit "that the minds of philosophers sometimes act like those of other mortals, and that, having once been determined by diverse circumstances to adopt certain views, they then look for and naturally find reasons to justify these views."[16]

In addition to this personal element in philosophical novelty, Cohen also points to the way in which themes—like relation, functional, dynamic, experience, and evolution—move into and out of fashion. Thus it is that philosophy, in a fashion similar to literature, does not really 'progress' at all. Unlike science, where the past is in some real sense overcome, in philosophy the past is always potentially present, awaiting another chance to reenter the debate. "If a philosophic theory is once ruled out of court, no one can tell when it will appear again." He thus wants a philosophy that recognizes "its kinship with literature and with the social sciences . . ." Such a philosophy could "aim to be scientific, but it would not be afraid to go beyond science just as life and conduct must go beyond knowledge." Such an approach would carry philosophy back to an earlier time when it

---

[15] Ibid., 404–5.
[16] Ibid., 405–7.

saw as its task "mediating between the *lebensanschauung* of literature and the social sciences, and the *weltanschauung* of the natural sciences." This approach would also return philosophy to a concern with the broader aspects of education and give renewed significance "to the teaching of it in our American colleges." In order for it to remain possible for our institutions of higher education "to train men rather than entomologists or geometers," Cohen maintains that "we need some integrating study that shall keep apace with and balance the progress of specialization."[17] As we all know, the associations did not follow this advice; and we shall see an expansion of the 'scientific' understanding of philosophy, and the desire for philosophical progress, in our consideration of the organized discussion sessions in the next few chapters.

---

[17] Ibid., 408–9. Cf. James Hayden Tufts's remarks to the graduate students at the University of Chicago in 1898: "You are now planning to teach language or history or science. I feel confident that you will come to place the emphasis rather on teaching *men* and *women*" (*Selected Writings*, 21).

Hugo Münsterberg

8

The Discussion Sessions I

In our consideration of the papers read at the early meetings of the associations in chapter 7, one of the ongoing themes was the growing feeling that philosophers needed to specify exactly what philosophy was. This self-consciousness was a sign of disciplinary maturity. When the profession was first emerging, it had been enough to know that philosophy was an activity that was neither religious nor theological. The usual way used to describe this emerging philosophy was to call it 'scientific,' as in Charles Sanders Peirce's call to replace the cluster of tenacious, authoritarian, and a priori methods familiar in religious and theological thinking with the method of science[1]; but describing philosophy as vaguely and generally 'scientific' provided no lasting answer. As we have seen in our consideration of the new realism, for some a 'scientific' philosophy would have to approximate the narrowness of focus and the unity of method of such sciences as mathematics and physics. For others, like Morris Raphael Cohen, a 'scientific' philosophy needed only follow William James's call to pay closer attention to the richness of experience. As the associations continued to evolve, the need to establish an identity for philosophy grew as a means to both the progress of philosophizing as a human endeavor and to increasing professional respectability of the discipline. The clearest demonstration of this struggle to specify the meaning of philosophy can be found in the APA's discussion sessions, which began in the early years, peaked about 1917, and then were abandoned.

As we have seen, there was a clear distinction in the minds of at least some of the members and leaders of the APA between what they saw as its "work proper"—the reading and discussing of philosophical papers—and its other activities. With regard to the papers, there was great hope that the

---

[1] Peirce, *Collected Papers*, 5.377–87.

interaction of the assembled minds would result in high-quality individual work and collective progress for philosophy. There was also, however, an underlying recognition that these gains would not occur spontaneously: some guidelines for the papers would be necessary. The APA's secretary, Harry Norman Gardiner, reported that during the course of the first meeting the membership adopted a recommendation of the executive committee that suggested "that the readers of papers present the substance of their papers in as brief and direct a form as possible, omitting introductions and prefaces, and aiming not to exceed twenty minutes in the reading of the paper, so as to allow as much time as possible for discussion" (PR 11:266). It is perhaps no surprise to anyone who has ever attended an APA meeting that over the course of the years these expectations were frequently ignored. The record of any number of meetings gives some indication of a festering dissatisfaction with the (reading of) papers. Consider, for example, Gardiner's own comment at the conclusion of his account of the second meeting: "The papers were . . . of a very varied character, conducive to the maintenance of interest during the packed four sessions of the meeting," but because of this diversity of themes and approaches, "perhaps leaving a somewhat bewildering impression, if there were any one besides the president forced to listen to them all" (S 17:142).[2]

We can consider as well the following comments by Harold Chapman Brown that make up part of his report on the APA's 1908 meeting: "The meetings were, for the most part, interesting and well attended, but the opinion was generally voiced that there were too many presentations at each session . . ." (JP 6:45). Or we can consider Brown's reminder, in his account of the thirteenth meeting, of what should take place when a person reads a twenty-minute paper. The speaker, he writes, "should write a twenty-minute paper and not make extempore and not always intelligible omissions, or read against time at a speed far greater than human articulatory powers can master or human apprehension meet" (JP 11:58). Or we can consider Theodore de Laguna's account of a presentation by Wilmon Henry Sheldon entitled "Error and Unreality" at the meeting in December 1915. In this paper, the author set aside the "psychological" aspects of error—"the mental and physical processes that lead to it and constitute it"—and focused upon the "metaphysical" aspects that concern "the status of the illusory object" (PR 25:170). De Laguna notes that in this paper "Professor Sheldon contended that few had faced and none had solved the problem of the metaphysical status of the object of error; and he offered as his own solution the theory that it

---

[2] At the early meetings of the associations, there were only plenary sessions and the particular association's president was in the chair throughout the meeting.

is not an unreal being (which would be a contradiction in terms), but real." De Laguna is more concerned, however, to criticize Sheldon for the presentation. "Unfortunately in writing his paper he had paid no attention to the time which it would take to read it; and as a result his thesis was left in mid-air without any substantial support." He goes on to complain that "[t]his is an old and common offense, and it was repeated at this meeting. In my opinion it has been regarded altogether too leniently by the association" (JP 13:100). Or we can consider the comments of Albert G. A. Balz, who wrote after the 1916 meeting in favor of such proposals as publishing the papers, or at least circulating abstracts, before the meetings. He noted, however, that another simple step might "easily be taken," and that would be "that all who present papers endeavor so to limit their length that they can be read within the time assigned at a comfortable pace—comfortable for both reader and auditor" (JP 14:215).

The lingering sense of dissatisfaction with the practice of reading and discussing papers, so central to the original APA vision, was present throughout the period of its history under examination in this study. As further evidence of this dissatisfaction, we can consider the beginning of Helen Huss Parkhurst's account of the 1921 meeting: "There are two kinds of people who attend philosophical meetings: those who go because of the papers to be presented; and those who go in spite of them . . ." (JP 19:210). The next year, Horace L. Friess reports as follows:

> To attend a meeting of the Philosophical Association is a curious experience, like tasting some strange, outlandish fruit. It may not prove so very pleasant, nor so nourishing, but at least it is rare and difficult to get; we appreciate it as the pride of the fruiterer. Quite similar is the satisfaction derived from hearing speeches that are not exactly inspiring, nor informative, but which obviously represent the farthest thought can reach. It is wonderful to realize how far that is, and to see into what hidden nooks it can be deflected by the way, and in what odd corners it can be caught. (JP 20:68)

In his account of the APA's twenty-third meeting, John Herman Randall, Jr., wonders why we "put men to the labor of listening while others read papers whose import is either too great or too slight to be grasped in the allotted twenty minutes?" Could it be because philosophers "like to prepare long papers, cut them down until, in bare skeleton, they take only twice the prescribed twenty minutes to deliver, and then read them to their fellow-members in the full consciousness that they will never be able to transmit the peculiar urgency of the thought that is in them." Whatever the reason, he continues, "these men, all of them, are capable of much better things than any collective gathering of them has yet given evidence of . . ." Randall suggests that the papers "might well be printed before and not after the event." If this were to happen, "they could be carefully studied and pondered, and the ensuing discussion might be more pertinent" (JP 21:40–41, 50). Finally, in his summary account of the first twenty-five years, Gardiner, while maintaining that "we have reflected in our meetings the best thinking of American philosophers in our time," finds himself forced to admit that "the papers have not always added greatly to our insight and . . . discussion has at times seemed footless and fruitless. We have frequently been more bewildered than illuminated and sometimes . . . we have felt frankly bored or irritated."[3]

Over at the WPA, the process of reading and discussing papers seems to have been a bit more successful; the reports, at least, are less critical. The proceedings of the 1904 to 1906 meetings, authored by Arthur Oncken Lovejoy who served for those three years as WPA secretary, suggest a higher level of success at their meetings. He writes, for example, of the 1904 meeting that "[p]ains had been taken to avoid overcrowding the program; not more than two papers were presented in any one session; and the result of this wise policy was seen in unusually general and adequate discussions of most—unfortunately, not all—of all topics presented." He continues that the sole justification "for the oral delivery of technical papers" has to be "the promotion of criticism and a comparison of notes between workers in the same field, good discussions are of the essence of a good meeting; and in this respect the sessions at Columbia [MO] were more successful than those of previous years" (JP 1:269). In his account of the next meeting, we find a similar evaluation: "Pains having been taken not to overcrowd the program with formal papers, it was possible, in such a relatively small gathering of specialists, to have a full, vigorous and fairly general discussion of nearly all the topics presented, and to get the stimulating effect of genuine philosophical debate" (JP 2:377). Further, he writes of the sixth meeting, "At most of the sessions there was extended and vigorous discussion of the papers read . . ." (JP 3:318). Perhaps Lovejoy's accounts of these meetings had been too rosy, or perhaps the procedures at the WPA slipped over the years; in any case, dissatisfaction soon set in. At the business session of the ninth meeting in 1909, the membership felt it necessary to enact by vote "that the time of the papers shall be printed in the program and that twenty minutes shall be the maximum limit unless by vote of the executive committee; . . . that abstracts be submitted to the secretary previous to the meeting at which the paper is to be read; . . . [and] . . . that special sessions be held for the more technical papers in experimental psychology and philosophy respectively . . ." (JP 6:403–4).

If we assume that the aim of the meetings was to bring together experts in philosophy for an annual session of comparison and evaluation of ideas

---

[3] Gardiner, "First Twenty-Five Years of the APA," 157.

in the hope that this stimulating interaction would lead to philosophical advance, there seems to have been little sense that this plan was succeeding. There was a generally felt need to do something to make the meetings better. We have already seen a number of suggestions for improving the individual papers: their length must be controlled, their content must be more focused and hearer-friendly, perhaps the papers should be pre-printed so that they could be studied in advance and thus would only need to be summarized rather than read prior to discussion at the meetings, and so forth. There was the further belief, however, that even if the individual papers could be improved, the meetings themselves would still lack focus. They were too crowded with diverse topics, too fragmented. As Gardiner said of the APA's second meeting, the overall program left "a somewhat bewildering impression." In the hope of bringing more focus to the meetings, and thereby philosophical advance, a number of strategies were adopted over the first twenty-five years of the associations. The first of these was the APA's decision to select a theme for the annual meeting. This theme would be developed through a narrowly defined and well-organized symposium—called over the years the 'discussion session' or the 'debate'— that would bring together a number of major figures to explore an issue of central philosophical importance. These symposia were never fully successful; but the goal of advancing philosophical inquiry was felt so powerfully that the APA continued to tinker with these sessions in the hope of improving them.

The discussion sessions were initially intended to embody the vision of contemporary philosophy as a cooperative enterprise, modeled however vaguely on the natural sciences. Gardiner writes, "At first the topic was chosen and the leaders in the Discussion were selected by the executive committee, and those taking part in the debate were allowed to develop the subject in their own way." These discussion sessions were a common feature in the early years of the APA; he notes, "at six of the first ten of our meetings there were Discussions arranged for in advance . . ."[4] By my count, there were seven discussion sessions, or perhaps eight, during the first decade—a number of which have been considered previously. At the second meeting, Dickinson Sergeant Miller, Josiah Royce, Francis L. Patton, and William Torrey Harris addressed the issue: "What Should be our Attitude as Teachers of Philosophy toward Religion?" (PR 12:172–73). At the next meeting in 1903, the issue under examination was: "What Place has Aesthetics Among the Disciplines of Philosophy?" Speaking on this topic were George Santayana, William A. Hammond,

---

[4] Gardiner, ibid., 154–55; cf. Pitts, *Profession of Philosophy*, 144–49; Daniel J. Wilson, "Professionalization."

DISCUSSION SESSIONS AT THE APA

1901)

1902) "What Should be our Attitude as Teachers of Philosophy toward Religion?"

1903) "What Place has Aesthetics Among the Disciplines of Philosophy?"

1904) [Kant commemoration]

1905) "The Affiliation of Psychology with Philosophy and the Natural Sciences"

1906)

1907) "The Meaning and Criterion of Truth"

1908) "Realism and Idealism"

1909) "The Problem of Time in its Relation to Present Tendencies in Philosophy"

1910) "The Platform of Six Realists"
       "The Value for Philosophy of Mathematical Methods and Ideals"

1911) "The Relation of Consciousness and Object in Sense Perception"

1912) "Agreement in Philosophy"

1913) "The Standpoint and Method of Psychology"
       "Existence and Value"

1914) "Constitutional and Political Guarantees"

1915) [Royce celebration]

1916) "'Mental' and 'Physical'"

1917) "Ethics and International Relations"

1918) "Mechanism and Vitalism"

1919) "The Nature of Community"

DISCUSSION SESSIONS AT THE EASTERN DIVISION OF THE APA

1920) "The Role of the Philosopher in Modern Life, with reference both to teaching and to research"

1921)

1922) "Mind-Body"

1923)

1924)

1925) "Time"

Ethel D. Puffer, and Frank Chapman Sharp (PR 13:184–88). When the APA gathered in 1904, meeting in part with the AΨA and the SSPP, there was no discussion session; but, as we saw in chapter 7, the program presented a commemoration of the centenary of the death of Kant on 12 February 1804, with papers by Royce, Edward Franklin Buchner, William Caldwell, James Hayden Tufts, and George William Knox (PR 14:171–76). At the APA's fifth meeting in December 1905, which met jointly with the AΨA at the new Emerson Hall at Harvard, there was a discussion session on the topic: "The Affiliation of Psychology with Philosophy and the Natural Sciences." APA president John Dewey presided and the speakers were Hugo Münsterberg, Granville Stanley Hall, James Rowland Angell, A. E. Taylor, and Frank Thilly (PR 15:173–77). There was no discussion session the next year; but, as we saw in chapter 7, at the 1907 meeting James, James Edwin Creighton, Charles Montague Bakewell, John Grier Hibben, and Charles Augustus Strong discussed "The Meaning and Criterion of Truth" (PR 17:180–86). At the APA's eighth meeting, "Realism and Idealism" was discussed by Royce, Dewey, Frederick J. E. Woodbridge, Bakewell, and Norman Kemp Smith (PR 18:182–86). In 1909, Lovejoy, Woodbridge, and Royce discussed "The Problem of Time in its Relation to Present Tendencies in Philosophy" (PR 19:180–83). There were two discussions at the APA's tenth meeting in 1910. The first, considered in chapter 7, explored "The Platform of Six Realists" and was led by Dewey and Ralph Barton Perry; the second, "The Value for Philosophy of Mathematical Methods and Ideals." Leading this discussion were Hibben and Brown (PR 20:187–89).

While these discussion sessions seemed to have brought more unity to the APA programs, they did not eliminate dissatisfaction. For one thing, as a result of time restraints and other practical pressures, these symposia were not always well organized.[5] Perhaps more importantly, to their critics these symposia did not seem to be contributing to philosophical advance. At the 1908 meeting, two of these critics, Karl Schmidt and Christine Ladd-Franklin, each offered a plan to facilitate philosophical progress. In his paper, "Concerning a Philosophical Platform," Schmidt begins with a consideration of the role played in contemporary thought by such notions as evolution, change, and flux. He emphasizes especially how these themes tended to encourage a kind of passivity on the part of

---

[5] As an example of inadequate preparation, we can consider the discussion session at the eighth meeting. In a letter of 3 November 1908 to APA president Münsterberg, APA secretary Thilly requested Münsterberg's preference for a topic for the session that was less than two months away. On 19 November, Thilly wrote to announce that the topic and participants had finally been settled, although he names Calkins instead of Dewey (Münsterberg Papers, Boston Public Library).

philosophers, a forsaking of any goal of deliberate direction. He maintains, however, that "philosophy itself is called upon to act, and . . . therefore it is incumbent upon every age to make up its mind, to occupy and maintain some definite stage in this process of evolution that philosophy is undergoing, and not to use the idea of evolution as a convenient excuse for indefiniteness and absence of a doctrine and recognized school in philosophy." At the present time, philosophers were not performing "the *social* function and duty of philosophy in the republic of knowledge . . ." Here, Schmidt compares philosophy unfavorably with mathematics, whose practitioners have established "axioms" and "first principles" and "fundamental concepts" for its practice, and have begun to develop methods for the social evaluation of these practical tools and a clearer sense of the nature of their discipline as a science. Philosophers, on the other hand, have as yet made no such progress: each thinker works on "*his* philosophy" and "all is controversial . . ." If philosophy is ever to move ahead, it must become more cooperative and adopt more fixed viewpoints that would allow its practitioners to work together on common projects. In science, he calls these tentative frameworks "schools" which, though in process, still make cooperation possible. "The momentum of the school acts like a fly-wheel to keep a science from erratic and premature changes." He thus calls for "a recognized doctrine and school; or, if you please, a ruling party, which shall transact the business on hand, until it (which means its principles) is replaced by the opposition party . . ." Schmidt maintains that "[t]he state of anarchy" that has prevailed in philosophy for centuries "must end; this we all feel and the necessity for action demands it." Philosophers must learn to imitate the advances in the sciences and "choose a system as authority with which we can start, which we can criticize, measure by certain ideals, change, mend, supplement or finally discard for a better, but all with due deliberation and for definite, specific reasons." He believed that the APA meetings would provide "a suitable opportunity" for advancing this platform. He continues on to make explicit some sense of what the form and content of such a platform might be. More important, however, is his overall point of the need to overcome "the petty criticizing spirit prevailing among us philosophers by the mutual understanding of cooperation" and develop future philosophy "as a system, not of individuals, but of humanity itself."[6]

The other pro-platform speaker at the 1908 meeting was Ladd-Franklin, whose title was "The Doctrine of Histurgy: an Epistemology for the Scientist and the Logician." "It is an old reproach to philosophy that

---

[6] Karl Schmidt, "Concerning a Philosophical Platform," 674–80, 685; cf. PR 18:166–67; Elkus, "Philosophical Platform," 19.

it fails to make progress," she writes. "The hallmark of science, on the other hand, is that its acquisitions are cumulative from generation to generation . . ." Philosophy fails to progress, she continues, because of its tolerance of individual positions. "The distinguishing mark of philosophy, hitherto, has been that 'everything goes.' In other branches of learning, absurd hypothesis and creed are quickly weeded out by ruthless criticism . . . In science, wrong doctrines, once disproved, are disproved forever; there are no 'systems,' save temporarily and upon the outskirts . . ." She indicates that two developments had enabled science to rise from its former stagnation. The first was "the discovery of strict principles of method . . . that brought it [science] suddenly into a position such that its progress has been, for the last two centuries, by leaps and bounds." Philosophy, of course, was operating without any such method; and "[i]t may well be," she writes, "that it is a total lack of scientific method which is responsible for the condition in which philosophy finds herself to-day." Second, she points to the fact that science is a cooperative activity: "there is one criterion which science considers indispensable, and which philosophy, much to its loss, has hitherto been content to go without,—viz. the ability to secure *common assent* among those . . . who are in a condition to form well-grounded judgments in a given domain—to obtain . . . 'the consensus of the competent.' This it is which philosophy is conspicuously lacking . . ."[7]

Ladd-Franklin was unwilling to grant that philosophy is "not a branch of knowledge," that it is merely a kind of "enjoyment" or poetry; and she calls for fundamental changes in philosophical practice. In particular, she calls for "a commission, whose task should be simply to propose some few fundamental principles so well founded that they may be handed over to the outsider as at least a program—a platform—which may have some chance to command the consensus of the competent among the philosophers, and to meet the severe tests for validity which are matter of course among the logicians and the scientists." Membership on this commission should be selective, with the commissioners being chosen "not so much for their proved prolificness as philosophers . . . as for their powers of logical acumen, for their keen scent for the detection of fallacy." She then offers her own understanding of what the "common doctrine" produced by such a commission might contain. She calls this doctrine "*Histurgy*," a philosophical perspective that includes a theory of reality, a reformed psychology, a theory of truth, and a theory of judgments. In particular, she presents knowledge as "a woven tissue": "knowledge is an net-work . . .

---

[7] Ladd-Franklin, "Epistemology for the Logician," 664–66. (The abstract of her paper [PR 18:180–82] notes that it had been part of the program at the Third International Congress of Philosophy in Heidelberg, earlier in 1908. For a fuller picture of her remarks, I am relying on the proceedings of that congress.)

truths hang together, and . . . it is the confirmation (by instances) of the countless cross-connections (conclusions of syllogisms) which exist between our 'items of knowledge' that give us the immense confidence we feel in its validity as a whole." Her own position is, of course, less important to Ladd-Franklin than her overall proposal to help make philosophy more progressive.[8]

Discussing these two presentations early in 1909, Creighton notes that they had both emphasized the potential advantages to philosophy from the adoption "of a body of doctrines and principles that might be regarded as at least provisionally established." Primary among these advantages was a growth of scientific stature: "it would remove from philosophy the standing reproach that it has arrived at no certain conclusions, and is therefore unworthy to be called a science . . . it would enable philosophy to take its place and perform its proper function in the development of scientific thought and social practise." He further points to the general currency that this criticism had among the scientifically inclined members of the academic community:

> It is, of course, a notorious fact that philosophers do not agree; and this is commonly regarded as a proof that no objective certainly is possible regarding the problems with which they occupy themselves. The lack of any established body of results which can be summed up in a series of definite propositions that an outsider can directly appropriate and apply in some field of practise, is doubtless another source of the wide-spread conviction that philosophy neither bakes bread nor can any longer give us "God, freedom, and immortality."

As might be anticipated, however, Creighton's own position was somewhat different. "As students and teachers of philosophy," he writes, "we do not, of course, admit the truth of these charges." For him, on the contrary, philosophy "is not one of the special sciences, dealing with a particular field of the phenomenal world, but is an attempt to understand and evaluate the standpoint and results of all the sciences and the meaning of experience as a whole." As a consequence, "[f]rom the very nature of philosophy, it ought to be evident that such a platform is neither desirable nor possible of attainment."[9]

Further, while he rejects "an officially established creed in philosophy," Creighton denies the claim that philosophy is without agreement. Some level of agreement, he writes, "especially regarding the nature of the prob-

---

[8] Ibid., 666–67, 670. Throughout her presentation, she draws upon the work of Peirce and rejects contemporary pragmatism, the "nearest foe" to her position, as "not only immoral but also untrue" (ibid., 670; cf. Daniel J. Wilson, "Professionalization," 57–58).

[9] Creighton, "Idea of a Philosophical Platform," 141–42.

lems that can profitably and significantly be raised and the kind of answers which they demand, is an essential condition of the existence of a subject as a rational branch of human inquiry." If there were not some such sense of agreement among philosophers, "no fruitful cooperation or discussion would be possible." The source of this agreement is philosophers' shared participation in the history of philosophy. "To become a philosopher," he writes, a individual must "assimilate and reproduce in his own thinking the development of philosophical problems and answers as these are shown in the course of history." He notes further that "to comprehend the *development* of philosophical thought is to gain an understanding of the significance of philosophical problems and the true function and relations of the conceptions that appear in the course of its history. This involves an active process of philosophizing on one's own part: it requires us to interpret, reconstruct, and evaluate the historical results through our own thinking." The problem that Creighton would address, then, is not how to make philosophy approximate one of the special sciences. Rather, it is to improve, in the face of "the evident lessening of interest in historical studies among American philosophers at the present time," the teaching of the history of philosophy. It is through understanding its history, he believed, that philosophy will progress. "For the continuity of our thought with the past is at the same time our bond of union and basis of objectivity, and, as such, it, therefore, is the only thing that insures the reality of philosophy at the present time or that furnishes a guarantee for its future."[10]

The suggestion that philosophers use the APA programs to formulate a platform failed to gain support. Another proposal for philosophical advance was adopted at the tenth meeting. Gardiner describes this new attempt as follows: "in view of the difficulty of arriving at satisfactory results in the absence of agreement on the meaning of the terms, the executive committee was empowered to appoint a committee of five to prepare, after the selection of the subject for discussion at the next meeting, definitions of terms pertaining to that subject for the use of those participating . . ."[11] The "Report of the Committee on Definitions of the APA" appeared in *The Journal of Philosophy* in December 1911, just before the eleventh meeting. The committee—composed of Woodbridge (APA president), Thilly, Miller, Lovejoy, William Pepperell Montague, and Edward Gleason Spaulding (APA secretary)—had been "appointed to draw up a

---

[10] Ibid., 142–45. Cf. Leighton, "Philosophy and the History of Philosophy," 519–22; Karl Schmidt, "Concerning a Philosophical Platform"; PR 20:194–95.

[11] Gardiner, "First Twenty-Five Years of the APA," 155. There was also a short-lived Committee on Terminology, organized in 1915 "to cooperate with a similar committee of the American Psychological Association" (PR 26:195). This committee was discontinued at the 1919 meeting (PR 29:155).

plan for the principal discussion" at the upcoming meeting. The discussion topic itself—"The Relation of Consciousness and Object in Sense-Perception"—had been chosen by the executive committee "from among a large number of topics suggested by members of the Association . . ." In its deliberations, the committee on definitions saw as its task not the narrow one of simply "preparing definitions of the terms to be used in the debate," but the much broader task of "formulat[ing] somewhat precisely the issues involved and . . . indicat[ing] what appears to it to be, at the present juncture in philosophical discussion, the most promising mode of approach to those issues." As the report notes, "Such an extensive attempt at an organization of cooperative philosophical inquiry has not hitherto been made by this Association"; and, even should this attempt fail, the committee believes "such organized and cooperative inquiry to have important possibilities for the future of philosophical study." In the hope that the general membership would come to recognize this, the committee appealed to the membership to "enter into the spirit of the undertaking, to review the recent literature of the subject, and, in their participation in the discussion, to conform for the time being to the general plan of procedure herein suggested" (JP 8:701).

The committee begins its report by offering a series of definitions for the following terms: 'object,' 'real objects,' 'unreal objects,' 'perceived object,' 'unperceived object,' and 'consciousness.' As further background assumptions for the discussion, the committee postulates that "all members will agree in admitting (*a*) that there are individuated sequences or 'streams' of perceptions (*i.e.*, those of different persons), and (*b*) that any definable object which is at certain times present in a given individuated sequence of perceptions may at other times not be present in this." With these assumptions made explicit, the committee then proposes that the discussion be directed to the following "connected but discriminable questions." First: "What is the relation with respect to numerical identity or difference between the above defined classes of real and of perceived objects?" Finding that there are a number of possible answers here, the committee reformulates the initial question as follows: "*In cases where a real (and non-hallucinatory) object is involved, what is the relation between the real and the perceived object with respect (a) to their numerical identity at the moment of perception, (b) with respect to the possibility of the existence of the real object at other moments apart from any perception?*" The second question to guide the discussion deals with "the positive nature of the difference between the status of a given object at those moments when it figures in some particular individuated stream of perceptions, and its status at those moments when it does not figure in that same stream? In brief, what is the nature of consciousness, considered as a factor or aspect of any specific perceptual situation? and how is the answer to this question logically related to the first question?" Here the committee was able to list thirteen possible interpretations, drawing upon an attached bibliography of thirty-nine items, that it hoped might "serve as a basis for discussion and a point of departure" (JP 8:701–4).

The discussion of "The Relation of Consciousness and Object in Sense Perception" took place as scheduled at the eleventh meeting in December 1911. The speakers at this symposium were: Montague, Miller, Lovejoy, Thilly, Evander Bradley McGilvary, and Henry Rutgers Marshall (PR 21:199–204). In his account of this discussion, Harry Allen Overstreet reports that the meeting was "remarkable in two respects: First, for what it purposed but did not accomplish; second, for the unmistakable promise of a new type of accomplishment at future sessions." I would like to consider both of these aspects, beginning with the negative. He writes that the committee "had, with elaborate care, formulated and defined the main issue for discussion, and this same committee, with the exception of the *ex officio* member, had undertaken to debate this issue." The hope of all this work was "that by this means the discussion would be so narrowed that it would result either in clearly defined agreement or in equally clearly defined disagreement. This hope was far from realized." He continues that the debate was "not a sharp presentation of counter positions, but rather a presentation of the more or less complex and involved views of the individual debaters upon the various issues in question." When the session was opened up to contributions from the floor, the discussion went nowhere. As Overstreet writes, "In great part it was a discussion of what the discussion ought to have been but was not." In spite of the apparent failure, however, he reports positively that "the opinion strongly emerged that the method of debating a clearly formulated issue should by all means be continued as by far the most profitable mode of philosophic discussion." Overstreet's report continues that, in order to help foster future successful discussion, "the committee of five was continued in office with instructions to draw up a plan for the next meeting along lines similar to those laid down for this year's meeting. It is to be hoped that the lessons of this year will aid the committee in outlining a plan such as will make possible both a sharper joining of issue and a clearer effort of cooperation" (JP 9:101). APA secretary Spaulding offered the official version of the plan for the next meeting in the proceedings: "On recommendation of the Executive Committee it was voted to continue the present committee on the general discussion, this committee to have power to determine the subject of discussion for the next meeting, to arrange for the discussion, and to formulate a report prior to the next meeting, involving general points to be discussed" (PR 21:191).

Soon after the 1911 meeting, Royce published an essay entitled "On Definitions and Debates" that details the extent of his displeasure with the symposium that had occurred at that meeting. He begins by alluding to the fact that the APA had been expending a great deal of effort of late "to render its general discussions more unified, more profitable, and more conducive to the furtherance of agreement among students of philosophy." So far, however, there had been only the expense of much hard work without any corresponding payoff. "The issue involved is not their unquestionable sincerity and devotion," he grants, "but as to the future policy of the Association, and as to the best way of securing, in the discussions at our meetings, the right sort of philosophical communion and community amongst the members." Royce conceded that the topic chosen—"The Relation of Consciousness and Object in Sense Perception"— was a worthy one; his complaints were related to how the committee had developed this topic. While there was no question of the committee's authority or competency "to determine the rules of the proposed debate," he writes, the result was that many APA members were excluded from the discussion. In other words, no one was able to participate in this cooperative undertaking "unless he was willing to abide by the restrictions . . . The debater was required to follow the assigned rules of the game. He was not to discuss their value. He was to play under these rules." He then discussed, in great detail, the stipulated definitions and their uses by the committee to demonstrate the extent of their exclusionary power. In summary, he notes, "The Committee inadvertently excluded people whom of course they never consciously intended to exclude." And the number excluded by these restrictions made up "no small party." While his enumeration of the excluded may be padded a bit—he lists "[v]arious mystics, scholastics, Kantians, idealists, modern realists, and pragmatists"—his point is the simple one that to proceed in any kind of exclusionary fashion "is not the best way to secure general cooperation." Royce continued to believe that the discussion sessions, suitably modified, were a good idea. "The plan of having general discussions upon issues sharply defined and directly joined," he writes, "is a plan that promises great results for the future, if only we learn from our first attempts how to carry out that plan better than at first we did." What was necessary was that more effort would have to be put into developing rules that would enable all to participate.[12]

This openness was perhaps reflected at the next meeting. For the APA's twelfth meeting in 1912, the subject that had been chosen for discussion was "Agreement in Philosophy." The symposium was organized around the following central question: "Is a continuous progress towards una-

---

[12] Royce, "On Definitions and Debates," 85–87, 98; cf. Daniel J. Wilson, *Science, Community*, 135–41.

nimity among philosophers on the fundamental philosophical issues (*a*) desirable, (*b*) attainable?" Apparently assuming that philosophical agreement is desirable, the committee then went on to ask two series of questions about its attainability:

I. If not attainable: 1. What are the impediments to agreement in philosophy? 2. Should it be deemed the essential function of philosophy to serve as a means for expressing the reactions upon reality of differen[t] types of temperament? 3. What is the purpose of philosophical argumentation and discussion? 4. What, from this point of view, is the place and value of the study of the history of philosophy?

II. If agreement is attainable: 1. Upon what significant issues has it already been attained? 2. How is the failure to reach a greater measure of agreement in the past to be explained? 3. Is the study of the history of philosophy indispensable as a means towards the attainment of agreement? 4. What methods for the systematization of philosophical inquiry, or for organized cooperation in philosophizing, would help towards this end? 5. Are discussions of specific problems, with preliminary analyses and definitions, after the general manner of last year's discussion in this Association, serviceable towards this end? (PR 22:172).

The leaders of the discussion were Schmidt, de Laguna, Walter B. Pitkin, and Kemp Smith. In accordance with the ground-rules for the discussion sessions, all of the participants were to publish "preliminary statements of the principal topics to be brought forward" (JP 9:701). In the 19 December 1912 issue of *The Journal of Philosophy*, we find relevant material from three of the four leaders of the upcoming discussion on the topic of agreement in philosophy published in advance to help facilitate the discussion.[13]

In the first paper, "How Far Is Agreement Possible in Philosophy?" Kemp Smith opposes excessive efforts to foster present agreement. He begins with a long introduction aimed at reining in attempts to elide philosophy and science. Philosophy can legitimately be seen as "scientific," he writes, even if it is not among "those disciplines in which there is a working agreement as to principles, methods, and results" as long as it represents "thinking that is as rigorous, as enlightened, and as competent as our present knowledge of the factors involved in the problems dealt with will permit." Science as it is narrowly construed—for example, mathematics and physics—must be distinguished from philosophy. "Science deals with the isolable, philosophy with the non-isolable problems . . . Science is successful specialization." The philosophic human life, however, is more than

---

[13] De Laguna's paper was the missing one. For his abstract, see: PR 22:173–74.

specialization; and we will continue to need a broad vision. "Philosophy is still needed in order to enforce breadth of outlook and catholicity of judgment. It stands for the general human values as against excessive pretensions, whether in science, in religion, or in practical life, for the past and the future as against the present, for comprehensiveness and leisure as against narrowness and haste." The problems with which philosophy deals—the problems of logic, of consciousness, of morality—"involve considerations which reach out into all departments of life," Kemp Smith writes; and, more broadly, he maintains that "[t]he specific character of philosophical reflection is that in dealing with any of its problems it must simultaneously bear in mind the correlative requirements of all the others." Another aspect of the difference between philosophy and science is that, while the various scientists for the most part can overlook the history of their disciplines, philosophy cannot: "Philosophy is to be found only in the history of philosophy, and each new system fulfils its mission in proportion as it yields an enlightening reading of past experience, a genuine analysis of present conditions, and in terms of these a prophetic foreshadowing of its own future development."[14]

With these general themes as prelude, Kemp Smith turns to the issue of the lack of agreement among philosophers. "The really fundamental reason why equally competent philosophical thinkers may arrive at diametrically opposite results," he writes, is to be found not "in temperament, but rather in the complexity of the problems, and in the limitations which personal experience, necessarily incomplete and differing from one individual to another, imposes upon us." Philosophers, in other words, are addressing different problems that cannot simply be isolated from their contexts, and the philosophers who are addressing these problems are themselves limited by their partial experience. As a result, he continues, there will continue to be disagreements in philosophy, a situation that he thinks should not be seen as necessarily problematic: "The willing acceptance by the individual of mutually irreconcilable beliefs, *i.e.*, pluralism within the individual mind, is the 'happy despatch' of philosophy," he writes. "The cooperative pluralism of divergent thinkers may, on the other hand, prove its salvation." While it may be true that a kind of mutual agreement is "the ultimate goal," no such agreement can be anticipated soon; and "[s]hould it come about, by the tyranny (it could be nothing else) of a dominant school . . . philosophy itself would cease to fulfil its critical function . . ." Therefore, in the APA's discussions, philosophers should not "assume that we can start from points of agreement" but rather aim "at better mutual understanding of our points of difference, in the

---

[14] Kemp Smith, "How Far Is Agreement Possible?" 701–5.

hope that we may . . . thereafter be more clear minded in regard to our own tenets, and better appreciative of the more inward aspects of our opponents['] positions."[15]

In the second of the preliminary statements, "Is Agreement Desirable?" Pitkin reports to be bewildered that anyone would even pose the initial question of whether continuous progress toward unanimity on fundamental philosophical issues is desirable. Equating philosophic disagreements with the existence of philosophic doubts, he maintains that there is no question that agreement is desirable. "A doubt regarding any matter carries with it . . . the desirability of the doubt's annihilation," he writes. "The undesirability of doubt is a psychological axiom, just as the undesirability of pain is." He thus rejects the position that "debate on the committee's first question is *logically* possible . . ." Turning away from the committee's two follow-up questions about the attainability of agreement, Pitkin introduces a question of his own: "The Discussion Committee must raise the prior question for debate; *it must, in its first query, mean to ask us whether there are any fundamental philosophical issues or not.*" By such issues he means questions like "a problem of the immortality of the soul, or a problem of God, or a problem of the relation of mind to body, or a problem of the status and function of perception," each of which he considers to be "a certain matter of fact"; and he wonders about those who do not recognize such philosophical issues.[16]

The third of these preliminary papers, Schmidt's "Agreement," also takes issue with the question of the desirability of agreement, but focuses rather on "how much agreement is *necessary*" for philosophers to be able to work together. Those who advocate increased agreement "do not mean to stem the flux of time, to stop the growth of living thought," he writes; but there must be some minimum of agreement for philosophers to be able to interact profitably. As examples, he lists the following:

> (*a*) *There must be certain common problems* . . . (*b*) It is not necessary that our solutions of the same problem should be *identical*; on the contrary, it is much better that they should *not*; but they should be *equivalent* with respect to truth. (*c*) How is this possible unless there is a *common set of criteria* by which the solutions are to be judged? . . . (*d*) Such a set of criteria requires . . . that the solution be of a definite *type*, i.e., that there be agreement on the *structure* of the solution.

Schmidt is willing to go further, and he suggests that "an agreement on *method* seems quite possible." In this regard, he praises the work of the

---

[15] Ibid., 707–11; cf. PR 22:175–76.
[16] Pitkin, "Is Agreement Possible?" 711–15; cf. PR 22:174–75.

new realists, who consider "*analysis* as the prime method of exact thinking . . ."17

In his account of the 1912 meeting, James Bissett Pratt writes, "As had been the case with the two preceding meetings, the liveliest interest centered in the debate, which this year was upon the untechnical question of 'Agreement in Philosophy.'" After considering the roles of the supporters of agreement, Schmidt and Pitkin, and of de Laguna and Kemp Smith "who supported the negative side of the question," Pratt continues, "The discussion was prolonged throughout the morning session of Friday by a large number of speakers from the floor, and in the afternoon it was recommenced with three ten-minute papers by Professor [T. C.] Hall, Miss [Savilla Alice] Elkus, and Professor [Carl Vernon] Tower, after which the open debate continued until it had to be closed *in medias res* for lack of further time" (JP 10:91; cf. PR 22:176–78).

In the light of this apparent success, planning for the symposium at the APA's 1913 meeting began immediately. The proceedings from the twelfth meeting report the adoption of the following measures:

> 1. That the Executive Committee appoint a Discussion Committee which shall, before March 1, 1913, choose a topic for debate at the next annual meeting of the Association. 2. That the Discussion Committee shall announce the chosen topic, as soon as chosen, in the philosophical periodicals of this country, and shall invite essays and discussions on the topic, to be submitted to these periodicals for publication during the ensuing year. 3. That, on or before December 1, 1913, the Discussion Committee may, at its discretion, publish in pamphlet form such essays on the topic as it deems worthy of special publication, provided these same essays shall not have been published elsewhere. 4. That the sum which the Discussion Committee is empowered to expend for the printing of such essays shall not exceed two hundred dollars. 5. That two entire sessions of the next annual meeting of the Association be devoted to discussion of the chosen topic. (PR 22:166–67)

It is not clear how much of this elaborate plan came to fruition the next year, because the program developed in two directions.

The APA met for the thirteenth time in December 1913, in part with AΨA.18 There were two separate prearranged discussion sessions at this meeting. The first brought together members of both associations to consider the topic, "The Standpoint and Method of Psychology." This topic was developed by the executive committees of the two associations, and the results of this cooperative planning were published by AΨA president

---

17 Karl Schmidt, "Agreement," 715–16; PR 22:173.

18 This was the joint meeting that produced the Mecklin Report discussed in chapter 5.

Howard C. Warren and the APA secretary Spaulding, who called for "as much anticipatory and published discussion of the chosen subjects as possible." These subjects were:

> *Data of Psychology.*—Should psychology study unit-beings (selves, mind, consciousness), or inner states (e.g., sensations, feelings), or inner processes (e.g., sensibility, affectivity, association), or certain relations between unit-beings and their environment (e.g., reflexes, instincts), or several of these?

> *Method of Research.*—Should the psychologist obtain his data mainly by self-study (introspection by himself and others), or by studying the motor reactions of organisms? If both methods be admitted, what is their relative importance?

> *Philosophy of Psychology.*—Does a systematic psychology depend upon a specific world-view, or can it be developed, as are physics and biology, without a definite philosophic basis? In the latter case, do the results of empirical psychology compel us to adopt some specific philosophy?

In order to maintain as tight a focus as possible on these questions, Warren and Spaulding also requested that "[t]he question of the nature of consciousness, sensation, introspection, etc., should be discussed only in its relation to the standpoint that is taken concerning the above positions" (PR 22:461; cf. JP 10:335).

The four leaders of this discussion were Creighton, F. M. Urban, Dewey, and Münsterberg. Creighton began by indicating that, for him, "the type of psychology which is based upon the categories of physical science does not satisfy all the demands that may legitimately be made for an understanding of the mental life." No psychology can be adequate that does not make use of introspection, experimentation, and history, he continues, and he points to contemporary successes in "social psychology, the psychology of religion, myth, custom, and language, etc." Urban noted that "[t]he realm of philosophy is the entire field of experience," whereas psychology cultivates only "part of this field." He continued that philosophy can be of use to psychology, especially with "epistemological analysis" in such areas as introspection and psychometrics. Dewey discussed the presence of bad psychology in the philosophy classroom that results in a host of epistemological quandaries and the need to overcome bifurcations such as that of 'inner' and 'outer' worlds and the abstract notion of consciousness. Münsterberg began with some comments on the relation of philosophy and psychology in Germany and then turned to a distinction between what he called "causal psychology"—the psychology of the experimental laboratory that has little to do with philosophy—and "teleological psychology" in which "mental life appears as the expression of a meaning." The latter is "the only psychology which is directly related to philosophy";

but, since both types can provide useful information, he recommends the sort of resolution that is made possible by idealism (PR 23:190–92; cf. JP 11:63–65).

In addition to this APA/AΨA discussion session, there was also an APA discussion session focused on the topic of "Existence and Value." In advance of this discussion, the topic was refined by the executive committee—"in only the most general form and in such a way as will allow all parties to present their more specific points of view and to participate in the discussion"—as: "The Problem of the Relation of Existence and Value, including their relation both as facts and as concepts, and also the Relation of a Theory of Existence to a Theory of Value." The committee also requested that "brief analyses, formulations, and discussions of the problem, or longer papers, be submitted for publication." Further, a subcommittee consisting of McGilvary, Pitkin, Overstreet, and Spaulding offered a formulation of the problem that it hoped would connect the upcoming discussion with the prior one from 1912. This formulation consisted in a series of questions including the following: "Is Value . . . something which is ultimate and which attaches itself to 'things' independently of consciousness, or of an organic being with desires and aversions, or . . . is it a characteristic which a thing gets by its relation to the consciousness of an organic being, or to an organic being with desires and aversions? . . . may, or may not, a theory of the nature of things be successfully developed without reference to a theory of values, and *vice versa*? . . . Is there one fundamental standard of values, or are there more than one?" (JP 10:167–68). J. Frederick Dashiell also published "An Introductory Bibliography in Value" that consisted of eighty-six relevant items classified in thirteen categories (JP 10:472–76).

Before the 'debate' began, there were a number of papers presented on the theme of existence and value: Wilbur Marshall Urban, "Existence, 'Value,' Reality"; Ernest N. Henderson, "The Empirical Determination of a Value Scale"; Cohen, "History vs. Values"; Horace Meyer Kallen, "Value and Existence in Art and in Religion"; Tufts, "Social Factors in Value"; Montague, "A Neo-Realistic Conception of Value"; and Dashiell, "Values and Experience." The debate itself filled two sessions, beginning with papers by the leaders, Sheldon and Perry. Sheldon began with a paper entitled "An Empirical Definition of Value" that maintained that all cases of value—sensual, economic, aesthetic, moral, religious, and intellectual—consist in "the furthering or hindering of some given tendency." Thus, he continues, value is to be defined "in terms of a factual category—viz., potentiality. Every value which is not merely imagined but felt as a working influence is such a potentiality, tending to realize itself." In "The Definition of Value," Perry followed with an examination of claims that value is indefinable and of a series of inadequate definitions. He favored the attempt to define value in terms of "the fulfillment of interest," and explained why he believed that complaints against this view were misguided. These two papers led to a wide-reaching discussion of the topic (PR 23:178–90; cf. JP 58–63).

The next meeting of the APA, its fourteenth, was held jointly with the fifteenth meeting of the WPA at the University of Chicago in December, 1914. In his report on the meeting, Wendell T. Bush remarks, "Owing to the distance of Chicago from eastern centers, the majority of those attending the conferences were members of the Western Association" (JP 12:93). War had broken out in Europe in August; and, perhaps because of this, the meeting seems to have had a more social and political 'feel' than most APA meetings, even if there was little explicit mention of the war. The papers included: Tufts's joint presidential address, "Ethics of States"—to be considered in chapter 13—and Hartley Burr Alexander, "Justice and Progress"; Kallen, "Democracy and its Melting Pot"; McGilvary, "The Conflict of Moral Ideals"; and Overstreet, "What Philosophy can Contribute to the Conception of Justice." As at the previous meeting, there was a joint discussion session. This time, the WPA/APA met with the American Political Science Association and the Conference on Legal and Social Philosophy to discuss "Constitutional and Political Guarantees." The leaders of this discussion were George Herbert Mead and W. F. Dodd (PR 24:186–94). The following year at the APA there was no organized discussion session; the fifteenth meeting took its theme from the sixtieth-birthday celebration for Josiah Royce that was discussed in chapter 5.

Lovejoy was elected APA president for 1916, and he worked to reestablish the formal discussion sessions. In mid-1916, he published on behalf of the executive committee a detailed announcement of the topic for discussion upcoming at the sixteenth meeting in December. As the committee notes, one of the most significant recent developments in American philosophy and psychology was "the reaction against the traditional sharp division of the data of experience into the two classes of 'mental' (or 'psychical') and 'physical.'" Philosophers, psychologists, and psychiatrists have all attempted "to transcend, to mitigate, or to abolish the 'Cartesian dualism' and to substitute therefor the conception of a homogeneous 'world of pure experience,' or of a 'psychophysical continuum,' or of the fundamentally 'neutral' nature of the entities with which experience is concerned or out of which it is constituted." In response to these attempts, supporters of the "antithesis" have been busy as well. Therefore, the committee continues, it would seem to be a good time to examine this issue carefully and to attempt "to bring about a further clarification of the matter at issue, by means of a general but methodical and connected discussion." The committee thus proposed to examine in the discussion session these two general questions: "*A. Is the division of the entities present or involved in*

experience into two reciprocally exclusive classes of 'mental' (or 'psychical')
and 'physical' to be retained? B. If so, how is the distinction to be formulated?
In particular, what is the essential differentia of the class 'mental' or psychi-
cal'?" In order to base the discussion "upon a review of recent reflection," the committee then offered a series of eleven definitions of the term, *mental*, as drawn from an attached bibliography of forty-two items that had been published since 1904 (JP 13:573–74).

The committee suggests that this formulation was still a bit loose and "therefore, offers certain further suggestions, consideration of which by members, it believes, will be conducive to a more effective and connected discussion and to a more direct joining of issue between the representatives of different views." The first of these is that the discussants keep as one of their goals attempting "to decrease the prevalent diversity and confusion in the use of the terms 'mental' and 'physical.'" The second suggestion is related to the more important issue of attempting to decide whether the entities attached to the terms 'mental' and 'physical' "exist and are to be recognized by metaphysics and by psychology." Here, the committee offers a series of "supplementary questions" that it believes will help to illuminate the general questions: whether nonphysical entities exist; and, if they do, what they might be: selves? awareness? conations? processes? sense-qualities? secondary qualities? ideas? meanings? universals? and so forth. The third suggestion from the committee, based upon the acceptance of nonphysical entities, runs as follows: "do those which exist (or any among them) exist only in, or in connection with or dependence upon, those complexes known as the 'experiences' of individual persons or organisms?" The final suggestion from the committee deals with definitions and wonders whether it was possible to define 'physical' first and then define 'mental' or 'psychical' as nonphysical functions of organisms. In spite of all this framing of the issues, the committee still admits that "the possible range of the discussion is extremely and perhaps excessively wide." While it may be so, the committee suggested that comprehensiveness would seem to be an advantage to an initial consideration of the topic (JP 13:576–78).

With these topical questions settled, the committee went on to announce the plan for conducting the discussion session in December 1916. The arrangements were as follows: (1) the committee will select six individuals to lead the discussion; (2) these six individuals "will either publish brief papers in advance of the meeting, on the topic of the discussion, or will indicate already published articles or passages, by themselves or others, expressing the theses which they desire to maintain," and the announcement of the program will note their whereabouts; (3) they will present at the meeting "papers not more than twenty minutes in length"; (4) they will "before the meeting, exchange briefs indicating the considerations which it is their purpose to present"; (5) the general membership will be given full opportunity to discuss these papers and to present papers of their own as long as they focus upon this topic; and (6) at least two sessions of the meeting will be devoted to the discussion (JP 13:579). At the meeting at Union Theological Seminary in New York, the first session (on Wednesday afternoon) contained the following: a presentation by Cohen on idealism, materialism, dualism, and neutral monism, Boyd Henry Bode's paper "Meaning of the Psychical," R. F. Alfred Hoernlé's paper "Confessions of an Old Idealist," and Warner Fite's discussion of consciousness. At the second session (on Thursday morning) five more papers were read: Pratt, "Confessions of an Old Realist"; Grace A. de Laguna, "The Limits of the Physical"; Wilbur Marshall Urban, "Meaning in Modern Psychology and the Problem of the Existence of the Psychical"; Durant Drake, "An Unlisted Definition of the Psychical"; and H. G. Hartman, "A Definition of Dualistic Entities." The topic was then opened up to general discussion; and, among others, Mary Whiton Calkins, John Elof Boodin, Montague, Overstreet, and the leaders themselves took part (PR 26:199–206; JP 14:207–13).

The uneven results of all this effort on behalf of organizing the discussion session were discussed by Albert G. A. Balz in his account of the 1916 meeting. The executive committee, he writes, "is certainly not at fault if its labors were not crowned with that convergence of the discussion upon the same issues and that focusing of interest and inquiry upon the same or closely related topics for which it planned." Part of the problem was that the intended prior interaction among the leaders of the discussion, to establish "some measure of inter-adjustment and articulation of the positions maintained," did not take place as planned. "Owing to insufficiency of time," he writes, "this plan miscarried." Similarly, the intention to publish the papers of the discussion leaders before the meeting was not fulfilled. As a result, Balz continues, "the positions expounded by the leaders started from different bases, were addressed to different issues, and the underlying similarity of interest and the nuclei of agreement and precise points of disagreement were obscured. Besides, the committee was unable to determine the logical order in which the papers should be read . . ." Consequently, without any success in these premeeting efforts, "it became the task of the meeting to disclose whatever unanimity of purpose and identity of idea existed, and to secure the focalization of the lines of thought, instead of taking its departure from whatever common fund of agreement concerning issues, methods of approach, and delimitations of subject that might have been attained beforehand by a favorable outcome of the committee's designs." He concludes that "the meeting closed at the point at which the discussion might conceivably have opened." In spite of his dissatisfaction with the conducting of this discussion session, however,

Balz still believed in the overall approach of pre-organized discussion sessions as a means to facilitate philosophic advance. As he writes, "something would undoubtedly have been gained in the way of clarified issues had the scheme adopted been carried out." As a result, he endorses further attempts to make these discussion sessions work in the future: "The experience of this meeting, therefore, should indicate that an earlier announcement of the topic of discussion, coupled with the circulation of abstracts prior to the meeting, would render more effective the meetings of the association" (JP 14:202).

The proceedings of the sixteenth meeting contain the following statement of the APA's intention to get more serious and to try once again to present an organized and effective discussion session in 1917:

> It was voted that the Association recommend to the Executive Committee that, for next year's meeting, (1) there shall be a prearranged discussion, (2) the topic shall be selected and announced as early as possible, and (3) other subjects shall be provided for . . . It was also voted that the Executive Committee be instructed, that one session of next year's meeting shall be devoted to the continuation of the discussion of the topic of this year. It was further voted, that a committee of twelve on discussion be appointed by the President, with the approval of the Executive Committee. (PR 26:198–99)

At this point, we may well ask why this commitment to the possibilities of the discussion session continued. The record was one of annual dissatisfaction followed by modifications, more dissatisfaction the next year and further fine-tuning. In the face of a series of at best modest successes that had come at the cost of a great investment of time and effort, the mood of the APA—or at least of its leadership—was to continue to try harder until the process was perfected and these sessions finally began to yield the anticipated philosophical progress. We may further wonder about the sense of philosophical progress that is operating in this escalating series of efforts to make the discussion sessions work. The best locus for encountering an explicit statement of this vision of philosophy and its potential progress is Lovejoy's presidential address, delivered on Wednesday evening, between the two sessions of the discussion on the mental and the physical at the APA's sixteenth meeting.

ARTHUR ONCKEN LOVEJOY

9

The Goal of Philosophical Progress

One way to classify presidential addresses is according to their theme. Sometimes, the theme of the address is an elaboration of the overall views of that year's president. As examples of this type of presidential address, we can consider Josiah Royce's attack on pragmatism contained in his 1903 address to the APA, "The Eternal and the Practical," or William James's call for greater appreciation of humans' unrecognized potential contained in his 1906 APA address, "The Energies of Men." Less frequently, presidents use their address to consider a topic that they believe is important to the association itself. One example of this latter sort is James Edwin Creighton's address at the first meeting of the APA in 1901, "The Purposes of a Philosophical Association," considered in chapter 4. Another is the 1916 address of Arthur Oncken Lovejoy.

In December of that year Lovejoy read his APA presidential address, "On the Conditions of Progress in Philosophical Inquiry."[1] He opened up his presentation with an indication that he intended to talk not so much about philosophy as about "philosophizing." He continues that the occasion of his presidential address "has brought on in me what may be called an attack of professional self-consciousness and self-searching, has given rise to some sobering reflections on the nature and the difficulties and the disappointments of the business of being a philosopher." In particular, he wanted to discuss with his professional colleagues the disappointments that result from the lack of philosophical progress. Turning autobiographical, Lovejoy notes that he was drawn as an undergraduate into the web of idealism and its presentation of final answers to life's questions under the guidance of George Holmes Howison at Berkeley. He was not alone. "I

---

[1] The address was published under the more modest title, "On Some Conditions of Progress in Philosophical Inquiry."

165

suppose," he writes, "that nearly all that was academically respectable and most that was intellectually vigorous, in philosophical teaching in America of the late [eighteen-] eighties and early nineties, professed and called itself idealistic . . ." Other philosophical perspectives, like "Platonic realism had a purely archaeological interest; and Kant, Fichte, and Hegel were names that few except William James dared utter without some bating of the breath." He continues that times, or fashions, had changed over the next two decades; and, looking back, he notes that there had appeared many different answers to philosophy's fundamental questions in the meantime:

> the secret of the universe has been discovered I know not how many times—thrice, at least, in America alone—and each time differently . . . Not many of the things which, in the early nineties, had been forever settled, have stayed settled; . . . many of the views which most of the enlightened would then have deemed impossible paradoxes . . . are now maintained by considerable and respectable bodies of philosophers, teaching from the chairs of our universities . . . How many *überwundene Standpunkte* [defeated views] have, in these decades, risen from the too shallow graves in which earlier generations had hopefully interred them![2]

As a result of philosophy's failure to abandon positions that had been defeated, Lovejoy finds it necessary to admit that it has made no progress. More significantly, philosophers seem little bothered by their failure to move ahead.

What sort of a 'business' is it to be a philosopher, Lovejoy wonders, if "[u]pon what appear to be plain, and also unescapable questions, trained specialists of high abilities find themselves unable to reach any common conclusion"? While he admits that "disagreement among experts is a common enough phenomenon in other sciences also, especially in their more general or theoretical portions," he reminds his audience that in philosophy "the theoretical portion is equal to the whole; if we fail to achieve a measurable amount of agreement and a consecutive and cumulative progress there, we fail altogether." This is exactly what has been happening in philosophy, he continues, and this failure must be admitted. "The fact remains, then, a standing scandal to philosophy, bringing just discredit upon the entire business in which we are professionally engaged." He admits that some philosophers remain unbothered by such continuing disagreements; but, from his point of view, such romanticism forces the philosopher into a difficult position: "Certainly the philosopher who argues—which is to say, the philosopher—and at the same time professes to regard a philosophy as essentially and desirably a disclosure of unstan-

---

[2] Lovejoy, "On Some Conditions," 126–28.

dardized private reactions upon the universe, a species of lyric cry, puts himself into a rather curious posture." If philosophers are not seeking agreement, "and as much of it as possible . . . why argue?" Lovejoy is willing to grant the likelihood that there will always be disagreements between and among philosophers; but he still maintains that philosophy is more than a private matter. And, as long as philosophers claim to be engaged in the pursuit of "verifiable truths" or to be "cultivating anything of the nature of science," it is "sheer dishonesty of us not to play *that* game according to the rules . . ." Thus, we should not allow ourselves "to be content with any lower degree of rigor in scientific method, any smaller measure of established and agreed-upon results, any greater infusion of the idiosyncracies of our private personalities, than the nature of the case and the imperfections of the human intellect render inevitable." To remain content with these deficiencies would continue to prevent philosophical progress.[3]

Lovejoy's explanation for the persistent stagnation of philosophy was that philosophy has been attempting "to perform two seemingly identical, but practically incongruous, functions": providing edification and enforcing a critical distance. As he writes, the philosopher, perhaps because of his earlier role as minister-president of the college expounding on the evidences of Christianity, "is, or is popularly expected to be, a creature of equivocal race, partaking somewhat of the preacher and somewhat of the skeptical inquirer, a queer hybrid of the prophet and the professor." The persistence of this dual function is what has set philosophy off from the other sciences and has made it nonprogressive. "In the investigations of specialists in the other disciplines," he writes, "it is not required that their conclusions shall edify or exhilarate; it is required only that they shall be reached by the honest application of the most exact methods of technical inquiry which the existing state of the science permits." Lovejoy maintains that it is at this point that change in the work of professional philosophers is necessary:

> If philosophy *is* to be treated as a science, but a science still in the making; if it is agreed that it is worth while for society to maintain a small body of men for the purpose of ascertaining, with as much care and exactitude of procedure as possible, what can be known about certain of the largest and most difficult

---

[3] Ibid., 128–33. George Santayana, for one, suggests that philosophers should not argue: "a system of philosophy is a personal work of art which gives a specious unity to some chance vista in the cosmic labyrinth. To confess this is to confess a notorious truth; yet it would be something novel if a philosopher should confess it, and should substitute the pursuit of sincerity for the pursuit of omniscience" ("Philosophical Heresy," 564). The similar position of Morris Raphael Cohen was considered in chapter 7.

questions that present themselves to the human intellect—then society must not confuse this purpose with a wholly different one, that of furnishing impressive, imaginative, edifying, emotionally stirring, popular discourse about these same problems. The public must learn to distinguish the two types of values; must not deem a man a good philosopher *merely* because he is a good metaphysical poet or a good preacher . . . success in something like this sense, though perhaps not attained by the same methods, not infrequently passes for success in the business of being a philosopher.

He believes that this emphasis upon the progressive possibilities of philosophy reflects its future. As he writes, "the confusion of philosophy and edification appears to be a waning error . . ." The scientific temper is becoming more prevalent among philosophers, and "the primary requisite for the conversion of philosophy into a science, and for the realization of that orderly and consecutive progress which is appropriate to a science, has already been attained."[4]

Lovejoy admits that there remains a tolerance for philosophical disagreements on the part of "a more or less large number of respected colleagues"—although, as he slyly remarks, this tolerance fails to produce any "doubt concerning the correctness of one's own conclusions." While these philosophers may believe that those colleagues who fail to agree with them are suffering from "the natural inertia of the human intellect" or "the aberrations of the younger generation" or some other personal failing that will eventually be overcome, Lovejoy is of a different opinion. On the one hand, he sees the belief that philosophical differences "will spontaneously diminish in the future" to be "a touching triumph of hope over experience . . ." On the other, he sees the attitude that tolerates such differences itself to be "the chief obstacle, not only to increase of agreement among us, but to . . . a progressive clarification of our problems." Philosophers need to start thinking more like scientists, for whom differences of opinion represent not insights but problems. As he phrases this point: "If two astronomers, observing the same object, get variant results, neither of them insists that his own (uncorrected) observation is the true one, no

---

[4] Lovejoy, "On Some Conditions," 133–38. Cf. George Stuart Fullerton: "philosophies are brought forward because it is believed or hoped that they are true . . . If the philosopher frankly abandons the attempt to tell us what is true, and with a Celtic generosity addresses himself to the task of saying what will be agreeable to us, he loses his right to the title. It is not enough that he stirs our emotions, and works up his unrealities to something resembling a poem. It is not primarily his task to please, as is it not the task of the serious worker in science to please those whom he is called upon to instruct. Truth is truth, whether it be scientific truth or philosophical truth. And error, no matter how agreeable or how nicely adjusted to the temper of the times, is always error" (*Introduction to Philosophy*, 282). For a defense of edification, see Van Riper, "Philosophy and Edification."

matter how clearly and distinctly he saw what he reports." What is true for the scientist should be true for the philosopher: I am not entitled "to assume confidently the correctness of my observation of a given logical fact, if my learned colleague, whose ability and general competency I cannot doubt, reports a different observation." This sense of self-doubt is not frequently found among philosophers, who too often remain confident following their own insights.[5]

Lovejoy goes on to point out what he takes to be "the most important of the typical subjective causes of the error in philosophical reasonings which is evidenced by our relatively high degree of disagreement" in the hope that these "accidental errors" can be largely removed by the "good will and determination on the part of philosophers." The first step in philosophical progress, he writes, is to remember that, contrary to the view of the general public, philosophy does not deal with "esoteric mysteries." Like "the other sciences," philosophy's job is to gather and analyze data, to engage in what he calls "logical observation." In explaining this notion further, he notes "the philosopher's task, broadly stated, is to observe as completely and exactly as possible . . ." The work of the philosopher "is a task of collating and focussing the data necessary for deciding as to the preponderance of evidence in relation to a given well-formulated question . . ." The philosopher performs this task well or ill—and thereby advances or retards philosophical progress—"according to the degree of comprehensiveness of the collation and the degree of precision with which the several data have been observed." Lovejoy continues, "The first thing needful, then, for the secure progress of philosophical inquiry—after the business of inquiry has been separated from the business of edification—is the development, or the very great intensification among us of a certain habit of mind—of the caution, and the sense of the probable multiplicity and elusiveness of the circumstances to be taken account of, which characterize the trained inductive investigator." The other sciences are very careful in their data-gathering, he maintains, and this is why they progress. Philosophy, on the other hand, is not. In general, he writes, philosophers have no "precautionary technique," even though their need for "such checks and precautions is manifestly greater than the need of the specialist in any physical science can be, precisely because our data are more abstract, more elusive, easier to overlook, less capable of forcing themselves upon our attention, than are the objects of physical observation." If philosophers were to adopt "the inductive investigator's habit of mind," if they were to operate with "a certain self-distrust, a sense that eternal vigilance is the price of sound philosophizing, an appreciation, in particular, of the fact

---

[5] Lovejoy, "On Some Conditions," 138–41.

that there are in all probability *many* 'considerations' to be looked for, brought into relation, and probed, before a conclusion can be legitimately reached," their philosophizing would be transformed.[6]

To approximate the inductive investigator would mean to reject what he calls "the 'happy-thought' method of philosophizing," the method that sees philosophy as providing edification through the transmission of illumination and insight. Lovejoy was willing to admit the continued attractiveness of this bankrupt tradition from philosophy's prescientific past, noting that perhaps all of us "have experienced something of that intoxicating sense of revelation, that metaphysical inebriety, which comes at these moments." Whatever the comfort value of illumination and insight might be, however, we must resist. Such comforts, he writes, "are, no doubt, among the chief rewards of the philosopher's life, but are also the chief dangers to philosophy itself" because they bring with them to the mind "a potency and charm that is likely ever thereafter to dull the edge of the critical sense and to impart to bad logic a strange plausibility, incomprehensible to those who have not had the experience." Thus, rather than following our insights, we need to distrust what seems to be so obvious to us as individuals and submit our intellectual creations to more severe testing. He writes that "only a Spartan discipline in the rigors of inductive inquiry . . . can suffice to overcome the natural fondness of parents, and secure that prompt extirpation of the logically unfit, without which philosophy is likely to the end to be a mere mob of private convictions." This sort of philosophical infanticide would prevent the continued development of positions grounded solely in comfortable self-evidence. Lovejoy thus advocates "the establishment of a sort of metaphysical testing laboratory, where the materials to be used in the construction of philosophical engines are first systematically subjected to all conceivable strains and stresses . . ." This testing would be the first step towards philosophical progress; or, as he writes, one way that we hope that "our dialectical locomotion will be made reasonably secure and continuous."[7]

In addition to adopting a stance of philosophy as a critical scientific undertaking, Lovejoy further suggests a series of other changes in how philosophy is conducted. The first was that it was necessary, and possible, "to treat individual philosophical problems in isolation, to deal with the general field of our inquiries piecemeal." Certainly, he writes, this is the procedure followed elsewhere, where "[t]he isolation of problems is a necessary part of *all* scientific procedure" and where there is no tolerance of the view current among some philosophers that "nothing could be known,

---

[6] Ibid., 140–43, 148, 143–44.
[7] Ibid., 144–48.

or even profitably discussed, until everything was known . . ." Another suggested procedure is that philosophers need to undertake "a deliberate and systematic attempt at exhaustiveness in the enumeration of the elements of a problem, of the 'considerations' pertinent to it—and, even, of all that any relatively sane minds have ever conceived to be pertinent considerations." In order to even approximate this goal of exhaustiveness, philosophers will need to work more cooperatively to share their contributions. Philosophy, he writes, "is—by the nature of the task, though not, perhaps, by the nature of its practitioners—more than any other science a cooperative enterprise"; and once philosophers come to recognize that "real philosophizing is a collective process," many of its half-baked pronouncements would disappear. Cooperative activity would function "to prevent people from having philosophies—that is, from having premature and personal philosophies which they suppose to be objectively tested ones." Third, cooperative activity would force more attention upon the need for fostering better discussions. Lovejoy reminds his audience "how hard it is to insinuate a philosophical idea in its exact and entire meaning into the mind of another human being, even though he be himself a philosopher." Then, turning to the specific meaning of this point for his APA audience, he continues that, fourth, philosophers need the adoption, "at least for the purposes of a particular discussion, of a common and unambiguous terminology, and—if so much be within human power—of a common set of initial postulates" and, fifth, they need "to organize discussion upon a sufficiently large scale and to provide for its prosecution over a sufficiently long time and with the requisite orderliness and sequentiality." Once again advocating the better use of techniques that we have already seen—the prechosen topic, focused teaching, and prepublished positions—Lovejoy maintained that if these measures were to be adopted "we should then have an approach to a suitable organization of cooperative philosophical inquiry in America."[8]

Adopting these five procedures, along with the stance of philosophy as a science, would finally make the discipline progressive. Lovejoy maintains that he has no simple notion of success and he admits that he does not anticipate that, with the close of each December's APA meeting, "every New Year's Day would see one of the ancient problems finally disposed of, by universal consent." Rather, what he has in mind is that "we should secure a more precise joining of issue, a far more real contact of mind with mind, a richer accumulation and convergence of pertinent 'considerations,' a more tenacious following of the argument, a better understanding, at the

---

[8] Ibid., 155, 157, 149–50, 152–55. The theme of cooperation was also central to James Edwin Creighton's presidential address discussed in chapter 4.

worst, of the precise nature and grounds of our differences, than would be attainable by any other means." Moreover, on occasion, "we should perhaps witness that rare and admirable spectacle of a philosopher of mature years converted by argument to a new opinion . . ."[9]

In his presidential address, Lovejoy also proposed an additional project as part of his vision for philosophical progress: "the preparation, through cooperative effort of many philosophers of differing schools, of a comprehensive *catalogue raisonné* of 'considerations' . . . a modern *Summa Metaphysica* of an undogmatic and non-partisan kind." In this volume would be found a complete display of what he calls "considerations"— "not terms, or systems, or doctrines, or even problems"—but the elements that are "the ultimate units of our inquiry . . ." These are "the logically distinguishable and significant presuppositions, arguments, 'considerations,' in a word" that make up the familiar philosophical systems. The ongoing problem is that a philosophical system "is often a highly accidental and highly unstable compound" of logically distinguished units that "frequently owe their conjunction more to peculiarities of the author's mind or of his historical situation than to any purely dialectical necessity." Lovejoy's proposal to overcome this weakness is "that the history of philosophy (including contemporary philosophy) be disarticulated, that these logical units into which it is resolvable be discriminated, set down each under the historic thesis, or diverse theses, to which it is relevant, and methodically and unequivocally correlated with all complementary, qualifying or contrary considerations relevant to the same thesis."[10]

What Lovejoy had in mind for this *Summa* was to produce an exhaustive enumeration of the elements of philosophy. On the positive side this would mean a "complete and just presentation of the considerations tending to support any philosophical thesis . . ." This would include offering "[f]or each argument . . . a series of precise references to the passages in other writings in which, to the present-day representatives of the view in question, it seems to have found its most satisfactory or its most influential formulations." Then "the negative considerations, real or supposed" would be discussed: criticisms of the proofs of the thesis, questions of the internal consistency in the conclusion, possible external criticisms, and so on. Finally, "the counter-considerations" would be offered by the supporters. When completed, this *Summa* would serve as a handy catalogue of ideas, as a tool to further philosophical thinking. He maintains that "it would be no part of the undertaking of the modern *Summa* to state a final conclusion. It would merely present, in the

---

[9] Ibid., 155.
[10] Ibid., 159–60.

manner indicated, the state of the argument, leaving the judicious reader to conclude for himself."[11]

Lovejoy admits that there are some who might see this overall project as "convert[ing] the living substance of philosophy into a *hortus siccus* [garden of dried flowers] of dried, abstract, depersonalized arguments and counter-arguments, destitute of all charm of style and arrayed in tedious formal schemes of classification and antithesis . . ." His response to such individuals is that they misunderstand the nature of the philosopher's task. We must, he maintains, see philosophizing as the intellectual work of discrimination and classification. He continues that we must do so

> unless we are prepared frankly to abdicate our customary pretension to be dealing with objective, verifiable and clearly communicable truths, and are content to acknowledge that all our brave parade of philosophizing is nothing more than an exploiting of our temperamental idiosyncracies, disingenuously masquerading in the garb of impersonal reason; unless, in short, we philosophers are willing to be classified, not as men of science, but as practitioners of what it would be necessary to call *belles lettres* if only it were not, on the other hand, usually so sadly lacking in beauty.

To those in his APA audience who were in general agreement with him, however, Lovejoy held forth the possibility of philosophical progress. Problems surely existed; but "whatever there be that is disappointing in the present state of philosophy, there is reason to believe that the cause lies, not in the nature of our task, but in our way of going about that task . . ." If philosophers were willing "to adapt the methods of our collective effort to the distinguishing peculiarities and difficulties of the philosophic enterprise," progress would finally be ours.[12]

Lovejoy's 1916 presidential address was published in the March 1917 issue of *The Philosophical Review*. The level of interest that the address sparked was evidenced by the fact that the next issue of the journal contained a series of five responses.[13] First in line was Ernest Albee, who wrote

---

[11] Ibid., 161–62.

[12] Ibid., 162–63; cf. Daniel J. Wilson, *Arthur O. Lovejoy*, 85–93.

[13] Cf. Herbert Wallace Schneider: "Philosophising, because it has been largely undisciplined, is contentious rather than scientifically productive. Prof. Lovejoy pleads for the development of a technique of cooperative inquiry. There is a great deal of irony about the whole plea, for its immediate result was to call forth fresh contention, and not cooperation. The discussion which followed . . . , however, marks the conscious recognition of an important fact, viz., that philosophy to-day is a curious mixture of 'the art of philosophising' and of a number of scientific (psychological, logical, metaphysical) problems for *inquiry* . . . The recognition of this is significant, because recent philosophy (at least that of 1917) has been (with a few notable exceptions) *inquiry* rather than *art*, science rather than philosophy in the narrower sense; and the conscious recognition of this and endeavor to develop scientific techniques is a genuine turning-point, or crisis, in philosophical thinking" ("Philosophy," 539).

that Lovejoy's address "illustrates a tendency which has become increasingly marked since the later development of the special sciences, viz., a tendency on the part of certain metholodogists to apologize for philosophy because it is not something else." Albee maintained that philosophy is not a science like mathematics, physics, or biology; and it should not attempt to become one. "If philosophy should ever sacrifice the broad humanism that has been one of its most admirable traits in the past for an abstractly conceived 'scientific' method," he writes, "the result could be nothing less than disastrous." He continues that "philosophy has relations to art, more particularly to literature, as vital and significant as those which it is universally recognized as having to science." Further, Albee maintains that "philosophy comes into closest relations with life," when it attempts to approximate art rather than science. "This is one reason," he writes, "why a de-personalized philosophy is sure to be a gloomy failure." With regard to the specific issue of the discussion sessions, he is very critical, describing it as potentially "a 'Frankenstein' invention" capable of "casting its shadow over the whole year . . ." Among other costs of this shift to narrow, pre-arranged, cooperative work would be a loss of original treatises. How successful, he wonders, would Kant have been if he had been obliged "to spend endless time discussing fundamental problems with contemporaries, most of whom would probably have been unable to understand him?"[14]

A similarly critical stance was taken by Charles Montague Bakewell. He repeats the point about the misguided attempts of philosophers to imitate the sciences. Further, he maintains that as a goal, philosophy should not seek unanimity. Philosophers' answers are always multiple, he writes, even when they share a vision and cooperate in 'schools.' The new realism, for example, is really best understood as an interweaving of the perspectives of six different realists. This diversity within philosophy is a result of the nature of the endeavor: "for better or for worse, philosophy is always an individual venture. Each philosopher must always build for himself from the ground up." What saves philosophy from a decline into solipsism is that "the hypothesis the philosopher is trying out is always one of a certain cosmic sweep." Bakewell admits that philosophy would benefit from more mutual understanding among philosophers; but, in his view, the suggested approach is not the way to attain it. Lovejoy, he writes, would have us attempt to resolve our philosophical problems

> into their simple elements, which could then be defined by accredited philosophic lexicographers. The eligible problems could then be formulated, the pitfalls noted, the thoroughfares and culs-de-sac, the relevancies and irrelevancies. Each philosopher could then pick his fragment for logical observation . . . We

---

[14] Albee et al., "Progress in Philosophical Inquiry," 315–16, 319–20.

are advised to suspend judgment on all the larger issues, and to content ourselves for the present with constructing a sort of map of philosophy . . . What Professor Lovejoy is suggesting is nothing more or less than a contemporary *Sic et Non*, compiled not by a single Abelard but by a group of them, and with scientific instead of theological *parti pris* [prejudice].

Bakewell suggests that, if Lovejoy's plan were adopted, philosophy would "take on the appearance of a Desert of Sahara, with scarcely a redeeming oasis . . ." While he admits that this result would not necessarily invalidate Lovejoy's method, he writes that it is "pertinent to suggest that had the philosophers of the past followed this pathway, not one of the great visions that are our philosophical heritage would be ours."[15]

The third response was from Theodore de Laguna, who offered a series of critical responses to specific points in Lovejoy's talk. One of them was the reminder in the face of his charge of a lack of progress that, in addition to present philosophy, past philosophy has also produced the special sciences. Another was the point that "[n]either agreement nor disagreement is intrinsically the better. The agreement of established knowledge is better than the disagreement of error. But the disagreement of independent inquiry is better than the agreement of narrow prejudice. Whoever welcomes disagreement, welcomes it as a means of finding truth, not as an end in itself." Overall, however, de Laguna seems to be, in large measure, in agreement with Lovejoy; and he closes with the following point: "The further practical recommendations, for the improvement of our annual meetings and for the compilation of an encyclopedia of philosophy, appear to me to contain much that is excellent—provided too much is not expected from them. The *Summa Philosophica* is surely a noble conception."[16]

William Ernest Hocking offered the most favorable response of the five. He begins by commenting, "Anybody who believes that philosophy seeks knowledge must accept, it would seem to me, the main positions of Professor Lovejoy's Address." Hocking continues: "The proposition that a man's philosophy is a function of his temperament . . . is worthless . . . as a rule of philosophic method . . . To accept philosophy as a common effort at objective truth need neither ignore the role of temperament, nor admit it to any voice in the control of method." In addition to this appreciation of the importance of method, he also looked favorably on Lovejoy's emphasis on cooperation, writing that "if it is possible to get ahead at all in philosophy, mutual and organized effort must be added to solitary and unorganized effort." Further, he supports the *Summa*: "The idea of a

---

[15] Bakewell, in Albee et al., "Progress in Philosophical Inquiry," 321–22; Bakewell, "On the Meaning of Truth," 579.

[16] De Laguna, in Albee et al., "Progress in Philosophical Inquiry," 327, 329.

compendium of 'relevant considerations' strikes me as a proposal of imaginative common-sense." Hocking does offer critical comments as well. Some are directed at what he takes to be Lovejoy's simplistic understanding of philosophical progress. Such progress, he writes, "cannot be pictured as the ascent of a staircase of fixed length in which everything is to be won by making sure of one tread at a time. It is partly a stair, and partly a lift; but the stair is one whose treads multiply as we go, and taken alone would let us sink as we climb." He was also critical of Lovejoy's apparent failure to recognize that he is in effect calling for "another era of general system-making." Hocking himself was not opposed to system-building; but he maintained that it is not normally a cooperative activity. Finally, he sees the philosophers' failure to cooperate to be due not to "lack of willingness, but lack of time." Here he suggests that Lovejoy is mistakenly putting his emphasis on efforts at early, rather than later, cooperation. Later cooperative interaction seems to come after a book has been published, which is not too late. "A book is no longer regarded as a final and unchangeable expression," he writes. "It is rather a circumspect and shapely presentation of an idea, entirely tentative, and an invitation for the searching attention of the colleague in his capacity as reviewer."[17]

The final response was from Edmund Howard Hollands, who, like Albee and Bakewell, rejected the science analogy. Lovejoy, he writes, wants us "to map out and divide our problems, and attack them cooperatively and successively, eliminating the personal equation, and adopting the hypothetical methods of mathematics." Such efforts cannot succeed, however, because philosophy—although it does seek "impersonal truth"—cannot be made into a "depersonalized science." The sciences may be able to do their work, progressing "fact by fact, little by little"; but "philosophies, aiming at the whole and final truth, are made individually and all of a piece, like works of art." Philosophy reaches down to the roots of living by "the internal necessity of free reflection itself"; and the philosopher "cannot 'depersonalize' his work, if this means to make it deal with facts and existences *to the exclusion* of meanings and values." Similarly, Hollands maintains that philosophy's problems cannot be isolated and dealt with in sequence because the philosopher, unlike the scientist, cannot "take the general presuppositions and character of his science for granted, and attend to his special problem alone." For him, philosophical reflection is "the regress of theory, analytic and synthetic at the same time, *behind* all such results, in the attempt to think them and all the real together." He continues that these elements "do not fall together of themselves into the

---

[17] Hocking, in Albee et al., "Progress in Philosophical Inquiry," 329–31.

total system which philosophy must aim at; if they did, either there would be no need for any philosophy in addition to the special sciences, or philosophy would be, as is sometimes suggested, merely the name for the discussion of questions as yet unanswered or unappropriated by the sciences . . ." In spite of Hollands's overall critical stance, however, he notes that Lovejoy's *Summa* "would undoubtedly be an honorable undertaking for American philosophers . . ."[18]

As might have been expected, Lovejoy replied forcefully to these criticisms. He maintained that some of the critics did not correctly understand his position, attributing to him "arguments or proposals nowhere to be found in the discourse under consideration, and even some which I had therein rejected with explicitness and emphasis." For example, *contra* Albee, he writes that he never intended to import the methods of the sciences into philosophy, but only to suggest "the requirements of a *specifically* philosophical method . . ." Similarly, he rejects Bakewell's "weird caricature" of his projected *Summa*. He writes that "the purpose of the suggested encyclopedia was primarily to serve as a sort of logical *aide-mémoire*—to assist the patient and open-minded philosophical investigator to make sure that he has not by inadvertence overlooked or misapprehended any considerations which have thus far occurred to other philosophers as relevant to his problem." Overall, his response consisted mostly of restatements and refinements of aspects of his presidential address. In particular, Lovejoy returns to his goal of philosophical progress. "I remain unpersuaded that the difficulty lies exclusively in the nature of philosophy," he writes, "and I find myself more convinced than ever of the needfulness of such improvements in the technique of philosophical discussion as may enable us to attain at least a higher degree of mutual intelligibility." To attain philosophical progress, we need to be clearer about what we are doing as philosophers.[19]

Part of this clarity means "an agreement as to which problems are open to impersonal and scientific inquiry, and which are not." Lovejoy continues that "a great part of philosophical writing is too 'appreciational,' too poetic, to be good logic, and too (ostensibly) logical to be good poetry." These two endeavors, he believes, must be kept separate:

---

[18] Hollands, in Albee et al., "Progress in Philosophical Inquiry," 331–34, 336, 338. Cf. Harold Chapman Brown: "The scientist can take his problems piecemeal, the philosopher must solve his synthetically. The scientific spirit now dominates and philosophy suffers accordingly . . . James used to say that ideas came to him as the charcoal sketches of pictures and that the detailed filling in arrived gradually. Certainly no picture could be produced by dividing the canvas into square inches and completing each one as a special problem" ("Philosophic Mind," 190).

[19] Lovejoy, "Progress in Philosophical Inquiry," 537–39.

I can conceive of no rule of philosophic method more primary than that the philosopher should always be perfectly clear in his own mind, when philosophizing, as to whether he is functioning as artist or as man of science—whether he is engaged in 'appreciation' or in rigorous, objective and conceptually communicable reasoning. Most philosophers whom I have met usually have the air of arguing. If it is upon quite other business that they are really engaged, one could wish to be warned of the fact in advance, that one may not waste time in applying logical criteria to their utterances.

Lovejoy believes that among the problems that are particularly open to impersonal and scientific inquiry are those of epistemology and metaphysics. Still, he maintains the broader point that "for my thesis, it makes little difference *what* part of philosophy is conceded to be akin to science in its purpose and ideal to aim at depersonalized and universally verifiable truth." So whether the focus is to be epistemology or metaphysics, or some other area(s) of philosophy, "[i]f only there be *some* such part, then to that part, and to all of it, and to it alone, the contentions advanced in my discourse apply . . . this part, whatever its extent, seems to me the one which alone rightly deserves the name of 'philosophy.'" Given these claims, attaining progress in philosophy will require a shift away from how it is currently practiced—it is often seen as "the most anarchical and chaotically individualistic of the provinces of thought"—to what it remains in principle—"the arch-enemy of intellectual caprice, of unchastened prejudice and of undisciplined individualism." He contends that all that he wanted to do was to make philosophy live up to this principle. "I find it hard to understand the attitude of those who are, practically if not avowedly, indifferent to the endeavor to realize some actual progress towards such a consummation," he writes. Lovejoy is further unable to understand those philosophers "who see occasion for alarm in the simple proposal that American philosophers shall make an organized effort to think more cooperatively and thereby to diminish the 'probable error' of their individual inquiries," who are consequently reluctant to "by voluntary consent, devote a fraction of their time each year to connected reflection, and to a genuine meeting of minds, upon some common and specific problem." He thus finds himself unable to understand his colleagues who are unwilling to devote some portion of the meetings of the APA to advance this goal.[20]

------

[20] Lovejoy, "Progress in Philosophical Inquiry," 543–44. Cf. Lovejoy: "Philosophy seems to me essentially a collective and cooperative business. Effective cooperation among philosophers consists, it is true, primarily in disagreement. For, given a sufficiently well defined problem, philosophy can really get forward with it only by bringing together in their logical interconnection all the considerations which have occurred, or are likely to occur, to acute and philosophically initiated minds as significantly pertinent to that problem . . . The

The only decidedly new strain in Lovejoy's reply is an emphasis on the professionalization of philosophy, in which he seems to be deliberately driving a wedge between the work of academic philosophers and the intellectual interests of the general, educated public. He begins by developing another aspect of the analogy between philosophy and science. "The investigator in the natural sciences does not primarily address himself to the public at large," he writes. "He reports the results of his inquiries in the first instance to fellow-specialists; the man who makes haste to proclaim his great discoveries to the laity (which has no competency to judge the evidence for them) before they have been submitted to the judgment of his peers and have passed through the ordeal of technical discussion, is usually looked upon as a charlatan." In a similar fashion, then, philosophy—or at least epistemology and metaphysics—should bypass the uninformed "laity" and lay its findings before the experts. This scientific procedure was not, however, being followed by the philosopher. "It is often at the general reader that his books are chiefly aimed"; and this is a problem because "the qualities which the general reader most values in philosophical books are not, as a rule, 'scientific' qualities." The general public's interest in metaphysics is like its interest in poetry: "for the moods that it awakens, for the personality which it expresses, for the uses of edification to which it can be put, for the sense of being in the presence of vastnesses and profundities which it affords, often for the mere pleasure of being mystified." The importance of vigorous thinking and the evaluation of arguments do not interest the broader audience. "At best, it is in the philosopher's *conclusions*, rather than his reasons for them, that the average cultivated reader is interested."[21] This sort of thinking constitutes what he had previously derided as "edification" and "happy-thought philosophy," an approach to philosophizing that professional, academic philosophers must reject for their own, and for their discipline's, sake. Lovejoy continues:

> It is thus entirely possible for a philosopher to attain reputation and influence, to 'stamp himself upon his age,' by virtue of essentially literary rather than philosophical merits. His 'success,' as that is often reckoned, is not conditioned

---

true procedure of philosophy as a science—as distinct from the philosophic idiosyncracies of individuals—is thus that of a Platonic dialogue on a grand scale, in which the theses, proposed proofs, objections, rejoinders, of numerous interlocutors are focused upon a given question, and the argument gradually shapes itself, through its own immanent dialectic, to a conclusion" (*Revolt against Dualism*, ix–x).

[21] Lovejoy, "Progress in Philosophical Inquiry," 541. Cf. William James: "a man's vision is the great fact about him. Who cares for Carlyle's reasons, or Schopenhauer's, or Spencer's? A philosophy is the expression of a man's intimate character, and all definitions of the universe are but the deliberately adopted reactions of human characters upon it" (*Pluralistic Universe*, 14; cf. Cohen, "Later Philosophy," 249).

upon abundance of knowledge, closeness and circumspection of reasoning, or even genuine logical perspicacity. And this fact makes it still easier for the philosopher to slur his processes of verification. The plausible notion which has captivated him is still more likely, if skillfully presented, to impress, and perhaps to captivate, the great public. And how doubly hard it is for the philosopher who has once found disciples to be seriously sceptical of the 'insight' which has brought him so grateful an experience!

Because philosophers are in greater danger "of mistaking the plausible for the proved" than the experimentalist is, philosophers who have any regard for philosophical progress must remain cognizant of the necessity "of caution, method, patience and rigor in the testing even of the seemingly most promising and persuasive of 'insights.'"[22]

---

[22] Lovejoy, "Progress in Philosophical Inquiry," 541–42; Daniel J. Wilson, *Science, Community*, 144–45. I have discussed the theme of philosophical progress in "Arthur Lovejoy and the Progress of Philosophy."

FREDERICK J. E. WOODBRIDGE

Image courtesy of James Woodbridge

10
The Discussion Sessions II

Despite Arthur Oncken Lovejoy's passionate defense of his conception of philosophical progress, his was not the only one. Other philosophers saw advance to lie in different directions. For Boyd Henry Bode, for example, progress in philosophy was related to careful attention to what is problematic in our situation. In his review of Mary Whiton Calkins's *The Persistent Problems of Philosophy*, he writes that "the attempt to solve problems without reference to the conditions in which they arise makes philosophy a repository for 'persistent problems' that ought to be recognized as dead and entitled to decent burial." To have once been a philosophical problem does not necessarily make something a philosophical problem now, and we cannot progress if we allow such past problems to persist.

> That Descartes's doubt, taken as a reaction against the claims of authority, was of enormous significance, is not, of course, in dispute. A similar significance attaches to Locke's insistence that direct experience must be the touchstone of theory, and to the idealistic formulation of the doctrine that man is the measure of things. These doctrines were significant precisely because they provided an outlook upon life that gave promise of a more effective control of experience. It is when theory lapses from its proper function of giving us a better leverage on the facts of experience and becomes a means of perpetuating artificial problems that we have a close parallel to the procedure of a hidebound lawyer whose vision is limited to the letter of the law.

Other philosophers, like George Herbert Palmer, were less concerned that philosophy progress. He notes that, should we consider books on the physical sciences, we would find that "most of those written fifty years ago are entirely superseded to-day. They are dead things. What is asserted in them is not true." On the other hand, books on theology and philosophy are full of "the speculations and pronouncements of more than two thousand years" that remain "vital still."[1] Progress in philosophy remained a complex issue for philosophers and for the associations; and, as the adopted method of philosophical advance, the discussion sessions continued.

The seventeenth meeting of the WPA took place on 6–7 April 1917. The American entry into the war had been brewing for some time; and the United States declared war on Germany on the first day of the meeting. Aside from George Herbert Mead's presidential address "The Instinct of Hostility," to be discussed in chapter 13, the content of the papers seems to have been largely unaffected by wartime events. In his account of the meeting Edward Leroy Schaub notes: "The morning and afternoon sessions of the first day were devoted to papers and general discussion centering about three questions formulated by the executive committee as follows: (1) In what sense does the human person possess independence of his physical organism and environment? (2) What reality has the history of the world as the physical and biological sciences present it? (3) Does any being exist that plays the part assigned to God in theistic religion?" Among the individuals who took up these themes were Edmund Howard Hollands, Roy Wood Sellars, Addison Webster Moore, Bode, and Edward Scribner Ames, who addressed these themes from the points of view of idealism, pragmatism, and realism (JP 14:403–8).

In August of 1917, James Edwin Creighton published a criticism of recent APA programs. The substance of his remarks was that, in the sixteen years since its creation, the APA—*his* APA—had lost its way. He noted a "loss of interest," and even "a mild sense of grievance," on the part of some members who had become uncomfortable with "the subordination of the other parts of the programme to the discussion of some specific subject, of interest to a particular group, and oftentimes defined so narrowly in terms of the presuppositions of that group as to render the discussion unmeaning, and to a considerable extent unintelligible, to others." He admitted that there is a great deal to be gained from the meetings—even "apart from the programme"—from "the social and informal side of the meetings"; but he still maintained that the general membership of the APA should not be, or even feel, railroaded by some members' attempts to mandate their understanding of philosophical progress.

> It was hoped that by setting to work more systematically, by "organizing" a discussion which should be continued through two or three sessions,—prescribing the channels in which it should run, and defining the terms to be employed—to compel the opposing forces to abandon their trenches and

---

[1] Bode, "Why Do Philosophical Problems Persist?" 174; Palmer, introduction to *Contemporary American Philosophy*, 42.

engage in open battle at a fixed predeterminable point. And if such an engagement could be brought about, so it was argued, there ought to be some definable result—a victory for one side or the other, and the consequent acceptance of the part of the association of a final philosophical truth, which as the "fruit" of the discussion would, of course, be a comforting mark of progress and might enable the "philosopher" to hold up his head in a company of "scientists."

To Creighton's way of thinking, however, the process of conducting these discussions was beginning to resemble "scholasticism over again . . . the disputations of the medieval schools . . ." As instances of this developing scholasticism, he pointed to the "extreme artificiality" introduced to the discussions by attempts to circumscribe the issues and to define the terms.[2]

Creighton was willing to admit that "a closely defined and specialized form of philosophical discussion can be carried on successfully only among the members of a group who accept in common (at least provisionally) certain assumptions, and who are sufficiently familiar with one another's accepted logic and terminology to concentrate attention upon the details and technique of the arguments employed." His complaint was based upon the belief that the APA's membership did not constitute such a narrow group. It was, rather, a broad association with interests far beyond those of the approaches to metaphysics and epistemology that Lovejoy had just proclaimed to be real philosophy. More importantly for the meetings of the APA, these individuals were unlikely to have much interest in any discussion designed to mandate this sort of philosophical advance. Creighton, in other words, was not opposed to philosophers attempting to advance what might be seen as narrow philosophical interests, just to their highjacking of the APA meetings to do it. He offered two suggestions. The first was that the APA think more in terms of informal discussions that could still make use of "the opportunities afforded by the meetings for such intimate discussion of particular points." His second suggestion, perhaps more realistically in tune with those members "who believe that they can most profitably employ a large share of the days devoted to meetings in 'close and prolonged debate,'" was to abandon the APA's longstanding practice of favoring plenary sessions at the meetings.[3] Creighton thought that organizing "simultaneous sections" during parts of the APA meetings would make room for "those who believe in a less formally defined mode of cooperation, and who perhaps attach more importance to viewing contemporary problems in the light of the great historical systems" to advance a different understanding of "philosophical scholarship which, through the

---

[2] Creighton, "APA and Its Programmes," 472–74.

[3] Ibid., 475. There had long been concurrent sessions when the various academic societies held joint meetings.

great emphasis laid upon the discussion, has very largely been lost sight of in our recent meetings."[4]

At the APA meeting in December 1917, the only meeting of the APA while the United States was fighting in World War I, the topic of the discussion, to be considered in chapter 13, was "Ethics and International Relations." In his presidential address, entitled "The Opportunity of Philosophy," Moore returned to the issue of science and philosophy that had been the core of Lovejoy's presidential address at the previous meeting, and of the various responses to his address. He began with a rejection of "the wide-spread apprehension that philosophy is in danger of losing its job," either because it is "capitulating to science" or because it is "surrendering to inspiration and edification—to religion and art." For him, such uncertainties are "the inevitable accompaniment of any period of pronounced reconstruction such as that through which philosophy is now passing and should be hailed as sure signs of life." For his own part, Moore maintains that "philosophy has never shown greater vitality nor had a greater opportunity than now." To bring this opportunity to fruition, however, it was necessary that the inherited bifurcation between facts and values, between tradition and science, be abandoned. If we understand this Darwinian point properly, he writes, "it does not signify that philosophy is to be made more scientific and science more philosophic by substituting mathematical or logical conceptions for eternal values as the objects of philosophic vision." On the contrary, the true meaning of a 'scientific' philosophy will appear when, "instead of attempting to substitute scientific concepts for values, or conversely, philosophy shall proclaim science as the method of its values." He continues that "science, forced by the old tradition to expend its energies in developing a purely existential and physical world, is now called in as a mercenary to furnish so much hired force in the form of high explosives, barbed-wire, and poisoned gas, to serve values and purposes that, by the same tradition, have been formed largely by more or less sublimated survivals of tribal custom . . ." For Moore, on the contrary, science should not be called "to the defense of values born of instinct, custom and myth." Rather, "scientific intelligence must be operative in the *formation* of the values and purposes of our social life."[5]

The question that philosophers (and others) must face is whether we are prepared for the transformation that the scientific method will have on philosophic practice: "Are we ready to take toward our social, political and religious values the same experimental attitude, subjecting them in principle to the same tests of international scrutiny and criticism, which we

---

[4] Ibid., 474–76.
[5] Addison Webster Moore, "Opportunity of Philosophy," 117–18, 127–28.

demand in our scientific procedure?" This shift, Moore writes, is nothing less than "the democratization of values." This transformation of philosophy, moreover, is not specific to one school or another. Rather, it requires "an idealism that is more than a sanctuary, a realism whose reals are more than mathematical and logical entities, and a pragmatism whose practice is not confined to 'bread and butter needs.'" All that is necessary to take part in this great opportunity to transform philosophy is a commitment to developing a science of values. Especially in the midst of the war, Moore thought that this commitment would be strong. As he writes, "what could be more edifying than the prospect of substituting reason for shrapnel as the method of dealing with the problems involved in the formation and in the conflicts of our human values and purposes?"[6]

The Committee on Discussion that had been set up at the 1916 meeting and chaired by the immediate past-president, Lovejoy, also offered its final report at this meeting.[7] In this report, the committee recommended further measures to finally make the discussion sessions successful. In a kind of a preamble, the committee discussed what it took to be three "characteristic objects" of the APA. The first was "to promote what may be called philosophical scholarship—the study of the history of speculative thought and its interaction with other phases of human culture." The committee granted that this historical work had been underrepresented at recent meetings. The second aim of the APA was to improve teaching. "Since the membership of the Association consists in the main of teachers in colleges and universities," the report notes, "it falls within the natural province of the society to consider from time to time the pedagogical aspects of the subject—to discuss methods of effectively teaching philosophy . . ." The committee's interest in improving instruction was modest, however; and the report continues that "this object should be kept decidedly subordinate to the other two . . ." The final aim of the APA, and in the committee's eyes the most important, was to improve research: "The Association exists chiefly for the promotion of philosophical inquiry. Its principal purpose is to assist towards the attainment of a progressively better understanding of philosophical problems themselves, by means, primarily, of a better understanding by philosophers of the results of one another's reflections" (PR 27:166).

The committee then indicates that, for "fruitful and cumulative inquiry," there were three requirements. The first was that "fresh ideas shall actually be furnished through the spontaneous and original activity of individual

---

[6] Ibid., 132–33; cf. JP 15:179–80.

[7] The committee consisted of Lovejoy (chair), Bakewell, Boodin, Calkins, Creighton, Drake, Montague, Moore, Perry, Sabine, Sheldon, Spaulding, and Guy Allan Tawney. Lovejoy had earlier offered a preview of the plan (JP 14:719–20).

minds . . ." This requirement the committee saw as a matter of individual effort. The second and third requirements of fruitful philosophical inquiry—"that these ideas shall be rigorously tested . . . [and] . . . that, in so far as they emerge successfully from their testing, they shall be developed, correlated, and articulated with other and older insights"—were understood to be "social processes," possible only if there is "the convergence of many competent and instructed minds . . ." Therefore, the committee continues, "one of the principal functions of this society is to bring about a genuine meeting of minds upon actually *identical* points of the logical universe, or to come as near to that result as is possible; in other words, to promote the coherent, methodical, mutually intelligible, and constructive discussion of common problems." To help this kind of discussion take place, the committee suggests that, as part of the annual program,

> one or more of the regular sessions of each meeting should continue to be devoted to the discussion of topics selected and announced beforehand—and as long beforehand as is practicable; that leaders should also be chosen in advance, and as nearly a year in advance as may be; and that every effort should be made both to bring as many minds as possible to convergence upon the same specific questions, and also to bring about a direct and unequivocal *joining of issues* in the discussion of those questions (PR 27:166–68).

It was thus the position of the committee that past failures of the discussion sessions did not reflect a problem with the idea of symposia but rather were the result of inadequate planning and execution.

The committee then moved on to offer its plan for organizing future discussion sessions, a plan which, it believed, "should in any case . . . be given a trial for a period of two years." The prearranged discussion was to occupy at least one session per meeting (the executive committee would be empowered to add a second session, or to carry the topic over to the next meeting, if it were deemed necessary). The executive committee was to pick the topic for the next meeting; but, beginning in 1918, the members at the meeting would choose the topic for upcoming meetings from a list offered by the executive committee (based upon members' suggestions). As part of the annual meeting's business, the incoming executive committee was to choose one member to organize the next meeting's discussion. This individual would be empowered to determine the leaders of the discussion by selecting several other members of the association, taking care "that different angles of approach to the problem under discussion be represented." Over the ensuing year, these leaders were to plan the upcoming discussion—meeting at least once during the course of the year at the APA's expense—giving "special consideration" to such matters as: the question of definitions and the value of the common usage of terms, formulating principles and presuppositions of agreement and indicating the disagreements that are crucial "for the settlement" of the main issue, and delineating the several theses to be maintained. These leaders were then to notify the membership about these developments by mid-July (PR 27:168–69).

At this point, the broader preparation for the discussion session could begin. This planning would include a number of activities. First, "[a]ll members, including the leaders, shall be invited to publish, in philosophical journals or in some other manner, papers on the subject to be discussed, or to send to the Secretary abstracts of arguments, the substance of which shall be communicated by him to the membership in advance of the annual meeting." Second, "[t]eachers and students of philosophy throughout the country shall be asked each year to give some special attention, in their courses or discussion clubs, during the fall term, to the subject proposed for the discussion at the ensuing meeting of the Association." Third, "[a]ll members of the Association shall be invited by the Secretary to contribute papers to the discussion at the annual meeting." Further, a bibliography of relevant materials was to be published by the leaders no later than the beginning of September and the program for the meeting issued no later than mid-December. This report was challenged during "interesting and lively discussion," and the preamble was eventually withdrawn. Despite his prior dissent, Creighton suggested that the upcoming discussion at the APA's 1918 meeting be organized in accordance with the report; and, after some further discussion, the report was adopted (PR 27:169–71).[8]

The topic selected by the executive committee for the 1918 discussion session was "Mechanism *versus* Vitalism," and the discussion was led by R. F. Alfred Hoernlé, Walter T. Marvin, Lawrence J. Henderson, H. S. Jennings, and H. C. Warren. (The first two were philosophers; the others represented, in order, physics and chemistry, biology, and psychology.) The various procedures for preparation and publicity were more-or-less followed, in spite of the fact that the entire system of American higher education was virtually nationalized in the fall of 1918 and the Armistice came only six weeks before the meeting.[9] First, Hoernlé was chosen as organizer of the session. He presided over a two-day meeting of the principals in June at Harvard, where they spent five or six hours each day "planning the general scope of the discussion and outlining the arguments" that each was to present at the meeting. In August, they published an eight-point "common *basis of reference*" that they hoped would "exhibit the place of 'mechanistic' concepts in the existing system of the Natural Sciences, and thus

---

[8] Cf. Pitts, "Profession of Philosophy," 145–48.
[9] For a consideration of these war matters, see chapter 11.

. . . define the general theoretical context within which the problem of the nature and status of 'life,' or rather of living beings, arises, and to which all attempts at a solution must be relevant." At the same time, they published their abstracts. Hoernlé, for example, maintained that the overall setup of the session would offer "a good opening for discussing how far, and in what sense, a *unified* theory of the universe is possible," without falling victim to either pure mechanism or "absolute discontinuities." He also announced that he would argue "for the 'autonomy of life,' *i.e.*, of the characteristic concepts which biology needs in order to give an adequate theory of the living as distinct from the non-living" and "for mechanical and biological concepts as complementary and 'cumulative,' not as mutually exclusive" (JP 15:459, 467). In September, the committee published a collective bibliography of seventy-six items on mechanism versus vitalism (JP 15:550–53). Irwin Edman reports that the first session began with vitalism being "discredited at the hands of purely neutral scientific inquirers offering evidence of an unequivocal nature from their special fields." Marvin followed with a strong attack on vitalism as bearing "all the earmarks of that animism and magic whose painful slow obliteration has been synchronous with human progress." He further noted that "[b]iological mechanism is part of the creed of science." For his own part, Hoernlé offered a modest defense of vitalism, maintaining "the philosophical legitimacy of teleological categories in a world discoverably mechanistic," and argued for "the autonomy of teleological categories in biology . . ." Edman reports that there was displeasure with the mostly one-sided presentations. One of the attendees, for example, protested, "The symposium had been heralded as a convocation on mechanism and vitalism," but "it had turned out to be a paean of unanimity for mechanism." When the philosophers re-gathered for the second session, vitalism seems to have been treated more favorably; the whole discussion ended, however, with a general sense of dissatisfaction (JP 16:129–31).[10]

The APA secretary, Harry Allen Overstreet, reports that at the 1918 meeting a series of potential topics were under consideration for the discussion planned for the APA's nineteenth meeting: "The Executive Committee presented for the consideration of the Association three discussion topics chosen from among those submitted to the Committee by the members of the Association: Contrasted Theories of Beauty; The Nature of Community; Contrasted Theories of Time." The membership present chose the middle one (PR 28:177, 181). The preparations for this

---

[10] A symposium at the WPA's nineteenth meeting in 1919 on "The Function of Philosophy in Social Reconstruction" will be considered in chapter 15.

symposium consisted in the early selection of six leaders and the publication by five of them of either an abstract or the paper itself just before the APA met in December 1919. Those chosen to lead the discussion were: Morris Raphael Cohen, Mary Parker Follett, Harold J. Laski, Roscoe Pound, James Hayden Tufts, and Wilbur Marshall Urban.

The first of the abstracts was by Urban, for his paper "The Nature of the Community, A Defense of Philosophic Orthodoxy." In this piece, he introduced the discussion by interpreting "the 'traditional and orthodox' conceptions of community and state . . ." His focus was upon two conceptions of the state: the organic and the monistic. The former has the advantages of indicating to us that the community is not "an aggregate, conscious construction" and of offering a ground for group values. The monistic theory of the state, on the other hand, offers the best means of understanding the relationship between the state and the community. "The main contention" of his paper, however, is that "social and political formulas are by their very nature more than descriptions of historical fact. As expressions of the meaning of the social order, the traditional and orthodox formulas still represent the *sensus communis* in it deepest moments and highest reaches." The second abstract was by Follett. Relying upon recent biological and psychological research, she maintains that "community, the essential life process, is the activity of integrating . . . a genuine inter-weaving where each individual has its full part in the whole a-making." In her view, community "creates personality, purpose, will"; and with these "appear freedom and law." She criticizes both idealists and pluralists for putting "the individual outside the process: the idealists when they would have us 'choose' the universal community, the political pluralists when they would have us 'choose' the 'nearest' group." For Follett, on the contrary, "the community process . . . is continually producing both society and the individual" (JP 16:713–16).

Laski, a political scientist, chose as his topic "The Pluralistic State." His abstract was divided into five points. The first was that philosophers, as distinct from political scientists, have overemphasized "rather the form than the substance of the state"; and, as a result, philosophers have overemphasized the purpose of a state "as distinct from the fulfillment of purpose." His second point was that philosophers thus resemble lawyers. Third, he notes that "a state in which sovereignty is single is morally inadequate and administratively inefficient" because "it depends upon an intellectualistic view of the state which is not borne out by the facts . . . [and] . . . It does not see that the rules of administration are dependent upon certain psychological factors." Fourth, "[t]he pluralistic state is an attempt to remedy these defects by substituting coordination for a hierarchical structure." Laski believes, for example, that the way in which various "functional and territorial" interests work together suggests "the necessarily federal character of all government." Finally, he maintains that liberty is "unattainable in a monistic state upon the present administrative scale except for a small governing class." In the abstract of his paper, "The Community and Economic Groups," Tufts points to "two opposing tendencies at work." The first is the growing control of economic power "over all living conditions" that is in the eyes of some "rendering political power obsolescent." He points specifically to both capitalist groups and labor unions as examples of this power. The second tendency which he considers is a series of recent decisions from courts and legislatures that restrict the actions of these two centers of economic power. Tufts then points to the advantages and disadvantages of both tendencies. With regard to the former, he points to its great flexibility, "since it is unhampered by precedents or constitutions," and to "its devotion to special group interests, often to the ignoring of general interests . . ." With regard to the latter, he points to the political and legal system's inclination "toward general interests, toward equality and responsibility" and its difficulties "with new issues . . ." (JP 16:717–19).

Cohen published his full paper, entitled "Communal Ghosts and Other Perils in Social Philosophy." Among other themes, he considers the danger that "becoming absorbed in the passionate social problems of the day, we may forget philosophy altogether and become partizan journalists, propagandists, economists, reformists or politicians—anything but philosophers." While he admits to appreciating the value of respecting "competent" social thinkers, he maintains that philosophy's function is distinct: "pure philosophy, the true love and fearless pursuit of fundamental truth for its own sake, is in itself one of the greatest blessings of human life, and, therefore, never to be entirely subordinated to the solution of social problems . . ." He further maintains that "philosophy is in a sense more important than the solution of social problems," and that it can "best aid those actually engaged in the more concrete human problems by vigorously maintaining just that spirit of impartiality and aloofness so frequently and thoughtlessly condemned by those whose business it is to think." Philosophers have no particular training or expertise to take on the specific social problems with which society is struggling; their focus should be elsewhere. He continues:

> Philosophy, by detaching men from current prejudices or the idols of the tribe and the forum, tends to give men a truly liberal attitude to current controversies; but that only makes the genuine philosopher humbly aware of his insufficiency for a task which the community has assigned to others . . . there generally is a practical conflict between the interests of the moment and the more permanent interests of human life, and that those engaged in fighting the issues of the day are apt to overlook the more permanent interests which give meaning and purport to these temporary conflicts.

Adopting a series of medical metaphors, Cohen notes that while "a modern critical philosophy can no longer pretend to be in possession of elixirs for eternal life or panaceas for all human ills, it may still usefully function as a general antiseptic or disinfectant of intellectual life." In this spirit, it remains ever necessary "to warn the social philosopher that in trying to save the world he may lose that which has been one of the most valuable contributions of philosophy to human culture, the critical spirit." As a consequence, he concludes, "the philosopher should not undertake to cure the ills of humanity before he has learned to disinfect himself and his instruments."[11]

When the APA eventually gathered in late December 1919 in Ithaca, perhaps because of concerns about illness[12] or because of the weather, Laski, Pound, and Tufts were not in attendance. In her commentary on the meeting, Helen Huss Parkhurst notes that in general for many members "zero weather and remoteness of place proved insuperable barriers." She continues, "The theme that commanded principle attention was the nature of the community"; and she notes that, since three of the discussants failed to appear, "some at least of the challenges of Miss Follett, Professor Urban, and Professor Cohen were safe from counter-challenge, and the time left over was used for a more extensive discussion from the floor than would otherwise have been possible" (JP 17:94, 96–98). While Parkhurst is quite possibly right that the interactions that occurred at the 1919 meeting were a success on their own terms, the failure of half of the discussants to appear prevented a fully successful discussion session. Thus, it seems that in this particular instance, the attempt to hold an organized symposium failed not for organizational or philosophical reasons but for the more mundane reasons of climate and health.

Looking forward to 1920, the topic selected for the discussion session at the twentieth meeting was philosophy teaching: "The Executive Committee presented for the consideration of the Association four discussion topics chosen from among those submitted to the Committee by members of the Association: The Nature of the Self; Types of Idealism; Contrasted Theories of Beauty; Aims and Methods in Teaching Philosophy. It was moved and carried that the topic for the ensuing year be: Aims and Methods in Teaching Philosophy" (PR 29:157). By the time that the discussion took place in December, however, the chosen topic had somehow been transformed into: "The role of the philosopher in modern life, with reference both to teaching and to research." This symposium included five speakers, whose abstracts were published in advance. The firstspeaker was

---

[11] Cohen, "Communal Ghosts," 673–75. The final scheduled participant, Roscoe Pound, did not offer an abstract.

[12] The 'Spanish flu' epidemic killed over 500,000 Americans, and perhaps fifty million worldwide, during 1918–19. Cf. Crosby, *America's Forgotten Pandemic*; and Kolata, *Flu*.

Richard C. Cabot, a social ethicist, whose sketchy remarks suggested the importance of increased seriousness both on the part of instructor and students. He indicated, for example, that it is "difficult but necessary to get students to *practise* the task of conceiving new ideas or arranging old ones as they would practise a musical instrument." The second speaker, Thomas Reed Powell, a law professor, urged philosophers to consider the values of interdisciplinary approaches for students. Philosophers, he thought, could help students of the law uncover and trace previously unquestioned assumptions. Conversely, philosophy students could gain as well from the study of law understood as "a series of human judgments." He continued, "A study of authoritative human judgments is a study of ethical ideals or of practical compromises that are matters of fact and not merely of aspiration." The third speaker, John Moffatt Mecklin, now at Dartmouth,[13] maintained that "what men want is not so much a reasoned interpretation of the universe as light upon immediate and pressing social issues." As a result, he suggested the importance of attempting to develop scientific method and "a sense of social responsibility" in students, concentrating upon "phases of the social question" and discounting the role of philosopher as "traditional system-builder." The fourth speaker was James Bissett Pratt, whose position was that the philosopher is a specialist in four areas— psychology, ethics, logic, and metaphysics—and that as such the philosopher has little to offer to the discussion of public affairs. In addition, for him, the philosopher

> should refrain from spending more than a little of his time on practical issues for still another reason, namely because he has other things of importance to do; and if he devotes himself largely to solving the world's practical difficulties he will perforce neglect some of his more special duties and will bring pure philosophy into disrepute. The practical applications of philosophy are merely its by-product. The chief function of the philosopher consists in championing and keeping alive the spiritual life of man.

The final speaker, Frederick J. E. Woodbridge, emphasized the critical aspects of philosophy; and, while recognizing the difficulties inherent in addressing social questions, he thought that "[p]hilosophers can do much to promote the freedom of the mind" both inside the classroom and out. The latter activities, however, require "writing of a different sort from that which now largely prevails among our philosophers." Philosophers were writing for other philosophers, he noted, "with the result that they are not widely read and have little influence . . . to be socially effective philosophers must write for society, about the things which interest society, and in a language society can understand" (JP 17:688–92).

---

[13] Mecklin's dismissal from Lafayette in 1913 was discussed in chapter 5.

This discussion session—although wide-ranging and at times impassioned—does not seem to have been very successful either. In her subsequent report on the meeting, Parkhurst found this discussion session to have been upsetting, writing that "when disagreement extends to something so fundamental as the very constitution and aims of philosophy itself . . . there is cause for actual alarm." The chief offender seems to have been Durant Drake, to whom she attributes the view that "while the contemplation of ideas is justifiable in that it satisfies a harmless human impulse, it is valuable only as a genteel substitute for chess—the really important thing, the one valuable thing, being the solution of social problems." Parkhurst indicates that this "anti-intellectualistic" analysis, that she also attributes to others besides Drake, found little or no support among the panelists. For example, Pratt rejected the participation of philosophy in "political propaganda"; and Mecklin emphasized that philosophy was not social reform but "untrammelled theorizing activity . . ." At some point in this lively discussion, Parkhurst reports that "Professor Woodbridge disturbed the serenity of those engaged upon the definition and praise of the philosopher by his protest that it was pitiful indeed if at this our twentieth celebration we could do nothing more useful or more self-respecting than to ask what it is to be a philosopher." This protest apparently sent the discussion off in another direction: a consideration of *historical* research and teaching the *history* of philosophy. Even here, however, Parkhurst could report no consensus; and, while she was willing to grant that disagreements between idealism and realism, or between materialism and vitalism, are "probably advantageous for the search for truth," she continues "that on such a question as the significance of historical research in philosophy for philosophy itself there should be sharply opposed opinion, is quite another matter." Rather that paying less attention to the history of philosophy, she maintained that recent developments in thought—especially those of an evolutionary sort—suggest the importance of paying more. "More than any previous age of human life," she writes, "this is an historical age" (JP 18:153–56).[14]

Interest in continuing the discussion sessions was clearly decreasing. Looking forward to 1921, the APA's secretary, A. H. Jones, writes: "The

---

[14] Drake later clarified the position he expressed at the APA's 1920 meeting as follows: "all philosophy can be divided into two parts, the one containing those problems that have appreciable practical bearings, the other containing those whose solution would make no or slight difference to practise. That there are problems of this latter class I am convinced; among them I place the epistemological problem . . . the devotion to such impractical problems I called 'play,' in the broad sense of the term. That is, it is an activity that exists not as a means to something else, but for its own sake. It is its own excuse for being, like the greater part of our artistic activity, our games and sports, and much of what we call 'culture.'

following topics for discussion at the next meeting were presented for consideration: The Place of Feeling in the Life of Reason; The Philosophical Basis of Aesthetic Criticism; Critical Realism; The Relation of Logic (1) to Philosophy and (2) to Psychology; Types of Idealism; The Logic of Philosophy, or what Form of Comprehensibility should Philosophy Aim At?" Perhaps as a result of the diversity of suggested topics, or as a consequence of greater than usual dissatisfaction with what had just occurred at the 1920 meeting, any decision about the upcoming meeting was postponed. "The Executive Committee recommended that the program for the next meeting be selected by the incoming Executive Committee on the basis of such expression of opinion as may be offered at the present meeting of the Association, or subsequently obtained by the Committee." The membership recommended further "that the Executive Committee consider holding meetings of longer duration with a view to allowing longer and freer discussion of papers, and freer arrangements. It was moved and voted that the recommendations, as amended, be adopted" (PR 30:195). Perhaps as a result of these uncertainties, however, the 1921 meeting had no discussion session.

At the joint meeting of the APA and the WPA, in New York City in December 1922, John Dewey offered the initial Paul Carus Lectures.[15] These three lectures, one each day of the meeting, overshadowed all the other events; and the discussion session reappeared in a greatly reduced form. In his account of the meeting, Horace L. Friess writes: "On the last day of the conference there were two discussion meetings held simultaneously, the first devoted to some problems of the mind-body relation, and the second to a miscellaneous group of topics" (JP 20:74). The latter— comprised of four papers that dealt with, *seriatim*, poetics, American law, the rationality of democracy, and epistemology—was obviously not really a 'discussion session.' The former session was unified around the theme of

---

Metaphysics is not only a 'genteel' substitute for chess, it is a glorious, exhilarating substitute . . . it is yet too soon in the world's history for us to dally too exclusively with play. There are millions of men and women suffering or dying for lack of the prevalence of reason in the ordering of human life. The student of philosophy is in a position to help. He can formulate and teach insights that will have their part in bringing order out of confusion, in replacing injustice and cruelty by justice and happiness. It is by no means calling the philosopher aside from his historic function to ask him to consider these more practically urgent problems. On the contrary, the historic philosophers have often been of very great service in this way . . . My plea [at the meeting] was that we spare more time from the discussion of these fascinating and time-honored problems for the investigation of our actual human interests, and the means to their realization . . . The rational ordering of human life on earth is a task that needs the economist, the statesman, the sociologist, and a hundred others; but it need the philosopher too" ("Philosophy as Work and Play," 442–44).

[15] The establishment of the Carus Lecture series will be discussed in chapter 14.

mind and body; but it does not seem to have had any of the recommended preparations, and it ran concurrently with the other session. Looking ahead to 1923, the proceedings announce that: "A motion to instruct the Executive Committee to arrange a discussion for the next meeting being defeated, it was voted that the Executive Committee arrange the program for the next meeting and decide where it shall be held" (PR 32:199); but at neither the 1923 meeting nor the 1924 meeting was there a discussion session. In 1925, there was a symposium on the topic of "Time." The speakers were Alfred North Whitehead, William Pepperell Montague, and Wilmon Henry Sheldon. In his report on the meeting, John Herman Randall, Jr., notes that "the symposium on Time, so eagerly looked forward to, proved on retrospect somewhat disappointing. It was not a symposium, nor was there any real discussion . . ." He held the speakers largely responsible: Whitehead's paper "had to be curtailed through lack of time; and its ideas proved too novel to awaken any response"; Montague offered "a wealth of metaphor and imagery that placed him in another realm from his predecessor, and fairly startled his audience"; and Sheldon "endeavored to puncture by the hard-headed empiricism of the nominalist a number of accepted notions making of time a mysterious entity." Randall concludes his remarks with the disappointed admission that "the members dispersed without any measurable clarification of ideas . . ." (JP 23:45–46).

After twenty-five years of meetings, and endless rounds of tinkering, the hope that these highly organized symposia would bring philosophical progress had vanished. Many in the APA and the WPA had hoped that, through focused and cooperative examinations of narrowly defined topics, a way would be found to convert philosophy into a progressive science like the many others that had developed in the emerging university context. These hopes, however, had not materialized. The carefully constructed discussion machinery proved unworkable or unproductive, and no consensus ever developed about how to repair it. Further, doubts continued in many minds, not just philosophers', about the potential mission of this new philosophy profession. William Adams Brown, for example, writes in 1921 that "to many serious men of science the group of studies with which the philosophical department of our universities is concerned is regarded as a luxury rather than as a necessity, legitimate for those who have the time to give to such things but not worthy any longer of the structural place in the organism of university study which in their introductory lectures as to the nature of philosophy all philosophers with one accord claim for it."[16] These doubts had been made worse by the events surrounding the war. It is to a consideration of these developments that we now turn.

---

[16] William Adams Brown, "Future of Philosophy," 673; cf. Daniel J. Wilson, "Professionalization," 54–55.

G. STANLEY HALL

11
World War I and American Academic Life

The war that began in Europe in late summer 1914, and that eventually spread around the world, resulted in the deaths of millions of people and the destruction of the lives of millions more. While the decades that have passed since the Armistice have left many important questions unanswered, I intend to offer here no overall interpretation of the causes, results, or meaning of World War I. Rather than focusing on such issues as British propaganda, German tactics, the American munitions lobby, or other matters of national or international importance, in the next few chapters I will consider the relatively less important question of what the war meant to the development of American philosophy and the philosophical associations. In the context of the issues of global import that the fighting unleashed, my concern with matters academic and philosophic may seem misguided; and I make no claims about its relative importance. Still, if our goal is to understand the early development of the APA, events related to the war must be considered.

While the Great War that destroyed Europe between 1914 and 1918 was in hindsight not unexplainable, it was certainly not expected, at least by American academics. To these individuals, many of whom had traveled and studied there, Europe represented the height of culture and provided the model of progress for the twentieth century. In May 1919, APA president Hartley Burr Alexander published a paper, "Wrath and Ruth," that he had read six months earlier at the eighteenth meeting of the APA. In this paper he asks "what philosopher, in the fall of 1918, can write of human nature and achievement as he would have written in the spring of 1914?" He continues:

> The world has changed since 1914; the Titanism in human nature which we who call ourselves the civilized had deemed to lie deeper than Orcus has made

WORLD WAR I TIMELINE

1914

9-10 April	**The WPA meets in Chicago**
19 April	Death of Charles Sanders Peirce
28 June	Assassination of Archduke Franz Ferdinand in Sarajevo, Bosnia
29 July	War begins
4 August	Germany invades Belgium
19 August	Woodrow Wilson: "impartial in thought as well as in action"
23 August	Germany destroys Louvain
5–9 September	First Battle of the Marne
2 November	Great Britain declares a war zone in North Sea
28–30 December	**The WPA and the APA meet jointly in Chicago**

1915

18 February	Germany declares submarine war zone around Great Britain
7 May	Sinking of the *Lusitania*: 1,200 die (128 Americans)
28–30 December	**The APA meets in Philadelphia**

1916

20 Feb.–20 Oct.	Battle of Verdun
21–22 April	**The WPA meets in St. Louis**
14 September	Death of Josiah Royce
16 December	Death of Hugo Münsterberg
27–28 December	**The APA meets in New York City**

1917

22 January	Woodrow Wilson: "peace without victory"
1 February	Germany returns to unrestricted submarine warfare
11–15 March	Russian revolution; provisional government
6–7 April	**The WPA meets in Ann Arbor**
6 April	US declares war on Germany
26 June	American troops reach France—175,000 by the end of the year
7 November	October Revolution in Russia
7 December	US declares war on Austria-Hungary
15 December	Central Powers conclude armistice with Russia
27–28 December	**The APA meets in Princeton**

WORLD WAR I TIMELINE (CONT'D.)

1918

8 January	Woodrow Wilson: Fourteen Points
3 March	German-Russian Treaty of Brest-Litovsk
21 March	German offensive on Western Front
29–30 March	**The WPA meets in Evanston**
18 July–6 August	Second Battle of the Marne
August to mid-1919	Influenza pandemic—25–50 million die worldwide
1 October	Nationalized system of higher education
11 November	Armistice—2,000,000 American soldiers in Europe
27–28 December	**The APA meets in Cambridge, MA**

1919

18–19 April	**The WPA mets in Iowa City**
28 June	Treaty of Versailles signed

---

the lands to tremble and has lighted cities with lurid flame; fanes are shattered and the old images are overthrown . . . the ideals of 1914 seem shot through with the bizarre, the puerile, the presumptuous. Then we believed, with all our ostensible souls, in human self-sufficiency; we believed in hard reason and practical realities, in the panacean powers of science and in the substantial good of properties acquired; we believed, gaily, inflatedly, in our superiority over all that was humanly past and in our ability to insure progress through the future . . .

For Alexander, and many others, those beliefs were viable no longer. In spite of humanity's expectations and hopes, disaster came in the summer of 1914. In the words of Vernon Louis Parrington, "the war intervened and the green fields shriveled in an afternoon."[1]

In our attempt to understand the relationship between the war and American philosophy, it will be perhaps a good starting point for us to consider the intellectual mood of American higher education in the years before the United States entered the war. One good indication of this mood would be to consider the public pronouncements made about the war by some of the university presidents whom we have encountered previously in this study. What were the positions of such individuals in the

---

[1] Alexander, "Wrath and Ruth," 253; Parrington, *Main Currents in American Thought*, 3:412.

years between the assassinations in Sarajevo on 28 August 1914 and the entry of the United States on 6 April 1917? One such figure, Nicholas Murray Butler, the philosopher and president of Columbia, writes in 1915 of the incongruity of this European war. "The peoples who are engaged in this titanic struggle are not untamed barbarians or wild Indians of the virgin forest," he notes. "They are the best-trained and most highly educated peoples in the world. They have had every advantage that schools and universities can offer, and they have been associated for generations with literature and science and art and everything that is fine and splendid in what we call civilization." His interpretation was that the war demonstrated that the civilizing roots of culture did not reach deeply into the marrow of humanity. Rather, "under this thin veneer of civilization the elementary human passions of jealousy, envy, hatred, and malice were so lightly confined that at the touch of a magic spring they burst forth to overwhelm everything that seems to make life worth living."[2] The events of the years before had been enough to release these passions, and the future possibilities for the advancement of humankind had been thrown into doubt.

The former president of Harvard, Charles William Eliot, seems to have had a more specific interpretation of the meaning of the European War. In early 1915, he published a volume entitled *The Road toward Peace* that, as its title suggests, was a survey of what had gone wrong and an indication of what was needed to bring the world out of the present calamity. He writes that "the probable causes of the sudden lapse of the most civilized parts of Europe into worse than primitive savagery" are "secret diplomacy" and "autocratic national executives." He also includes imperialism as one of "the underlying causes of the horrible catastrophe the American people are now watching from afar," and further he condemns the militarism that offers executives "immense armaments and drilled armies held ready in the leash." What is most pronounced in his account of the war, however, is his belief that, despite the tidal-wave of propaganda from all the belligerents, the guilt lay demonstrably on one side. Which side can be determined from the following representative passage from his pen: "Should Germany and Austria-Hungary succeed in their present undertakings, the civilized nations would be obliged to bear continuously, and to an ever-increasing amount, the burdens of great armaments, and would live in constant fear of sudden invasion . . ." As a result, Eliot continues, the American people "are not, and cannot be, neutral or indifferent as to the ultimate outcome of this titanic struggle. It already seems to them that England, France, and Russia are fighting for freedom and civilization."[3]

---

[2] Butler, *World in Ferment*, 89–90.
[3] Eliot, *Road toward Peace*, 60, 63, 66–67, 69.

Thus, while Eliot is willing to grant that the war is "the most horrible calamity that has ever befallen the human race, and the most crucial trial to which civilization has been exposed," he is quick to point to the fact that "the gigantic struggle of these times [is] between the forces which make for liberty and righteousness and those which make for the subjection of the individual man, the exaltation of the state, and the enthronement of physical force by a ruthless collective will. It threatens a sweeping betrayal of the best hopes of mankind." The reestablishment of peace thus requires both the defeat of the Central Powers and a fundamental change in the relations among states. He writes that "thoughtful Americans can see but one possible issue of the struggle, whether it be long or short, namely, the defeat of Germany and Austria-Hungary in their present undertakings, and the abandonment by both peoples of the doctrine that their salvation depends on militarism and the maintenance of autocratic executives entrusted with the power and the means to make sudden war." Eliot is careful to point out that the enemies of peace are not the people of the Central Powers, especially the Germans, but rather the political system that controls them. "American sympathies are with the German people in their sufferings and losses," he notes, "but not with their rulers, or with the military class, or with the professors and men of letters who have been teaching for more than a generation that Might makes Right." Eliot continues that Americans "believe that Germany will be freer, happier, and greater than ever, when once she has got rid of the monstrous Bismarck policies and the Emperor's archaic conception of his function, and has enjoyed twenty years of real peace." Once liberated from Prussian hands, Germany would rejoin the community of progressive nations. Furthermore, with the end of Prussian control could come real liberty for the German people, because this new freedom would overcome the "efficiency which takes hold of every child in Germany at birth, and follows every youth and every man and woman through life until death . . . which has prevented the last two generations of Germans from knowing anything about liberty."[4]

In December 1915, another university president, Granville Stanley Hall of Clark, spoke to a conference on his campus about the problems and lessons of the war. He stressed American neutrality—"real neutrality"— and sought to understand what could be learned if the war were approached as an educational experience. His spirit of neutrality toward Germany enabled him to offer praise for German education, business and municipal organization, and thinkers and writers; but this spirit of neutrality did not go much further. Hall writes that "now that she [Germany] has elected to grasp the sword to enlarge her borders and increase her influ-

---

[4] Ibid., 151–52, 92–93, 95–96, 191.

ence by force, she seems in a sense turning her back upon the spiritual kingdom and reversing the great choice that Jesus made between material and political rule, and that of the spirit of truth . . ." He further remarked that there were aspects of the German philosophical tradition that must be considered in our attempts to understand Germany's military actions:

> Kant made will the very apex of the human soul. According to his pragmatism, reason can never prove or disprove even such things as God, soul, freedom, or immortality. Nevertheless, they are truer than anything else because as postulates they work best. Man attains his highest end by acting as if they were true. Duty Kant made the sublimest word in the whole vocabulary. It must be done in the face of every natural inclination, in order to be pure, so that the moral rigorism of the categorical imperative filtered down through Schiller and many others into the folk-consciousness as a potent influence for culture, both expressing and moulding the national consciousness. Fichte, too, fired the German soul with the idea of duty, while Schopenhauer even identified will with the force and energy of the natural world . . .

While Hall thus casts blame across a large portion of the German philosophical tradition, the focus of his comments was on Nietzsche, whom he considered to be the thinker underlying current German policies. For him, Nietzsche's message ran as follows: "Man is a bridge . . . It is vicious to serve the meanest, the humblest. All effort must be focussed on the *elite*, so that we shall in the end develop a species as much superior to modern man as he is to the troglodytes . . . as Germany is superior to other races, she has responsibility for the higher development of other countries . . ." If this is how we are to understand the spirit of modern Germany—and Hall thought that it was—then understanding of the outbreak and conduct of the war could not be difficult.[5]

As our final presidential source, we can consider Charles Franklin Thwing, the historian of education and president of Western Reserve, who writes in October 1915 that "[t]he sympathy of at least nineteen-twentieths of all academic people is with the Allies. The most common remark made about Germany is that she is obsessed. The feeling toward her is rather one of pity than of anger, and rather one of anger than of hatred." With regard to philosophy in particular, he notes, "One finds it hard to accept the fact that the nation of Kant has so far forgotten herself as to be at war with the lands in which the influence of Kant has been so mighty." Still, Thwing continues that Fichte "has in his idealistic and egoistic philosophy laid a very deep and almost forgotten cause of the present obses-

---

5 Hall, foreword to *Problems and Lessons of the War*, xxiv, xi, xiv–xvii; cf. "Practical Relations," 12, 14.

sion," and that Schopenhauer, "in presenting the world as will, has had a formative and evilly inspiring force far greater than is commonly recognised in either England or the United States."[6] Thus, we find in the ideas of such academic figures as Butler, Eliot, Hall, and Thwing a general sense of American academic opinion in the years before the United States joined the war. They suggest to us a social mood that contains a tilt toward Great Britain and her Allies and away from Germany and Austria-Hungary. Germany was especially suspect because of its perceived arrogance and its conduct of the war; and German philosophy, or at least the general play of German ideas, was felt to be somehow implicated in Germany's actions.

While this sampling of university presidents cannot fully represent the ideas of all American intellectuals, it seems to have been representative of the majority. While ambiguity and doubts persisted, the war against the Central Powers was seen to be a necessary one and one that increasingly required American participation. Immediately after the United States entered the war in April of 1917, whatever resistance might have existed among the academics dissolved (or at least disappeared from view). Speaking of the actions of those who opposed American participation in the war, Butler declared in June: "What had been folly was now treason."[7] We can consider, as an example of this pro-war enthusiasm, a small volume entitled *Handbook of the War for Public Speakers*, edited in 1917 by Albert Bushnell Hart, the Harvard historian, and Arthur Oncken Lovejoy, the philosopher at Hopkins and immediate past-president of the APA, for the private patriotic organization, the National Security League. Hart and Lovejoy saw the purpose of this volume to be one "of informing the understanding, of awakening the moral vision and the moral passion, of the entire people, concerning the cause for which they fight." In this regard, it was necessary "to bring to the mind of every honest and loyal citizen the momentousness of the present crisis; to make him or her understand what deep concerns of humanity are at stake; to bring all to feel that

---

[6] Thwing, "Effect of the European War," 79–80, 83; cf. *American Colleges and Universities*, 180–81. Cf. Carol S. Gruber: "Pro-Ally sentiment among professors was comprised of two complementary elements: an identification of American interests—political, economic, cultural, and strategic—with those of Great Britain and a view of Germany as the aggressor nation, whose political system and world political ambitions represented a threat to those interests and to world peace . . . From the private correspondence and the publicisitic and scholarly writings of professors, a picture emerges of Germany, bent on challenging British naval, commercial, and colonial supremacy, seizing the opportunity presented by the 1914 diplomatic crisis to do so, and engaging in outlaw tactics under dubious justifications of 'might makes right' and military necessity" (*Mars and Minerva*, 52, 56; cf. Curti, "The American Scholar in Three Wars," 247).

[7] Cited in Metzger, *Age of the University*, 499; cf. Angoff, "Higher Learning Goes to War," 179–83.

America has never entered upon a more just or more necessary war."
Among the points that they emphasized was the assertion that the war was
necessary because of "hostile acts against us committed by the German
Government"—submarine attacks, espionage, sabotage, and so forth—and
because of "the character of the future to which we would have to look forward, the kind of world in which we and those who come after us would
have to live, in the event of the victory of Germany and her allies." Hart
and Lovejoy further maintained that "every man, woman and child in the
country has his own part in the war . . . to obey the laws, to pay their taxes,
and to render to the country all the service that is within their power."[8]

There were many other examples of this pro-war enthusiasm emanat-
ing from academia; and, while there seems to have been nothing quite as
extraordinary as the "Call to the Civilized World" of ninety-three German
intellectuals,[9] there was much that was more enthusiastic than true. We

---

[8] Hart and Lovejoy, *Handbook of the War for Public Speakers*, 3, 28, 95. Cf. Daniel J.
Wilson: "the *Handbook* was little more than a propaganda tract . . . [it] . . . demonstrated the
enormity and finality of German guilt, extolled the idealism and righteousness of the Allied
cause, and exhorted America to 'subordinate thoroughness of discussion to celerity of
action'" (*Arthur O. Lovejoy*, 126; cf. William Roscoe Thayer, introduction to *Out of Their
Own Mouths*, Grattan, "Historians Cut Loose," 419–21).

[9] The "Call to the Civilized World" ["Aufruf an die Kulturwelt"] of 4 October 1914 was
a statement signed by 93 German intellectuals—including Rudolf Eucken, Ernst Haeckel, Karl
Lamprecht, Max Planck, Alois Riehl, Wilhelm Röntgen, Wilhelm Windelband and Wilhelm
Wundt—in defense of German policies. In part, it read: "As representatives of German Science
and Art, we hereby protest to the civilized world, against the lies and calumnies with which
our enemies are endeavouring to stain the honour of Germany in her hard struggle for existence—a struggle which has been forced upon her . . . *It is not true* that Germany is guilty of
having caused this war . . . *It is not true* that we trespassed in neutral Belgium . . . *It is not true*
that the life and property of a single Belgian citizen was injured by our soldiers without the
bitterest self-defense having made it necessary . . . *It is not true* that our troops treated Louvain
brutally . . . *It is not true* that our warfare pays no respect to international laws. It knows no
undisciplined cruelty. But in the east, the earth is saturated with the blood of women and children unmercifully butchered by the wild Russian troops, and in the west, dumdum bullets
mutilate the breasts of our soldiers. Those who have allied themselves with Russians and
Serbians, and present such a shameful scene to the world as that of inciting Mongolians and
Negroes against the white race, have no right whatever to call themselves upholders of civilization . . . *It is not true* that the combat against our so-called militarism is not a combat
against our civilization, as our enemies hypothetically pretend it is . . . We cannot wrest the
poisonous weapon—the lie—out of the hands of our enemies. All we can do is to proclaim to
all the world, that our enemies are giving false witness against us . . ." (Lutz, *Fall of the German
Empire*, 1:74–75). For the German text, see: Böhme, *Aufrufe und Reden*, 47–49.

John Dewey offers the typical American academic response: "I doubt if anyone can
reread . . . the Address to the Civilized World, without being again overcome by those old
sensations of incredulity and amazement. Was it possible that men to whom we had been
trained to look up could lend their names, even in a moment of patriotic fervor, to such a far-
rago?" ("Our Educational Ideal in Wartime," 180; cf. Thwing, *American Colleges and
Universities*, 193–94; Gruber, *Mars and Minerva*, 66–69).

can consider, for example, a few of *The University of Chicago War Papers*, a series of eight pamphlets attacking Germany. Harry Pratt Judson, the university president, wrote the first of these. It was published in January 1918 with the title "The Threat of German World-Politics." This essay is clear in its hatred of Germany: "The German Empire as now organized and as now administered is an enemy of the world by reason, first, of its controlling forces; by reason, secondly, of the far-reaching, piratical aims of those forces; by reason, thirdly, of the methods by which the imperial government of Germany seeks to attain these ends." Judson concludes this essay as follows: "We are dealing, therefore, with a vast world-wide conspiracy which has for its end the subversion in the long run of the liberty of practically every free nation, and which means, if the conspiracy succeeds, the overthrow of the independence of the United States. In other words, we are engaged in a great battle for the liberty of all free countries." In the second of these *War Papers*, this militant spirit continues. The author, Albion Small of the sociology department, writes that "[n]ever in history has the moral principle at issue in a war been clearer than in the present struggle." He further notes:

> *The central, supreme, paramount issue of this war is whether civilization is to instal the principle of aggression as its highest law; whether for a defiant epoch morality is to be suspended; whether, during an era of the most cynical apostasy that the record of mankind will have registered, that nation is to be greatest which can mobilize the most terrific force and use it in the most savage way.*

The Central Powers, aggressive and amoral, have thus removed themselves from the community of civilized countries. "The world is divided today between a group of nations whose units have delivered themselves over to the dictation of an artificial, arbitrary, anti-moral, militaristically imposed code, according to which force is the arbiter of right," he continues, "and another group of nations driven by the instinct of self-preservation into championship of a morality which makes its appeal to justice as its standard . . ." The United States and the Allies, the latter group, were thus fully justified in their war effort.[10]

Of course, this pro-war enthusiasm on the part of American academics, or of Americans in general, is not the whole story. From the beginning of the conflict, the diverse attachments of Americans had led to divisions between those who favored an Allied victory and those whose sympathies lay with the Central Powers. Using as their backdrop the belief

---

[10] Judson, "Threat of German World-Politics," 4, 15; Small, "Americans and the World-Crisis," 3, 22, 4. There were similar series produced at Columbia, Illinois, North Carolina, Princeton, and Wisconsin (cf. Grattan, "Historians Cut Loose," 424).

that Americans were fundamentally a British people,[11] however, the former group focused upon the 'dangerous' divided loyalties of immigrants, who were derided by Theodore Roosevelt and others as 'hyphenated Americans' for maintaining some fondness for the countries of their birth. In particular, there were the German-Americans, whose loyalties to the *Vaterland* left them particularly vulnerable. As hostilities widened and lengthened, and the United States was finally drawn into the war, social fusion increased; and with it, a frenzy of patriotic excesses ensued, ranging from firings and arrests to eliminating German-language instruction and renaming foodstuffs.[12]

In academia, these same forces played themselves out. While the vast majority of American professors were not immigrants, a few of them were, including such philosophers as: James Edwin Creighton, Frederick J. E. Woodbridge, Roy Wood Sellars, and Albert Ross Hill (from Canada), Harry Norman Gardiner and Alexander Meiklejohn (from England), Hugo Münsterberg, Max Carl Otto, and Felix Adler (from Germany), Morris Raphael Cohen (from Russia), and John Elof Boodin (from Sweden). Except in the case of the German-born, however, there was little immigration-based trouble. The real problem was that many of the professors were—or at least had been—so deeply influenced by German academic life. Germany meant *Wissenschaft* and the *Universität*, some of the forces that had transformed the American educational system toward the end of the nineteenth century that we considered in chapter 2. Many of the American professors had taken a portion of their own education in Germany, and not a few had earned their doctorates there. With regard to philosophers, moreover, the attachment to the German philosophical tradition was in many cases stronger still. Hall—who characterizes himself as "one of the thousands of American teachers who have been more or less

---

[11] For example, Josiah Royce, whose parents were born in England, had written as follows in 1900: "Nations as near to each other, not only in blood, but in their whole spiritual kinship as are America and Great Britain, can never view each other's fortunes and issues considerately and justly without learning from each other. Our destinies, despite very strong contrasts, are of necessity closely akin. Our hopes and interests, despite all that might tend to keep us apart, are intimately bound together . . . Our own civilization had an English stamp, and always, I believe, will retain that stamp . . . we have been forced, as time went on, to try to make that civilization meet the needs of great numbers of foreigners, whose traditions were not our own . . ." ("Some Characteristic Tendencies," 195–96; cf. Read, "England and America," 5–6).

[12] Cf. Henry Louis Mencken: "During World War I an effort was made by super-patriots to drive all German loans from the American vocabulary. *Sauerkraut* became *liberty cabbage*, *hamburger steak* became *Salisbury steak*, *hamburger* became *liberty sandwich*, and a few extremists even changed *German measles* to *liberty measles*" (*American Language–Supplement I*, 429; cf. Kolbe, *Colleges in War Time*, 101–6, 200–201; Thwing, *American Colleges and Universities*, 181–84; Angoff, "Higher Learning Goes to War," 187).

'made in Germany'"—describes the wartime strain upon the German-trained as follows: "Like so many of my class, I have felt my soul almost torn in two between a sense of loyalty to and admiration of civic and cultural Germany, from whom we have yet so much to learn, and German militarism."[13] Still, in spite of whatever intellectual respect they might have retrained for things German, most American academics did demonstrate a high level of support for America's entry into, and America's efforts during, the war. Those who did not—the 'disloyal' and the 'slackers'—paid a high price.[14]

The American system of higher education became fully involved with the war when it was virtually nationalized in 1918. In that year, the federal government expanded upon the Reserve Officers' Training Corps (ROTC) that had been established in 1916 in two directions. One was the training of carpenters, auto mechanics, telephones linesmen, sheet metal workers, and the like, through the vocational division, or "Section B" of the Students' Army Training Corps (SATC). This program, paid for by the War Department, used the facilities of colleges and universities to house, feed, and instruct the recruits; and, by the summer of 1918, there were over 30,000 men in 140 training centers. A second program had an even stronger impact of American higher education. When enlistments and the lowering of the draft age to eighteen in the summer of 1918 threatened to empty campuses of male undergraduates for the upcoming academic year, the government stepped in. "Section A" of SATC was the collegiate-level program that was designed to take high school graduates through two years of instruction to insure a continued supply of officer candidate material throughout this war of uncertain length. Again, colleges and universities were paid to house, feed, and instruct the recruits. On 1 October 1918, when this program officially began, there were over 140,000 men enrolled and stationed on 400 campuses around the country. About this latter program, Thwing writes, "The colleges became, like the railroads, essentially government institutions. All [male] students who entered the American colleges in the autumn of 1918, either as freshmen or as upper-

---

[13] Hall, foreword to *Problems and Lessons of the War*, xi.

[14] Cf. Walter P. Metzger: "The crisis of 1917 plunged the academic profession into vast and unheralded new difficulties. A mob fanaticism arose that put every freedom in jeopardy. The American university, always vulnerable to the opinions of the community, could not escape its coercive spirit. Indeed, professors, being by tradition and usually by disposition somewhat more detached from mass obsessions, became the particular targets of the country's enthusiasm and anxiety. All over the nation, patriotic zealots on boards of trustees, in the community, and on the faculties themselves, harassed those college teachers whose passion for fighting the war was somewhat less flaming than their own" (*Age of the University*, 495–96; Kuklick, *Rise of American Philosophy*, 446; Curti, "American Scholar in Three Wars," 255–56).

classmen, being eighteen years of age and of physical fitness, became by
their entrance, soldiers of the United States . . . An essential military camp
was established on every campus. The *Campus Academicus* became the
Campus Martius." Parke Rexford Kolbe further notes: "The War
Department . . . said: 'During the war you are no longer degree-giving
institutions, but rather short-course training schools for the specific purpose of preparing officers for the army and navy.'"[15] Of course, the war
ended soon after he program began, on 11 November 1918; and the
SATC was demobilized on 26 November 1918.

While it was in existence, however, the SATC was a remarkable, if brief,
moment in the history of American higher education. Of particular interest to us is what was called the "War Issues" course. Frank Aydelotte, the
director of this aspect of the SATC, described this course as follows:

> The purpose of this course was to build up the morale of the soldiers who were
> being trained under the direction of the Committee [on Education and Special
> Training] by giving them an idea of what the war was about and of the reasons
> for our participation in it. As planned and conducted by the Committee, the
> course was not so much a statement in propaganda form of the official reasons
> for our participation in the war as an attempt to provide the men with a basis
> of the facts upon which our cause rested and a further attempt to induce them
> to form their own opinions by discussion.

Emphasizing the democratic traditions of the American people, and down-
playing the obvious restraints of the military context, Aydelotte continues,
"Lecturers were not told what to say nor were men told what to think."
The war issues course, part of the program of all of the students in both
sections of the SATC, was designed to advance the morale of "a democratic army" by demonstrating to the men—or allowing them to demonstrate
to themselves—the importance of the institutions for which they were
about to fight. "Our attempt from the very start was to lead the men to
formulate their own opinions by discussion," he writes, "rather than to
furnish them with opinions ready made."[16] Many philosophers, who had
little to offer in other areas of SATC instruction—health and sanitation,
military tactics, engineering, drill, and so forth—found in the preparation

---

[15] Thwing, *American Colleges and Universities*, 57–59; Kolbe, *Colleges in War Time*,
196–197. See also the symposium on "Problems Presented by Students' Army Training
Corps, and the Future Military Training of Students" at the December 1918 meeting of the
Association of American Universities, with presentations by General Robert I. Rees, Richard
C. MacLaurin, and Frank Aydelotte, and comments by, among others, Arthur Twining
Hadley, Abbott Lawrence Lowell, and Creighton (*Journal of Proceedings and Addresses of the
Twentieth Annual Conference*, 106–29).

[16] Aydelotte, *Final Report*, 7, 9.

and teaching of their war issues course an attractive outlet for their efforts to advance the war and several past or future presidents of the two associations took administrative jobs with SATC. William Ernest Hocking, for example, was the director of the vocational section of the war issues course for districts one (New England), two (New York and New Jersey), and three (Pennsylvania, Maryland, Delaware, and the District of Columbia), and director of the collegiate section for district two. James Hayden Tufts was the director of the collegiate section of the war issues course for district seven (Michigan, Wisconsin, and Illinois); George Herbert Mead, for district nine (Missouri, Kansas, Colorado, and Wyoming).[17]

---

[17] For their final reports, see: Aydelotte, *Final Report*, 88–90, 101–3, 106–7.

MARY WHITON CALKINS

Courtesy of Wellesley College Archives. Photo by Partridge.

12

The War and Three American Philosophers

While any simple distinction between thinking and doing is illegitimate, no one would dispute that philosophers are primarily thinkers. On issues of fundamental human importance—like the nature of well-being or the causes of suffering—philosophers respond by attempting to understand. The American philosophers' response to the World War was thus to consider the meaning of this great human tragedy. Their discussions sought to find justice among the conflicting claims, or direction within the competing policy suggestions, or reconciliation beyond the hatred.

Many American philosophers addressed the issues of the war in their writings. The best known of the books are John Dewey's *German Philosophy and Politics* (1915) and George Santayana's *Egotism in German Philosophy* (1916). There were many other war related books, among them: Hugo Münsterberg's *The War and America* (1914), *The Peace and America* (1915), and *Tomorrow: Letters to a Friend in Germany* (1916); Ralph Barton Perry's *The Free Man and the Soldier* (1916), and *The Present Conflict of Ideals* (1918); Mary Whiton Calkins's *The Good Man and the Good* (1918); and Hartley Burr Alexander's *Liberty and Democracy* (1918). While these and related volumes deserve more careful study,[1] in this chapter I want to explore the war-related volumes of three other American philosophers, chosen in part for the diversity of their responses to the events in Europe. One of the figures, George Stuart Fullerton, is now virtually forgotten; the second, Josiah Royce, remains one of the major figures in American philosophy; the third, William Ernest Hocking, is still carefully studied, although for other of his writings.

---

[1] I have sketched out Dewey's and Münsterberg's positions on the war in "Dewey and German Philosophy in Wartime."

George Stuart Fullerton was a widely published philosopher/psychologist who had long taught at Pennsylvania and, since 1903, served as a research professor at Columbia. He was a charter member of the APA, and his AΨA credentials included his election as its fifth president for 1896. Fullerton had spent a good deal of time in Europe, especially in Germany; and he served as Columbia's exchange professor at the University of Vienna for the winter semester of 1913-1914. At the outbreak of the war, he was in Munich and he seems to have remained in Germany until the war ended.

Early on, Fullerton published a pamphlet entitled "Why the German Nation Has Gone to War: An American to Americans." Published in Germany and dated 1 November 1914, this pamphlet was designed "to set the American in the place of the German." He maintains that "no class, either in Germany or in Austria, desired to precipitate this terrible war. Peace was desired, and earnestly desired, for economic reasons. But war was for[c]ed upon both nations." While rejecting the charges of "German militarism" and the view that the Germans are "an aggressive and predatory people," Fullerton maintains that they all support the war now that it has come. Setting the American "in the place of the German" requires that the former recognize that the Germans live in a dangerous place and must defend themselves. On the East lies Russia, "a great land with a vast population of more than one hundred millions, under an autocratic government, boasting, even in time of peace, an immense army." On the West lies France, a wealthy and industrialized country fully prepared for modern warfare that has "for forty years made no secret of the fact that it was animated by a bitter sentiment of resentment . . . and hoped some day to have its revenge." Germany's third enemy is England, "inaccessible by land" and yet in control of Germany's "only available outlets to the sea." In contrast to Germany, surrounded by an alliance of hostile powers, America is large and safe. As Fullerton phrases it, "we have no more need for the German army than has a Philadelphia Quaker, at his Yearly Meeting, for a revolver." His point is that our situation is very different from Germany's, and he suggests that "we Americans, under the same circumstances, would have done just what the Germans have done." That is, Americans would have militarized; and, when war was pressed upon them, they would have gone forward just as Germany had done.[2]

In 1915 Fullerton expanded upon these themes in a book published in America entitled *Germany of To-day*,[3] which he dedicates "[t]o those who

---

[2] Fullerton, "Why the German Nation," 9, 4–5, 7–8, 11.

[3] This book was also published in English in Munich with the title *The Truth about the German Nation* (1915). There was a German translation as well: *Die Wahrheit über Deutschland*, published in Germany in 1916.

desire a mutual understanding among civilized nations and who work for the cause of international conciliation." In this volume, he offers "a collection of facts that may easily be verified by anyone who has access to a public library." Writing as one whose family "has been American as long as there has been an American nation," he aims to overcome misconceptions "among my countrymen" by offering them "a just conception of the political and social constitution of the German nation and of the spirit with which it is penetrated." Fullerton's ultimate hope was to improve mutual understanding between the two countries. As he continues: "United Germany is a young and vigorous nation. So is the United States of America. The better the two understand one another, the better for both."[4]

In *Germany of To-day*, Fullerton offers chapters on the general nature of the German empire—which he calls "The United States of Germany"—the political situation of German citizens, the German education system, two chapters on militarism and one on imperialism, and a concluding discussion of the future. We can consider these themes in order. Politically, he writes, Germany was a combination of "twenty-two states, three free towns [Hamburg, Bremen, and Lübeck], and the imperial territory of Alsace-Lorraine [Elsaß-Lothringen]. There are four kingdoms, six grand duchies, five duchies, and seven principalities." In spite of Germany's monarchical and heredity government, Fullerton works very hard to suggest similarities between it and the United States: "the fact that the chief executive of the German nation is an emperor, inheriting his title, and the fact that the same individual is king of Prussia . . . have caused in the United States a widespread misconception, even among well-informed people, as to the imperial office." He maintains, however, that the correct understanding of the situation is that "the German Emperor is virtually the president of the confederation of the German States."[5]

German citizens, Fullerton continues, were not being crushed under some presumably oppressive 'Prussian' system, but were living lives that were quite similar to those of Americans. As he writes, "the average German does not appear to be more restlessly discontented than the average American, who is usually agitating for reforms of some sort . . ." While he points to some dissimilarities between the German and American situations—for example, "the political rights of the Germans are not identical with ours"—he also suggests that the Germans were certainly no worse off than Americans. Modifying Lincoln, he writes of Germany that "a government, which the average American would not be inclined to describe as *of*

---

[4] Fullerton, *Germany of To-day*, iii–vi.
[5] Ibid., 1, 8, 14–15.

the people and *by* the people, may, nevertheless, be most emphatically a government *for* the people . . ." Particularly with regard to social legislation, Fullerton writes that he found the German system preferable. This meant, of course, that the involvement of the government in citizens' lives was greater in Germany; but this was not necessarily an evil. As he writes, "although the German is very thoroughly governed, he is governed in his own interests."[6]

In his consideration of the educational system, Fullerton writes, "It is education that has made Germany what it is, and Germany knows it." Part of this education is content-oriented, involving the mastery of the data that science was yielding about the nature of the world, and part of it is more properly understood as socialization. "The German is trained to discipline from his earliest years. He learns when young to obey, and this discipline is capped later by his [two] years of military service." The German is taught that he has a place, that he is a part of something larger than himself. "All are taught to obey; all have their burdens to bear. The German belongs to the state and he is educated to believe that he owes something to the state and that the state owes him a good deal." All of this consideration of the centrality of the national state might raise for some the issue of militarism; but, for Fullerton, "the standing army of Germany is no more and no less than a school. The officers, commissioned and non-commissioned, correspond to the teachers." Once again, what is gained in military service is not the technical skills of soldiering so much as the general social benefits of "discipline, orderly habits, cleanliness and prompt obedience . . ." Moreover, he again maintains that if America faced the geopolitical realities that Germany faced, Americans would better appreciate the potential value of a standing army themselves.[7]

Fullerton's final two themes are imperialism and post-war reconstruction. He recognizes that the term 'empire' has a negative sound to Americans, especially when it means "the control exercised by a nation over peoples which cannot properly be regarded as belonging to it and truly sharing in its national life." Under this definition, however, he maintains that the great imperialist country was not Germany but Great Britain, followed closely by France and Russia. The German empire, on the contrary, was not like that of the British; but consisted of "a homogeneous people, having the same blood, the same speech and much the same traditions." In this, Germany was like the United States: "both nations represent confederations of civilized states which naturally belong together; and . . . certain dependencies remote from [their] own shores," and neither has been "compelled to seize the lands of foreign peoples." Another

---

[6] Ibid., 26, 33, 35–36, 55.
[7] Ibid., 60, 81, 55–56, 86–87.

similarity between the two was that neither the United States nor Germany accepted the map as configured prior to its birth. "Did we accept the *status quo* when we dispossessed the Indians?" he asks. "Did we bow down before the principle when we published our Declaration of Independence in 1776?" The Americans had expanded to fill the continent and, more recently, to move overseas; the Germans were simply doing the same thing.[8]

In each case the *status quo* was upset; but, in itself, this is not wrong. "The *status quo* makes for peace," Fullerton grants under normal circumstances; "but, if conditions change beyond a certain point, the peace may reveal itself as a frozen immobility which nations with life in them will reject as intolerable." Such nations, which he further describes as "developing nations, civilized nations whose growth in wealth and power signifies a contribution to the total wealth of the world and to the richness of its civilization," must be allowed to expand even if their expansion destabilizes the current situation. As he puts it, "such nations should have a place made for them . . ." Germany's possible expansion had been prevented in large measure because Great Britain had the most to lose in any such change and because its naval power controlled the oceans. This clash between Germany's legitimate rights of expansion and Britain's selfish policies had led to the war; and, when it ends, some "flexible system of international organization that growth may take place unaccompanied by convulsions and the rupture of the system" will have to be instituted. Fullerton believed that Americans and Germans, if they "work together in harmony for the welfare of the whole family of nations" and do "not fall, through blindness, into useless and harmful conflict," could make this new international system easier to attain. His message to his fellow Americans in 1915, therefore, was that they should stay out of the war.[9]

Josiah Royce, elected the tenth president of the AΨA for 1901 and the third president of the APA for 1903, studied in Germany as a young man, as we saw in chapter 2, and pursued throughout his life a vision of the philosophical life that drew strongly upon the German tradition. Just after the war broke out, he published a small volume entitled *War and Insurance*. This volume represents his attempt to carry the Peircean ideas on the communities of interpretation that he had developed in *The Problem of Christianity* (1913) into the new reality that had emerged after the assassinations in Sarajevo. *War and Insurance* presents Royce as a neutral figure,

---

[8] Ibid., 135, 1, 150–51, 158.

[9] Ibid., 161–62, 173, 181. Unable to return from Germany, Fullerton resigned from Columbia during the course of the war. He later took up a position at Vassar and continued to write. His volume, *A Handbook of Ethical Theory*, was published in 1922. He committed suicide on 23 March 1924.

working "to understand better than we now do the depth, the gravity, and the true nature of the motives which have thus far made warlike tendencies so persistent in the life of mankind" and "to discover, if we can, methods not yet tried, whereby the wars of the nations may be gradually rendered less destructive, and less willful." In particular, what drew him was the issue of loyalty to one's community, an ideal that he took to be just as important as hatred of the enemy. "War's other aspect," he writes, "what one may call its spiritual aspect, is the loyalty to which it gives active employment, the fearless faith in life which it converts into works, the endurance which it transforms into creative deeds." He continues that because the relations of loyalty are "the highest human relations," relations that "express the best in man" and that "often lead to the worst of warlike hatreds," a more fundamental answer to the question of how loyalty can be redirected was necessary.[10]

For Royce, the solution is triadic in form. It requires us to rise above the conflict of opposing sides. He writes that "if ever relief is to come to humanity's great woe of combat, it will come not merely through a cessation of hate and a prevalence of love for individual men . . ." What is required, rather, is "the growth of some higher type of loyalty, which shall absorb the men of the future so that the service of the community of all mankind will at last become their great obsession . . ." When this "world-patriotism" comes, he continues, it will be a powerful force that "will remain still as active, and on occasion as militant and as businesslike in its plans and in its devotion as is now the love of warring patriots for their mutually hostile countries." His approach involves the recognition that "the *dyadic, the dual, the bilateral relations of man and man, of each man to his neighbor, are relations fraught with social danger.*" Each of these pairings gives rise to what he calls "*an essentially dangerous community*"; and, in the place of these dangerous dyads, he emphasizes the social need for the development of triads like families. Similarly, on the international scale, it was his position that war persisted "*because the nations still cultivate dyadic relations too exclusively.*" To prevent future wars, he believed, countries would have to adopt the triadic stance of interpreters: "*if the world's peace is to be furthered, such progress must take the form of creating and sustaining certain definable communities of interpretation.*" Returning to the domestic level, Royce maintains that the interpreter is the most important member of the community because it is the neutral interpreter who fosters cooperation and solidarity among all the other members of the community. The interpreter, whom he named 'B,' "desires, just as any reasonable agent desires, not to do A's will alone, nor C's will alone, *but at once to*

---

[10] Royce, *War and Insurance*, 1, 19, 21.

create and to make conscious, and to carry out, their united will, in so far as
they both are to become and remain members of that community in which he
does the work of the interpreter." As examples of the sort of interpreters
whom he finds active on the domestic level, he points to the judge in the
legal community, and to the banker in the business community.[11]

On the international level, Royce suggests that the position of neutral
interpreter could be filled by expanding the work of another triadic institution that is currently in place: insurance. At the present time, he writes,
the insurance community works to safeguard individuals from loss; and he
hopes to develop this community to address the problem of war. "*Apply to*
international relations, gradually and progressively, that principle of insur-
ance which has been found so unexpectedly fruitful and peaceful and power-
ful and unifying in the life and in the social relations of individual men."
His proposal was fairly simple: nations should place their 'premiums' in
neutral hands (he suggested Sweden and Switzerland); and, at the conclusion of a war, individual nations would receive payments to rebuild only if
they could demonstrate that they had not started the war:

> if large enough, *this community of mutual international insurance could insure*
> *its members progressively against more and more of the evils and destructive*
> *calamities due to war*, by the simple addition of one very important rule to the
> rules so far laid down: If a nation had a war with another, the insurance trustees
> would never directly inquire as to the moral justification of this war, but would
> ask: *Who committed the first act of war? No nation would receive insurance com-*
> *pensation for any expenses due to a war in which it committed the first act of war.*

Thus, if nations could gain access to reconstruction funds only for wars
that they had not started, Royce believed that no wars would be started.
Perhaps convinced by expectations from Europe that the war, however
destructive, would be over by the end of 1914, he suggests that his proposal be adopted at the war's end. His idea was that, whichever side won,
the larger community of nations would support structural changes to prevent the outbreak of future conflicts. He thus proposes that the victors,
instead of dedicating the indemnity extracted from the vanquished to
fund preparations for future wars and thereby fostering further hatred by
the vanquished, put the money to a better use. "*When it is paid, let the*
victors at once and actively establish the first mutual insurance company
against national calamities, including wars. Let them devote this whole
indemnity to forming the initial fund of this company." Thus, instead of
being the down payment on the next war, the indemnity would become
"*the fund of the community of all mankind.*" Royce concludes his call for

---

[11] Ibid., 24, 30, 40, 49, 52.

neutral interpretation as a means to overcome war with his own paraphrase of Lincoln: "My thesis is *that whenever insurance of the nations, by the nations, and for the nations begins, it will thenceforth never vanish from the earth, but will begin to make visible to us the holy city of the community of all mankind.*"[12]

The war did not end in 1914; and, as it raged on in Europe, Royce became increasingly angered by German conduct. He notes for example in early 1916 that "we in America have long loved and studied German civilization, and would be loving it still but for its recent crimes." Although he did not live long enough to see the American entry in 1917, he championed an increasingly belligerent response in the last months of his life. We can consider this position as it is to be found in a series of his public lectures that were gathered together after his death in a volume entitled *The Hope of the Great Community*. In a piece entitled "The Duties of Americans in the Present War," he praises the faithfulness of "bleeding and devoted Belgium,—that suffering servant of the great community of mankind," and he condemns "the moral attitude which has been deliberately and openly assumed by Germany since the outset of the war." This attitude, that he believes "will remain until the end of human history, one great classic example of the rejection, by a great and highly intelligent nation, of the first principles of international morality," was what he characterized as "the rejection of international duty, the assertion that for its own subjects, the State is the supreme moral authority, and that there is no moral authority on earth which ranks superior to the will of the State." He rejects the claim found in Fullerton that America was the victim of anti-German propaganda. In Royce's view, "not Germany's enemies, but Germany herself, her prince, her ministers, her submarine commanders, have given us our principal picture of what the militant Germany of the moment is, and of what Germany means for the future of international morality."[13]

Royce was especially hard hit by the sinking of the *Lusitania* on 7 May 1915 that drowned some 1,200 people, including 128 Americans. In this same piece on American duties, he writes that "the young men, the women, the babies, who went down with the *Lusitania* were our dead." More specifically, he continues, "[a]t least I know—some of whose pupils were amongst the victims of the *Lusitania*—that they were my dead." In a piece entitled "The Destruction of the Lusitania," published a few months earlier, he had written that one result of the attack on the *Lusitania* was an end to any attempt on his part to remain neutral. After

---

[12] Ibid., 66–67, 77–80.
[13] Royce, *Hope of the Great Community*, 12, 4–6.

the attack, it was "both necessary and advisable to speak out plainly many things which an American professor in my position has long felt a desire to say upon occasions when he still supposed it to be his duty not to say them." In a world in which the *Lusitania* could be so callously torpedoed, "I am no longer neutral, even in form," he writes. "The German Prince is now the declared and proclaimed enemy of mankind . . ." Royce maintained that because of what Germany—"the enemy of mankind"—had done, because of "the infamies of Prussian warfare," Americans of all backgrounds were coming to recognize "that utter ignorance of human nature and of its workings which the German propaganda, the German diplomacy, and the German policy have shown from the outset of the War." As a particular instance of German cruelty, Royce focused upon the work of the U-boats. "Submarines these people may understand," he continues, "certainly not souls." Returning to the theme of the infamous *Lusitania* attack on the first anniversary of its sinking, he derided those Germans and German-Americans who had celebrated "their glorious victory over the women and children who sank with her" and attacks them as the "enemies of our country and of mankind."[14]

In his discussion of "The Duties of Americans in the Present War," Royce calls upon his fellows to abandon any lingering neutrality: "Neutral, in heart or in mind, the dutiful American . . . will not and cannot be. He must take sides." Considering what Germany had done, and was continuing to do, in Belgium with its army and on the high seas with its submarines, "Germany, as at present disposed, is the wilful and deliberate enemy of the human race." Even though the United States had not yet entered the war, he thought it was necessary to become more involved in the support of the opponents of the Central Powers. "In the service of mankind," he writes, "we owe an unswerving sympathy not to one or another, but to all of the present allied enemies of Germany." He continues, "We owe to those allies whatever moral support and whatever financial assistance it is in the power of this nation to give." Particularly with regard to munitions of war, he writes that "it is not merely a so-called American right that our munitions-makers should be free to sell their wares to the enemies of Germany. It is our duty to encourage them to do so, since we are not at the moment in a position to serve mankind by more direct and effective means." We should thus provide the Allies with monetary and military assistance, he maintains, overlooking any inconveniences such assistance might cause us. Such efforts would both help "to lift up the hearts that the Germany of to-day has wantonly chosen to wound, to betray, and to make desolate" and to relieve us of some of the shame and

---

[14] Ibid., 10, 15, 22, 16, 20, 96, 98.

guilt for failing to "stand beside Belgium, and suffer with her for our duty and for mankind . . ." America was not yet completely ready to heed Royce's call; and, when he died on 14 September 1916, it was with his hope for the Great Community unfulfilled.[15]

When the war broke out, Royce was fifty-nine years old and Fullerton was fifty-five. William Ernest Hocking was forty-one, not quite at the start of his career, but still a dozen years away from his 1926 presidency of the Eastern Division of the APA. He had studied in Germany in 1902–1903, and earned his Ph.D. at Harvard the next year. He returned from teaching philosophy at Yale to the Harvard faculty in 1914. After military training at Plattsburg, New York, Hocking was commissioned as a captain in the U.S. Army in 1916 and taught ROTC at Harvard in 1916–1917. He spent the summer of 1917 in England and touring the battlefields in France; and, as we have seen in chapter 11, he later served as a district supervisor of the war issues course for SATC. In the course of all of these war-related activities, he wrote *Morale and Its Enemies*. In the preface dated 6 November 1918—just five days before the Armistice—he describes the impact of that summer of 1917 spent in Europe. The body of the text draws upon material that he presented in lecture form at Williams late in 1917 and Yale earlier in 1918. Hocking tells us that the purpose of this volume is not to condemn the Central Powers, or even to discuss the issues behind the war. Rather, his aim is simply "to deal with the psychology of war-making": "This book is an attempt to help—the soldier first, and also the civilian—in this task of understanding one's own mind, under the special stresses of war."[16]

In spite of his disclaimer, however, *Morale and Its Enemies* is loaded with a full array of criticisms of Germany and Austria that indicate that he at least was completely convinced of their guilt. He notes, for example, that "[c]onfidence, determination, endurance, and discipline may exist in a perfectly bad cause: for four years all these qualities were present in the Austro-German command." Further, he notes that German officers demand deference from civilians in occupied territories, and the German high command lies to its own troops and tries to control their spirit by a kind of "scientific management." He continues that "the leaders of Germany could have won the nation to war neither in 1870 nor now without a plausible show that their war was a war of defense"; but he maintains that "as the facts gradually oust the now well-rooted falsehood, the will to

---

[15] Ibid., 10–13. Cf. George Herbert Palmer: Royce's "belief in the crimes of Germany, the land of his spiritual birth, pursued him day and night and had considerable influence in bringing about his death" ("Josiah Royce," 8; cf. Clendenning, *Life and Thought of Josiah Royce*, 381–95).

[16] Hocking, *Morale and Its Enemies*, 61, vii.

war of the Central Powers weakens . . ." Hocking maintains further that German morale "would weaken faster but for the dread that the wrath of the world may indeed make their fight now one for national existence." Much of his criticism of Germany is grounded in his belief that the country had abandoned truth in the interest of pragmatic success. His interest in improving morale will not allow the violation of truth, because he believes that to do so would ultimately destroy "the morale of both army and people at its roots." The *Realpolitik* of the Central Powers had no place in his vision for America.[17]

The causes of the war were, for Hocking, easy to uncover. The German government and its general staff, "attitudinizing in mediaeval armor before the glass of their own conceit," had lost touch with the realities of contemporary political life. What was directing Germany was "a state of mind supported by a false science and a materially pragmatic philosophy, a perverse interpretation of history and a morbid dramatization of dead ideals of rulership and empire, blind to the fact that new methods are already born and that the solution of public dilemmas already in germ exists." Further, he notes that the German conduct of the war has been without honor and that the Americans have only too slowly come to accept the reported evils of the Germans war machine. He writes that "we could not believe the criminal as black as he was painted: men's eyes have to get used to this kind of darkness also." Recognizing that most of their information was received via British censors, Americans were reluctant to believe. "The portrait of the designing, unscrupulous, spy-setting, world-claiming, treaty-wrecking, humanity-spurning Germany seemed a partisan caricature . . . There must be, we thought, another side: no modern nation could give itself to a policy quite so evil, so cynical, so quixotically pretentious." As the tales of horror mounted, however, belief became easier. He further maintained that the German state of mind omitted the restraints of practical living. "The German people are far more inclined to commit themselves to a theory, and are less likely to be saved by the vaguer inner monitors (all more or less intuitive; such as, humor, taste, virtue, etc.) from the excesses of the intellect." In the world that the Germans have created, *Realpolitik* is triumphant; and "the very plausible principle that States must be guided by 'real' rather than imaginary goods and considerations" is subverted by the dangerous view that "the 'real' goods are the solid substances of economic advantage and prestige, as opposed to the purely imaginary or ideal properties of honesty and good-will . . ." As he characterizes this situation, what is primary in Germany is "the principle . . . that just in the great affairs of inter-state relations, principles do not count." Hocking, of course,

---

[17] Ibid., 10, 22, 29, 37.

rejects this *Realpolitik*. "To do otherwise," he writes, "is to give up the tendency of social evolution toward a more thoughtful, lawful, and consistent world; it is to accept the defeat of a moral control of history at the hand of the cruder and simpler fact. It is to give Germany the right."[18]

To return to Hocking's original topic of understanding military morale, he writes that "[m]orale is the practical virtue of the will to war." For him, no war in history has relied so strongly on morale. Victory will depend upon "the endurance, the initiative, the power of sacrifice, the loyalty, the ability to subordinate personal interest and pride, the power of taking the measure of the event, of discounting the unfavorable turn, of responding to frightfulness with redoubled resolution rather than with fear, of appreciating the real emergency and rising instantly to meet it." Morale remains, however, a complex force. On the one hand, he maintains that purely material factors do not explain victory in wartime; on the other, that morale cannot be decisive alone. "Morale wins, not by itself, but *by turning scales*: it has a value like the power of a minority or of a mobile reserve." Moreover, morale is not the sort of thing that can be "tested by the methods of the psychological laboratory." While there are mental tests that can be used "to distinguish the promising soldier from the unpromising," Hocking maintains that "the critical elements of morale elude them." This elusiveness is the result of the fact that "[m]orale, for all the greater purposes of war, is a state of faith; and its logic will be the superb and elusive logic of human faith." This is why truth must be respected over the short-term pragmatic advantages of convenient deceptions. For there to be a fully effective "*mental mobilization*," citizens must have faith in their cause as it is presented to them. As he writes, "morale, while not identical with the righteousness of the cause, can never reach its height unless the aim of war can be held intact in the undissembled moral sense of the people."[19]

Hocking then takes up the psychological question of building morale. Recognizing the basic fact that morale "cannot be simply distilled from the atmosphere," he wants to know how to get a greater contribution to the war effort out of each human component, and this is always a question of more or less. "The most important distinction affecting morale among our people, in or out of the army," he writes, "is not that between the loyal and disloyal, but that between the whole-hearted and the half-hearted or the three-quarters-hearted . . ." To get the greatest possible contribution out of each individual, he stresses the importance of training, discipline and willing obedience to the soldiers' sense of belonging to

---

[18] Ibid., 51, 56, 62–63, 70.
[19] Ibid., ix, 8–9, 17–18, 23, 43, 23.

a unit. Hocking further recognizes the special power of the momentous task at hand:

> the occasion of war excites instincts deep-laid in human nature . . . The fighting-instinct is coupled with another, the instinct of the herd. A new and far-flung fraternity is in the air: for there is the haunting knowledge that the herd is in motion, is attacking or being attacked,—and if attacking, then being attacked,—in any case, then, in danger. To know that is enough. The neighbor is no longer the indifferent mortal he was yesterday: he belongs with us to the tribe, the nation.

The individual who has yielded to "the tide of war-feeling" will come to recognize "that he has surrendered something of his mind as well as of his will to the keeping of the mass." Unlike those who fight for personal causes, "he who fights in company with his community may read his own conviction in the eyes of his neighbors on every hand. His critical faculty is disarmed by the momentum of common consent . . ." When 'my' cause becomes 'our' cause, "[t]he genuine devotion one gives to the community, the loyalty, the labor and the sacrifice, lend their color to the cause itself . . . The herd-impulse tends of itself, automatically, to sanction and sustain the fighting-impulse." In addition, the role for hatred of the enemy and for its "threatening, inhuman, treacherous, arrogant, or otherwise intolerable" actions contributes to the strength of morale.[20]

Hocking recognizes that the war would someday end; and, when that happened, our efforts to advance "universal justice"—what he calls "the aim of the war"—would move to a new level and require a different sort of morale. He points out, for example, that we will need to recognize that racism and profiteering are crimes against the common good that we are trying to advance. To fully realize this common good, he maintains that we will have to overcome our traditional American individualism and recognize the lasting importance of the state and of patriotism. "The modern State," he writes, "cares more about the individual man than does the economic order; its laws and courts aim to provide that no wrong shall be done to him; and its charities that no ultimate misfortune shall deprive him of the plain necessities of living." In other words, "the State, when it is what it should be, acts as a sort of over-parent . . ." Rejecting the familiar *laissez-faire* approach that social goods necessarily result from individual strivings, Hocking maintains that "all common interests *must be enacted*. The fundamental social fact is the *enactor*, and that being, in developed societies, is the State." Without the sort of direction that the state offers ,"human experience would be a perpetual recurrence of ancient mistakes

---

[20] Ibid., 10, 13, 25, 33, 31, 27.

. . ." He emphasizes that our highest happiness is to be found in what we "do and give," rather than in what we get; and he maintains that through the social creation of common interests, "the State creates the conditions that make sacrifice significant" because it provides "the moral framework within which acts of sacrifice, all labors and offerings for the common good, may become significant . . ." It is thus necessary to develop a more permanent morale, or social faith, and to overcome our "State-blindness," if we are to win the war and to benefit fully from the possibilities of peace.[21]

---

[21] Ibid., 66, 83–84, 87–88, 90, 78.

JAMES HAYDEN TUFTS

Image courtesy of Special Collections Research Center, Morris Library,
Southern Illinois University Carbondale

13

The War and the Philosophical Associations

It is hard to anticipate how a national academic association will respond to a tragedy as massive as a world war. Outsiders' perceptions of the usefulness of particular sorts of expertise play an important role, no doubt, as do insiders' commitments to their discipline and their general modes of attempting its advance. The efforts of the philosophical associations with regard to the war were—beyond some minor steps like contributing their modest treasury surpluses to the Liberty Loan program[1] and discussing war-related themes at their annual meetings—exclusively the individual efforts of the members. As examples of these individual efforts, we have just considered the written work of a trio of philosophers. In chapter 11 we considered the contributions of Arthur Oncken Lovejoy to develop a pro-war public opinion, and of other philosophers to the Students' Army Training Corps (SATC) as organizers and instructors in the war issues course. Other philosophers functioned as mathematics or language instructors. And, of course, many younger philosophers, like Ralph Barton Perry and Clarence Irving Lewis, served in the military. The sorts of inquiries in which professional philosophers engaged, however, precluded any collective efforts by the associations to advance the war effort.

In this regard, the philosophers ranked far behind the contributions of their cousins in psychology, where the possibilities of mental testing were just being recognized. In January 1917, Walter Bowers Pillsbury, a former president of the WPA and the AΨA, pointed to the "dream" of the psychologist for a society "in which each individual should be measured and assigned to the place for which he is best fitted, and then instructed in the

---

[1] The APA bought two $100 war bonds on 16 August 1918 and held them until 1926, earning $8.50 per year in interest (PR 28:176–77; PR 36:58). The WPA bought forty $5 War Savings Stamps at a cost of $167.38 in 1918 (JP 16:463).

best and most economical use of his capacity in the performance of the task that has been given him."[2] While he did not necessarily share this dream in its entirety, other psychologists did; and they saw in the war the dual opportunity of advancing the national defense and proving psychology's practical value. Robert Mearns Yerkes, a Harvard psychology professor and the 1917 president of the AΨA, entered the army along with a group of other psychologists in August 1917 to organize a pilot study to develop standards for testing all future recruits. The psychologists thought that they would be able to assist the military with such tasks as sifting for intellectual deficiencies, matching abilities to military assignments, evaluating for psychopathological tendencies, and finding candidates for positions of authority. The results of this pilot study were accepted and testing, using the deeply flawed alpha and beta tests, progressed, eventually examining over 200,000 recruits per month.[3]

In his presidential address at the twenty-sixth meeting of the AΨA in December 1917, Major Yerkes discusses the theme of "Psychology in Relation to the War." In introducing his topic, he quotes from his earlier letter to the AΨA's Council dated 6 April 1917, the day that the United States entered the war. "In the present perilous situation, it is obviously desirable that the psychologists of the country act unitedly in the interests of defense," he wrote at the time. "Our knowledge and our methods are of importance to the military service of our country, and it is our duty to cooperate to the fullest extent and immediately toward the increased efficiency of our Army and Navy." He then outlined a series of planned steps that he hoped would bring together the AΨA "as a professional group . . . to render our professional training serviceable." Yerkes continues his address with a description of the actions of the military psychologists on behalf of science and national defense, noting how "[p]sychologists who develop methods or accumulate information which promises to aid us in winning the war are shortly appointed to positions which give them opportunity to apply their special knowledge effectively." Thus were the psychologists able to apply their training to enhance the effectiveness of the activities of the military. "Everyone who has had opportunity to share in the work," he writes, "obviously feels that he has contributed to our military progress and has rendered more substantial service through the application of his professional training than would have been possible in any other line."[4] The War Department was not totally convinced of the mili-

---

[2] Pillsbury, "New Developments," 66.

[3] Cf. Yerkes, *Psychological Examining*; Yoakum and Yerkes, *Army Mental Tests*; Brigham, *Study of American Intelligence*; Kevles, "Testing the Army's Intelligence"; Kennedy, *Over Here*, 187–89.

[4] Yerkes, "Psychology in Relation to the War," 86-87, 113, 115.

tary value of the contributions of these academics; but, by the end of 1918, the war was over and the psychologists had proven to themselves and to much of the broader society the potential contribution of their new science to social advance.

A somewhat different approach to war work was adopted by historians with the establishment of the National Board for Historical Service (NBHS) in April 1917. This organization, while not an official organ of the Government or of the American Historical Association, was established to facilitate and coordinate the efforts of individual historians. The July 1917 issue of *The American Historical Review* contains the following description of the NBHS:

> The main function of the board will be to serve the nation, in a time when the national problems of war and of ultimate peace cannot receive their best solution without the light of historical knowledge, by mediating between the possessors of such knowledge on the one hand, and on the other hand the government and the public who need it; in a word, to mobilize the historical forces of the country for all the services to which they can be put.

Elsewhere in that same issue, the managing editor, John Franklin Jameson, notes the importance of finding "[a]part from such services as can be rendered equally well by any other able-bodied or intelligent man," what "the 'history man'" can do for his country in war time, "of things for which he is especially fitted by his professional acquirements and habits of mind . . ." He continues that both the government and the public are aware of what scientists can do, while at the same time "both are prone to regard the historian as occupied only with the dates and details of remote transactions having no relation to the fateful exigencies of the present day." In response to such opinion, Jameson notes, "the mind of the virile historical student protests with all his might." What could be, he wonders, "more essential to the successful prosecution of a great national war than an enlightened, unified, and powerfully-acting public opinion?" and "how can public opinion in America be enlightened, homogeneous, and powerful, in a crisis which is in the plainest way the product of historical forces, if it is not informed in the facts and lessons of history?" This task of informing the public requires the historian "to come out from his cloistered retirement and to use for the information of the public whatever knowledge of European history he may possess—and to use it energetically and boldly." The present climate presented much bad history, and professional historians were the only ones who could rectify the situation: "history *will* be invoked, whatever we do, is being invoked every day, and if the public is not guided by sound historical information, it will be guided by unsound." Jameson thus calls upon American historians to contact the NBHS in Washington and help to carry out its work. The *Annual Report of the*

American Historical Association for 1919 details the sort of efforts that were made by historians under the aegis of this board during the course of the war, including: research into particular problems of relevance to the war effort, publications and lecturing, educational work (including SATC), governmental service, and the collection and preservation of materials.[5]

Philosophers, as I have said, were unable either to carve out an official niche in the war efforts of the country, as did the psychologists, or to create, as did the historians, an unofficial 'board' to coordinate their individual contributions. Thus, the philosophical associations had no collective impact upon the war, and this left them at a professional disadvantage when compared to the psychologists and historians, and to the many other disciplines that were even more centrally engaged in war work. Turning our inquiry around, we can examine the philosophical content of the meetings and papers of the associations to attempt to judge the impact of the war in Europe on the associations.[6] Soon after the war began in August 1914, the WPA and the APA met together at the University of Chicago (28–30 December 1914). This meeting had a distinctly political theme, with a number of papers on democracy and on justice[7]; but there seems to have been no particular war-focus among the submitted papers.[8] In his presidential address, however, James Hayden Tufts—who had earned his Ph.D. in Freiburg in 1892 and was serving as president that year of both associations—discussed "The Ethics of States."

Tufts begins with the consideration a paradox related to the state. "On the one hand," he notes, "no institution has commanded nobler devotion or inspired loftier art; on the other, none has lent itself so ruthlessly to the destruction of every human interest and value, or has practiced so consistently what in common life we all call crime." States, in other words, do themselves what they prevent their own citizens from doing; and he won-

---

[5] *American Historical Review* 22, no. 4, 918; Jameson, "Historical Scholars in War-Time," 831–33; cf. Leland, "National Board for Historical Service"; McLaughlin, "Historians and the War"; Blakey, *Historians on the Homefront*, 16–21; Hutchinson, "American Historian in Wartime."

[6] Another interesting line of inquiry would be to consider the impact of military metaphors on philosophical discussions. In chapter 10, for example, we saw James Edwin Creighton's 1917 criticism of the discussion sessions for attempting "to compel the opposing forces to abandon their trenches and engage in open battle . . ." ("APA and Its Programmes," 474). The lasting impact of such metaphors can be seen in the case of, for example, Ralph Barton Perry, who in 1930 described his teachers as follows: "Royce was the battleship, heavily armoured, both for defence and offence. James combined the attributes of the light cruiser, the submarine, and the bombing aeroplane" ("Realism in Retrospect," 188).

[7] This joint meeting was discussed in chapter 8.

[8] The proceedings of this joint meeting suggest that the members were more interested in APA/WPA unification, a topic that will be discussed in chapter 14.

ders "[h]ow can we explain the contrast between private and public conduct?" He rejects a number of simple explanations—for example, the
Machiavellian suggestion that the realm of politics should be considered
amoral—because he believes that such an explanation cannot adequately
explain the demonstrated "anxiety of states for moral approval." His own
answer to the paradox is that Western morality broadly conceived is "a con-
glomerate of several codes" among which are: "(1) The code of self interest . . . (2) . . . the code of honor . . . (3) A third code, of legal standards
. . . (4) . . . the code of family behavior . . . (5) . . . some more ideal code
inspired by some cause, some personality, some imaginative vision, some
response to personal relations of friendship, or of a wider human group
than that of honor." The problem results from the fact that nations generally consider self-interest to be the primary value, followed by honor and
only then legal standards, whereas in private conduct the rankings are felt
to operate in reverse order. Tufts further believes that, whatever justifications are offered, "[p]ractically all modern European states have arisen
through conquest" and only slowly is the citizens' role changing from obedience to authority to participation in the society's decisions.[9]

While recognizing the power of the nation-state, Tufts believes that it
is still possible to evaluate its conduct. On the positive side, "the state is
more than the individual. It is in its idea the organization of men through
which they achieve what is impossible for them singly." As examples of
such achievements, he points to social practices like restraining violence,
enforcing contracts, and protecting rights. None of these practices could
be carried out by separate individuals; but collectively, social institutions
create the possibility of peaceful and progressive interaction. On the negative side, however, the evils from which the nation-state suffers are, "in
part at least, due to the unregulated and only very partially responsible
organization for power." He maintains that it is this power focus, and the
lack of international structure, that leads to warfare; and he rejects the
assumption of progress present in the claim that success in war is to be
evaluated like success in business. Tufts's quick response is that "an army
is no better test of a nation's character than a football team of a university
. . ." Developing this response into a longer answer, he reminds his audience that "[w]hile success may be secured by public service it may also be
secured by strangling competitors, and for this latter purpose the moral
virtues are not the qualities chiefly necessary," and that "despite all our
own inefficiency in national, state and city government, we of America still
believe there is a value in self-government." Further, he challenges the
view implicit in the unbridled struggle mentality that the last to survive

---

[9] Tufts, "Ethics of States," 131–35.

would be vindicated. "Unless we are ready to go the whole way and deny that anything that exists is evil," he notes, "we must use some other standard of value than existence . . ."[10]

Tufts then turns from the question of self-interest to a consideration of honor. While recognizing its power to touch "deep chords in the natures of all of us," he points out that, at least on the individual level, honor has fallen in rank in recent times, noting the demise of formerly accepted social customs like dueling and feuds, and the belief that physical labor is taboo. On the international plane, however, honor still remains primary: "we are hypnotized by the words 'honor' and 'the flag' without asking whether honor may not have other standards than repute for strength, other supports than the sword." Still, he points to the possibility of international law and of higher public consciousness to create a world where law could surpass national self-interest and honor. As he writes: "no student of history can doubt the influence of law upon the formation of a moral consciousness. Law has been the schoolmaster to develop the consciousness of duty, and we need not be too cynical in our judgment upon the morals of nations which have lacked this education." Progress has been made on many fronts; and, despite the current war in Europe, there remains the possibility of building "a higher public conscience." When we come to reassess our situation, we will recognize, Tufts believes, "the need of adding to political codes of self preservation and honor the further codes of justice toward others, of friendly intercourse, and even, remote as it may seem, of devotion to the uniting ideals of mutual understanding, mutual aid, common sympathy, and common humanity . . ."[11]

Having met twice in 1914—in April and in December—the WPA did not meet at all in 1915. The APA met in December 1915; and, while the program did not officially address the war raging in Europe, it played an important role in Josiah Royce's autobiographical remarks, discussed in chapter 5, when he suggested that "unless the enemies of mankind are duly rebuked by the results of this war" he did not wish "to survive the crisis."[12] At the WPA's sixteenth meeting in April 1916, "the philosophy of the state" was chosen as the main topic of the meeting, and papers related to this broad theme predominated. Among the papers presented were: L. L. Bernard, "War and the Democratic State"; Edmund Howard Hollands, "Nature, Reason, and the Limits of State Authority"; Horace C. Longwell, "Philosophia Ancilla Civilitatis"; Hartley Burr Alexander, "Liberty and Democracy"; and George H. Sabine, "Liberty and the Social System." Their overall tenor was reported by Alexander and Boyd Henry Bode as follows:

---

[10] Ibid., 137, 139, 142–45.
[11] Ibid., 145–49.
[12] Royce, *Hope of the Great Community*, 132.

The problems foremost in the papers and in the discussions may be summarized: (1) The meaning of individualism and the place of initiative in the Hegelian and other German conceptions of the state; especially, are liberty and progress possible in a state organized as a logically closed system? (2) Liberty in relation to democracy: what are the guarantees of freedom, and indeed what is the meaning of freedom in a democracy? (3) The relation of economic and political freedom, and the possibility of adjusting these without disrupting democratic institutions. (4) The definition of nationality: if race, language, religion, politics do not make the state, what is it?

They note that on the whole "both in papers and discussions there was more of a tendency to set and define problems than to suggest solutions" (JP 13:374–80).

In addition to these papers at the WPA's sixteenth meeting, the presidential address of Alfred Henry Lloyd, "The Doctrinaire in Time of Crisis," focused upon the war, and offered a defense of the admittedly impractical and seemingly irrelevant activity of philosophers. The "doctrinaire," whom he describes as "the man of far vision," may seem out of place in the modern world, especially at a time when "military preparation and scientific efficiency" are called for from all sides. Because of their vision, however, such individuals are more important than practical thinkers: "before war one cannot prepare, during war one cannot fight and, above all, after war one cannot live by soldiers or munitions alone." He thus indicates the important possibilities and responsibilities that exist for philosophers in a neutral country and praises the level of thinking that was demonstrated in the many political papers that were being read at the meeting. Lloyd also offered his praise for another group of doctrinaires: the pacifists. Although widely regarded as guilty "of abstraction and sentiment," of dreaming "of a most visionary future," and of blindness to "present facts," he regards them as a necessary counterbalance to "the equally unreasoning abstraction . . . in the present cult of preparedness." Further, he sees their essential role in a neutral nation as helping to prepare for the post-war world, by recognizing "the possibility that the struggle itself has created of a new and better way of international living." In good Wilsonian fashion, he writes that "[s]taying out of the war with dignity," a neutral nation "must fight for the best results of the war . . . to make the results true to its best genius and vision." This struggle, Lloyd thought, was largely in the hands of the philosophers and other doctrinaires.[13]

Again at the December 1916 meeting of the APA, the European War was largely lost among other considerations: the deaths of Royce and Alexander Thomas Ormond, the attempts to chart the future direction of

---

[13] Lloyd, "Doctrinaire in Time of Crisis," 493, 482, 495, 497–99.

the association, and contingency plans to unify the various philosophical associations. The following motion by Morris Raphael Cohen, however, was passed:

> Recognizing that international cooperation in science and philosophy has been at the basis of what is most valuable in civilization, and that the animosities aroused by the present war threaten to make such cooperation impossible in the future, we reaffirm our faith in international cooperation in the search for truth, and we pledge ourselves to do all in our power to the end that the community of philosophy, as typified by such institutions as the International Congress of Philosophy, be restored as soon as possible. *Resolved*, that a committee be appointed to report on ways and means in which the American Philosophical Association may be made to serve that end (PR 26:197).

Out of this resolution arose the Committee on International Cooperation that will return in chapter 15.

On 6–7 April 1917, the WPA met in Ann Arbor. On the first day of the meeting, the United States—as had been expected—declared war on Germany. The meeting itself, however, gave little reflection of this solemn time. The sole war-related presentation came that very evening, when George Herbert Mead delivered his presidential address, "The Instinct of Hostility."[14] Mead's theme is the power and the danger that hatred of the outsider has for forging social solidarity. He begins with a consideration of the origin of a group's sense of itself that develops in a context of great mutual adaptation, and a group's sense of itself that develops in the face of a hostile enemy. He notes that "the consciousness of self through consciousness of others is responsible for a more profound sense of hostility— that of the members of the groups to those opposed to it, or even to those merely outside it." This hostility for outsiders "has the backing of the whole inner organization of the group" and "provides the most favorable condition for the sense of group solidarity because in the common attack upon the common enemy the individual differences are obliterated." In the mental state of the endangered group we lose our selves as individuals and reemerge as the defenders of group values. "The cry of 'stop thief' unites us all as property owners against the robber," he continues. "We all stand shoulder to shoulder as Americans against a possible invader."[15]

There is a problem with this sort of solidarity, however, because "[j]ust in proportion as we organize by hostility do we suppress individuality." Moreover, this hostility or hatred aims solely at the elimination of the dangerous enemy and thus cannot work towards eventual reconciliation

---

[14] Mead's paper, "The Instinct of Hostility," was never published as such, although its themes appeared soon after in "The Psychology of Punitive Justice."

[15] Mead, "Psychology of Punitive Justice," 215–16, 228.

and larger community. Mead notes further that, while this "attitude of hostility" towards the external foe gives the group a strong sense of solidarity "which most readily arouses like a burning flame and which consumes the differences of individual interests," the costs to the society of this stance are "great and at times disastrous." A society that has fused itself into one in the face of a foreign menace is a society that cannot adapt to the full range of social experience. The same processes that allow the individual to adopt "the attitude in which he undergoes suffering and death for the common cause" also incline the collective to actions that, because they represent "the attitude of self-assertion of a self which is fused with all the others in the community" are not as circumspect as those of a free and diversely-thinking society. Mead's message, then, as American society was reaching for the sword was to avoid, as much as possible, the kind of social fusion that results from the attitude of hostility to the enemy.[16]

The seventeenth meeting in December 1917 was the only APA meeting while the United States was at war. In his account of the meeting, Irwin Edman begins by noting, "Philosophers, as somewhat amorphously defined by the popular imagination, are profound irrelevant people totally and absurdly unaffected by considerations of time and space." As such, it was possible to have expected that the American entry into the war would have no effect on them. As Edman phrases the point, "the mere fact of there being current under the forms of time and space a war that was occupying the attention and the energies of the whole world should have made no difference at the Christmas meeting of the Association . . ." Such was not the case, however, and this meeting was "a War Meeting" concerned especially with international relations. In a parallel account of the meeting, Warren Fite noted that "even philosophers, accustomed to view the world *sub specie eternitatis*, are more deeply moved by a topic referring to the temporary tragedy of the present time . . ." (JP 15:177–78, 181). In his presidential address, "The Opportunity of Philosophy," for example, Addison Webster Moore points to the severity of the struggle—"we are in the midst of a war . . . in comparison to which all others have been mere skirmishes"—and indicates that only a post-war transformation that eliminates unscientific "idols" in such areas as politics and religion can prevent future destruction. As he writes, "The world can never be made 'safe for democracy' so long as tribal survivals can avail themselves of a theory which places values above or below, at any rate beyond, scientific treatment on the ground that they are either 'unique' or 'universal' . . ." What

---

[16] Ibid., 228–29, 235. For other of Mead's war related writings, see: "The Psychological Bases of Internationalism"; "The Conscientious Objector"; "Social Work, Standards of Living and the War."

needs to occur, he continues, is the expansion of "the democratization of values."[17]

The discussion session at this meeting was built around the topic of "Ethics and International Relations," with papers by Tufts, William Ernest Hocking, Harry Allen Overstreet, and Lovejoy. Tufts's contribution to the discussion was a paper entitled "Ethics and International Relations" that resembles in many ways his presidential address from the joint meeting of the WPA and the APA in December 1914. He begins with a quick indication of his belief that there must be some sort of connection between the two: "If there can be no genuine moral principle that does not hold good for all rational beings, if consequences of happiness or well being for all rationals must be reckoned with, if good and bad are properties of things independent of opinion, or if good is the transcendent and eternal—on any of these ethical theories right and good should not be determined by national frontiers." His longer answer is in three parts, beginning with a consideration of responsibility. He admits that there are many individuals at present who maintain that there should be a complete split between moral and social questions. Why then, he wonders, do states make moral appeals? If moral questions are separated from social ones, why does the state act as if "moral justification is necessary strategy" and attempt to "make its wars appear wars of self defense . . ."? Other individuals admit a relationship between morality and the actions of states; but they reject the individual interpretation of ethics for another that allows for 'higher' struggles. Under this interpretation, he continues, heroism and struggle and suffering are moral in a 'higher' way, and "[m]orally, as legally, the state can do no wrong." As an example, he points to the belief that the human's highest duty is to the state. "Englishmen and Americans, [Hugo] Münsterberg explains, are too hedonistic and egoistic in their ethics to apprehend such a superindividual object of loyalty." Tufts's response here is direct. "I can only wonder," he writes, "whether those who have actually been close enough to the trenches and the empty homes to take in the full experience of such a war as this, will still regard it as the best life." For him, ethics and international relations must be connected; and one of the tasks "of ethics in relation to international relations, is to discover and point out how far intelligent methods of co-operation may supersede conflict as an international process." Just as business competition can be socially beneficial or cutthroat, so can international relations be either military and dominating or cooperative in nature. Concluding his consideration of responsibility, he writes, "the doctrine of the state as naked power issues in an ethics of power which doubtless has claimed admiration, but

---

[17] Addison Webster Moore, "Opportunity for Philosophy," 118, 132. This address was considered more fully in chapter 10.

which when universalized . . . becomes too horrible a thing for most men to tolerate, and which even in its own test of power ignores the greater power of co-operation and good will as compared with conflict." For Tufts, the connection between ethics and international relations is plainly required by responsibility, for "if the world is to remain tolerable for man no single group or organization, whether it call itself 'state' or by less pretentious name, can claim exemption from moral responsibility."[18]

The second part of Tufts's discussion of ethics and international relations considers the topic of justice, especially with regard to issues of growth versus the *status quo*. While this issue was, of course, prominent in German demands for room to grow and for empire, he discusses other instances in which the *status quo* was upset as well. He considers, for example, the European dispossession of Native Americans. He defends that process, maintaining that "the right of the whites to the territory controlled by the United States rests less on any treaties with the Indians than on the fact that under the civilization of the whites the land supports a hundred millions and may support many more, whereas under the Indian . . . it was far less fruitful." Thus, while he emphasizes that "individual Indians ought to have been treated with consideration and humanity," he rejects the claim that "the collective units, the tribes, ought to be preserved forever in their original states of exclusive occupancy of the whole continent." (He suggests that this case is similar to the mechanization of production: "Individual workers ought not to bear the burden of readjustment, but society cannot refuse to accept inventions on the ground that some men will lose their employment in tasks for which they have acquired special skill.") Tufts believes that it would be unjust for the native Americans to have prevented the changes that were necessary for the larger group's progress. The American situation, however, differs from contemporary German demands for territory because the Germans do not claim to represent a *larger* community but only a *better* one, and because economic adjustments are now possible without conquest. As he writes, "it is increasingly unnecessary for a nation to own mines or forests or soil in order to obtain heat and metal, wool and wheat."[19]

The final section of Tufts's paper is directed toward the issue of the ultimate values of either aristocracy or democracy. While recognizing that blanket statements have exceptions, he writes that the Central Powers favor the former, whereas the Allies favor the latter. Those who control the Central Powers "maintain or accept the militarist scheme of subordination of civil to military power. The dominating forces of the opposing group are

---

[18] Tufts, "Ethics and International Relations," 299, 302–3, 305–7. For Münsterberg's position, see: *Peace and America*, 57–86.

[19] Tufts, "Ethics and International Relations," 308–9.

increasingly democratic and have no disposition to allow military forces the decisive word in national policy." Aristocracy he associates with feudalism, with permanent classes and passive resignation. "A feudal morality," he writes, "finds in loyalty to a superior complete satisfaction and sufficiently ethical sanction for any act . . . feudal morality is the *Herrenmoral* of a ruling class." Democracy, on the other hand, he associates with the modern world, with change and possibility. "Democracy believes in experimenting with human nature, in taking chances, that new powers may unfold." The former accepts the power of some over others; the latter the benefits of equality. In all three of these areas—responsibility, justice and ultimate values—Tufts suggests that international relations must recognize the importance of ethics, and that in fact ongoing trends demonstrate this recognition.[20]

The second speaker, Hocking, also took the position that states are not beyond the realm of morality. In his abstract published before the meeting, he suggests how he sees sovereignty to be compatible with the acknowledgment of moral obligation by nation-states. For him, sovereignty is no bar to moral responsibility. "The idea of sovereignty," he writes, "indicates a kind of equality among sovereign states which alone makes obligation applicable." Thus, a sovereign state is not emancipated from moral concerns. Rather, it possesses a "finality of decision" on the part of its leaders—political, legislative, judicial—that is "analogous to the independence implied in maturity, not to the independence implied in the 'state of nature.'" Moreover, there is to his mind a kind of collective responsibility among these sovereign nations to uphold international morality. Here, Hocking is pointing to "a permanent nucleus of common principles" to be upheld by sovereign nations, thus preventing what he characterizes as a "Darwinian struggle for survival among states . . ." Among these principles are developing "a common body of international goods" and recognizing "the common obligation of all states to intervene by force in the maintenance of this rule and of these goods" (JP 14:698–700).[21]

The published version of Hocking's remarks, "Sovereignty and Moral Obligation," is far ranging. In this paper, he proposes a way of understanding the relationship of the individual and the state that makes the state a necessity and ongoing component to moral interactions. Part of his position comes from his belief that the sovereign state represents the final-

---

[20] Ibid., 310–13; cf. JP 15:181–82. For other of Tufts's war related writings, see: *The Real Business of Living*; *The Ethics of Cooperation*; and "Wartime Gains for the American Family."

[21] In the proceedings of the APA's 1917 meeting, Hocking's abstract is mistakenly replaced by part of Tufts's abstract (PR 27:175–76; JP 14:720–21).

ity of decision. If we are to act together, decisions must be made; and the power to make them must be localized somewhere. Another aspect of his position comes from his belief that political interests have what he calls "*psychological priority*" to such other interests as "recreation, industry, religion, professional fraternity, etc." He continues: "the state is on a different psychological plane than other groups . . . The state does not *include* the end of religion, commerce, industry. It is not quite the case that it *provides the conditions* which makes them possible." The state thus represents to Hocking a kind of "supervisory mind" that is required to coordinate society's various experiments. When this political will, or sovereignty, is exercised, however, it must be used in accord with accepted domestic or international moral standards. Thus, he writes that the moral relations of sovereign states are "precisely analogous to those of sovereign persons." Drawing out this parallel, he continues that just as "children and other wards" are not seen as fully responsible moral beings, "the world naturally divides itself into sovereign and part-sovereign states *on the basis of maturity*. States are recognized as sovereign precisely because they are morally responsible,—the very reverse of supposing them sovereign because they are above moral obligation."[22]

The final aspect of his position is that we cannot simply apply codes of personal justice to international affairs because our contemporary standards of justice—legality that would continue the *status quo* and equity that would shatter it—are unsatisfactory for the international realm. His proposal here is the development of an international conscience that could clarify moral issues among nation states. He notes that "the third kind of justice we need is no other than the familiar justice of the family, which in giving gifts to children does not feel obliged to make the gift to A identical with the gift to B for equity's sake . . ." The obvious problem is that sovereign states, comfortable with inherited ideas of autonomous amorality, seem not yet ready to adopt this view of international morality. Consequently, no state seems now able to rely upon such a public mind: "it is very doubtful whether it yet exists *in sufficient volume* to justify any state in entrusting its interests to the keeping of international conscience." This situation, however, might well be changing. To trust in the international defense of a family sense of justice—Hocking's interpretation of "[t]he deliberate self-sacrifice of Belgium"—might seem foolhardy and negligent; on the other hand, it "might conceivably be the opposite of folly and crime, if it were a necessary sacrifice to arouse a slumbering world-conscience into competent action." The latter position is clearly his.[23]

---

22 Hocking, "Sovereignty and Moral Obligation," 320–22.
23 Ibid., 325–26; cf. JP 15:182–83.

In his paper, "Ethical Clarifications through the War," Overstreet discusses a series of four factors that had contributed to the war and that he believes would be understood differently after peace returned. The first of these was the process of economic expansion, especially as business enterprise had "overleaped national boundaries" and brought with it various forms of diplomatic and eventually military intervention to protect these international investments. After the war, he suggests, there would have to be "free trade, free markets, free investment opportunities . . ." The second factor to which he points was the increasing level of nationalism and the desire for greater cultural unity within national borders. He thinks that these narrowings would be replaced by "the free development of all authentic life in the light of standards increasingly internationalized . . ." His third theme is the political claim made more frequently by nation states in recent years "to a finality of rights and powers" that he thinks must give way to the recognition that "there is a jurisdiction above that of the separate states" and that "jealous independence is to give way to a generous and effective leaguing of nations in co-operative rights and obligations." Overstreet calls his final point "temperamental," and he means by this particularly the temperament of Prussianism, "a temper, an attitude, a way of regarding things and of getting things accomplished. It is the temper which is the opposite of the urbane, the conciliative, the generous." The Prussian temperament would be replaced by the development of "a frank willingness to let all life, big and little, have its full opportunity of productive satisfaction." Such changes as these four represent "the hope of a sanely reconstructed world"; and he believes that at least a significant portion of these four changes "will be realized as the immediate outcome of the war."[24]

Lovejoy's contribution—"The Limits of the Analogy between Personal and Social Ethics"—does not seem to have been published, nor did he provide an abstract.[25] Based on Warner Fite's discussion, Lovejoy's presentation dealt with the fact that while property rights and national sovereignty both appear to be absolute, claims of property rights are in fact limited by the national power of eminent domain. Thus, no claim to limitless national sovereignty can be drawn from such an analogy. While there is at present no such power at the international level to restrain claims of sovereignty, the argument would seem to indicate the eventual presumption of limitations on national sovereignty (JP 15:183–84). The discussion

---

[24] Overstreet, "Ethical Clarifications through the War," 327, 346, 337, 346, 342, 346; cf. JP 15:183.

[25] This failing seems remarkable in the light of Lovejoy's ongoing work on behalf of the discussion sessions, as we have seen in chapters 8 through 10, and can only be attributed to the pressures of his war work.

of these four papers involved, in addition to the principals, Fite, R. F. Alfred Hoernlé, Mary Whiton Calkins, William Kelley Wright, James Edwin Creighton, James H. Dunham, and Cohen; and Fite reports that this discussion session was successful and stimulating, and that "it ended all too quickly" (JP 15:181; cf. 184–87).

In March 1918, the only meeting of the WPA while Americans were fighting the war in Europe took place. A number of papers dealt with its impact, including: Clarence E. Ayres, "Intellectual Reconstruction after the War"; Albert E. Avey, "The Problem of Philosophical Methodology in the Light of the War"; Edward Leroy Schaub, "Ethics and Social Reconstruction" (JP 15:522–25). The Armistice was signed on 11 November 1918. Six weeks later, the APA met at Harvard. Edman describes the mood of the meeting as follows:

> Perhaps it is because the war is over that philosophy has felt free to relax, and return as of old to its privileged triflings with eternal things. Perhaps even with the armistice signed, peace genuine and enduring comes only with the perspective of eternity. Certainly there was much less in evidence at this year's meeting of . . . that passionate and purposeful concern with the reconstruction of reality which has been a latter day preoccupation of philosophy . . . Philosophers seemed to have felt that they had done their bit (the records of the War Department will bear them out, as did the presence of uniforms at the meetings), and were entitled now to the glorious dissipation of problems at once provocative and insoluble.

He continues, "Peace was celebrated with irresponsible irrelevance by a revival of the controversy as to the primacy of mind or matter, stated in its modern equivalence, mechanism *versus* vitalism" (JP 16:127), in a discussion session that was considered in chapter 10. In spite of this account, a few of the papers read dealt with social and political themes. Among them were Alexander's lament, "Wrath and Ruth," with which I began chapter 11, and Wilbur Marshall Urban's "How Are Moral Judgments on Groups and Associations Possible?" At the business meeting, the Committee on International Cooperation, established at the 1916 meeting, was continued. In addition, the following motion of Horace Meyer Kallen was read but tabled: "*Resolved*: That it is the sense of the American Philosophical Association that the indispensable instrumentality of a just and lasting peace is a League of Free Nations democratically organized and administered and designed to serve the common interests, economic and political, of all nations. Be it further resolved that notice of this resolution be sent to the President and to the Senate of the United States" (PR 28:178–85). There is no indication that this motion was ever taken up for further consideration.

HARTLEY BURR ALEXANDER
Photo courtesy of Archives and Special Collections,
University of Nebraska–Lincoln

14

The Unification of the Associations

Had America's philosophers been asked in the early twentieth century how many general philosophical associations were necessary, I suspect that few would have responded that America needed more than one. America, of course, had two; and, while it seems that there was a general feeling that unification was desirable, advance toward this goal eluded them. We have seen in chapters 4 and 5 that, from the very founding of the WPA and the APA, there was a good deal of discussion about effecting some sort of affiliation between the two associations. This initial flurry of effort toward amalgamation failed to produce any positive results, however, and, as the two associations developed, the topic disappeared from discussion for the next decade. After a dozen or so years of existence, the two associations again began to exert efforts toward unification. A number of unsuccessful plans were introduced and debated over the next decade before a national APA was created in 1927. We can consider these halting steps in sequence.

The first of these was a curious development that occurred at the thirteenth meeting of the APA in 1913, when one of the members proposed that the APA authorize the creation of regional branches. The motion, offered by Walter B. Pitkin and passed by the membership, ran as follows:

> I. That the Executive Committee be authorized to organize at its discretion, branches of the American Philosophical Association upon application for such action by members of the Association resident in or near the place of organization. II. No branch society thus organized shall be allowed to elect members to the Association nor to itself. III. No branch society shall be allowed to hold a meeting within two weeks of the date on which the current annual meeting of the Association shall be held (PR 23:177).

What, if anything, the executive committee did with this new power is not reported in the proceedings of this meeting. Nor is there any record of the committee acting upon this power later. Moreover, this plan for regional meetings seems to have never returned in subsequent discussions.

A more promising step toward unification occurred at the joint meeting of the two associations—the first such meeting—that took place in December of 1914 at Chicago. In his report on this meeting, Wendell T. Bush writes, "It had long been felt that the title, American Philosophical Association, was too comprehensive to be properly the name of any single society." As we have seen, however, over the prior decade little had been done to resolve the situation, except to reserve the topic for discussion at the first joint meeting of the two associations. "The meeting just held at Chicago being the first joint meeting, the question was automatically revived" (JP 12:108). With James Hayden Tufts in the chair as president of both the APA and the WPA for that year, the discussion turned to the terms of unification of the two associations, with an additional twist. In the proceedings, we read that the association "discussed at some length the matter of the present organization of the philosophical interests of the country into three associations, The American, The Western, and The Southern, and considered such questions as the advisability of amalgamating these into one association, an American, with three sections, and, accordingly, of changing the name of the present American Philosophical Association." One of the suggested plans was that following this unification there could be "both general and sectional meetings" to be held in some alternating arrangement. The whole matter was referred to a committee "with instructions that this committee receive suggestions and invite discussion" (PR 24:185). The twist here is the surprising inclusion of the SSPP, simplified as a 'philosophical' association. As far as I can determine, the SSPP had expressed no interest whatever in affiliating with the APA and/or the WPA. This society was founded as an explicitly philosophical and psychological association, and as an explicitly Southern one; and it had (and has) maintained the mutual nourishment of its dual emphases with its deliberately regional focus.

The merger discussions of December 1914 seem to have gone nowhere. The WPA, having met twice in 1914, did not meet in 1915. When the APA met in December of that year, the interest of the membership was focused on celebrating the sixtieth birthday of Josiah Royce, discussed in chapter 5. When the WPA met again in April 1916, the topic of unification returned and "a resolution was passed requesting the American Philosophical Association in conjunction with the Western and Southern Philosophical Associations to formulate a scheme of amalgamation into a single national society" (JP 13:375). At its December 1916 meeting, the APA responded with the following tentative but explicit unification plan that had been prepared by a committee of three appointed by the APA president, Arthur Oncken Lovejoy, and chaired by the APA secretary, Edward Gleason Spaulding:

TENTATIVE PLAN FOR THE AMALGAMATION OF THE AMERICAN
PHILOSOPHICAL ASSOCIATION,
THE WESTERN PHILOSOPHICAL ASSOCIATION, AND THE SOUTHERN
PHILOSOPHICAL ASSOCIATION.

I. The three Associations to become the Eastern, Western, and Southern branches of one new Association to be called the American Philosophical Association.

II. The American Association to have a meeting once in *three* or *four* years, the first or second week in September, at a place as geographically convenient as possible.

Comment.—This plan allows each of the three sections to have its usual meeting at Christmas, and will not deprive them of the opportunity of such a meeting as they would be deprived of, if the general meeting of the *new* Association were held at the holiday season. It also allows members to attend such a general meeting at a period which is at the end of the summer vacation and before the beginning of the academic year in most institutions. The sessions at the general meeting would be, perhaps, only one or two a day, and last four or five days, and possibly longer.

III. Each section to continue essentially its present organization and collection of yearly dues. The dues of the *new* organization to be one dollar for the period from meeting to meeting.

IV. The Executive Committee of the new Association to consist of two members of each sectional Association, together with the President, Vice-President, and the Secretary-Treasurer of the new Association.

V. The President, Vice-President, and Secretary-Treasurer of the Western Association to act as the officers for the first meeting, new officers to be elected at this meeting. The remaining members of the Executive Committee to hold office until the first meeting, and to be elected by each section of the Association at an early date before the first meeting of the Association.

Comment. This would be, seemingly, the most feasible plan for taking care of the first meeting, since this would most likely be held in the vicinity of Chicago as a central city, probably at some summer resort.

VI. The first meeting of the Association to be held in Sept., 1918.

VII. Each section to elect its own members as heretofore, these members thereby becoming members of the American Association.

VIII. This scheme to be submitted to each Association at as early a date as possible, and to go into effect only if all Associations accept it (PR 26:195–96).

The proceedings of the APA's 1916 meeting indicate that this proposal was not well received: "On motion of Professor Cohen, the report of the committee was accepted and the committee thanked. The report was then laid on the table with the request that the secretary notify the other associations of this action, and of the reasons therefor." In explanation of this action, Morris Raphael Cohen portrayed the thinking of the executive committee as follows:

1. While joint meetings of all the three philosophical societies were highly desirable, it did not seem that the proposed plan of holding such meetings was feasible, and, in any case, joint action by the three societies can always bring about a joint meeting whenever conditions are such as to make such a joint meeting practicable.

2. The proposed abandonment of the name American Philosophical Association by our society, and the adoption of such a name as the Eastern Philosophical Association would seriously interfere with the effectiveness of our present organization (which includes a large number of western members) and would not be of any help to the Western Philosophical Association. The majority of the members of the latter (41 out of 75) are now members of our Association; many of these have attended our meetings, read papers, or served as our officers. To change our name so as to emphasize the locality of the majority of our members would tend in the long run to cut us off from these valued western members without increasing the membership of the Western Association (PR 26:196–97).

Thus it was that the first explicit plan for unifying the associations was explicitly rejected. As we shall see, a decade of further attempts at unification were better received, but still failed to win approval.

Four months later, at the seventeenth meeting of the WPA in April 1917, the issue of amalgamation was again considered; and a resolution calling for further discussions was adopted unanimously. The three-point resolution ran as follows: "That the President-elect [Hartley Burr Alexander] be instructed to appoint a committee of three to state to the officials of the American Philosophical Association the regret of this association for the disposal of the report of their [own] committee proposing a union of the Eastern and the Western Associations; to request a conference with a committee of that association to discuss further plans for the formation of a national organization; and to act as the representatives of this association in this conference" (JP 14:403). Alexander carried the matter of unification forward with a long letter in September 1917 published in *The Journal of Philosophy* that in part addresses the relationships among the country's philosophical associations: "Members of the Western Philosophical Association are by no means satisfied with the attitude of the American Association toward their [own] plan of amalgamation, and hope for a reconsideration of that plan or for the suggestion of some other, perhaps more generally agreeable." In his mind, unification and further expansion was a practical necessity. "In a country territorially so vast as is the United States," he writes, "it is obvious that regional associations must grow in number with the passage of time; indeed, all North America ought to be the continental field for a single group of related associations, all gathering strength from their community of interest, and, if possible, of organization." He envisioned the continuation of the separate annual meetings with "a triennial meeting of all, or of large delegations from all, at Washington, or some other accessible point." Further, he envisioned that these general meetings would incorporate more than just philosophy. "If at the same time related sciences, especially the whole group of the sciences of man (psychology, anthropology, sociology, political science, and economy), could meet along with their mother, philosophy, the triennial meeting could assume the proportions of an important congress, of much significance for the learning of the continent." Believing that it was clear that "one of the great problems of the civilization of the continent is the common understanding of its ideals or that the bond of such understanding should be the universities," Alexander wonders, "what science is in better position to prepare the way than is philosophy?"[1] However rational this plan may have been, there is no indication that it piqued the interest of any discipline outside of philosophy; and, even within philosophy, this plan seems to have had little or no impact.

As a response to the WPA's resolution and to Alexander's letter, the following occurred at the APA's seventeenth meeting in December 1917: "On motion of Professor Tufts, it was voted that the Executive Committee, either directly or through a special committee, consider further, in connection with the Western and Southern Associations, the problem of securing more fully national and widely representative occasional meetings" (PR 27:170). A special committee was established, with Tufts as its chair; but the WPA was unsatisfied with this response, and at its next meeting it decided to apply some pressure. "The association resolved that a committee be appointed to communicate to the American Philosophical Association a definite plan of federation of American philosophical associations, and to formulate an alternative plan (involving a change of name) for the reorganization of the Western Philosophical Association, to be submitted at the next annual meeting, in case the American Philosophical Association refuses federation . . ." To carry out this plan, the WPA formed a committee composed of five individuals who were members of both associations: the outgoing WPA president Alexander, the WPA secretary Edward Leroy Schaub, Tufts, Henry Wilkes Wright, and Boyd Henry Bode (JP 15:519, 700). Their plan for the federation of the philosophical

---

[1] Alexander, "Letter from Professor Alexander," 643–44.

associations was published in *The Journal of Philosophy* a few weeks before the APA's 1918 meeting. The committee suggested that its objective was "primarily to find some form of workable organization for an association strong enough to maintain itself without weakening the work of the sectional groups" so that philosophy would have in America "a public unity of organization proportionate to the opportunities for influence that are opening out." This plan, while "provisional" in form and even including occasional "alternate suggestions," was then presented for the immediate consideration of the APA (JP 15:697).

In the preamble, the WPA committee suggests that to advance philosophy in America "as an educational discipline and as a social force" a national federation was necessary. The objectives of this federation were listed as three. The first was "[t]he advancement of philosophical learning through the closer cooperation of its professional teachers and students, as by means of congresses, special publications, councils and the like." The second objective of the proposed federation was "[t]he encouragement of philosophical activities amid the general public, especially by emphasis upon the social, political and religious bearings of philosophical thought." Finally, the committee called for "[t]he closer union of philosophy with the other sciences, if possible by means of a periodic congress in which should join representatives of all the branches of learning for the discussion of their common problems and related programmes." In order to achieve these objectives, the committee proposed "a federation, continent-wide in its scope" that would incorporate the APA and the WPA—and the "Southern Philosophical Association" if it were willing—and eventually expand further to include other geographical areas (JP 15:697–98). The nine-article plan ran as follows:

Articles of Organization

ARTICLE I. The name of the federation of the Philosophical Associations of North America shall be "The American Philosophical Association."

ARTICLE II. The federation shall comprise the Eastern Philosophical Association (hitherto known as the "American"), the Midwestern Philosophical Association (hitherto known as the "Western"), and such other American societies as shall be duly admitted thereto.

Note.—Invitation is hereby extended to the Southern Philosophical Association to join the federation; while, at the earliest opportunity, the officers of the federation are expected to encourage the formation of subsidiary societies, especially, a Northern (or Canadian), a Western (or Pacific Coast), and a Middle American (or Mexican-Antillean) Association.

ARTICLE III. The regular members of the federal association shall be the regular (but not the associate) members of the federated associations. There shall be an associate, or subscribing, membership to the federal association, to be filled by nomination and election by the regular membership. Associate, or subscribing, members, shall have all the privileges of membership in the federal association, excepting that they shall have no right to vote in the transactions.

ARTICLE IV. The officers of the federal association shall be president, first and second vice-presidents, and secretary-treasurer (or, secretary and treasurer). Their term of office shall be from the meeting of the association at which they are elected to the next ensuing regular meeting. They shall be elected by a majority vote of a quorum of the regular members; and the regular members present at any such meeting shall be regarded as constituting a quorum of the association membership.

ARTICLE V. The council of the federal association shall consist of its officers and of the executive officers (not more than two in each case) of the federated associations. (Or, the council of the federal association shall consist of not less than six or more than twelve members, each federation to be represented by an equal number of councillors, to be elected at their regular meetings.) It shall be the duties of the council to fix the time and place of all meetings, to arrange for and supervise programmes, to superintend the issuance of publications, and to advise the executive officers in all matters of business or policy coming up in the intervals between regular meetings.

ARTICLE VI. The regular meetings of the federal association shall be biennial. The time and place of such meetings shall be fixed by the council, as per Article V.

ARTICLE VII. The biennial dues of each member of the federal association shall be five dollars. In the case of regular members, two dollars (equivalent to the present regular annual fee) shall be retained in the treasuries of the federated associations to which the members belong, and three dollars shall pass to the treasury of the federal association. In the case of associate, or subscribing, members, the total amount shall pass to the treasury of the federal association.

Note.—This Article is regarded doubtfully by some members of the committee, on account of the amount of the fee. It seems certain, however, that publication of the Proceedings of the biennial meetings can not be if the fee is lowered (and the Proceedings ought to be worth the price). Associate membership in the federated associations could provide for those who do not care to become members of the federal association.

ARTICLE VIII. The Proceedings of each biennial regular meeting of the association shall be printed in the form of a volume, a copy of which shall be sent to each regular and associate member whose dues are fully paid.

Note.—It has been suggested that the federal association undertake the publication of a philosophical journal, subscription to which could be included in the membership fee; or that it make arrangements with some journal at present published in America, which should become its official organ. Possibly, the association could advance the interests of all or a number of these journals by offering its members a clubbing rate, assuming

certain financial obligations toward them, and in return receiving elective
editorial representation on their staffs.

ARTICLE IX. The council of the federal association shall encourage joint
meetings of the American Philosophical Association and other societies
devoted to the advancement of learning (JP 15:698-700).

At the APA's December 1918 meeting—just after the War had ended—
discussion of unification took place under the rubric of the report of
Tufts's APA committee, somewhat extravagantly named the "Committee
on the Possibility of Securing More Representative and Inclusive Meetings
of those Interested in Philosophy." This committee consisted of five APA
members: Tufts and Alexander—both of whom were serving on the WPA's
federation committee[2]—the current APA president, Mary Whiton Calkins,
Harry Allen Overstreet, and Albert Lefevre, the 1909 president of the
SSPP. This APA report begins historically with the recognition that "[t]he
present situation with three organizations, none of them completely inclusive, seems to be largely due to accident." There is a reference to the AΨA,
"[o]ur first organization," from which the APA separated because of what
were characterized as "increasing professional interests aided perhaps by
the increasingly technical character of psychology . . ." Similarly, there is a
reference to the WPA that was founded "[a]t about the same time," showing the same mix of philosophical and psychological interests. The committee mentions as well, and misidentifies, the "Southern Philosophical
Association" (PR 28:178).

The point of the committee's survey is to suggest the cause of the profession's current institutional disarray: "whereas the American Psychological Association, like similarly named associations in other fields, is a
general all-inclusive association, there are three philosophical associations
which overlap in part." The APA, while largely eastern, was never exclusively so in either its members or its officers. Further, as a result of this disarray, "we recognize that the American [Philosophical] Association at
present does not fully perform the service rendered by similarly named
associations in other fields." Especially with regard to the meetings, the
APA "does not bring together so many as ought to come together"
because the East Coast meetings attract few from the West, and vice versa.
Moreover, the report continues: "Meetings [of the APA] have not been
arranged with a view to cover all parts of the country so as to distribute the

---

[2] Tufts and Alexander eventually served as presidents of what were to become the three
divisions of the national APA. Tufts served as the sixth and fifteenth presidents of the WPA,
the fourteenth president of the APA, and the twelfth president of the Pacific Division of the
APA. Alexander served as the eighteenth president of the WPA, the nineteenth president of
the APA, and the sixth president of the Pacific Division of the APA.

expense of attending meetings somewhat equally over all sections." Rather, meeting locations had been determined "more by offers of hospitality, by the convenience of a majority of members, and by the thought that western and southern members had their own association" (PR 28:178–79).

Turning from these historical considerations to the future, the overriding theme of the rest of this report was that the philosophers of America had a larger role to play in the post-war world and that their associations(s) and meetings needed to have a higher profile. As the report continues, "in a republic a profession like ours has a duty not only to seek truth and to teach the young but also to contribute towards shaping institutions and public opinion." While admitting that part of this social role is satisfied by the publication of books and articles, the committee continues that "a comprehensive organization holding widely representative meetings would furnish additional opportunity and tend to call out the best thinking and most effective presentation." Balancing off the advantages of "larger gatherings" and the consequential "more comprehensive organization of the profession" against what was seen as the greatest disadvantage, the reality of travel expenses, the committee called for "a general meeting once in two or at most three years." Assuming that "a general meeting is worth some effort and sacrifice," the committee then offered three proposals, the first two of which were merely working sketches,[3] designed to make such meetings possible on a regular basis. The first plan called for increasing the scope of the APA to make it a national organization by:

(1) enlarging its membership, *e.g.*, by including all now enrolled in other Associations and some not now enrolled in any; (2) arranging a schedule of meetings for some years in advance, to be held in the several sections of the country with the understanding that the biennial or triennial meetings should be of especial importance; (3) constructing a program for these special meetings which should give prominence in at least one session, to the public as contrasted with the more purely technical aspects of philosophy; (4) making definite provisions for publishing papers, carrying out more completely the policy of the last and of this present meeting.

The second plan of Tufts's committee called for closer affiliation of the associations rather than for their amalgamation. Under this option, there would be biennial or triennial joint meetings under the leadership of individuals chosen by all three societies and the establishment of some modest ongoing structures to enable the three to work more closely in the future. The third plan, the fully articulated plan for a federation of philosophical

---

[3] The committee members had only been able to discuss the relative merits of the plans by mail.

organizations was the one contained in the WPA proposal that had been published just prior to the meeting.[4] The committee expected that the first plan would be the most controversial, because neither of the others "would interfere with the present excellent work of the respective Associations" (PR 28:179–80). In any case, the committee was adamant that something had to be done; and it further suggested that a general meeting of American philosophical associations should be held in 1919 if possible.

After its acceptance, the report was considered by the APA membership. Among the speakers was Warner Fite, who favored adopting the second plan. Durant Drake then proposed:

(1) That we instruct the committee of which Mr. Tufts is chairman that it is the wish of this Association to join with the Western and Southern Philosophical Associations in constituting an inclusive association, and thereupon to change the name of our existing Association, that the new inclusive Association may bear the name "American Philosophical Association." (2) That we instruct said committee to confer with a committee of the Western Association upon the problems involved in creating the inclusive association, and upon the proposal that congresses of the inclusive association shall be held, reporting the results of this conference to this Association as its next annual meeting.

Overstreet, a member of Tufts's committee, proposed to delete "and thereupon to change the name of our existing Association, that the new inclusive Association may bear the name 'American Philosophical Association'" from the proposal; this was approved, and the amended motion was carried. In response, Drake proposed the following amendment to the APA constitution, in an attempt perhaps designed to set the process in motion: "The name of this organization shall be the Eastern Division of the American Philosophical Association" (PR 28:181–82). This proposed amendment to the constitution was automatically scheduled for a vote at the next meeting.

Four months later, at the WPA's nineteenth meeting in April 1919, a report was read by the "Committee on the Federation of Philosophical Associations," presumably still led by Alexander. As modified and adopted,

---

[4] Alexander, the WPA president and chair of the committee that produced the WPA plan, summarized it at the APA's 1918 meeting as calling for "a general federation of all philosophical societies in America. The name of the federation was to be 'The American Philosophical Association.' It was to have, besides the regular officers, a Council, consisting of these officers and the executive officers of the federated associations. The regular meetings were to be biennial; biennial dues to be five dollars, apportioned between the federal and the federated associations. The Proceedings were to be printed in the form of a volume" (PR 28:180).

this report contained four resolutions. The first was "[t]hat a committee be appointed to confer with the committee of the American Philosophical Association in the interest of formulating a workable plan of union or federation of the several philosophical associations of the United States." The second was that, although the WPA favored "some such plan as that presented by our committee to the American Philosophical Association," it was willing "to enter into a less binding or formal or a more provisional type of association than is there offered should this seem advisable to the joint committee." The third resolution was that, should the APA change its name at its upcoming meeting, the WPA should similarly change its name to "American Philosophical Association, Central Branch" to express "the assumption that we have formed at least a nominal union with the American Association." The final resolution dealt with plans for the future of this new federation:

> That we recommend for the consideration of the joint committee the following propositions: (A) that biennially or triennially there shall be held a Congress of the several Philosophical Associations, or branch associations. (B) That the date of such Congress should fall some time during the summer, preferably in early September. (C) That the place chosen for such Congress should be an attractive vacation or summering place, or, if the conditions seem to favor, some college or university. (D) That a feature of each Congress should be one or two series of lectures or a symposium to be arranged by the joint committee. (E) That the first such Congress be held in the eastern part of the United States in September, 1920, and that the committee of this association be empowered to act with committees of the American and Southern associations for the arrangement and supervision of the meeting, subject to similar authorization of the committees of the American and Southern Associations by their respective memberships (JP 16:462–63).

The Committee on Federation with the addition of the new WPA president, Norman Wilde, was continued in existence for another year.

At the APA meeting in December 1919, with Alexander now in the chair as APA president, the matter of the constitutional amendment proposed by Drake the year before was considered and passed. Article I, Section I, of the association's constitution now read: "The name of this organization shall be the Eastern Division of the American Philosophical Association." The association had thus voted to become part of a nonexistent organization, a move that seems to have caused no particular puzzlement among the assembled ontologists. It was further moved and carried "that the matter of closer association between the Western, Eastern, and Southern Associations be referred to the Committee on Organizing and Attendance," with Tufts as chair (PR 29:156). At the WPA meeting a few months later in April of 1920, there was another report of the Committee on the Federation of Philosophical Associations, of which Alexander was the Chair, that after slight modifications, was accepted. The report began with the notification of the WPA members that "no definite response" to the offer of closer affiliation with the SSPP had been received, although some of its members had expressed their approval. Then the report turned to the events that had transpired at the 1919 APA meeting, especially the name change of the APA to the "Eastern Division of the American Philosophical Association" and the Eastern Division's continued interest in "closer association." In response to these actions, the committee recommended that the WPA change its name to the "Western Division of the American Philosophical Association" and that the association express its "cordial appreciation of the courtesy of the members of the Eastern Division of the American Philosophical Association, and the hope that the change of name may be the foretoken of a more intimate association of the memberships of the two Divisions." Going further, the committee also recommended the following:

> (*a*) That the matter of securing a joint meeting be continued with a committee appointed for this purpose, to act in consultation with the committee similarly empowered by the Eastern Division. (*b*) That the members of the Western Division express their hope that the first joint meeting, or congress, may be arranged to be held in the first or second week of September, 1921, on the campus of some university of the eastern states. (*c*) That the Western Division believe that the joint meeting should be made the occasion for the extending of an invitation to some American philosopher to deliver there a series of not less than five lectures upon some philosophical topic, the lecturer to be chosen by the committee organizing the programme. (*d*) That they also suggest the desirability of inviting the presence of delegates from other philosophical societies, American or foreign, thus giving the meeting the character of a philosophical congress (JP 17:317–18).

While the WPA carried through on its pledge to change its name to the Western Division of the as yet nonexistent APA, it could effect nothing further on its own; and the glacial advance toward the goal of closer unification between the divisions might, in the fashion of one of Zeno's paradoxes, still be going on had it not been for the incentive provided by the Paul Carus Foundation. Telling the story of the beginnings of the Carus Lectures requires a brief detour from the question of APA unification.

Paul Carus was born in Ilsenburg, Germany, in 1852. After his education in Strassburg and Tübingen, where he earned his Ph.D. in 1876, he moved to the United States. Once established in La Salle, Illinois, he made a philosophical career for himself outside of academe, as had a number of philosophers in America before the turn of the twentieth century. He became the editor of the magazine *Open Court* in 1888, and later founded

The Monist as a more technical philosophical journal. Carus was elected to membership in the APA in 1903. After his death in February 1919,[5] his family established the Paul Carus Foundation as a means of carrying on his work. One of the activities of this foundation was to fund a series of lecture and publication projects that we now know as the Carus Lectures. These philosophical lectures, unrestricted as to theme or content, were to be given on an ongoing basis by individuals chosen by a committee made up of representatives of the divisions and the Carus family. As such, the Carus Lectures thus constituted the first effective cooperative project between the divisions.

In Schaub's report on the 1920 WPA meeting, that we have just been considering, we read that "Mrs. Carus had generously made the offer of an honorarium, in memory of Dr. Paul Carus, for a course of lectures to be given on the occasion of the first joint meeting of the Divisions." This notion, as we have seen, was incorporated in the report by Alexander's committee. Further, in the business session, the membership decided to gratefully accept the offer: "The generous offer of Mrs. Paul Carus of an honorarium, in memory of Dr. Paul Carus, for a course of lectures to be given at the first joint meeting with the Eastern Division, was enthusiastically accepted and the secretary [Schaub] was instructed to convey to Mrs. Carus the deep appreciation of the Division" (JP 17:316, 318). At its 1920 meeting, the Eastern Division's Committee on Organization and Attendance, with Tufts as chair, reported that the division's efforts for developing "closer association between the Western, Eastern, and Southern Associations" had been carried a bit further and that the two divisions had "agreed that if the joint meeting should be arranged, they would favor inviting Professor John Dewey to give the lectures" (PR 30:193–94). The planning continued to inch forward slowly—contributing to the holdup was the fact that Dewey was then in China[6]—and at its 1921 meeting, the executive committee of the Eastern Division recommended that John Dewey be invited to lecture under the terms of the Carus gift on a philosophical topic of his choosing (PR 31:166).

The greatly anticipated joint meeting of the Eastern and Western Divisions of the APA took place in December 1922 at Union Theological Seminary in New York City. At this meeting, Dewey offered the inaugural Carus Lectures. He delivered, without discussion from the assembled philosophers, three lectures—on 27, 28, and 29 December—that contained the essence of chapters 2, 3, and 4 of his volume *Experience and*

---

[5] Carus's memorial at the APA's 1919 meeting was discussed in chapter 5.

[6] Dewey left for Japan in January 1919 and moved on to China in May. He returned to the US in July 1921. For some of the negotiations, see: Tufts to Dewey, 1 April 1921, *Correspondence of John Dewey*, #07208.

Nature.[7] In the business session of the Eastern Division just before Dewey's first talk, the question of the continuance of the lecture series, and closer affiliation of the divisions, was considered. On the recommendation of its executive committee, the membership voted to authorize the committee "to appoint three members, who, with three members appointed by the Western Division, shall constitute a committee which shall present to this Division at its next meeting a plan for an organization that shall effect a working relation between the two Divisions, and that shall have the legal power to receive and administer the Carus Lecture Fund . . ." Further, this committee would, "together with representatives of the Open Court Publishing Company . . . select the next lecturer on the Carus Foundation." Similarly, at its own business session that was meeting concurrently, the membership of the Western Division reiterated these themes. For the Western Division representatives on the Carus Committee, president Schaub selected Tufts, Alexander, and Guy Allan Tawney, all three of whom were also members of the Eastern Division (PR 32:199–200).

At the Eastern Division meeting in December 1923, the report of Tufts's Joint-Committee of the Eastern and Western Divisions was read. It recommended "that the next lecturer on the Carus Foundation be Professor J. E. Creighton of Cornell University" (PR 33:172). The membership of the Eastern Division approved of this choice of the founding President of the APA and longtime editor of *The Philosophical Review*; but how far the preparation of these lectures proceeded is not clear since Creighton died at the age of sixty-three on 8 October 1924. As a replacement for Creighton—although this characterization is hardly fair—former WPA and APA president Lovejoy was chosen to offer the second series of Carus Lectures. He did so at the joint meeting of the divisions in December 1927 at the University of Chicago, under the title: "A Critical Examination of the Contemporary Revolt Against Dualism" (PR 37:162).[8]

We left the unification story in April 1920, with the WPA's acceptance of the long report by Alexander's committee on the federation of the philosophical associations. At the Eastern Division meeting in December 1920, there was another report from Tufts's Committee on

---

[7] Cf. JP 19:720–21; 20:71–72. The volume was published by Open Court in February 1925.

[8] The resulting volume, *The Revolt against Dualism: An Inquiry concerning the Existence of Ideas*, was published by Open Court in 1929. There had been a suggestion that some European scholar(s) be chosen to replace Creighton, and that the second series of Carus Lectures be delivered at the planned Sixth International Congress of Philosophy (Cf. Hartley Burr Alexander to Catherine Cook, 15 October 1924, *Correspondence of John Dewey*, #17132).

Organizing and Attendance related to developing closer associations among the Western, Eastern, and Southern Associations. Among the matters considered in this report were: the suggestion that the members of the Eastern Division take note of the recent WPA actions; the announcement that agreement had been reached with the Western Division to ask Dewey to deliver a series of lectures at a joint meeting if it could be arranged; a request for "an expression of opinion from the members of the Eastern Division here present, (*a*) as to the possibility of a joint meeting to be held either in September [1921] or at some other time, (*b*) as to whether in case such a meeting is held, it would be preferable to hold it on the campus of an urban or a rural university or college"; and a recommendation "in case the opinion of the Association is favorable to further action," that the committee be authorized to proceed in cooperation with the committee of the Western Division (PR 30:193–94). Approval was given to pursue a joint meeting with the Western Division, and the arrangements were put in the hands of Tufts's committee and the division's executive committee, in consultation with the relevant representative of the Western Division. At their meeting in March 1921,[9] the members of the Western Division approved pursuing a joint meeting of the Eastern Division, preferably at Cornell in early September 1922. As we have seen, that joint meeting did not take place until December 1922 and in New York City. At the Eastern Division meeting at Vassar in December 1921, "[t]he Executive Committee recommended that the Association hold during 1922 one meeting, and that meeting (provided the Western Division agrees) to be a joint meeting with the Western Division at such time and place as shall be agreed upon by the Executive Committees of the two Divisions; and that Professor John Dewey be invited to lecture on some philosophical subject under the terms of the Carus gift" (PR 31:166).

The long-awaited joint meeting of the Eastern and Western Divisions of the APA in December 1922 produced the first joint *Proceedings* of the (national) APA, although there appears to have been no national business beyond pledges by the Eastern and Western Divisions to continue efforts at cooperation (PR 32:199–200). The Western Division did not meet in 1923; and by the time that the Eastern Division meeting took place in December 1923, there were few lasting traces of the flush from the prior joint meeting. The *Proceedings* themselves are again reported as those of the Eastern Division; and, while there was some discussion of the second series of Carus Lectures, there was no record of any further movement

---

[9] At this twenty-first meeting of the Western Division, Mrs. Carus was recognized for her support of philosophy in America and of the Western Division: "In recognition of her interest in the work of the Division and in the development of philosophical thought in American, Mrs. Mary Hegeler Carus was elected to honorary membership in the Division" (JP 18:436).

toward unification (PR 33:172). Similarly, in the account of the meeting of the Western Division in April 1924, there is no mention of either the Carus Lectures or further amalgamation.[10] At the Eastern Division's 1924 meeting in December 1924, however, the issue of unification returns. Among the various Eastern Division activities reported on at the business session, we read the following: "Contact with the Western Division has been established through Professor [Frederick J. E.] Woodbridge[11] as their representative, through the presence on the [joint] Organization Committee of Professors [Evander Bradley] McGilvary and Tufts, and through report from Professor [Andrew Campbell] Armstrong to Professor Tawney, Secretary of the Western Division, for their Annual Meeting of 1924. While no formal action was taken, their concurrence in plans made seems assured" (PR 34:167–68). Presumably, at least one of these plans was a publication project, the consideration of which is worth another slight detour. First, however, it is necessary to examine the founding of the Pacific Division.

The Journal of Philosophy reported in late 1924 that the first meeting of the Pacific Division of the APA had occurred on 28–29 November of that year at California. This association was a successor to the ill-fated Southwestern Philosophical Society that had met semiannually a number of times in California in the early 1920s.[12] The new association was founded at a meeting of philosophers from the University of California, Stanford, and the University of Washington in April 1924 at which "it was decided to organize a Philosophical Association which would offer to such properly qualified persons as reside in the far-western states, advantages and opportunities similar to those provided by the Eastern and Western Divisions of the American Philosophical Association in the East and Middle West." The individuals selected as the organizing committee for this new society were: George Plimpton Adams, Robert M. Blake, Harold Chapman Brown, William Ray Dennes, Curt John Ducasse (chair), Jacob Loewenberg, Stephen Coburn Pepper, Donald Wight Prall, William

---

[10] After the twenty-fourth meeting, the numbering of the Western Division's meetings goes awry. Guy Allan Tawney, the association's secretary-treasurer, mistakenly believing that there had been a meeting in late 1899, decided to call the April 1925 meeting at Illinois the 'twenty-sixth' although it was in fact only the twenty-fifth. This mistake led to the misnumbering of subsequent Western Division meetings for decades. See: Charles A. Morris to Tawney, 21 March 1930; Tawney to Morris, 4 April 1930 and 29 April 1930 (APA Western Division Archives, University of Illinois).

[11] While Columbia's Woodbridge might seem like an unlikely choice for this assignment, he had worked for unification when he was the president of the WPA in 1902, while he was at Minnesota before his move to New York City in 1902. He had also been APA president in 1911.

[12] Cf. PR 31:212; 32:119; JP 19:722.

Savery, and Henry Waldgrave Stuart. At the Pacific Division's first meeting in November of 1924, there was no president and, consequently, no presidential address, although Brown offered the keynote address to the twenty or so assembled philosophers. His title was "The Material World—Snark or Boojum?" Eight other papers were also read. At the business session on the first day of the meeting, a constitution was adopted and officers were elected for the upcoming year. The president was to be George Rebec; the vice-president, Brown; and the secretary, Ducasse. The executive committee was to consist of this trio plus Adams, Loewenberg, Bernard Capen Ewer, and Ralph Tyler Flewelling. Also a committee consisting of the newly elected president Rebec, Ducasse, and Prall was established to facilitate the development of relations with the Eastern and Western Divisions "on all matters of common interest." As expressed in its resolution the association desired "to establish with the American Philosophical Association the same affiliation that already exists between the Eastern and Western Divisions thereof, and to be permitted by it to assume officially the name of Pacific Division of the American Philosophical Association" (JP 21:719–21). I hesitate to remind the reader at this point that the APA is still a nonexistent association, however many divisions it might acquire.

The signs of a closer affiliation seemed favorable when the next month at the twenty-fourth meeting of the Eastern Division "[i]t was voted that this Division send greetings to the newly-organized society for Philosophy on the Pacific coast, and express the hope that this society will affiliate with the existing divisions as the Pacific Division of the American Philosophical Association" (PR 34:169). In addition, by the time that the second meeting of the Pacific Division occurred on Thanksgiving weekend, 27–28 November 1925 at Stanford, it had been invited to take part in the *Contemporary American Philosophy* project. At the Pacific Division's second meeting, President Rebec "reported that, in harmony with action taken by the Eastern Division at its last meeting, he had appointed Professors G. P. Adams, H. C. Brown, and C. J. Ducasse as members from this Division to a joint committee of the three Divisions, to consider the feasibility of a volume or volumes concerning contemporary American philosophy, similar to the recently published volumes concerning German philosophy." The presidential address by Rebec was entitled "Back to the Antinomies." After the election of new members, forty-three philosophers were listed as members of the division, at least two of whom were women.[13] Further business included the election of Stuart as the president for 1926, and the expression of support for the 1926 International Congress at Harvard (PR 35:173–75).

---

[13] The women were Georgiana Melvin and Ethel Sabin-Smith (PR 36:176–77).

It is now time to consider the cooperative publication project. At the Eastern Division's 1924 meeting, the executive committee recommended that the membership "consider the feasibility of a volume, or volumes, concerning contemporary American philosophy, similar to the recently-published volumes covering contemporary German philosophy[14]; this committee to report next year if possible, and if the project is found feasible, to include in its report the list of those intended to contribute." The plan was to select three members from the division who would then work together with an equal number from the Western Division and the newly organized Pacific Division. This plan was accepted by the membership, and president Alexander Meiklejohn was authorized to select the three representatives. He chose Edgar Sheffield Brightman, Maurice Picard and, as chair, William Pepperell Montague (PR 34:166; 35:163). At the Eastern Division's twenty-fifth meeting, this committee recommended:

> I. That the project for the publishing of a volume of Contemporary American Philosophy be approved. II. That the contributions consist of personal or autobiographical statements of each contributor's philosophical creed, and of the causes as well as the reasons that led to its adoption. III. That the kind offers made by Professor J. H. Muirhead and Herr Felix Meiner to bring out the volume in their respective countries be gratefully recognized by any committee of the Association entrusted with the management of the project; and that favorable consideration be given to the possibility of arranging for simultaneous editions of the volume in America, England and Germany, with suitable forwards by the foreign associate-editors as well as by the American editors.

This report was accepted and the committee was requested "to proceed to the selection of contributors to the volume" (PR 35:163). In 1926 Montague reported continued progress (PR 36:59), and the next year he reported that "[i]t now seems probable that two volumes will be published to include thirty-five or forty contributions" (PR 37:165). Finally, at the 1928 meeting, Montague reported that almost all of the invited essays had been received and that the two volume set of essays would be published by Macmillan "at an early date" (PR 38:161).

Contemporary American Philosophy: Personal Statements was published in two volumes by Macmillan in New York in 1930. The volumes were edited by Adams and Montague, who represented the Pacific and Eastern Divisions of the APA respectively. (Alfred Henry Lloyd was to have served

---

[14] These volumes, *Die deutsche Philosophie der Gegenwart in Selbstdarstellungen*, edited by Raymund Schmidt, had appeared in 1921. There was also a two-volume British equivalent, *Contemporary British Philosophy: Personal Statements*, edited by John Henry Muirhead, that appeared in 1924–1925.

as the third editor—representing the Western Division—but he died on 11 May 1927.) In the preface, Adams and Montague indicate that "[t]he contributors to the volumes were selected on the basis of a referendum vote of the membership of the three Divisions of the American Philosophical Association." They expressed their regret "that either through the more or less accidental omissions in this hastily taken referendum or through sudden illness, as in the case of Professor Addison Moore [d. 25 August 1930], a number of colleagues whose essays would have been greatly valued are not here represented." With regard to the content of the essays, the editors note that "[e]ach contributor was requested to state his principal philosophic beliefs, the reasons supporting them, and the manner in which he had reached them."[15] Volume one contains sixteen essays, including one by the dedicatee, George Herbert Palmer. The other authors were: Adams, Alexander, Armstrong, John Elof Boodin, Brown, Calkins, Morris Raphael Cohen, Gustavus Watts Cunningham, Drake, Ducasse, Walter Goodnow Everett, Warner Fite, William Ernest Hocking, Theodore de Laguna, and Joseph Alexander Leighton. Volume two contains eighteen essays, authored by: Dewey, Clarence Irving Lewis, Loewenberg, Lovejoy, McGilvary, Montague, De Witt Henry Parker, Ralph Barton Perry, James Bissett Pratt, Arthur Kenyon Rogers, George Santayana, Roy Wood Sellars, Edgar Arthur Singer, Jr., Charles Augustus Strong, Tufts, Wilbur Marshall Urban, Robert Mark Wenley, and Woodbridge.[16]

Returning from this fruit of closer affiliation to the ever-lengthening process of completing the unification of the divisions, we find little in the records of the next few business sessions. The big breakthrough occurred at the Eastern Division meeting at Harvard in September 1926, which was held as part of the Sixth International Congress (to be considered in chapter 15). It was at this meeting that a draft of a national APA constitution was adopted. "It was then voted that the Western Division and the Pacific Division be invited to approve this constitution" (PR 36:62). This constitution was similarly adopted at the third meeting of the Pacific Division in November 1926 and the twenty-seventh meeting of the Western Division in April 1927, thus establishing a national APA (PR 36:175, 357). In early 1928, the APA offered the first of its national publications: *Proceedings of the American Philosophical Association, 1927*, containing a report of the Board of Officers of the APA and the proceedings from the three divisions for the preceding year. It also contained the text of the newly approved constitution:

[15] Adams and Montague, preface to *Contemporary American Philosophy*, 1:9.

[16] The reviews of these volumes considered such themes as: the centrality of Harvard, the significance of religion, and the pluralism of the contributions. See, for example, Costello, review of *Contemporary American Philosophy*; Gotesky, review of *Contemporary American Philosophy*; Otto, review of *Contemporary American Philosophy*; Phelan, "Catholicism or Delusion."

CONSTITUTION OF THE AMERICAN PHILOSOPHICAL ASSOCIATION

ARTICLE I. *Name.*

The name of this organization shall be the American Philosophical Association.

ARTICLE II. *Membership.*

1. The membership shall be divided into three divisions—Eastern, Western, and Pacific.

2. Each division shall elect its own members.

ARTICLE III. *Officers.*

1. The officers of this Association, hereafter known as the Board of Officers, shall consist of the following duly elected officers of the several divisions—the Presidents and Secretary-Treasurers—*ex officio*. The President of the Western Division shall become the first chairman of this board for one year. The following year the President of the Pacific Division shall be chairman and the third year the President of the Eastern Division shall be chairman and thereafter in rotation annually. In a similar manner the Secretary of the board shall be selected *ex officio* and by rotation from the Secretary-Treasurers of the divisions beginning with the Secretary-Treasurer of the Eastern Division. The Secretary's term of office shall however be for three years. In calculating the terms of office for members of the Board of Officers the calendar year beginning January 1 shall be the unit.

2. The Secretary shall collect annually from the Treasurer of each division, at the rate of twenty-five cents per member, money to defray the necessary expenses of the Board of Officers. The Secretary shall also apportion, collect and transmit the Association's dues for membership in the American Council of Learned Societies.

3. The Board of Officers shall transact all legal business for the Association, coordinate the interests of the several divisions and act for the association as a whole (1) in International correspondence, (2) in the election or appointment of delegates to the American Council of Learned Societies or similar societies, (3) in the administration of permanent funds now or hereafter belonging to the Association.

ARTICLE IV. *Publications.*

The association shall publish annually the proceedings and presidential addresses of the divisions together with the combined list of members and a report of the Board of Officers. This publication shall be in charge of the Secretary who shall furnish a copy to each member. The expense of publication shall be borne *pro rata* by the several divisions.

ARTICLE V. *Amendments.*

Amendments to this constitution may be made by a concurrent majority vote of the members of each division present at its regular annual meeting (PR 37:156–57).

With the adoption of this constitution by the three divisions in 1926–1927, the story of the unification of the APA into a national organization is completed. Of course, the APA was not much of a national organization—it had no national meetings, no national office or president, no official journal—but the philosophers of America, after a quarter-century of effort, had finally constructed a national organization.

About this time, institutional changes had caught up with the Carus Committee; and, in the *APA Proceedings* for 1927, we find Tufts reporting to the APA Board of Officers on behalf of the Committee on the Carus Foundation that it was necessary to reconstitute the committee under the provisions of the new national constitution. The committee "proposed that the new committee be composed of nine members, six to be appointed by the Board of Officers and three by Mrs. Carus." This proposal was approved (PR 37:159). In the *APA Proceedings* for 1928, we read that Mrs. Carus had appointed Schaub (chairman), Alexander, and herself.[17] We also read that "Professor George H. Mead has been chosen by the committee to deliver the third series of lectures" at a time and place to be determined by "a committee consisting of the lecturer, a representative of the Department of Philosophy at the University of California, and H. B. Alexander" (PR 38:153). The next year, the date for these lectures was announced to be "at the time of the annual meeting of the Pacific Division at Berkeley, California, in 1930" (PR 39:191). Mead's three Carus Lectures were delivered to what was called "[a] general meeting of the Association" that included the thirty-first meeting of the Western Division and the seventh meeting of the Pacific Division—but not the Eastern Division—at California on 29–31 December 1930. Even though the Carus Lectures had been initiated to facilitate joint meetings of America's philosophical associations, at about the same time that Mead was lecturing to the Western Division and the Pacific Division, the Eastern Division was holding its thirtieth meeting at Virginia (PR 40:170, 174).[18]

----

[17] The six members appointed by the APA Board of Officers in December 1928 were: Adams, Lewis, and Cunningham (for two years each), and Dewey, Tufts, and Lovejoy (for four years each). (Harvey Gates Townsend to John Dewey, 11 January 1928, *Correspondence of John Dewey*, #05847).

[18] Mead died at the age of sixty-eight on 26 April 1931. *The Philosophy of the Present*, containing the lectures and some "supplementary essays" by Mead, was edited by Arthur Edward Murphy and published by Open Court in 1932. The next four Carus Lecturers, along with the published titles of their lectures and the dates of their delivery and publication, were: William Pepperell Montague: *Great Visions of Philosophy* (1933/1950); Evander Bradley McGilvary, *Toward a Perspective Realism* (1939/1956); Morris Raphael Cohen, *The Meaning of Human History* (1945/1947); Clarence Irving Lewis, *An Analysis of Knowledge and Valuation* (1945/1946).

JOHN DEWEY

15

International Relations

In chapters 11 through 13, we considered the impact of World War I on American academic life, on its philosophers and philosophy, and on the philosophical associations. The war strongly influenced the philosophers, and other intellectuals, toward a new consideration of the world and America's place in it. In particular, the false but widely tolerated notion that America stood apart from Europe was explicitly rejected; and thinking about international issues became an important, if passing, theme in the later years of the first quarter-century of the philosophical associations. Shortly after the war ended on 11 November 1918, the APA met at Harvard. Although much of the APA's attention had already turned inward, at this meeting there was still a modest amount of interest displayed in matters international including the continuation of the Committee on International Cooperation that had been established in December 1916.

Soon after this meeting, on 13 February 1919, a series of articles was published in *The Journal of Philosophy*, alerting the body of American philosophers to one aspect of post-war life in Europe. The first is by V. R. Savic, a Serbian government official, who calls upon American, British, and French thinkers to help the citizens of the newly established Jugoslavia to create "a national philosophy" by writing articles that, after translation, could be "immediately applied to the life of a young struggling democracy which still has to find its way to a larger life of humanity." In response to this appeal five Americans, although recognizing that the appeal might seem strange to the average American academic, offered their support. Wendell T. Bush, for example, notes that life is "the subject matter of philosophy" and thus "philosophers in America ought to be able to offer some fruits of the freedom we admire." Harold Goddard thought it important to remind Savic that "philosophy is not in the custody of the professional metaphysicians," and that he might be better off broadening his scope to "survey American periodical literature, both learned and popular, as widely as possible . . ." James Hayden Tufts suggests a possible shift in philosophy teaching in America "to give in our various institutions a course on fundamental values of life as they appear to us in the light of the past four years, and on the important ends—social, educational, national, legal, economic, moral, religious—which we may reasonably work for after the war." He further proposes that philosophers "drop—or hold in abeyance—for a time some questions we have loved, and follow the tradition of Plato and Aristotle, Locke, Descartes and Kant, not by discussing their problems, but by attacking the most vital public questions of our day." Such a shift in classroom activities, he thinks, would benefit both Americans and Jugoslavs. Hartley Burr Alexander wonders what academic philosophers in America might have to offer "that is of social and moral and humane value to our fellows overseas"; his conclusion is that there was very little. He offers two reasons for this failing. The first is "the narrowness and distortion which comes from a merely pedagogic horizon." Rather than functioning as "leaders of public life, at least as being its heard critics," philosophers in America "are instead occupants of scholastic 'chairs,' heroes of seminars, and wordy astonishers of youth." He calls upon his colleagues to free themselves from "scholastic seclusion and dependency" and to earn the right "to speak with authority for America" by sharing with other citizens "the whole peril and adventure of civic creation . . ." The second part of Alexander's critique is the converse of the first: Americans were not listening to what our philosophers had to say. As he writes, "the average American has neither the zeal nor wit to follow strenuosities of reasoning remote from his obvious interests . . ." Americans were not skilled in seeing how ideas matter to their lives; and the ideas that philosophers had been offering surely did not matter. The post-war world, however, had set the stage for new work by American philosophers; as Alexander writes, "never in our history was there such an opportunity for the thinker as is now." Finally, Harry Allen Overstreet reiterated the point that rising to the challenge would do American philosophers good: "To attempt now to write or to help write a philosophy for Serbia is to plunge again into all the stimulating perplexities. It is to revalue what has been valued. It is to help build up from the ground and to build better . . . Few tasks could be more salutary for American philosophy" (JP 16:89–95).[1]

---

[1] Cf. Henry T. Moore: "the appeal of the new Serbian democracy to American philosophy for leadership in its hour of need finds our philosophers frankly embarrassed" ("Reply to 'The Defect of Current Democracy,'" 576).

The WPA met for the nineteenth time in April 1919; and, according to the account of Edward Leroy Schaub, "the major emphases fell on political philosophy and on the present obligations and opportunities of philosophy in the fields of educational and, more generally, of social reconstruction." The presidential address of Henry Wilkes Wright, "The Social Purpose of Education" maintained that "the primary function of education consists in developing capacities and experiences which will enable individuals to share, and also to promote, the social life" of technical achievements, art, science, and knowledge (JP 16:461–62). This meeting of the WPA also contained a symposium on "The Function of Philosophy in Social Reconstruction," with presentations by Alfred Henry Lloyd, Tufts, George Thomas White Patrick, and Gustavus Watts Cunningham. Lloyd maintained that the war had ended "the era of science and of science's calculating rationalism" and that the possibility of a philosophical era had emerged. By this, he did not mean an era directed by philosophers, but an era in which "the spirit of philosophy" would permeate "all parts of life and all classes of society . . ." In this new era, the reconstructive power of philosophy could serve to combine "vision and vitality, hope and hunger, or spirituality and reality." Lloyd had no doubt that social reconstruction was coming; the only question was how: "whether it come cataclysmically and with great loss and delay or not must depend on which of the two agencies of change, intelligence or violence, is first to get the better of the frightened and resisting established order."[2] In his paper, Tufts discussed two results of the war. One was the growth of class consciousness; the other, the recognition of the possibilities of collective action in science and industry. The role that philosophy could play here, as he saw it, was "to interpret the meanings and responsibilities of power" as these new realizations worked their way through social consciousness. In his presentation, Patrick took to task philosophers (and others) who propose "idealistic plans" for social reconstruction that are "based hardly at all on a study of human nature . . ." A serious study of human "instincts, passions and primal interests" shows, he notes, that humans are not likely to "live or work contentedly in a standardized economic world under scientific management and the rule of efficiency." Cunningham called for a reemphasis away from "internationalism, labor, government, groups within states, *etc.*" that he saw as "secondary and derivative" and toward more work on the fundamental principles of the social order without which no progress could be possible. A number of other papers at this meeting also dealt with international themes, including: John Elof Boodin, "The Unit of Civilization"; Edmund Howard Hollands, "The General Will"; and Max Carl Otto, "The Two Ideals" (JP 16:465–71).

---

[2] Lloyd, "Function of Philosophy in Reconstruction," 509, 512–13.

At the APA's 1919 meeting, the recently ended war and related issues had faded from view, at least as far as the content of the papers presented went. At the business session, however, two items of international concern were considered. One matter had to do with the question of joining the proposed American Council of Learned Societies. The problematic issue that had arisen was that the constitution of the proposed International Organization of Learned Societies Devoted to Humanistic Studies contained the following article: "The Union is open to the learned societies of all the countries which are not excluded for an indeterminate period because of the war (*i.e.*, the enemy countries)." Going beyond the recommendation of the executive committee that the APA join the ACLS but protest against this article as "inconsistent with the ideals of international culture," the membership voted to postpone joining the ACLS and to investigate the issue further (PR 29:155). (The next year the investigating committee returned with a favorable recommendation and "[i]t was moved and carried that the Association join . . ." [PR 30:194]). The second matter of international importance was the emergence of the Committee on International Cooperation, chaired by Andrew Campbell Armstrong. This committee was to become the APA's longtime instrument for matters international; and, as we shall see, it grew in importance in the 1920s, especially with regard to the International Congress of 1926 and to efforts at international relief.

The WPA met for the twentieth time in April 1920, and there were only a few papers on international themes. Among them were: Edgar Lenderson Hinman, "The Ethical Import of Nationalism"; and George H. Sabine, "The Concept of State Power." The presidential address of Norman Wilde, "The Attack on the State," was a critique "of recent pluralistic theories, and a defense of the view that political sovereignty must be interpreted as very genuinely supreme and unitary" (JP 17:316, 321–23). At the Eastern Division's meeting in 1920, it was proposed that the Committee on International Cooperation be instructed "to draw up, in conjunction with the Executive Committee, and to publish, a statement of the faith of this Association that the time has come to resume international cooperation in science and philosophy"; but the motion was tabled (PR 30:194). At the next meeting, the Committee on International Cooperation was authorized to spend $200 "for the purpose of supplying Russian and other European libraries and teachers with American books and periodicals" (PR 31:166). By December 1922, when the joint meeting took place in New York City, Armstrong, the chair of the committee, was able to report to the Eastern Division business session "the expenditure of the funds voted for the purpose of supplying European teachers and libraries with American books and periodicals." Further, the committee "recommended that One Hundred Dollars be appropriated from the funds of the [Eastern] Division to be expended in assisting European Philosophical Journals in financial distress, and in supplying American Philosophical Journals to European libraries." This recommendation was accepted. At the business session of the Western Division, that took place upstairs at the same time, it was also voted "that seventy five dollars be contributed from the treasury of the Western Division through the Committee on International Cooperation toward a fund for the *Archiv für die Geschichte der Philosophie*" (PR 32:199–200).[3] In December 1923 Armstrong again reported for the Committee on International Cooperation requesting "authority to expend these [previously appropriated funds] in connection with the Emergency Society for German and Austrian Science and Art, that Society to care for the Journals, our committee to donate books." This request was approved. Then the committee discussed with the membership the similar need of Japanese universities and schools for books and journals. "It was voted that the Executive Committee be authorized to appropriate and place in the hands of the Committee on International Cooperation for this purpose any amount they might decide after reviewing the finances of the Division" (PR 33:172). Upon review, the executive committee determined that the treasury was not able to grant any additional funds.

At the Eastern Division's twenty-fourth meeting in December of 1924, Armstrong reported further on the money matters, indicating that "pursuant to the vote of the Division last year, it had applied the moneys then to its credit to the sending of books to Germany and Austria." The donations had amounted to $229.09: $154.09 from the Eastern Division and $75.00 from the Western Division. He continued: "In view of the vote passed last year concerning Japanese relief, and of the fact that no funds were available for this purpose in the Treasury, the subcommittee, after consultation with [1923] President Montague and [1924] President Meiklejohn, issued an appeal for individual donations for Japan, as well as one in behalf of German and Austrian libraries." This appeal, Armstrong reported, had yielded an additional $300 from members and nonmembers of the APA, resulting a total of $529.09 available for book purchases. Armstrong continues:

---

[3] A public appeal for Germany and Austria, prepared by the committee of Armstrong, Cohen, and Evander Bradley McGilvary read in part: "At the Annual Meeting in 1922 both Divisions of the American Philosophical Association voted to aid German and Austrian Philosophy. Inquiry has shown that the most effective way in which we can do so is to send recent American philosophical publications which, owing to the impoverished condition and the unfavorable rate of exchange, are not otherwise procurable in Central Europe. For this purpose we appeal for further gifts of money, books, or current philosophical periodicals, which will be forwarded free of charge to the *Notgemeinschaften* [Aid Societies] of Germany and Austria. Books may be sent and checks drawn to the order of *Professor Morris. R. Cohen, College of the City of New York*" (PR 33:324).

Various gifts of books and generous discounts by publishers, in agreement with authors, made a contribution of at least $500.00 more. Expenses of printing and issuing the appeals and of shipping the books, were not charged against the funds. Actual expenses for books to date are $584.76. This leaves a deficit of $55.67, to be covered by a further gift, assured through Professor Cohen, of about $100.00 which will also enable purchase of some books not yet ordered.

The ratio for the distribution of these books, Armstrong reported, was to be approximately 75 percent to Germany and Austria, and 25 percent to Japan. He further noted that through arrangements that it had established with the Germanistic Society of America, the American philosophical journals, *The Philosophical Review*, *The Journal of Philosophy* and *The International Journal of Ethics*, "have been sent to between twenty and thirty German and Austrian libraries, in particular to the libraries of universities" (PR 34:166–67). At the 1925 meeting, Armstrong again reported for the committee, noting "the completion of the literary aid to Germany and Austria, and the shipment of books, without further expense, to Japan" (PR 35:162).

The other main activity of Armstrong's Committee on International Cooperation in the 1920s was its successful effort to bring an international philosophical congress to America. That congress, the sixth in a series of such congresses, eventually took place in Cambridge, Massachusetts, in September 1926. (The Fifth International Congress was to have taken place in England, in September 1915; but it was canceled because of the war.[4] It eventually took place in Naples in 1924.[5]) In December 1922, Armstrong's committee was instructed "to make informal inquiries in regard to the possibility of renewing the sessions of the International Congress of Philosophy in 1925" (PR 32:199). After its report at the 1923 meeting, the efforts of this committee were directed toward advancing the

----

[4] The cancellation by the English Organizing Committee of December 1914 runs as follows: "The war in Europe has made it impossible to carry through the arrangements for the Fifth International Congress of Philosophy, which was to have been held in London in September, 1915. Before July of the present year (1914) the arrangements for the meeting had, to a great extent, been completed. The leading Universities of many nations had appointed delegates, and a very large number of distinguished Continental and American scholars were preparing to take part in the proceedings . . . In announcing the necessary abandonment of the arrangements for the Congress of 1915, we, Members of the General Organising Committee, desire to express an earnest hope that the confederacy of the entire philosophical world, which has subsisted since the inauguration of the series of Congresses in 1900, and seemed to have attained the rank of a permanent institution, will not be set aside for a longer time than outward circumstances render absolutely imperative . . ." (Brightman, *Proceedings*, xv).

[5] The earlier congresses had taken place in: Paris (1900), Geneva (1904), Heidelberg (1908), and Bologna (1911) (ibid., xvi).

possibility of an international congress of philosophy in 1925, even though the prior British site seemed unlikely. "It was voted that the Division approves the idea of holding an international congress of philosophy in America, and authorizes the Committee on International Cooperation, at their discretion and in consultation with the Executive Committee, to proceed with the formulation of plans" (PR 33:172). W. Wildon Carr, the Honorary Secretary of the English Organizing Committee reports, in April 1924 that he had received "a proposal from Professor A. C. Armstrong . . . to take over the arrangements for this Congress and to hold it in America in one of the principal universities in 1925 or 1926." In recommending to the members of the permanent International Committee and the English Committee that this offer be accepted, Carr notes that the advantages of this American offer were "obvious and irreproachable. The invitation will come from a country outside the complications of the impoverished European nations and from a people who can offer generous assistance to the delegates without offending any national susceptibilities."[6] In November of 1924, *The Philosophical Review* published an announcement that the APA had been authorized "by the Permanent International Committee, as constituted at the Congress of Bologna, 1911, and by the English Organization Committee of 1915, to convene the next International Congress in the United States." Therefore, the Eastern Division of the APA invited "the philosophers of all nations to meet with it in the United States in the second week of September, 1926." The location of the congress, although not yet determined, "will be at one of the Eastern Universities, not far from New York" (PR 33:627).[7]

Soon thereafter at the Eastern Division meeting, Armstrong reported on the activity of the Committee on International Cooperation during 1924. The first item was the establishment of an organizing committee, to be headed up by Columbia president and APA member Nicholas Murray Butler, with Armstrong serving as honorary secretary, and John Jacob Coss of Columbia as corresponding secretary and treasurer. Additional favorable developments included the beginning of coordination with the Western Division, positive replies from various foreign societies, and the "authorization for the Congress . . . from the Permanent International Committee and the British Organizing Committee of 1915." At the request of individuals abroad, the congress had been delayed a year, and was scheduled to begin on 13 September 1926. The location, too, had

---

[6] Ibid., xvi–xvii.

[7] One possibility that was floated was to hold the congress in conjunction with the 1926 Philadelphia Sesquicentennial that was to commemorate one hundred and fifty years of the Republic (Hartley Burr Alexander to Catherine E. Cook, [15 October 1924], *Correspondence of John Dewey*, #17132).

been decided: "In order to diminish travelling expenses of foreign members, it seems necessary to meet on or near the Atlantic seaboard. The Committee has voted that the invitation extended by the President of Harvard University, through members of the Department of Philosophy, should be accepted." Funding for the congress was being sought, and the broad outlines of the program had been set. As Armstrong described it, "[g]eneral sessions upon outstanding questions, with selected speakers, are planned, as well as sectional meetings with more special topics and more general discussion." He also suggested that the program committee was open to further suggestions, and that they should be communicated to Ralph Barton Perry or to Coss (PR 34:167–69).

At the twenty-fifth meeting of the Eastern Division in December 1925, much of the business session was taken up with matters relating to the upcoming congress. It was voted, for example, that the annual meeting of the division be merged with the congress. Further, "[i]n view of the possibility that there might be no adequate opportunity at this meeting in 1926 for the Presidential Address and the election of new officers, the Executive Committee recommended that in reckoning the terms of all officers of the Division, the period from December, 1925, to December, 1927, shall count as one year." After some discussion, it was decided "that this matter be left to the Committee with power to act after conference with the Program Committee of the Congress, and that the Committee be instructed that their decision should depend on the question whether suitable sessions of the Division, with Presidential Address, can be held in connection with the Congress" (PR 35:160).[8]

In the report of the Committee on the Sixth International Congress for Philosophy, Armstrong listed the successful articulations with the other two divisions of the APA and with national boards in Great Britain, France, Germany, and Italy. He further announced that the program committee had just about finished its work. The program itself had been divided into four divisions: (A) Metaphysics, with a general session on "Emergent Evolution" as well as other sessions; (B) Logic, Epistemology, and the Philosophy of Science, with a general session on "Continuity and Discontinuity among the Sciences" as well as other sessions; (C) Ethics and the Theory of Values, with a general session on "Philosophy and International Relations" as well as other sessions; and (D) History of Philosophy, with a general session on "The Role of Philosophy in the History of Civilization" as well as other sessions. Armstrong also reported on money matters—indicating that over $13,500 had been gathered but

---

[8] At the business session during the Congress, "it was voted that the next regular meeting be held in December, 1927, and that the present officers of the Association hold over until January 1, 1928" (PR 36:62).

that a further $6,000 was still needed—and he noted that the committee had accepted an offer of cooperation from the Russian Information Bureau in Washington, and had requested from it "the addresses of Russian colleagues needed in the arrangements for the International Congress" (PR 35:160–62). The Congress itself was a great success[9]; and, at the Eastern Division's 1927 meeting, the Organizing Committee for the Sixth International Congress offered its final report. In it, Armstrong noted that the *Proceedings* had been published earlier that year, edited by Edgar Sheffield Brightman, whom the committee commended for his efforts. Further, Armstrong announced that the congress would probably end up with a surplus of about $1,270 after expenses of some $17,000.[10] The committee then reported that no new business had come before it in 1927. "It was voted to discharge the Committee with thanks" (PR 37:165).

---

[9] Cf. Ralph Barton Perry: "The congress numbered 450 active and 275 associate members, of whom upwards of 60 represented countries other than the United States . . . This being one of the early congresses in which representatives of the Allied and Central Powers met intimately on the neutral ground of learning, it helped materially to restore the international amity of scholars" (Palmer and Perry, "Philosophy," 23–24).

[10] The final surplus was $1,958.39, and it was decided to use this money to subsidize the anticipated Seventh International Congress (PR 38:1262). That Congress was held at Oxford, England, 1–5 September 1930.

16
The Professionalization of Philosophy

In this study, we have been considering moments in the early history of the (national) American Philosophical Association. Perhaps some other emphases could have been selected and different themes more carefully explored; but I doubt that the overall story of the first twenty-five years of the philosophers' association would change much. In this chapter, however, I would like to step back a bit and evaluate this critical period in the history of the APA, especially with regard to the professionalization of philosophy. About this theme there is likely to be more diversity of opinion.

We began with a focus on what it meant to be a philosophy teacher in nineteenth-century America, especially as that role was being modified by the shift from the model of the old-time college to that of the new university. Then we explored the relationship between the emerging disciplines of philosophy and psychology around the turn of the twentieth century in the context of a group of four academic associations—the American Psychological Association, the Western Philosophical Association, the (regional) American Philosophical Association, and the Southern Society for Philosophy and Psychology—that were founded around that time. Some of the diverse activities of the early years of the WPA and the APA were then detailed, including efforts to advance the understanding of the history of American philosophy and to improve teaching, leadership and membership issues, memorials for recently deceased members, and the question of academic freedom. In addition to these organizational matters, we also considered the general shape of American philosophical life during those years through an exploration of the interactions of idealism, pragmatism, and realism. The next focus was upon the so-called discussion sessions, a decades-long attempt to direct the work of the annual meetings to the discussion and debate of preselected topics in the hope of fostering greater philosophical progress. An examination of the impact of World War I upon American academic life and American philosophers, and upon the efforts of the philosophical associations, followed. Then we considered the long-felt desire, and the years of effort required, to form a unified national organization that would finally realize the ideal contained in the name of the American Philosophical Association. The most recent chapter discussed other post-war activities, especially those of the Committee on International Cooperation. In this concluding chapter, we will be considering some contemporary evaluations of this new philosophy profession by some philosophers who were part of its growth.

My story of the APA is, of course, incomplete. Part of its incompleteness is due to my failure to uncover all of the available pieces of the APA's history. Another part of its incompleteness results from the fact that many of the pieces that would be necessary to make this story complete—like the WPA constitution—were never preserved, or later mislaid by those who did not recognize their historical value. (Other records—like the APA's original invitation to membership—were only accidentally preserved, as we saw in chapter 4.) Additional examinations of the early years of the APA may be able to advance this story by uncovering some of these lost materials.

My story is also a distorted one. Part of this distortion results from my own blind spots and from my failure to interpret to a contemporary audience, in the sense that Royce advocated in chapter 12, the full meaning of these events of a century ago. Another part of this distortion results from my unavoidable need to rely primarily on published materials. While it may not be true, for example, that the WPA was the lesser of the two philosophical associations, certainly its activities were not as well chronicled as those of the (regional) APA, and my story reflects this imbalance. Similarly, the secondary materials with which I was able to work tend to overemphasize elite institutions and prominent individuals. This literature simplifies as it celebrates, and the pieces of the APA history that are not yet part of the secondary literature are seldom part of my story. (Further, I urge readers to contemplate on their own the importance of the obvious, but here unemphasized, fact that the APA, and the system of higher education of which it has been a part, have never offered a representative picture of American society as a whole.)

I hope that these flaws in my story are not major ones. In any case, we have now come to the end of this history of the first quarter-century of the APA. What had begun in obscure gatherings in unlikely locales had by the mid-1920s blossomed into a national organization of over four hundred members that could bring to the United States an international gathering of the world's philosophers, and make a profit doing it. This is a story of great advance that should be better known, at least by contemporary American philosophers. During this quarter-century, there had been a major shift in the direction of America's philosophical thinking. Idealism's primacy had been challenged by the human urgencies championed by the pragmatists, and undermined by the analytical epistemology of the realists. There had also been many changes in the institutional situation of philosophy in America. Philosophy had completed its move from the old-time college to the new university, where it had secured its own place—in terms of distinct departments, graduate study, and specialized journals—among the many other professionalizing disciplines. This was a wondrous time to be a philosopher.

The APA had played a role in both of these processes, although its causal efficacy in either process should not be exaggerated.[1] In terms of philosophical interests, the APA had built its programs around the evolving ideas of its members, although these were ideas upon which the association's activities surely had some impact. In terms of academic life, the APA had functioned during this period as an outside certifier of the work of American philosophers. In this informal role, it had performed two functions. The first was to vouch for the professional respectability of particular pieces of philosophic work; the second, to demonstrate that philosophy—whether as the idealistic harmonizer of the work of the sciences or later as the clarifier of the work of each individual science—was playing a role in the emerging academic world. In neither of these functions, however, was the APA able to offer much guidance. Even if philosophers accepted all that the Eastern Division's founding president, James Edwin Creighton, had to say about the progress of philosophy—namely, that progress in philosophy requires the production of new work and that a professional association of philosophers should take this as its focus—they still remained unsure about what philosophy is or what they should be doing to help it progress.

The professionalization of American higher education, to which the APA (and its sister associations in the other disciplines) had contributed, helped to improve academic life in America. Among other results, the professionalization of philosophy raised the technical quality of philosophic work: graduate study and academic specialization enabled philosophy teachers to attain levels of sophistication of which their predecessors could not even dream. Similarly, the professionalization of philosophy eliminated, or at least marginalized, the amateur and the dilettante, denying especially to the theologian his traditional retreat into the philosophy classroom. Professionalization also downplayed the personal aspects of candidates for the academic life and emphasized their philosophical expertise. This made it possible for individuals like Mary Whiton Calkins and Morris

---

[1] For two conflicting views, see: Gardiner, "First Twenty-Five Years of the APA," 157; Daniel J. Wilson, "Professionalization," 69.

Raphael Cohen and George Johnson—and less difficult for those who followed them—to secure a foothold in an academic world that previously would have had places only for white, Christian men. The regularization of evaluative procedures that came with these new professionalized arrangements offered philosophy teachers some ongoing job security, improved their remuneration, and gave them a modicum of social status versus increasingly powerful administrators. All in all, as I hope this study has indicated, the new professionalized situation made it possible for philosophers to pursue their philosophical goals while at the same time making a living.

By the mid-1920s, philosophy in America had thus become a specialized academic profession with some level of personal security and professional respectability. There were, of course, costs related to these changes, many of which are more obvious to us now than they were at the time. With specialization upon topics of primarily philosophical interest comes the possibility of hyperspecialization, the micro-focusing of philosophers' work upon topics of almost exclusively philosophical interest, particularly upon the topics of methods in logic and epistemology. Realism, dedicated to *finding truth*, was much more successful living in isolation from the wider community than idealism or pragmatism ever had been. This was so because it was a kind of contemplative intellectualism, uninterested in *advancing wisdom* or in *creating truth*. Realism could be quite satisfied with recording and analyzing 'propositional truths' that were uncovered by means that aspired to approximate 'science.' Focusing on topics of professionally narrowed philosophical interest minimizes the likelihood of outside evaluation of the content of philosophers' efforts and thus opens the way for the administrative commodification of their 'output' that gives research further primacy over teaching and public service, and that makes publication—regardless of the content of the message or the breadth of the potential audience—a central requirement for holding continuing academic appointments.[2] Similarly, this hyperspecialization can lead to the routinization of philosophical practice. Bereft of any possibility of social rescue, myopic professional philosophers are free to adopt as their evaluative reference group other experts from within the profession and to turn their backs upon the concerns and contributions of outsiders, who, even if listened to, remain outsiders. Bruce Kuklick offers us a good sense of both aspects of this mood when he writes that "[t]he order of the day was tech-

---

[2] Carl Lotus Becker indicates this understanding of 'professional philosopher' when he writes in 1932 of "professors of philosophy whose business it [is] to publish, every so often, systematic and stillborn treatises on epistemology and the like subjects" and of "professional philosophers sitting in cool ivory towers for contemplative purposes only . . ." (*Heavenly City*, 35, 122; cf. Knight, "Mass Production of Ph.D.'s," 236).

nical specialized research published for technically competent audiences in technical journals, with popularizations in all areas of speculation frequently relegated to hacks, incompetents, and has-beens."[3]

Clearly the most remarkable instance of this spirit of professionalization—though far from the only one—in the APA's early history was Arthur Oncken Lovejoy's extraordinary presidential address of 1916. As we have seen in chapter 9, in this address he called for the abandonment of the social half of the philosophers' traditionally dual task of public edification and intellectual criticism; and, in a later defense of this address, he advocated that philosophers relinquish any concern for the interests of the "laity" and the "general reader"—and any lesser sort of philosopher—so that real philosophy could get about its own business and could finally make some 'progress.' Again, the question of the APA's causal efficacy in these negative processes remains as open as it does in the positive ones. Surely, this address did not decide the issue; as we have seen, it did not even stand unchallenged. Rather, the multifaceted inertia of the emerging university was carrying American higher education, and American philosophy with it, away from its potential role as the focal point for thinking about the vital needs of the larger society. The ideal of the self-directing professionalized academic was blinding America's philosophers to the dangers of their increasingly isolated life; and Lovejoy's address helped to furnish the younger generation with 'progress' as a justification for abandoning any lingering doubts that might be present. While the APA, the professional organization of philosophers in a professionalizing academia, was not the cause of this social myopia, it did not do enough to advocate the search for wisdom rather than for professional success. As we saw, for example, in chapter 14, nothing became of the WPA's emphasis upon philosophy's potential "as a social force" in the plan for unification that it presented in 1918.

There was no widespread sense of the costs of professionalization as the APA completed its first quarter-century, none at all if we limit ourselves to the more 'official' APA sources. We can examine three. First, Harry Norman Gardiner, in his celebratory retrospective at the Eastern Division's twenty-fifth meeting in 1925, "The First Twenty-Five Years of the American Philosophical Association" that we have considered repeatedly during the course of this study, discusses the personalities and events in an almost purely positive light. A second source is the presidential address at this meeting by Wilbur Marshall Urban, who chose as his topic "Progress in Philosophy in the Last Quarter Century." Urban takes the occasion to consider "the state of philosophy in America and in the world," although

---

[3] Kuklick, *Rise of American Philosophy*, 565.

he neither makes a sharp distinction between the two nor offers any direct consideration of the APA itself. In exploring the meaning of the term 'progress,' he rejects the simple definition of industry and art, and even "technical" philosophy, that progress means "the development from simplicity to complexity." For him, real philosophical progress requires overall advance such that it recognizes "the relevance of all problems" rather than the "mere elaboration of one . . ." In this broader sense of progress, he maintains that philosophy had greatly advanced—far more, in fact, than had science—through the fundamental recognition engendered by evolutionary thinking. He notes that "the specific task of this period has been to work out an intelligible concept of Evolution," and he continues that "no one can write philosophy in the same way, and no one can attempt to evaluate our thought of this period who does not orient it with reference to this problem." Urban then offered a survey of recent Western philosophy that put emphasis upon aspects of the impact of evolution, considering work in the genealogy of values and in the genealogy of knowledge, recent realism, and the problems of intelligible evolution. His survey shows that he was less than fully satisfied with the philosophy that had been produced. "In the last twenty-five years we have perhaps unlearned as much as we have learned," he writes, and much of what had been done seems to have been "the building up of card houses for the pleasure of knocking them down again." He was confident, however, that "the children's play is over," and that there was welling-up a renewed interest in metaphysics and "a truly speculative attitude" that was bringing with it "a new need and a new appreciation of Finality and System."[4]

Neither Gardiner nor Urban offered, in their survey of the prior quarter century of philosophical developments, any consideration of the emerging problems of professionalized higher education and how philosophy might respond. As a third possible source, we can consider the account of this meeting by John Herman Randall, Jr., which, although highly critical, directs its fire primarily at the practical problems of philosophy meetings. He sees the nature of the problem to be "the system of professional academic congresses which yearly brings together some of the teachers of the various college subjects . . ." He believes that those who attend such meetings, and even those who loyally read papers, "do not take themselves or their contributions too seriously." As indicators of the inadequacy of the meetings, he notes "many facts disquieting to an earnest soul." Among them, he points:

> to the slight nature of the papers read, to the total absence of any formal discussion worthy of the name; to the wholly inadequate intellectual reception

---

[4] Urban, "Progress in Philosophy," 93, 96–97, 99, 101, 120–21; cf. JP 23:40–41.

accorded to the two guests of honor on the occasion, the one the representative of a great philosophical tradition [the Thomist, James H. Ryan], the other one of the conspicuous leaders in the contemporary enterprise to make the foundations of present science intelligible [Alfred North Whitehead]; in general, to the inescapable impression of perfunctoriness, futility, and even triviality that hung over the sessions.

Randall did not think that these problems were new ones for the association, nor problems soon to be overcome. He even confesses that these weaknesses are themselves problematic "only if one surveys the American scene with the high hopes and with that touch of proudly idealistic blindness so admirably expressed by President Meiklejohn last year" (JP 23:36–37).

The year before at the 1924 meeting, Alexander Meiklejohn, the former president of Amherst, had suggested in his presidential address, "Philosopher and Others," that philosophers had a larger mission than professional advancement. While it might appear to some as idealistic blindness to maintain that philosophy "can save the world," Meiklejohn was convinced that "unless philosophers can do their part, our present scheme of human living will go to smash." Rejecting the view that scholars belong "in the ranks of those who spend their time at solitaire, at crossword puzzles, at playing the fiddle for their own amusement," he maintains that scholars, especially philosophers, have a job more central to the welfare of society. "Philosophers must rule," he writes, otherwise "the world must go its way in darkness." Of course, Meiklejohn is not proposing a dictatorship of the philosophers, a kind of "external authority by which to direct and control the work of other scholars." What he wants, rather, is a society in which thinking is "doing its proper part in the human endeavor to use for proper ends the world concerning which we think." In particular, he is concerned that philosophers take up their "most urgent duty," which is "to clarify and to direct other thinkers in clarifying that plan for human living which we call Democracy." More than a tool for selecting and controlling governments, he conceives of democracy broadly as "an experiment in the conduct of human living within which our political devices are only one relatively unimportant phase." Such a democratic society requires high levels of cooperation, equality, sharing and, of course, careful thought about these and other values. Meiklejohn thus points to the need to open up philosophical questioning to the nature of the world, human freedom, institutions, and "the human values because of which the venture must be tried, in terms of which we measure success or failure . . ." He did not believe that these questions were being answered, and schools and religious institutions were especially in need of philosophical assistance. In the former, the "older scheme of studies has broken down" and a replacement goes unbuilt; in the latter, dogmatism and sectarianism prevent the consideration of "things of ultimate concern . . ." In these areas and others, the task for philosophers was clear: "Philosophy must guide our thinking . . . Democracy, both in its spirit and its practice, rests on that."[5]

In his report on the 1924 meeting, Herbert Wallace Schneider indicates that he was not convinced by this presidential address. While he seems to have appreciated Meiklejohn's call for the primacy of philosophy not "by political or physical means, but by the compelling power of thought in stimulating and directing thought," he reports—as did Randall a year later—that he was skeptical. "For whatever conviction we may have of the divine mission of philosophy in the world," he writes, "it is impossible for most of us to keep a straight face when we are asked to believe in the American Philosophical Association as the Church of the Living God" (JP 22:42–43). This, of course, was not what Meiklejohn had envisioned; but, perhaps to the professionalizing philosopher, any reminder that there was a larger world beyond the campus and the discipline to which responsibilities were still owed might have felt unwelcome.

Following the series of reports at the culmination of the first quarter-century of the APA, it is also easy to infer that the costs of professionalized philosophy to which I have pointed, although actual by the mid-1920s, were not recognized by academic philosophers until a number of years later. This seldom-articulated but widely assumed date for the recognition of these costs seems to be sometime after World War II, and the costs are themselves often folded into the transformational effects of that war on American higher education. I hope that I have demonstrated, however, that by the time of the unification of the APA into a national organization in 1927 these costs were already being paid by American society and its philosophers. Any potential for broad social contributions by American philosophers had been lost as they had increasingly withdrawn from the search for social wisdom to concentrate on their own specialized and infinitely fascinating work, and as this work had itself increasingly narrowed into attempts to examine the internal workings of knowledge. And, while the APA witnesses upon whom I have called did not discuss the problems of professionalization, I can point to a substantial number of prominent American philosophers, most of whom were active figures in the APA, who were calling upon their colleagues to recognize and address these problems.

We are all familiar with William James's 1903 plea that more attention be directed to the teaching aspects of higher education that were being strangled by the tentacles of "the Ph.D. octopus," and with his later complaints about "[t]he over-technicality and consequent dreariness of the

---

[5] Meiklejohn, "Philosophers and Others," 264, 268–70, 273, 275, 277–79.

younger disciples at our american universities . . ."[6] Similarly, we all recall John Dewey's 1917 reminder that not everything that troubles a philosopher is necessarily important, especially when philosophers have lost sight of the problems of average men and women.[7] James and Dewey, of course, were not alone in their expressions of concern about the problems of the professionalizing of philosophy. The list of other Jeremiahs from the early years is long and distinguished.

George Santayana, for example, writes in 1894, five years after taking up his teaching duties at Harvard, that the professionalizing university was becoming a different sort of place from the one at which he had matriculated in 1882:

> the main concern of our typical young professor is not his pupils at all. It is his science . . . generally speaking, he wishes to be a scholar, and is a teacher only by accident, only because scholars are as yet supported only by institutions whose primary object is the education of youth. The pupils whom he really welcomes are those who have chosen his own profession and can encourage him in his labors by their sympathy and collaboration. His real colleagues also are not so much the other professors at the university as his *Fachgenossen* [expert colleagues] all the world over.

Uncomfortable with developments both on the campus and in the philosophy profession, Santayana retired to Europe in 1912. Henry T. Moore, whom we saw in chapter 15 criticizing the philosophers' response to the appeal for Jugoslavia, criticized as well their more general disregard for the problems of democracy. As he writes in 1919, "there is too elite a tradition surrounding our philosophers, a something that privileges them on occasion to play epistemological chess while Rome burns . . ." In 1920, Hartley Burr Alexander notes that, "[d]espite a creditable amount of serious reflection and of clever expression, the recent trend of professional philosophy, certainly in America, has been obtusely unrelated to the moving interests of men. Political and economic issues, never huger than to-day, seem impotent to call from philosophers forceful thinking . . ." What philosophers need to do, he continues, was to attempt to draw their wisdom "from the life and aspirations of our own communities . . ."[8]

---

[6] James "Ph.D. Octopus"; *Pluralistic Universe*, 13. Cf. James to Santayana, 2 May 1905; James to Dickinson Sergeant Miller, 10 November 1905, *Correspondence*, 11:27–28, 110–12.

[7] Cf. John Dewey: "Philosophy recovers itself when it ceases to be a device for dealing with the problems of philosophers and becomes a method, cultivated by philosophers, for dealing with the problems of men" ("Need for a Recovery," 46).

[8] Santayana, "Spirit and Ideals of Harvard University," 315; Henry T. Moore, "Reply to 'The Defect of Current Democracy,'" 576–77; Alexander, "Philosophy in Deliquescence," 617, 620.

William Adams Brown noted in 1921 that philosophy had largely turned away from being "a cultural study concerned with meanings and values" and had sought to become "a science among sciences." He points to the rise of two interests that have led philosophy astray. The first he calls "the trade interest"; the second, "the game interest." With regard to the former, Brown writes that "[l]ike all professionals who live by their trade the philosopher feels the need of showing that there is some particular thing that he can do that nobody else can do, in order to justify the salary which he draws . . . the teachers of philosophy . . . offer as their special subject matter the history of philosophy itself." With regard to the latter—the "game" interest—he notes that "[i]t is an interest that we all share to greater or less degree, but which in the philosopher takes a peculiar and original form." He continues:

> It is the interest of doing a thing for the sake of showing how well you can do it, irrespective of the end to be accomplished by the doing of it. In the philosopher it is the interest of thinking for thinking's sake, of defining and redefining, analyzing and reanalyzing, controverting and recontroverting, not for the sake of getting anything in particular accomplished by this elaborate paraphernalia but for the sake of showing that you are cleverer than the other fellow at the game you are both playing. Anyone who has attended meetings of philosophers when they were discussing such subjects as the theory of knowledge will understand what I mean . . .

In 1923, Harry Allen Overstreet writes in a similar fashion that "[t]he modern professional philosopher . . . is a great fellow to print head-splitting books on epistemology and on a kind of rarefied super-physics; but in this meticulous occupation he has ceased to be the sage." The professional philosopher has developed "his epistemological and metaphysical 'ologies' and 'isms.' No doubt these have their legitimate interest; but it is distressingly confusing to call them philosophy."[9]

At the Sixth International Congress at Harvard in 1926 that was discussed in chapter 15, William James Durant, neither an academic nor an APA member, maintained before the assembled philosophers that "[h]alf the charges against philosophy are due to its modern preoccupation with the problem of knowledge" and that "any rescue party formed to recap-

---

[9] William Adams Brown, "Future of Philosophy," 674–75; Overstreet, "Can Philosophy Come Back?" 324. Overstreet continues: "Perhaps the best conception of what philosophy is may be got by ceasing to use the noun and substituting the verb . . . To philosophize is to do something oneself; it is to go through a process; it is to develop a reflective, evaluating attitude toward life and things . . . To philosophize is to create and discover significances; it is to place oneself at an angle of approach that generates insights impossible for the mere seeker after facts" (Ibid., 325).

ture philosophy from the caves and bogs of epistemology, will have the blessing and imprimatur of all real lovers of the 'dear delight.'" At that same congress, Dewey attacked the isolation of philosophical practice from the broader life of society, noting that "philosophy, like politics, literature, and the plastic arts, is itself a phenomenon of human culture. Its connection with social history, with civilization, is intrinsic." A few years later, Thomas Vernor Smith, the philosopher and sometime politician, writes that our attempts to attain an Emersonian society of thinkers faced a severe obstacle in the widespread belief "that only great men have philosophy and that they can furnish it ready-made to humbler men." He continues that this assumption, one that seemed almost appropriate in an increasingly professionalized America—"If the highly specialized movie stars can furnish us our love and our morals, why not the wise men our philosophy?"—leaves philosophers with the false sense that, if we are to deal with nonphilosophers at all, it should only be to provide them with "some ready-to-wear garment . . ." In a similar fashion in 1930, John Elof Boodin writes that academic philosophers seem to be contributing little to the advance of society. Rather than seeing this as a problem, however, they stumble onwards, refusing to admit to themselves that "the chief end of academic philosophy is to furnish a living for professors of philosophy . . ."[10]

About the same time, George Herbert Mead notes, "It has long been a subject of comment, both within and without philosophic circles, that epistemology, the problem of knowledge, has excited not the slightest interest among scientists, whose profession is that of discovering what has been unknown." Philosophers, he thinks, have been led astray by a false hope of certainty and by their failure to appreciate the tentativeness of scientific practice. Our philosophical hypotheses must be tested against our everyday lives, "not by a world of ultimate reality but by a world within which we are living and acting successfully except at the point which has become problematic," he continues. "With this corrected, successful conduct can proceed until new problems arise." In 1933, James Hayden Tufts writes that "philosophy has suffered by its progressive withdrawal from field after field of broadly human interest" and further that "no profession can afford to hold itself immune from outside responsibility and criticism . . ." He expands this viewpoint five years later, when he notes that the forty-year period from roughly 1895 to 1935 "has seen philosophy in the United States occupied chiefly with the problem of knowledge" in spite of the fact that "during the past forty years extraordinary changes have been

---

[10] Durant, "Is Philosophy Doomed?" 159; Dewey, "Philosophy and Civilization," 3; Thomas Vernor Smith, *Philosophic Way of Life*, 179–80; Boodin, "Nature and Reason," 150; cf. Muirhead, "Place of Philosophy," 210–11.

taking place in industry and social classes, in government and the family, in science and education." Neglecting all of these fundamental changes, Tufts continues, "philosophy, as if to justify the ancient tradition of Thales, has for the most part calmly ignored such events and devoted its energies to the question, How is knowledge possible?" As one more example of those who early on recognized and spoke out against the serious problems resulting from the professionalization of philosophy, we can consider Max Carl Otto, who writes just as World War II was beginning: "As professional philosophers we are not interested in the world spread out before men's eyes . . . we look upon the world of daily experience as a dim vestibule to bright halls of true being. To these we press forward." Recognizing the fascinations of minute philosophical inquiry—as we all do—he notes that "we become absorbed in the technical and abstract; everyday interests and needs are forgotten; everyday objects and values drop from our attention or fade into the background as unworthy of concern."[11] Our narrow academic problems can supplant in this way any others that we as philosophers might more properly address.

We thus can see a powerful litany of dissatisfaction with at least some of the results of the professionalization of philosophy from well before World War II that indicates that a number of philosophers had long seen the situation developing negatively. Certainly by the time that the APA unified in 1927, these negative aspects were firmly in place. Later voices, right up to our own day, have echoed these criticisms again and again, failing only to emphasize their early onset. To consider just one more instance of commentary on the professionalization of philosophy, we can turn to the 1945 volume *Philosophy in American Education: Its Tasks and Opportunities* by Brand Blanshard, Curt John Ducasse, Charles W. Hendel, Arthur Edward Murphy, and Otto. This committee was selected by the APA and funded by the Rockefeller Foundation to examine "the present state of philosophy and . . . the role philosophy might play in the postwar world," given its dual functions "in liberal education and in the development of a free and reflective life in the community." The volume attempts to offer a clearly defined picture of the contemporary situation in America and in American philosophy, and of the possibilities of professional philosophy for worthwhile contributions both within the classroom and without. This extraordinary portrait presents us, for example, with Blanshard's recognition that many see philosophers as isolated "in their ivory towers . . . engrossed with solemn trifles," preoccupied with "such things as the status of sense data, the meaning of meaning, the reduction of the number of primitive propositions required for deductive logic, the

---

[11] Mead, *Philosophy of the Act*, 26, 280; Tufts, review of *Law and the Social Order*, 629; "Forty Years of American Philosophy," 433–34; Otto, *Human Enterprise*, 22.

question whether a priori statements are all of them, or only some of them, tautologous." While this criticism is not the whole picture that Blanshard offers, he recognizes that it is an important part of the picture, and that "[p]hilosophy was not always thus." In addition to this criticism of professionalized philosophy, however, this volume also contains defenses of it, including Murphy's position:

> Unless . . . he has some field of his own, on which venturesome outsiders trespass at their peril, it is hard to see how he can maintain his professional standing. And when he has, in fact, such a field, and keen delight in its intensive cultivation, it is to be expected that he will be tempted to accept this situation and leave to others—popularizers, pedagogues, and "applied philosophers"—the responsibility for supplying the comprehensive, over-all interpretation of life and experience which it had traditionally seemed the function of philosophy to present.

This invidious comparison between the real work of the philosophers—or the work of *real* philosophers—and the lesser work of "popularizers, pedagogues, and 'applied philosophers'" demonstrates the gulf between the practical concerns of the community and the ivory tower.[12]

In a consideration of *Philosophy in American Education*, Dewey indicates that the title of this volume "suggests that the Committee confined itself to the narrower of the two tasks confided to it" and only secondarily considered the issue of philosophy's role in the developing of a democratic community. He also saw in this volume a fairly accurate presentation of the predominant portion of the profession's understanding of philosophy as a kind of knowledge that is "more comprehensive, fundamental and ultimate" than the knowledge that is available to more mundane inquiries. Philosophy has consequently relegated the "practical problems" of contemporary life—"domestic, industrial, political"—"to a place that is subordinate and accessory to an alleged problem of knowledge." Dewey rejects this bifurcation, and he further rejects the understandings of philosophy as a kind of knowledge. For him, on the contrary, philosophy remains the search for wisdom and "wisdom differs from knowledge in being the application of what is known to intelligent conduct of the affairs of human life."[13] Professional philosophers, however, show little interest in

---

12 Blanshard et al., *Philosophy in American Education*, vii; Blanshard, "Climate of Opinion," 32; Arthur Edward Murphy, "Situation in American Philosophy," 56. While praising realism's "logical purification of the categories of philosophical inquiry" as "a great accomplishment, one of the greatest in the history of modern thought," Murphy admits that "this dialectical achievement has failed, so far at least, to eventuate in any corresponding philosophical wisdom or to make effective connection with the public mind" (Ibid., 55).

13 Dewey, "Problems of Men," 154, 156–57.

pursuing wisdom, preferring to leave such activities in the hands of "popularizers, pedagogues, and 'applied philosophers.'"

Academic philosophy in America, despite its admitted technical and institutional advances, has never attained its full potential because its strivings after a professionalized existence have continued to damage its roots in the life of the broader society, roots from which any institutionalized social practice must draw its challenges and sustenance. The APA, of course, is not alone here: many other academic associations have similarly flirted with self-deracination.[14] Nor is the APA solely responsible for philosophy's situation. It has, however, insulated philosophers from the question of their role in society by providing a veneer of professional success that has only in the last few decades cracked and fallen partially away. John E. Smith, in his Eastern Division presidential address in December 1981, points to the three abiding sins of our contemporary professional system of philosophy—the pursuit of certainty, the fetish of preparation, and the idolization of science—that have diverted philosophy "from its main task of relating the inescapable abstractions of thought to each other and to our primary experience of the world," and turned it "into a specialty concerned with purely technical matters bearing no direct relation to the perplexities confronting human beings in a precarious world."[15] In part because of Smith's manifesto, and because of the efforts of many other philosophers before and since, the APA and more broadly philosophy in American has made great progress in recent years. Philosophers have rediscovered the importance of philosophical inquiry into practical problems and few any longer consider such work as secondary to the 'real' work of philosophy. Similarly, philosophers have of late reacquired a greater appreciation for perspectives that do not share all of their assumptions about how philosophical inquiry might progress.

There remains a long way to go before American philosophy, and the larger sphere of American higher education, become the focal point for enduring and widespread thinking about the vital needs of our society and

---

[14] Cf. William Adams Brown: "the present difficulty with philosophy in our universities is specialization run to seed, but it would be a mistake to hold the philosophers responsible for this. What has happened to them has been happening to everybody else. We have all been too busy to see things in the large and to think whole thoughts. We have been immersing ourselves more and more in our narrow group interests, disciplines as we call them in our academic lingo, until the university has become an epitome of the larger world, a place where vested interests fight for their own rights because there is no one to stand for the rights of society as a whole. This vacant place the philosopher should fill. He should concern himself with those larger interests which belong to humanity as a whole. It is his function to interpret men to one another" ("Future of Philosophy," 676; cf. Wilshire, *Moral Collapse of the University*, 99; Jaggar, "Philosophy as a Profession," 112).

[15] John E. Smith, "New Need for a Recovery of Philosophy," 228; cf. 223.

the world. Part of the required shift is the incorporation of the Socratic lesson that we must ever continue to relearn, and to teach our students: that it is necessary to return from the wonder of philosophical inquiry to the problems of daily existence. Murphy admits the charge that philosophers' "provisional detachment becomes a kind of disorientation of the proper order and purpose of knowledge"; but he sees this charge as indicating a misunderstanding of the work of the philosophical profession. Dewey's understanding of the profession is, of course, different from Murphy's; and he cautions us to remain wary lest this provisional detachment become permanent. As he indicates metaphorically, in any philosophical inquiry we need to make sure that "the vine of pendant theory is attached at both ends to the pillars of observed subject-matter."[16] We can, in other words, never transcend the problem of professional isolation; but we must always work to minimize it. Perhaps the members of the APA, as they become more self-conscious of its past, will demand more from it in the future, and will remain cognizant that professional success—individual and collective—is hollow if the larger society does not benefit.

---

[16] Arthur Edward Murphy, "Professional Philosopher," 72; Dewey, *Experience and Nature*, 11.

APPENDIX
The Early Meetings of the Associations

1. American Psychological Association, 1892–1921

2. Western Philosophical Association, 1901–1920
   Western Division, American Philosophical Association, 1921–1930

3. American Philosophical Association, 1902–1919
   Eastern Division, American Philosophical Association, 1920–1930

4. Southern Society for Philosophy and Psychology, 1904–1930

5. Pacific Division, American Philosophical Association, 1924–1930

Appendix

1. AMERICAN PSYCHOLOGICAL ASSOCIATION

Founded in Worcester, MA, 8 July 1892

MEETING	DATE	LOCATION
Ψ1	27–28 Dec. 1892	University of Pennsylvania
Ψ2	27–28 Dec. 1893	Columbia College
Ψ3	27–28 Dec. 1894	Princeton University
Ψ4	27–28 Dec. 1895	University of Pennsylvania
Ψ5	29–30 Dec. 1896	Harvard University
Ψ6	28–30 Dec. 1897	Cornell University
Ψ7	28–30 Dec. 1898	Columbia University
Ψ8	27–29 Dec. 1899	Yale University
Ψ9	27–28 Dec. 1900	Johns Hopkins University
Ψ10 (with W2)	31 Dec. 1901–1 Jan. 1902	University of Chicago
Ψ11 (with A2)	30 Dec. 1902–1 Jan. 1903	Columbian [George Washington] University
Ψ12	29–30 Dec. 1903	St. Louis, MO
Ψ13 (with A4 & S1)	28–30 Dec. 1904	University of Pennsylvania
Ψ14 (with A5)	27–29 Dec. 1905	Harvard University
Ψ15 (with A6)	27–29 Dec. 1906	Columbia University
Ψ16 (with W8)	31 Dec. 1907–2 Jan. 1908	University of Chicago
Ψ17 (with A8 & S4)	29–31 Dec. 1908	Johns Hopkins University
Ψ18	29–31 Dec. 1909	Harvard University
Ψ19 (with W11)	28–30 Dec. 1910	University of Minnesota
Ψ20 (with S7)	27–29 Dec. 1911	George Washington University
Ψ21	30 Dec. 1912–1 Jan. 1913	Western Reserve University
Ψ22 (with A13)	29–31 Dec. 1913	Yale University
Ψ23 (with S10)	29–31 Dec. 1914	University of Pennsylvania
Ψ24	28–30 Dec. 1915	University of Chicago
Ψ25	27–30 Dec. 1916	Teachers College
Ψ26	27–29 Dec. 1917	Carnegie Institute of Technology
Ψ27	27–28 Dec. 1918	Johns Hopkins University
Ψ28	29–31 Dec. 1919	Harvard University
Ψ29	28–30 Dec. 1920	University of Chicago
Ψ30	28–30 Dec. 1921	Princeton University

1. The following set of abbreviations has been used for the sources: AJΨ: *American Journal of Psychology*; JP: *Journal of Philosophy*; P: *Proceedings of the American Psychological Association, 1892–1893*; PR: *Philosophical Review*; S: *Science*, new series; ΨB: *Psychological Bulletin*; ΨR: *Psychological Review*.
2. The asterisk indicates that the report contains a list of members.

PRESIDENT	SOURCE(S)[1]		
Granville Stanley Hall	P 3–14	PR 2:256	
George Trumbull Ladd	P 15–29	ΨR 1:214–15	
William James	ΨR 2:149–72	S 1:42–47	
James McKeen Cattell	ΨR 3:121–33	S 3:119–124	
George Stuart Fullerton	ΨR 4:107–41*[2]	S 5:206–215	
James Mark Baldwin	ΨR 5:145–71*	S 7:450–53	
Hugo Münsterberg	ΨR 6:146–79*		
John Dewey	ΨR 7:125–58*	S 11:132–35	
Joseph Jastrow	ΨR 8:158–86*	S 13:211–14	
Josiah Royce	ΨR 9:134–55*		
Edmund Clarke Sanford	ΨR 10:150–77*		
William Lowe Bryan	ΨB 1:33–45		
William James	ΨB 2:37–63	JP 2:57–77	
Mary Whiton Calkins	ΨB 3:37–75	JP 3:151–61	S 22:724–25
James Rowland Angell	ΨB 4:201–21		
Henry Rutgers Marshall	ΨB 5:33–52		
George Malcolm Stratton	JP 6:91–98	ΨB 6:33–54	
Charles Hubbard Judd	JP 7:185–91	ΨB 7:37–64	
Walter Bowers Pillsbury	JP 8:204–18	ΨB 8:33–62	
Carl Emil Seashore	JP 9:176–92	ΨB 9:41–92	
Edward Lee Thorndike	JP 10:95–103	ΨB 10:41–84	
Howard Crosby Warren	JP 11:85–109	ΨB 11:29–72	
R. S. Woodworth	JP 12:71–79	ΨB 12:45–81	
John Broadus Watson	JP 13:73–78	ΨB 13:41–100	
Raymond Dodge	JP 14:54–56	ΨB 14:33–80	
Robert Mearnes Yerkes	JP 15:96–103	ΨB 15:25–56	
J. W. Baird	ΨB 16:33–61		
Walter Dill Scott	JP 17:125–37	ΨB 17:33–82	
Shepherd Ivory Franz	JP 18:185–92	ΨB 18:57–108	
Margaret Floy Washburn	ΨB 19:65–115		

2. WESTERN PHILOSOPHICAL ASSOCIATION

Founded in Kansas City, MO, 1 January 1900

MEETING	DATE	LOCATION
W1	1–2 Jan. 1901	University of Nebraska
W2 (with Ψ10)	31 Dec. 1901–1 Jan. 1902	University of Chicago
W3	10–11 April 1903	University of Iowa
W4	1–2 April 1904	University of Missouri
W5	21–22 April 1905	University of Nebraska
W6	13–14 April 1906	University of Wisconsin
W7	29–30 March 1907	University of Chicago
W8 (with Ψ16)	31 Dec. 1907–1 Jan. 1908	University of Chicago
W9	9–10 April 1909	Washington University
W10	25–26 March 1910	University of Iowa
W11 (with Ψ19)	28–29 Dec. 1910	University of Minnesota
W12	5–6 April 1912	University of Chicago
W13	21–22 March 1913	Northwestern University
W14	9–10 April 1914	University of Chicago
W15 (with A14)	28–30 Dec. 1914	University of Chicago
W16	21–22 April 1916	Washington University
W17	6–7 April 1917	University of Michigan
W18	29–30 March 1918	Northwestern University
W19	18–19 April 1919	University of Iowa
W20	16–17 April 1920	University of Wisconsin

RENAMED: WESTERN DIVISION, AMERICAN PHILOSOPHICAL ASSOCIATION

W21	25–26 March 1921	University of Chicago
W22	April 1922	University of Nebraska
W23 (with A22)	27–29 Dec. 1922	Union Theological Seminary
W24	17–19 April 1924	University of Chicago
W25# [3]	9–11 April 1925	University of Illinois
W26#	1–3 April 1926	University of Chicago
W27#	14–15 April 1927	University of Minnesota
W28# (with A27)	27–30 Dec. 1927	University of Chicago
W29#	28–30 March 1929	University of Cincinnati
W30# (with A29)	30–31 Dec. 1929	Columbia University
W31# (with P7)	29–31 Dec. 1930	University of California

3. #: These WPA meetings are misnumbered one higher in the annual reports. For the explanation, see chapter 14, note 10.

PRESIDENT	SOURCE(S)	
Frank Thilly	PR 10:162–74*	S 13:393–94
(Thilly)	PR 11:152–69*	
Frederick James Eugene Woodbridge	PR 12:537–47*	
George Thomas White Patrick	PR 13:529–40*	JP 1:269–70
Albert Ross Hill	JP 2:252, 377–83	PR 14:518
James Hayden Tufts	JP 3:318–33	
Walter Bowers Pillsbury	JP 4:515–20	
Frank Chapman Sharp	JP 5:168	
Arthur Oncken Lovejoy	JP 6:403–11	
Carl Emil Seashore	JP 7:421–28	
Evander Bradley McGilvary	JP 8:232–42	
Addison Webster Moore	JP 9:350–57	
John Elof Boodin	JP 10:319–26	
Boyd Henry Bode	JP 11:337–52	
James Hayden Tufts	PR 24:184–203	JP 12:93–108
Alfred Henry Lloyd	JP 13:374–84	
George Herbert Mead	JP 14:403–14	
Hartley Burr Alexander	JP 15:519–28	
Henry Wilkes Wright	JP 16:461–71	
Norman Wilde	JP 17:315–26	

Edgar Lenderson Hinman	JP 18:433–41	
Edward Scribner Ames		
Edward Leroy Schaub	PR 32:200	JP 19:720–21
Roy Wood Sellars	JP 21:323–26	
Edmund Howard Hollands	JP 22:372–81	
Guy Allan Tawney	JP 23:289–96	
Rupert Clendon Lodge	PR 36:357–62*; 37:156–60, 166–79*	
Donald Ferdinand Swenson	PR 38:152–58, 163–76*	
DeWitt Henry Parker	PR 39:190–96, 200–214*	
Max Carl Otto	PR 40:168–74, 182–97*	
Gustavus Watts Cunningham	PR 41:180–87, 194–209*	

3. AMERICAN PHILOSOPHICAL ASSOCIATION

Founded in New York City, 2 November 1901

MEETING	DATE	LOCATION
A1	31 March–1 April 1902	Columbia University
A2 (with Ψ11)	30–31 Dec. 1902	Columbian [George Washington] University
A3	29–31 Dec. 1903	Princeton University
A4 (with Ψ13 & S1)	28–30 Dec. 1904	University of Pennsylvania
A5 (with Ψ14)	27–29 Dec. 1905	Harvard University
A6 (with Ψ15)	27–28 Dec. 1906	Columbia University
A7	26–28 Dec. 1907	Cornell University
A8 (with Ψ17 & S4)	29–31 Dec. 1908	Johns Hopkins University
A9	27–29 Dec. 1909	Yale University
A10	27–29 Dec. 1910	Princeton University
A11	27–29 Dec. 1911	Harvard University
A12	26–28 Dec. 1912	Columbia University
A13 (with Ψ22)	29–31 Dec. 1913	Yale University
A14 (with W15)	28–30 Dec. 1914	University of Chicago
A15	28–30 Dec. 1915	University of Pennsylvania
A16	27–28 Dec. 1916	Union Theological Seminary
A17	27–28 Dec. 1917	Princeton University
A18	27–28 Dec. 1918	Harvard University
A19	30–31 Dec. 1919	Cornell University

RENAMED: EASTERN DIVISION, AMERICAN PHILOSOPHICAL ASSOCIATION

A20	28–30 Dec. 1920	Columbia University
A21	28–30 Dec. 1921	Vassar College
A22 (with W23)	27–29 Dec. 1922	Union Theological Seminary
A23	27–29 Dec. 1923	Brown University
A24	29–30 Dec. 1924	Swarthmore College
A25	28–30 Dec. 1925	Smith College
A26[4]	13 September 1926	Harvard University
A27 (with W28)	27–30 Dec. 1927	University of Chicago
A28	27–29 Dec. 1928	University of Pennsylvania
A29 (with W30)	30–31 Dec. 1929	Columbia University
A30	28–30 Dec. 1930	University of Virginia

4. A26 was part of the Sixth International Congress of Philosophy discussed in chapter 15.

PRESIDENT	SOURCE(S)		
James Edwin Creighton	PR 11:264–86*	S 15:583–84	
Alexander Thomas Ormond	PR 12:163–86*	S 17:140–42	
Josiah Royce	PR 13:176–206*	JP 1:15–23	ΨB 1:46–56
George Trumbull Ladd	PR 14:166–94* ΨB 2:64–71	JP 2:41–55	S 21:98–101
John Dewey	PR 15:157–81*	JP 3:70–77	ΨB 3:76–82
William James	PR 16:50–69*	JP 4:64–76	ΨB 4:73–80
Harry Norman Gardiner	PR 17:167–90*		
Hugo Münsterberg	PR 18:164–90*	JP 6:44–51	
John Grier Hibben	PR 19:168–87*	JP 7:38–44	
Charles Montague Bakewell	PR 20:172–200*	JP 8:91–103	
Frederick James Eugene Woodbridge	PR 21:189–217*	JP 9:101–10	
Frank Thilly	PR 22:165–87*	JP 10:91–95	
Evander Bradley McGilvary	PR 23:176–202*	JP 11:57–67	
James Hayden Tufts	PR 24:184–203*	JP 12:93–108	
Andrew Campbell Armstrong	PR 25:168–81*	JP 13:97–102	
Arthur Oncken Lovejoy	PR 26:190–213*	JP 14:200–217	
Addison Webster Moore	PR 27:164–87*	JP 15:177–87	
Mary Whiton Calkins	PR 28:176–94*	JP 16:127–32	
Hartley Burr Alexander	PR 29:154–72*	JP 17:94–101	

Ralph Barton Perry	PR 30:192–208*	JP 18:152–60
Wilmon Henry Sheldon	PR 31:164–79*	JP 19:210–16
Walter Goodnow Everett	PR 32:198–207*	JP 19:720–21; 20:68–76
William Pepperell Montague	PR 33:171–81*	JP 21:40–51
Alexander Meiklejohn	PR 34:165–84*	JP 22:42–48
Wilbur Marshall Urban	PR 35:159–72*	JP 23:36–46
William Ernest Hocking	PR 36:58–70*	
(Hocking)	PR 37:156–59, 162–179*	
Felix Adler	PR 38:152–56, 159–176*	
Morris Raphael Cohen	PR 39:190–94, 197–214*	
Edgar Arthur Singer, Jr.	R 40:168–72, 174–179, 182–97*	

4. SOUTHERN SOCIETY FOR PHILOSOPHY AND PSYCHOLOGY

Founded in Atlanta, 23 February 1904

MEETING	DATE	LOCATION
S1 (with A4 & Ψ13)	27–28 Dec. 1904	Johns Hopkins University & University of Pennsylvania
S2	28 Dec. 1906	Montgomery AL
S3	26–27 Feb. 1908	George Washington University
S4 (with A8 & Ψ17)	30–31 Dec. 1908	Johns Hopkins University
S5	28 Dec. 1909	Charlotte NC
S6	27–28 Dec. 1910	Chattanooga TN
S7 (with Ψ20)	27–29 Dec. 1911	George Washington University
S8	8–9 April 1913	Johns Hopkins University
S9	31 Dec. 1913–1 Jan. 1914	Atlanta GA
S10	29–30 Dec. 1914	University of Pennsylvania
S11	30 Dec. 1915	Ohio State University
S12	12–13 April 1917	Randolph–Macon Woman's College
S13	*CANCELED BECAUSE OF THE WAR*	
S14[5]	May 1919	Vanderbilt University
S15	1920	New Orleans LA
S16	1921	
S17	1922	Memphis TN
S18	30–31 March 1923	Vanderbilt University & George Peabody College
S19	22–23 April 1924	Johns Hopkins University
S20	13–14 April 1925	University of North Carolina
S21	2–3 April 1926	University of Kentucky
S22	22–23 April 1927	University of Georgia
S23	5–6 April 1928	Virginia Military Institute
S24	29–30 March 1929	University of Kentucky
S25	19 April 1930	George Peabody College

5. Information on S14 through S17 comes from Pate, "Southern Society."

PRESIDENT	SOURCE(S)		
James Mark Baldwin	JP 2:56	PR 13:390	ΨB 2:72–80*
James Mark Baldwin	ΨB 4:80		
James Mark Baldwin	ΨB 5:97–108	JP 5:167–68	
J. MacBride Sterrett	ΨB 6:55–67		
Albert Lefevre	ΨB 7:65–74		
Edward Franklin Buchner	ΨB 8:63–76		
Shepherd Ivory Franz	ΨB 9:41–92		
Robert O. Ogden	ΨB 10:165–72		
H. J. Pearce	ΨB 11:73–79		
John Broadus Watson	ΨB 12:82–88		
J. C. Barnes	ΨB 13:101–8		
David Spence Hill	ΨB 14:145–47		
	ΨB 15:97		
E. K. Strong, Jr.			
Knight Dunlap			
John M. Fletcher			
Joseph Peterson			
Herbert C. Sanborn	ΨB 20:417–26		
Buford Johnson	ΨB 21:553–68		
John F. Dashiell	ΨB 22:649–58		
J. B. Miner	ΨB 23:609–30		
A. S. Edwards	ΨB 24:509–20		
Josiah Morse	ΨB 25:462–79		
L. R. Geisler	AJΨ 41:502–11		
Max F. Meyer	ΨB 28:325–41		

5. Pacific Division, American Philosophical Association

Founded April 1924

MEETING	DATE	LOCATION
P1	28–29 Nov.1924	University of California
P2	27–28 Nov.1925	Stanford University
P3	26–27 Nov.1926	Mills College
P4	25–26 Nov.1927	University of California
P5	30 Nov.–1 Dec. 1928	Stanford University
P6	27–28 Dec. 1929	University of Southern California
P7 (with W31)	29–31 Dec. 1930	University of California

PRESIDENT	SOURCE(S)
[none]	PR 34:209 JP 21:719–21
George Rebec	PR 35:173–75*
Henry Walgrave Stuart	PR 36:174–77*
George Plimpton Adams	PR 37:156–59, 161–62, 166–179*
Herbert Wildon Carr	PR 38:152–56, 158–59, 163–176*
Hartley Burr Alexander	PR 39:190–94, 196–97, 200–214*
Jacob Loewenberg	PR 40:168–72, 179–97*

Works Cited

Adams, George Plimpton, and William Pepperell Montague, eds. *Contemporary American Philosophy: Personal Statements.* 2 vols. New York: Macmillan, 1930.

Ahlstrom, Sidney E. "The Scottish Philosophy and American Theology." *Church History* 24, no. 3 (September 1955): 257–72.

Albee, Ernest, Charles Montague Bakewell, Theodore de Laguna, William Ernest Hocking, and Edmund Howard Hollands. "Progress in Philosophical Inquiry and Mr. Lovejoy's Presidential Address." *Philosophical Review* 26, no. 3 (May 1917): 315–38.

Alexander, Hartley Burr. "Letter from Professor Alexander." *Journal of Philosophy, Psychology and Scientific Methods* 14, no. 23 (8 November 1917): 643–44.

———. *Liberty and Democracy, and Other Essays in War-Time.* Boston: Marshall Jones, 1918.

———. "Philosophy in Deliquescence." *Journal of Philosophy, Psychology and Scientific Methods* 17, no. 23 (4 November 1920): 617–22.

———. "Wrath and Ruth." *Journal of Philosophy, Psychology and Scientific Methods* 16, no. 10 (8 May 1919): 253–58.

American Philosophical Association. Western Division Records, University of Illinois Archives.

American Philosophical Society Archives, Philadelphia.

American Psychological Association. *Proceedings of the American Psychological Association (1892–1893).* New York: Macmillan, 1893.

Ames, Edward Scribner. *The Psychology of Religious Experience.* Boston: Houghton Mifflin, 1910.

Anderson, Paul R. *Platonism in the Midwest.* Philadelphia: Temple University Publications, 1963.

Angell, James Burrill. "Religious Life in Our State Universities." *Andover Review* 13 (April 1890): 365–72.

———. *Selected Addresses.* New York: Longmans Green, 1912.

Angell, James Roland. *Psychology: An Introductory Study of the Structure and Function of Human Consciousness.* 4th ed. New York: Henry Holt, 1908.

305

Angoff, Charles. "The Higher Learning Goes to War." *American Mercury* 11, no. 2 (June 1927): 177–91.

Armstrong, Andrew Campbell. "Philosophy in American Colleges." *Educational Review* 13, no. 1 (January 1897): 10–22.

———. "Philosophy in the United States." *Educational Review* 11, no. 1 (June 1895): 1–11.

Association of American Universities. *Journal of Proceedings and Addresses of the Twentieth Annual Conference*, 4–5 December 1918.

Aydelotte, Frank. *Final Report of the War Issues Course of the Students' Army Training Corps*. Washington, DC: War Department, 1919.

Bakewell, Charles Montague. "On the Meaning of Truth." *Philosophical Review* 17, no. 6 (November 1908): 579–91.

———. "The Problem of Transcendence." *Philosophical Review* 20, no. 2 (March 1911): 113–36.

Baldwin, James Mark. *American Neutrality: Its Cause and Cure*. New York: Putnams, 1916.

———. *Between Two Wars, 1861–1921: Being Memories, Opinions and Letters Received*. 2 vols. Boston: Stratford, 1926.

———, ed. *Dictionary of Philosophy and Psychology*. 3 vols. New York: Macmillan, 1901–1905.

———. "Psychology Past and Present." *Psychological Review* 1, no. 4 (July 1894): 363–91.

Barber, Bernard. "Some Problems in the Sociology of the Professions." In *The Professions in America*, ed. Kenneth S. Lynn, 15–34. Boston: Houghton Mifflin, 1965.

Becker, Carl Lotus. *Cornell University: Founders and the Founding*. Ithaca, NY: Cornell University Press, 1943.

———. *The Heavenly City of the Eighteenth-Century Philosophers*. New Haven, CT: Yale University Press, 1932.

Berelson, Bernard. *Graduate Education in the United States*. New York: McGraw-Hill, 1960.

Bernard, L. L., and J. S. Bernard. "A Century of Progress in the Social Sciences." *Social Forces* 11, no. 4 (May 1933): 488–505.

Blakey, George T. *Historians on the Homefront: American Propagandists for the Great War*. Lexington: University of Kentucky Press, 1970.

Blanshard, Brand. "The Climate of Opinion." In Blanshard et al., *Philosophy in American Education*, 3–42.

———. "Speculative Thinkers." In *Literary History of the United States*, edited by Robert E. Spiller, Willard Thorp, Thomas H. Johnson, and Henry Seidel Canby, 2:1273–95. New York: Macmillan, 1948.

Blanshard, Brand, Curt John Ducasse, Charles W. Hendel, Arthur Edward Murphy, and Max Carl Otto. *Philosophy in American Education: Its Tasks and Opportunities*. New York: Harper, 1945.

Blau, Joseph Leon. Introduction to *The Elements of Moral Science*, by Francis Wayland, edited by Joseph Leon Blau, ix–xlix. Cambridge, MA: Harvard University Press, [1837] 1963.

———. *Men and Movements in American Philosophy.* Englewood Cliffs: Prentice-Hall, 1952.

Bliss, Charles M. "Proposed Changes in the American Psychological Association." *Psychological Review* 6, no. 2 (March 1899): 237–38.

Boas, Louise Schutz. *Women's Education Begins: The Rise of Women's Colleges.* Norton, MA: Wheaton College Press, 1935.

Bode, Boyd Henry. "Why Do Philosophical Problems Persist?" *Journal of Philosophy, Psychology and Scientific Methods* 15, no. 7 (28 March 1918): 169–77.

Böhme, Klaus, ed. *Aufrufe und Reden deutscher Professoren im Ersten Weltkrieg.* Stuttgart: Philipp Reclam, 1975.

Boodin, John Elof. "Nature and Reason." In Adams and Montague, *Contemporary American Philosophy,* 1:142–66.

Boring, Edwin G. *A History of Experimental Psychology.* New York: Century, 1929.

Brigham, Carl C. *A Study of American Intelligence.* Princeton, NJ: Princeton University Press, 1923.

Brightman, Edgar Sheffield, ed. *Proceedings of the Sixth International Congress of Philosophy: Harvard University, Cambridge, Massachusetts, United States of America, September 13, 14, 15, 16, 17, 1926.* New York: Longmans, Green, 1927.

Brodbeck, May. "Philosophy in America, 1900–1950." In *American Non-Fiction, 1900–1950,* edited by May Brodbeck, James Gray, and Walter Metzger, 3–94. Chicago: Regnery, 1952.

Brown, Harold Chapman. "A Philosophic Mind in the Making." In Adams and Montague, *Contemporary American Philosophy,* 1:169–95.

Brown, William Adams. "The Future of Philosophy as a University Study." *Journal of Philosophy* 18, no. 25 (8 December 1921): 673–82.

Brubacher, John S., and Willis Rudy. *Higher Education in Transition: An American History, 1636–1956.* New York: Harper, 1968.

Bryce, James. *The American Commonwealth.* Rev. ed. 2 vols. London: Macmillan, 1890.

Buchner, Edward Franklin. "A Quarter Century of Psychology in America: 1878–1903." *American Journal of Psychology* 14, no. 3–4 (July–October 1903): 666–80.

———. "Ten Years of American Psychology: 1892–1902." Pts. 1 and 2. *Science,* n.s., 18 (14 August 1903): 193–204; (21 August 1903): 233–41.

———. "The Work of the Southern Society for Philosophy and Psychology." *Journal of Proceedings and Addresses of the Southern Educational Association* 20 (1920): 249–51.

Butler, Nicholas Murray. "The American College." *Educational Review* 25, no. 1 (January 1903): 11–20.

———. "The Relation of the German Universities to the Problems of Higher Education in the United States." Introduction to *The German Universities: Their Character and Historical Development* by Friedrich Paulsen, ix–xxxi. New York: Macmillan, 1895.

———. *A World in Ferment: Interpretations of the War for a New World.* New York: Scribners, 1917.

Calkins, Mary Whiton. *The Good Man and the Good: An Introduction to Ethics.* New York: Macmillan, 1918.

———. *An Introduction to Psychology.* New York: Macmillan, 1901.

———. *The Persistent Problems of Philosophy: An Introduction to Metaphysics through the Study of Modern Systems.* New York: Macmillan, 1907.

———. "Unjustified Claims for Neo-Realism." *Philosophical Review* 22, no.1 (January 1913): 53–56.

Campbell, James. "The Ambivalence toward Teaching in the Early Years of the American Philosophical Association." *Teaching Philosophy* 25, no. 1 (March 2002): 53–68.

———. "Arthur Lovejoy and the Progress of Philosophy." *Transactions of the Charles S. Peirce Society* 39, no. 4 (Fall 2003): 617–43.

———. *The Community Reconstructs: The Meaning of Pragmatic Social Thought.* Urbana: University of Illinois Press, 1992.

———. "Dewey and German Philosophy in Wartime." *Transactions of the Charles S. Peirce Society* 40, no. 1 (Winter 2004): 1–20.

Capen, Samuel Paul. "The Dual Obligation of University and College." In *The Obligation of Universities to the Social Order*, edited by Henry Pratt Fairchild, 57–65. New York: New York University Press, 1933.

Carter, Franklin. *The College as Distinguished from the University: An Inaugural Address.* New Haven, CT: Tuttle, Morehouse and Taylor, 1881.

Cattell, James McKeen. "Address of the President before the American Psychological Association, 1895." *Psychological Review* 3, no. 2 (March 1896): 134–48.

———. "The Advance of Psychology." *Science*, n.s., 8 (21 October 1898): 533–41.

———. "Our Psychological Association and Research." *Science*, n.s., 45 (23 March 1917): 275–84.

———. "Psychology in America." In *Ninth International Congress of Psychology: Proceedings and Papers*, 12–32. Princeton, NJ: Psychological Review, 1930.

Clendenning, John. *The Life and Thought of Josiah Royce.* Madison: University of Wisconsin Press, 1985.

Coe, George Albert. "Philosophy in American Colleges." *Nation* 54 (14 April 1892): 282–83.

Cohen, Morris Raphael. *American Thought: A Critical Sketch.* Glencoe, IL: Free Press, 1954.

———. "Communal Ghosts and Other Perils in Social Philosophy." *Journal of Philosophy, Psychology and Scientific Methods* 16, no. 25 (4 December 1919): 673–90.

———. "The Conception of Philosophy in Recent Discussion." *Journal of Philosophy, Psychology and Scientific Methods* 7, no. 15 (21 July 1910): 401–10.

———. "Later Philosophy." In *Cambridge History of American Literature*, edited by William Peterfield Trent, John Erskine, Stuart P. Sherman, and Carl Van Doren, 3:226–265. 3 vols. New York: Macmillan, 1917–21.

———. *The Meaning of Human History.* La Salle, IL: Open Court, 1947.

———. "The New Realism." *Journal of Philosophy, Psychology and Scientific Methods* 10, no. 8 (10 April 1913): 197–214.

Costello, Harry Todd. Review of *Contemporary American Philosophy*, edited by George Plimpton Adams and William Pepperell Montague. *Journal of Philosophy* 28, no. 9 (23 April 1931): 244–49.

Coulter, John Merle. "The Contribution of Germany to Higher Education." *University* [of Chicago] *Record* 8, no. 11 (March 1904): 348–53.

Creighton, James Edwin. "The American Philosophical Association and Its Programmes." *Journal of Philosophy, Psychology and Scientific Methods* 14, no. 14 (16 August 1917): 472–76.

———. Discussion of "Aim of Philosophy Teaching in American Colleges." In *114th Annual Report of the Regents of the University of the State of New York: Administrative Department*, 35–38. Albany: University of the State of New York, 1900.

———. "The Purposes of a Philosophical Association." *Philosophical Review* 11, no. 3 (May 1902): 219–37.

———. "The Study of Philosophy." *Book Reviews* 3, no. 2 (June 1895): 29–33.

———. "Two Types of Idealism." *Philosophical Review* 26, no. 5 (September 1917): 514–36.

Crosby, Alfred W. *America's Forgotten Pandemic: The Influenza of 1918*. New York: Cambridge University Press, 1989.

Cunningham, Gustavus Watts. "A Search for System." In Adams and Montague, *Contemporary American Philosophy*, 1:251–74.

Curti, Merle Eugene. "The American Scholar in Three Wars." *Journal of the History of Ideas* 3, no. 3 (June 1942): 241–64.

Dewey, John. "Annual Address of the President to the American Association of University Professors." *Bulletin of the American Association of University Professors* 1 (1915): 9–13. Reprinted in Dewey, *Middle Works*, 8:104–8.

———. "Beliefs and Existences." *Philosophical Review* 15, no. 2 (March 1906): 113–19. Reprinted in Dewey, *Middle Works*, 3:83–100.

———. *The Correspondence of John Dewey*. Edited by Larry Hickman. Past Masters. Charlottesville, VA: InteLex, 1997–2003. Available online at http://www.nlx.com/titles/titldewc.htm and on CD-ROM.

———. "The Development of American Pragmatism." In *Studies in the History of Ideas*, 2:353–377. New York: Columbia University Press, 1925. Reprinted in Dewey, *Later Works*, 2:3–21.

———. *Early Works of John Dewey, 1882–1898*. Edited by Jo Ann Boydston. 5 vols. Carbondale: Southern Illinois University Press, 1969–1972.

———. "Education and Social Practice." *Psychological Review* 7, no. 2 (March 1900): 105–24. Reprinted in Dewey, *Middle Works*, 1:131–50.

———. *Experience and Nature*. Rev. ed. La Salle, IL: Open Court, 1929. Reprinted in Dewey, *Later Works*, vol. 1.

———. "From Absolutism to Experimentalism." In Adams and Montague, *Contemporary American Philosophy*, 2:13–27. Reprinted in Dewey, *Later Works*, 5:147–60.

———. *German Philosophy and Politics*. New York: Holt, 1915. Reprinted in Dewey, *Middle Works*, 8:135–204.

———. "The Influence of Darwinism on Philosophy." *Popular Science Monthly* 75 (1909): 90–98. Reprinted in Dewey, *Middle Works*, 4:3–14.

———. "Introductory Address to the American Association of University Professors." *Science*, n.s., 41 (1915): 147–51. Reprinted in Dewey, *Middle Works*, 8:98–103.

———. *Later Works of John Dewey, 1925–1953.* Edited by Jo Ann Boydston. 17 vols. Carbondale: Southern Illinois University Press, 1981–1990.

———. *Middle Works of John Dewey, 1899–1924.* Edited by Jo Ann Boydston. 15 vols. Carbondale: Southern Illinois University Press, 1976–1983.

———. "The Need for a Recovery of Philosophy." In *Creative Intelligence: Essays in the Pragmatic Attitude*, 3–69. New York: Henry Holt, 1917. Reprinted in Dewey, *Middle Works*, 10:3–48.

———. "Our Educational Ideal in Wartime." *New Republic* 6 (1916): 283–84. Reprinted in Dewey, *Middle Works*, 10:178–82.

———. "Philosophy and Civilization." *Philosophical Review* 36, no. 1 (January 1927): 1–9. Reprinted in Dewey, *Later Works*, 3:3–10.

———. "The Problems of Men and the Present State of Philosophy." In *Problems of Men*, 3–20. New York: Philosophical Library, 1946. Reprinted in Dewey, *Later Works*, 15:154–69.

———. *Psychology.* New York: Harper, 1887. Reprinted in Dewey, *Early Works*, vol. 2.

Dewey, John, et al. *Studies in Logical Theory.* Chicago: University of Chicago Press, 1903.

Dewey, John, and James Hayden Tufts. *Ethics.* New York: Henry Holt, 1908. Reprinted in Dewey, *Middle Works*, vol. 5.

Drake, Durant. "Philosophy as Work and Play." *Journal of Philosophy, Psychology and Scientific Methods* 18, no. 16 (4 August 1921): 441–44.

———. "The Philosophy of a Meliorist." In Adams and Montague, *Contemporary American Philosophy*, 1:277–97.

Drake, Durant, Arthur Oncken Lovejoy, James Bissett Pratt, Arthur Kenyon Rodgers, George Santayana, Roy Wood Sellars, and Charles Augustus Strong. *Essays in Critical Realism: A Co-operative Study of the Problem of Knowledge.* London: Macmillan, 1920.

Duncan, Elmer H. "Eighteenth-Century Scottish Philosophy: Its Impact on the American West" *Southwestern Journal of Philosophy* 6, no. 1 (Winter 1975): 131–48.

Durant, William James. "Is Philosophy Doomed?" In Brightman, *Proceedings of the Sixth International Congress of Philosophy*, 154–60.

Dysinger, Holmes. "Philosophy in the College Curriculum." *Science*, n.s., 22 (14 July 1893): 16–17.

Easton, Loyd D. *Hegel's First American Followers.* Athens: Ohio University Press, 1966.

Eliot, Charles William. "American Education since the Civil War." *Rice Institute Pamphlet* 9, no. 1 (January 1922): 1–25.

———. *Educational Reform: Essays and Addresses.* New York: Century, 1898.

———. "The New Education: Its Organization." Pts. 1 and 2. *Atlantic Monthly* 23, no. 2 (February 1869): 203–20; 23, no. 3 (March 1869): 358–67.

————. *The Road toward Peace: A Contribution to the Study of the Causes of the European War and of the Means of Preventing War in the Future.* New ed. Boston: Houghton Mifflin, 1915.

Elkus, Savilla Alice. "A Philosophical Platform from Another Standpoint." *Journal of Philosophy, Psychology and Scientific Methods* 7, no. 1 (6 January 1910): 19–20.

Evans, Rand B. "The Origins of American Academic Psychology." In *Explorations in the History of Psychology in the United States,* edited by Josef Brozek, 17–60. Lewisburg, PA: Bucknell University Press, 1984.

Fisch, Max Harold. *Peirce, Semeiotic, and Pragmatism: Essays by Max H. Fisch.* Edited by Kenneth Laine Ketner and Christian J. W. Kloessel. Bloomington: Indiana University Press, 1986.

Flower, Elizabeth, and Murray G. Murphey. *A History of Philosophy in America.* 2 vols. New York: Putnams, 1977.

Fullerton, George Stuart. *Germany of To-day.* Indianapolis: Bobbs-Merrill, 1915.

————. *A Handbook of Ethical Theory.* New York: Henry Holt, 1922.

————. *An Introduction to Philosophy.* New York: Macmillan, 1913.

————."The Psychological Standpoint." *Psychological Review* 1, no. 2 (March 1894): 113–33.

————. *The Truth about the German Nation.* Munich: Oldenbourg, 1915.

————. *Die Wahrheit über Deutschland.* Translated by Ernst Sieper. Munich: Oldenbourg, 1916.

————. "Why the German Nation Has Gone to War: An American to Americans." Munich: Süddeutsche Verlags-Druckerei, 1914.

Fullerton, George Stuart, Alexander Thomas Ormond, and F. C. French. "Aim of Philosophy Teaching in American Colleges." In *114th Annual Report of the Regents of the University of the State of New York: Administrative Department,* 8–34. Albany: University of the State of New York, 1900.

Gardiner, Harry Norman. Black Notebook. American Philosophical Association, University of Delaware.

————. "The First Twenty-Five Years of the American Philosophical Association." *Philosophical Review* 35, no. 2 (March 1926): 145–58.

————. Gardiner Papers. College Archives, Smith College.

————. "The Problem of Truth." *Philosophical Review* 17, no. 2 (March 1908): 113–37.

Geiger, Roger L. "The Rise and Fall of Useful Knowledge: Higher Education for Science, Agriculture, and the Mechanical Arts, 1850–1875." In *The American College in the Nineteenth Century,* edited by Roger L. Geiger, 153–68. Nashville: Vanderbilt University Press, 2000.

————. *To Advance Knowledge: The Growth of American Research Universities, 1900–1940.* New York: Oxford University Press, 1986.

Gilman, Daniel Coit. *University Problems in the United States.* New York: Century, 1898.

Gotesky, Rubin. Review of *Contemporary American Philosophy,* edited by George Plimpton Adams and William Pepperell Montague. *Outlook and Independent* 155, no. 12 (23 July 1930): 468–69.

Grattan, C. Hartley. "The Historians Cut Loose." *American Mercury* 11, no. 4 (August 1927): 414–30.

Gruber, Carol S. *Mars and Minerva: World War I and the Uses of the Higher Learning in America.* Baton Rouge: Louisiana State University Press, 1975.

Haldane, John. "American Philosophy: 'Scotch' or 'Teutonic'?" *Philosophy* 77 (July 2002): 311–29.

Hall, Granville Stanley. "American Universities and the Training of Teachers." *Forum* 17, no. 2 (April 1894): 148–59.

———. *Aspects of German Culture.* Boston: Osgood, 1881.

———. "Decennial Address." In *Clark University, 1889–1899: Decennial Celebration,* 45–59. Worcester, MA: Clark University Press, 1899.

———. "Editorial [on Experimental Psychology in America]." *American Journal of Psychology* 7, no. 1 (October 1895): 3–8.

———. "Editorial Note." *American Journal of Psychology* 1, no. 1 (November 1887): 3–4.

———. Foreword to *The Problems and Lessons of the War,* edited by George H. Blakeslee, ix–xxiv. New York: Putnams, 1916.

———. *Founders of Modern Psychology.* New York: Appleton, 1912.

———. *Life and Confessions of a Psychologist.* New York: Appleton, 1923.

———. "The Muscular Perception of Space." *Mind* 3 (October 1878): 433–50.

———. "The New Psychology." *Harper's Monthly Magazine* 103 (October 1901): 727–32.

———. "On the History of American College Text-Books and Teaching in Logic, Ethics, Psychology and Allied Subjects." *Proc. of the American Antiquarian Society* 9 (1893–94): 137–74.

———. "Philosophy." In *Clark University, 1889–1899: Decennial Celebration,* 177–185. Worcester, MA: Clark University Press, 1899.

———. "Philosophy in the United States." *Mind* 4 (January 1879): 89–105.

———. "Practical Relations between Psychology and the War." *Journal of Applied Psychology* 1, no. 1 (March 1917): 9–16.

———. "Psychological Progress." *The Liberal Club, Buffalo: 1893–94* (Buffalo: Matthews-Northrop, 1894): 13–47.

———. "Research the Vital Spirit of Teaching." *Forum* 17, no. 5 (July 1894): 558–70.

———. "Scholarships, Fellowships, and the Training of Professors." *Forum* 17, no. 4 (June 1894): 443–54.

———. "Universities and the Training of Professors." *Forum* 17, no. 3 (May 1894): 297–309.

Harlow, Victor E. *A Bibliography and Genetic Study of American Realism.* Oklahoma City: Harlow Publishing, 1931.

Harmon, Frances Bolles. *The Social Philosophy of the St. Louis Hegelians.* New York: N.P., 1943.

Harper, Robert S. "The Laboratory of William James." *Harvard Alumni Bulletin* 52 (5 November 1948): 169–73.

Harper, William Rainey. *The Trend in Higher Education.* Chicago: University of Chicago Press, 1905.

Hart, Albert Bushnell, and Arthur Oncken Lovejoy, eds. *Handbook of the War for Public Speakers.* New York: National Security League, 1917.

Herbst, Jurgen. *The German Historical School in American Scholarship: A Study in the Transfer of Culture.* Ithaca, NY: Cornell University Press, 1965.

Hilgard, Ernest R., ed. *American Psychology in Historical Perspective: Addresses of the Presidents of the American Psychological Association.* Washington DC: American Psychological Association, 1978.

Hill, Thomas English. *Contemporary Theories of Knowledge.* New York: Ronald Press, 1961.

Hinman, Edgar Lenderson. "The Aims of an Introductory Course in Philosophy." *Journal of Philosophy, Psychology and Scientific Methods* 7, no. 21 (13 October 1910): 561–69.

Hocking, William Ernest. *Morale and Its Enemies.* New Haven, CT: Yale University Press, 1918.

———. "Sovereignty and Moral Obligation." *International Journal of Ethics* 28, no. 3 (April 1918): 314–26.

Hofstadter, Richard. *The Age of the College.* Part 1 of *The Development of Academic Freedom in the United States,* by Richard Hofstadter and Walter P. Metzger, 1–274. New York: Columbia University Press, 1955.

von Holst, Herman E. "The Need of Universities in the United States." *Educational Review* 5, no. 2 (February 1893): 105–19.

Holt, Edwin Bissell. *The Concept of Consciousness.* New York: Macmillan, 1914.

Holt, Edwin Bissell, Walter Taylor Marvin, William Pepperell Montague, Ralph Barton Perry, Walter B. Pitkin, and Edward Gleason Spaulding. "The Program and First Platform of Six Realists." *Journal of Philosophy, Psychology and Scientific Methods* 7, no. 15 (21 July 1910): 393–401.

———. *The New Realism: Co-operative Studies in Philosophy.* New York: Macmillan, 1912.

Howison, George Holmes. "Philosophy and Science." *University* [of California] *Chronicle* 5, no. 3 (October 1902): 129–58.

———. "Josiah Royce: The Significance of His Work in Philosophy." *Philosophical Review* 25, no. 3 (May 1916): 231–44.

Hudson, Jay William. "The Aims and Methods of Introduction Courses: A Questionnaire." *Journal of Philosophy, Psychology and Scientific Methods* 9, no. 2 (18 January 1912): 29–39.

———. "Hegel's Conception of an Introduction to Philosophy." *Journal of Philosophy, Psychology and Scientific Methods* 6, no. 13 (24 June 1909): 345–53.

———. "An Introduction to Philosophy through the Philosophy in History." *Journal of Philosophy, Psychology and Scientific Methods* 7, no. 21 (13 October 1910): 569–74.

Hull, Richard T., ed. *Presidential Addresses of the American Philosophical Association.* 11 vols. Dordrecht: Kluwer / Amherst, NY: Prometheus, 1999–.

Hutchinson, William T. "The American Historian in Wartime." *Mississippi Valley Historical Review* 29, no. 2 (September 1942): 163–86.

Jaggar, Alison. "Philosophy as a Profession." *Metaphilosophy* 6, no. 1 (January 1975): 100–116.

James, William. *The Correspondence of William James*, edited by Ignas K. Skrupskelis and Elizabeth M. Berkeley. 12 vols. Charlottesville: University Press of Virginia, 1992–2004.

———. "The Energies of Men" [1907]. In *Essays in Religion and Morality*, 129–146. Cambridge, MA: Harvard University Press, 1982.

———. *Essays, Comments and Reviews*. Cambridge, MA: Harvard University Press, 1987.

———. *Essays in Radical Empiricism*. Cambridge, MA: Harvard University Press, [1912] 1976.

———. "Experimental Psychology in America" [1895]. In James, *Essays, Comments and Reviews*, 150–51.

———. "The Knowing of Things Together" [1895]. In *Essays in Philosophy*, 71–89. Cambridge, MA: Harvard University Press, 1978.

———. *The Meaning of Truth*. Cambridge, MA: Harvard University Press, [1909] 1975.

———. "The Ph.D. Octopus" [1903]. In James, *Essays, Comments and Reviews*, 67–74.

———. *A Pluralistic Universe*. Cambridge, MA: Harvard University Press, [1909] 1977.

———. *Pragmatism: A New Name for Some Old Ways of Thinking*. Cambridge, MA: Harvard University Press, [1907] 1975.

———. *The Principles of Psychology*. 3 vols. Cambridge, MA: Harvard University Press, [1890] 1981.

———. "The Social Value of the College-Bred" [1907]. In James, *Essays, Comments and Reviews*, 106–12.

———. *Talks to Teachers on Psychology and to Students on Some of Life's Ideals*. Cambridge, MA: Harvard University Press, [1899] 1983.

Jameson, John Franklin. "Historical Scholars in War-Time." *American Historical Review* 22, no. 4 (July 1917): 831–35.

Jastrow, Joseph. "The Reconstruction of Psychology." *Psychological Review* 34, no. 3 (May 1927): 169–95.

Johnson, George. *The Arithmetical Philosophy of Nicomachus of Gerasa*. Lancaster, PA: New Era, 1916.

Johnston, G. A. Introduction to *Selections from the Scottish Philosophy of Common Sense*, edited by G. A. Johnston. Chicago: Open Court, 1915.

Jordan, David Starr. *The Trend of the American University*. Stanford, CA: Stanford University Press, 1929.

———. "University-Building." *Popular Science Monthly* 61, no. 4 (August 1902): 330–38.

The Journal of Philosophy: Fifty-Year Index, 1904–1953. New York: Journal of Philosophy, 1962.

Judson, Harry Pratt. "The Threat of German World-Politics." In *The University of Chicago War Papers*, no. 1. Chicago: University of Chicago Press, 1918.

Kallen, Horace Meyer, ed. *Creative Intelligence: Essays in the Pragmatic Attitude*. New York: Henry Holt, 1917.

Kemp Smith, Norman. "How Far is Agreement Possible in Philosophy?" *Journal of Philosophy, Psychology and Scientific Methods* 9, no. 26 (19 December 1912): 701–11.

Kennedy, David M. *Over Here: The First World War and American Society.* New York: Oxford University Press, 1980.

Kernan, W. Fergus. "The Peirce Manuscripts and Josiah Royce—A Memoir, Harvard, 1915–1916." *Transactions of the Charles S. Peirce Society* 1, no. 2 (Fall 1965): 90–95.

Kevles, Daniel J. "Testing the Army's Intelligence: Psychologists and the Military in World War I." *Journal of American History* 55, no. 3 (December 1968): 565–81.

Knight, Edgar W. "Mass Production of Ph.D.'s." *Outlook and Independent* 155, no. 6 (11 June 1930): 209–11, 236.

Kolata, Gina. *Flu: The Story of the Great Influenza Pandemic of 1918 and the Search for the Virus that Caused It.* New York: Farrar, Straus and Giroux, 1999.

Kolbe, Parke Rexford. *The Colleges in War Time and After: A Contemporary Account of the Effect of the War upon Higher Education in America.* New York: Appleton, 1919.

Kolesnik, Walter B. *Mental Discipline in Modern Education.* Madison: University of Wisconsin Press, 1962.

Kraushaar, Otto F. "Introduction [to Josiah Royce]." In *Classic American Philosophers*, edited by Max Harold Fisch, 181–99. Englewood Cliffs: Prentice-Hall, 1951.

Kuklick, Bruce. *Churchmen and Philosophers: From Jonathan Edwards to John Dewey.* New Haven, CT: Yale University Press, 1985.

———. *The Rise of American Philosophy: Cambridge, Massachusetts, 1860–1930.* New Haven, CT: Yale University Press, 1977.

Ladd, George Trumbull. *Elements of Physiological Psychology: A Treatise of the Activities and Nature of the Mind.* New York: Scribners, 1887.

———. *Introduction to Philosophy: An Inquiry after a Rational System of Scientific Principles in Their Relation to Ultimate Reality.* New York: Scribners, [1890] 1896.

———. "The Mission of Philosophy." *Philosophical Review* 14, no. 2 (March 1905): 113–37.

———. "President's Address before the New York Meeting of the American Psychological Association." *Psychological Review* 1, no. 1 (January 1894): 1–21.

———. *Psychology: Descriptive and Explanatory. A Treatise of the Phenomena, Laws, and Development of Human Mental Life.* 3rd ed. New York: Scribners, 1896.

Ladd-Franklin, Christine. "Epistemology for the Logician." In *Bericht über den III. internationalen Kongress für Philosophie*, edited by Theodor Elsenhans, 664–70. Heidelberg: Carl Winters Universitätsbuchhandlung, 1909.

Leary, David E. "Telling Likely Stories: The Rhetoric of the New Psychology, 1880–1920." *Journal of the History of the Behavioral Sciences* 23, no. 4 (October 1987): 315–31.

Leighton, Joseph Alexander. "Philosophy and the History of Philosophy." *Journal of Philosophy, Psychology and Scientific Methods* 6, no. 19 (16 September 1909): 519–24.

Leland, Waldo G. "The National Board for Historical Service." In *Annual Report of the American Historical Association for the Year 1919*, edited by Newton D. Mereness, 1:161–89. Washington DC: Government Printing Office, 1923.

Lewis, Clarence Irving. *An Analysis of Knowledge and Valuation*. La Salle, IL: Open Court, 1946.

Lloyd, Alfred Henry. "The Doctrinaire in Time of Crisis." *International Journal of Ethics* 26, no. 4 (July 1916): 482–99.

———. "The Function of Philosophy in Reconstruction." *Journal of Philosophy, Psychology and Scientific Methods* 16, no. 19 (11 September 1919): 505–18.

Lovejoy, Arthur Oncken. "On Some Conditions of Progress in Philosophical Inquiry." *Philosophical Review* 26, no. 2 (March 1917): 123–63.

———. "Organization of the American Association of University Professors." *Science*, n.s., 41 (29 January 1915): 151–54.

———. "Progress in Philosophical Inquiry." *Philosophical Review* 26, no. 5 (September 1917): 537–45.

———. *The Revolt against Dualism: An Inquiry concerning the Existence of Ideas*. La Salle, IL: Open Court, 1929.

———. "A Temporalistic Realism." In Adams and Montague, *Contemporary American Philosophy*, 2:85–105.

———. "The Thirteen Pragmatisms." Pts. 1 and 2. *Journal of Philosophy, Psychology and Scientific Methods* 5, no. 1 (2 January 1908): 5–12; 5, no. 2 (16 January 1908): 29–39.

Lowell, Abbott Lawrence. *At War with Academic Traditions in America*. Cambridge, MA: Harvard University Press, 1934.

Lutz, Ralph Haswell, ed. *Fall of the German Empire, 1914–1918*. 2 vols. Stanford, CA: Stanford University Press, 1932.

Madden, Edward H. *Chauncey Wright and the Foundations of Pragmatism*. Seattle: University of Washington Press, 1963.

———. "Common Sense School." In *Routledge Encyclopedia of Philosophy*, 2:446–48. 10 vols. New York: Routledge, 1998.

———. "The Metaphilosophy of Commonsense." *American Philosophical Quarterly* 20, no. 1 (January 1983): 23–36.

Marsden, George M. *The Soul of the American University: From Protestant Establishment to Established Nonbelief*. New York: Oxford University Press, 1994.

McCosh, James. *American Universities—What They Should Be*. (Inaugural Address at the College of New Jersey, Princeton, October 27, 1868.) San Francisco: Turnbull and Smith, 1869.

———. *First and Fundamental Truths: Being a Treatise on Metaphysics*. New York: Scribners, 1894.

———. *The New Departure in College Education*. New York: Scribners, 1885.

———. *Psychology: The Cognitive Powers*. New York: Scribners, 1886.

———. *Realistic Philosophy: Defended in a Philosophic Series*. 2 vols. New York: Scribners, 1887.

———. "The Scottish Philosophy, as Contrasted with the German." *Princeton Review*, 4th ser., 10 (1882): 326–44.

———. *The Scottish Philosophy: Biographical, Expository, Critical, from Hutcheson to Hamilton*. Hildesheim: Georg Olms Verlagbuchhandlung, [1875] 1966.

McDermott, John J. *Streams of Experience: Reflections on the History and Philosophy of American Culture*. Amherst: University of Massachusetts Press, 1986.

McDougall, William. *An Introduction to Social Psychology*. Boston: Luce, 1926.

McGilvary, Evander Bradley. *Toward a Perspective Realism*, edited by Albert G. Ramsperger. La Salle: Open Court, 1956.

McLaughlin, Andrew Cunningham. "Historians and the War." *Dial* 62 (17 May 1917): 427–28.

Mead, George Herbert. "The Conscientious Objector." Patriotism through Education Series # 33. New York: National Security League, 1917.

———. "Josiah Royce—A Personal Impression." *International Journal of Ethics* 27, no. 2 (January 1917): 168–70.

———. *The Philosophy of the Act*. Edited by Charles W. Morris, John M. Brewster, Albert M. Dunham, and David L. Miller. Chicago: University of Chicago Press, 1938.

———. *The Philosophy of the Present*. Edited by Arthur Edward Murphy. La Salle, IL: Open Court, 1932.

———. "The Psychological Bases of Internationalism." *Survey* 33 (1914–1915): 604–7. Reprinted in *George Herbert Mead: Essays on His Social Thought*, edited by John W. Petras, 151–61. New York: Teachers Colleges Press, 1968.

———. "The Psychology of Punitive Justice." *American Journal of Sociology* 23 (1917–1918): 577–602. Reprinted in *Selected Writings*, edited by Andrew J. Reck, 212–39. Indianapolis: Bobbs-Merrill, 1964.

———. "Social Work, Standards of Living and the War." *Proceedings of the National Conference of Social Work* (1918), 637–44.

Mecklin, John Moffatt. "Letter from Professor Mecklin." *Journal of Philosophy, Psychology, and Scientific Methods* 10, no. 20 (25 September 1913): 559–60.

———. *My Quest for Freedom*. New York: Scribners, 1945.

———. "The Problem of Christian Ethics." *International Journal of Ethics* 23, no. 3 (April 1913): 298–310.

Meiklejohn, Alexander. "Is Mental Training a Myth?" *Educational Review* 37, no. 2 (February 1909): 126–41.

———. "Philosophers and Others." *Philosophical Review* 34, no. 3 (May 1925): 262–80.

Mencken, Henry Louis. *The American Language: An Inquiry into the Development of English in the United States*. 4th ed. New York: Knopf, [1936] 1962.

———. *The American Language: An Inquiry into the Development of English in the United States—Supplement I*. New York Knopf, 1945.

Metzger, Walter P. *The Age of the University*. Part 2 of *The Development of Academic Freedom*, by Richard Hofstadter and Walter P. Metzger, 275–506. New York: Columbia University Press, 1955.

Meyer, D. H. *The Instructed Conscience: The Shaping of the American National Ethic*. Philadelphia: University of Pennsylvania Press, 1972.

Mills, C. Wright. *Sociology and Pragmatism: The Higher Learning in America.* Edited by Irving Louis Horowitz. New York: Oxford University Press, 1964.

Mills, Eugene S. *George Trumbull Ladd: Pioneer American Psychologist.* Cleveland, OH: Press of Case Western Reserve University, 1969.

Miner, J. B. "The Twenty-Fifth Anniversary of the Southern Society for Philosophy and Psychology." *Psychological Bulletin* 28, no. 1 (January 1931): 1–14.

Montague, William Pepperell. "Confessions of an Animistic Materialist." In Adams and Montague, *Contemporary American Philosophy,* 2:135–59.

———. *Great Visions of Philosophy: Varieties of Speculative Thought in the West from the Greeks to Bergson.* La Salle: Open Court, 1950.

———. "May a Realist Be a Pragmatist? I. The Two Doctrines Defined." *Journal of Philosophy, Psychology and Scientific Methods* 6, no. 17 (19 August 1909): 460–63.

———. "Philosophy in the College Course." *Educational Review* 40, no. 5 (December 1910): 488–98.

———. "Professor Royce's Refutation of Realism." *Philosophical Review* 11, no. 1 (January 1902): 43–55.

———. *The Ways of Things: A Philosophy of Knowledge, Nature, and Value.* New York: Prentice-Hall, 1940.

Moore, Addison Webster. "Bergson and Pragmatism." *Philosophical Review* 21, no. 4 (July 1912): 397–414.

———. "The Opportunity of Philosophy." *Philosophical Review* 27, no. 2 (March 1918): 117–33.

———. *Pragmatism and Its Critics.* Chicago: University of Chicago Press, 1910.

Moore, Henry T. "A Reply to [Sheldon's] 'The Defect of Current Democracy.'" *Journal of Philosophy, Psychology and Scientific Methods* 16, no. 21 (9 October 1919): 574–77.

Muirhead, John Henry, ed. *Contemporary British Philosophy: Personal Statements.* London: Allen & Unwin, 1924.

———, ed. *Contemporary British Philosophy: Personal Statements,* Second Series. London: Allen & Unwin, 1925.

———. "The Place of Philosophy in American Universities." *Philosophical Review* 36, no. 3 (May 1927): 209–15.

———. *The Platonic Tradition in Anglo-Saxon Philosophy: Studies in the History of Idealism in England and America.* New York: Macmillan, 1931.

Münsterberg, Hugo. Hugo Münsterberg Papers, Boston Public Library.

———. *The Peace and America.* New York: Appleton, 1915.

———. "The Problem of Beauty." *Philosophical Review* 18, no. 2 (March 1909): 121–46.

———. *Tomorrow: Letters to a Friend in Germany.* New York: Appleton, 1916.

———. *The War and America.* New York: Appleton, 1914.

Murphey, Murray G. "Toward an Historicist History of American Philosophy." *Transactions of the Charles S. Peirce Society* 15, no. 1 (Winter, 1979): 3–18.

Murphy, Arthur Edward. "Philosophical Scholarship." In *American Scholarship in the Twentieth Century,* edited by Merle E. Curti, 168–206. Cambridge, MA: Harvard University Press, 1953.

———. "The Professional Philosopher." In Blanshard et al., *Philosophy in American Education*, 69–86.

———. "The Situation in American Philosophy." In Blanshard et al., *Philosophy in American Education*, 43–65.

Murphy, Gardner. *An Historical Introduction to Modern Psychology*. 2nd ed. New York: Harcourt Brace, 1930.

Newcomer, Mabel. *A Century of Higher Education for American Women*. New York: Harper, 1959.

Nichols, Herbert. "The Psychological Laboratory at Harvard." *McClure's Magazine* 1, no. 5 (October 1893): 400–409.

Ogg, Frederic Austin. *Research in the Humanities and Social Sciences*. New York: Century, 1928.

Ormond, Alexander Thomas. *Concepts of Philosophy*. New York: Macmillan, 1906.

———. "Philosophy and Its Correlations." *Philosophical Review* 12, no. 2 (March 1903): 113–29.

Otto, Max Carl. *The Human Enterprise: An Attempt to Relate Philosophy to Daily Life*. New York: Crofts, 1940.

———. Review of *Contemporary American Philosophy*, edited by George Plimpton Adams and William Pepperell Montague. *International Journal of Ethics* 41, no. 2 (January 1931): 230–34.

Overstreet, Harry Allen. "Can Philosophy Come Back?" *Freeman* 8 (12 December 1923): 323–25.

———. "Ethical Clarifications through the War." *International Journal of Ethics* 28, no. 3 (April 1918): 327–46

Palmer, George Herbert. Introduction to Adams and Montague, *Contemporary American Philosophers*, 1:17–62.

———. "Josiah Royce." In *Contemporary Idealism in America*, edited by Clifford Barrett, 3–9. New York: Macmillan, 1932.

Palmer, George Herbert, and Ralph Barton Perry. "Philosophy." In *The Development of Harvard University since the Inauguration of President Eliot, 1869–1929*, edited by Samuel Eliot Morison, 3–32. Cambridge, MA: Harvard University Press, 1930.

Parrington, Vernon Louis. *Main Currents in American Thought: An Interpretation of American Literature from the Beginnings to 1920*. 3 vols. New York: Harcourt, Brace, 1930.

Pate, James L. "The Southern Society for Philosophy and Psychology." In *No Small Part: A History of Regional Organizations in American Psychology*, edited by James L. Pate and Michael Wertheimer, 1–19. Washington, DC: American Psychological Association, 1993.

Paulsen, Friedrich. *Introduction to Philosophy*. Translated by Frank Thilly. New York: Henry Holt, 1895.

Peabody, Selim H., William E. Sheldon, James H. Baker, and John S. Irwin. "The Elective System in Colleges." *Addresses and Proceeding —National Education Association of the United States* (1888), 268–75.

Peirce, Charles Sanders. *Collected Papers*. Edited by Charles Hartshorne, Paul Weiss, and Arthur W. Burks. 8 vols. Cambridge, MA: Harvard University Press, 1932–1958.

Perry, Edward Delavan. "The American University." In *Monographs on Education in the United States*, edited by Nicholas Murray Butler, #6. Albany: Lyon, 1904.

Perry, Ralph Barton. "The Ego-Centric Predicament." *Journal of Philosophy, Psychology and Scientific Methods* 7, no. 1 (6 January 1910): 5–14.

———. *The Free Man and the Soldier: Essays on the Reconciliation of Liberty and Discipline*. New York: Scribners, 1916.

———. *The Present Conflict of Ideals: A Study of the Philosophical Background of the World War*. New York: Longmans, Green, [1918] 1922.

———. *Present Philosophical Tendencies*. New York: Longmans, Green, 1912.

———. "Prof. Royce's Refutation of Realism and Pluralism." *Monist* 12, no. 4 (July 1902): 446–58.

———. "Realism in Retrospect." In Adams and Montague, *Contemporary American Philosophy*, 2:187–209.

Phelan, Gerald B. "Catholicism or Delusion." *Commonweal* 13 (1 April 1931): 605–7.

Philosophical Review: Index to Volumes I–XXXV. New York: Longmans Green, 1927.

Pillsbury, Walter Bowers. "The New Developments in Psychology in the Past Quarter Century." *Philosophical Review* 26, no. 1 (January 1917): 56–69.

Pitkin, Walter B. "Is Agreement Possible?" *Journal of Philosophy, Psychology and Scientific Methods* 9, no. 26 (19 December 1912): 711–15.

Pitts, Edward I. "The Profession of Philosophy in America." Ph.D. diss., Pennsylvania State University, 1979.

Pochmann, Henry A. *German Culture in America: Philosophical and Literary Influences, 1600–1900*. Madison: University of Wisconsin Press, 1957.

Pollitt, Daniel H., and Jordan E. Kurland. "Entering the Academic Freedom Arena Running: The AAUP's First Year." *Academe* (July–August 1998): 45–52.

Porter, Noah. *The American Colleges and the American Public*. New Haven, CT: Chatfield, 1870.

Pratt, James Bissett. "Professor Perry's Proof of Realism." *Journal of Philosophy, Psychology and Scientific Methods* 9, no. 21 (10 October 1912): 573–80.

Read, Conyers. "England and America." *The University of Chicago War Papers*, no. 6 (Chicago: University of Chicago Press, 1918.

Reuben, Julie A. *The Making of the Modern University: Intellectual Transformation and the Marginalization of Morality*. Chicago: University of Chicago Press, 1996.

Riley, Isaac Woodbridge. *American Philosophy: The Early Schools*. New York: Dodd, Mead, 1907.

Robinson, James Harvey. "The Elective System Historically Considered." *International Quarterly* 6 (1902): 191–201.

Rogers, Dorothy. "Before the APA: Women in the Development of Academic Philosophy in America." Paper presented at the Society for the Study of Women Philosophers' session at the Eastern Division meeting of the American Philosophical Association, December 2006.

Ross, Dorothy. *G. Stanley Hall: The Psychologist as Prophet*. Chicago: University of Chicago Press, 1972.

Ross, Earle Dudley. *Democracy's College: The Land-Grant Movement in the Formative State.* Ames: Iowa State University Press, 1942.

Royce, Josiah. "The Eternal and the Practical." *Philosophical Review* 13, no. 2 (March 1904): 113–42.

———. *The Hope of the Great Community.* New York: Macmillan 1916.

———. Introduction to *La Philosophie en Amérique* by L. van Becelaere, ix–xvii. New York: Eclectic Publishing, 1904.

———. "On Definitions and Debates." *Journal of Philosophy, Psychology and Scientific Methods* 9, no. 4 (15 February 1912): 85–100.

———. *Outlines of Psychology: An Elementary Treatise with Some Practical Applications.* New York: Macmillan, [1903] 1908.

———. "Present Ideals of American University Life." *Scribners Magazine* 10, no. 3 (September 1891): 376–88.

———. *The Problem of Christianity.* 2 vols. New York: Macmillan, 1913.

———. "The Recent University Movement in America." *Trans. of the Aberdeen Philosophical Society* 3 (1900): 131–49.

———. "Some Characteristic Tendencies of American Civilization." *Trans. of the Aberdeen Philosophical Society* 3 (1900): 194–217.

———. *The Spirit of Modern Philosophy: An Essay in the Form of Lectures.* Boston: Houghton, Mifflin, 1892.

———. *War and Insurance.* New York: Macmillan, 1914.

———. "What Should Be the Attitude of Teachers of Philosophy towards Religion?" *International Journal of Ethics* 13, no. 3 (April 1903): 280–85.

———. *The World and the Individual.* 2 vols. *I—The Four Historical Conceptions of Being* [1899]; *II—Man, Nature, and the Moral Order* [1901]. New York: Macmillan, 1904.

Royce, Josiah, and W. Fergus Kernan. "Charles Sanders Peirce." *Journal of Philosophy, Psychology and Scientific Methods* 13, no. 26 (21 December 1916): 701–9.

Rucker, Darnell. *The Chicago Pragmatists.* Minneapolis: University of Minnesota Press, 1969.

Sabine, George H. "Philosophical and Scientific Specialization." *Philosophical Review* 26, no. 1 (January 1917): 16–27.

Santayana, George. *Egotism in German Philosophy.* New York: Scribners, 1916.

———. "Philosophical Heresy." *Journal of Philosophy, Psychology and Scientific Methods* 12, no. 21 (14 October 1915): 561–68.

———. "The Spirit and Ideals of Harvard University." *Educational Review* 7, no. 4 (April 1894): 313–25.

Schmidt, George P. "Intellectual Crosscurrents in American Colleges, 1825–1855." *American Historical Review* 40, no. 1 (October 1936): 46–67.

———. *The Old Time College President.* New York: Columbia University Press, 1930.

Schmidt, Karl. "Agreement." *Journal of Philosophy, Psychology and Scientific Methods* 9, no. 26 (19 December 1912): 715–17.

———. "Concerning a Philosophical Platform." *Journal of Philosophy, Psychology and Scientific Methods* 6, no. 25 (9 December 1909): 673–85.

———."Concerning a Philosophical Platform: A Reply to Professor Creighton." *Journal of Philosophy, Psychology and Scientific Methods* 6, no. 9 (29 April 1909): 240–42.

Schmidt, Raymund, ed. *Die deutsche Philosophie der Gegenwart in Selbstdarstellungen.* 2 vols. Leipzig: Felix Meiner, 1921.

Schneider, Herbert Wallace. *A History of American Philosophy.* 2nd ed. New York: Columbia University Press, 1963.

———. "Philosophy." In *New International Year Book* (1917), edited by Frank Moore Colby, 539–42. New York: Dodd, Mead, 1918.

Schurman, Jacob Gould. "Prefatory Note." *Philosophical Review* 1, no. 1 (January 1892): 1–8.

Scripture, Edward Wheeler, "Methods of Laboratory Mind-Study." *Forum* 17, no. 6 (August 1894), 721–728.

———. *The New Psychology.* New York: Scribners, 1897.

———. *Thinking, Feeling, Doing.* Meadville, PA: Flood and Vincent, 1895.

Sellars, Roy Wood. *Critical Realism.* Chicago: Rand, McNally, 1916.

———. *Reflections on American Philosophy from Within.* Notre Dame: University of Notre Dame Press, 1969.

Sharples, S. P. "Some Reminiscences of the Lawrence Scientific School." *Harvard Graduates' Magazine* 26, no. 4 (June 1918): 532–40.

Sheldon, Wilmon Henry. "The Defect of Current Democracy." *Journal of Philosophy, Psychology and Scientific Methods* 16, no. 14 (3 July 1919): 365–79.

Skillman, David Bishop. *The Biography of a College, Being the History of the First Century of the Life of Lafayette College.* 2 vols. Easton, PA: Lafayette College, 1932.

Sloan, Douglas. "The Teaching of Ethics in the American Undergraduate Curriculum, 1876–1976." In *Education and Values,* edited by Douglas Sloan, 191–254. New York: Teachers College Press, 1980.

Small, Albion. "Americans and the World-Crisis." *The University of Chicago War Papers,* no. 2. Chicago: University of Chicago Press, 1918.

Smith, John E. "The New Need for a Recovery of Philosophy." In *The Spirit of American Philosophy,* rev. ed., 223–42. Albany: SUNY Press, **1983**.

Smith, Thomas Vernor. *The Philosophic Way of Life.* Chicago: University of Chicago Press, 1929.

Sokal, Michael M. "Origins and Early Years of the American Psychological Association, 1890–1906." *American Psychologist* 47, no. 2 (February 1992): 111–22.

Solomon, Barbara Miller. *In the Company of Educated Women: A History of Women and Higher Education in America.* New Haven, CT: Yale University Press, 1985.

Stern, Sheldon M. "William James and the New Psychology." In *Social Sciences at Harvard, 1860–1920: From Inculcation to the Open Mind,* edited by Paul Buck, 175–222. Cambridge, MA: Harvard University Press, 1965.

Storr, Richard J. *The Beginnings of Graduate Education in America.* Chicago: University of Chicago Press, 1953.

Strong, Charles Augustus. "Nature and Mind." In Adams and Montague, *Contemporary American Philosophy,* 2:313–29.

Thayer, Horace Standish. *Meaning and Action: A Critical History of Pragmatism.* 2nd ed. Indianapolis: Hackett, 1981.

Thayer, William Roscoe. Introduction to *Out of Their Own Mouths: Utterances of German Rulers, Statesmen, Savants, Publicists, Journalists, Poets, Business Men, Party Leaders and Soldiers,* edited by William Roscoe Thayer, xi–xviii. New York: Appleton, 1917.

Thilly, Frank. *A History of Philosophy.* New York: Henry Holt, 1914.

———. "Modern University Problems." *University of Missouri Bulletin* 32, no. 2 (20 January 1931).

———. "Psychology, Natural Science, and Philosophy." *Philosophical Review* 15, no. 2 (March 1906): 130–44.

———. "The Theory of Interaction." *Philosophical Review* 10, no. 2 (March 1901): 124–38.

———. "What is a University?" *Educational Review* 22, no. 5 (December 1901): 498–506.

———. "What Is Philosophy?" *Popular Science Monthly* 60 (April 1902): 513–20.

Thomas, M. Carey, "Education of Women." In *Monographs on Education in the United States,* edited by Nicholas Murray Butler, #7. Albany: Lyon, 1904.

Thwing, Charles Franklin. *The American and the German University: One Hundred Years of History.* New York: Macmillan, 1928.

———. *The American Colleges and Universities in the Great War, 1914–1919: A History.* New York: Macmillan, 1920.

———. "The Effect of the European War on Higher Learning in America." *Hibbert Journal* 14, no. 1 (October 1915): 79–94.

———. *A History of Higher Education in America.* New York: Appleton, 1906.

Titchener, Edward Bradford. "Psychology." In *Encyclopedia Americana,* 16 vols., edited by Frederick Converse Beach, 12: six pages [unpaginated]. New York: Americana, 1904.

———. "Psychology (physiological)." In Baldwin, *Dictionary of Philosophy and Psychology,* 2:390.

———. "Psychology (the new)." In Baldwin, *Dictionary of Philosophy and Psychology,* 2:391.

Townsend, Harvey Gates. *Philosophical Ideas in the United States.* New York: American Book, 1934.

Tufts, James Hayden. "Ethics and International Relations." *International Journal of Ethics* 28, no. 3 (April 1918): 299–313.

———. *The Ethics of Cooperation.* Boston: Houghton Mifflin, 1918.

———. "The Ethics of States." *Philosophical Review* 24, no. 2 (March 1915): 131–49.

———. "Forty Years of American Philosophy." *International Journal of Ethics* 48, no. 3 (April 1938): 433–38.

———. "Garman as a Teacher." *Journal of Philosophy, Psychology and Scientific Methods* 4, no. 10 (9 May 1907): 263–67.

———. *The Real Business of Living.* New York: Henry Holt, 1918.

———. Review of Morris Raphael Cohen, *Law and the Social Order,* and Felix S. Cohen, *Ethical Systems and Legal Ideals. Journal of Philosophy* 30, no. 23 (9 November 1933): 628–31.

————. *Selected Writings of James Hayden Tufts*, edited by James Campbell. Carbondale; Southern Illinois University Press, 1992.

————. "Wartime Gains for the American Family." New York: Russell Sage, 1919.

————. "What I Believe." In Adams and Montague, *Contemporary American Philosophy*, 2:333–53.

Turner, James. "Secularization and Sacralization: Speculations on Some Religious Origins of the Secular Humanities Curriculum, 1850–1900." In *The Secularization of the Academy*, edited by George M. Marsden and Bradley J. Longfeld, 74–106. New York: Oxford University Press, 1992.

Urban, Wilbur Marshall. "Progress in Philosophy in the Last Quarter Century." *Philosophical Review* 35, no. 2 (March 1926): 93–123.

Van Riper, Benjamin W. "Philosophy and Edification." *Journal of Philosophy, Psychology and Scientific Methods* 14, no. 20 (27 September 1917): 550–54.

Veysey, Laurence R. *The Emergence of the American University*. Chicago: University of Chicago Press, 1965.

Ward, James. *Naturalism and Agnosticism*. New York: Macmillan, 1899.

Werkmeister. William H. *A History of Philosophical Ideas in America*. New York: Ronald Press, 1949.

West, Andrew Fleming. "The American College." In *Monographs on Education in the United States*, edited by Nicholas Murray Butler, #5. Albany: Lyon, 1904.

Wiener, Philip P. *Evolution and the Founders of Pragmatism*. Cambridge, MA: Harvard University Press, 1949.

Wilshire, Bruce. *The Moral Collapse of the University: Professionalism, Purity, and Alienation*. Albany: SUNY Press, 1990.

Wilson, Daniel J. *Arthur O. Lovejoy and the Quest for Intelligibility*. Chapel Hill: University of North Carolina Press, 1980.

————. "Professionalization and Organized Discussion in the American Philosophical Association, 1900–1922." *Journal of the History of Philosophy* 17 (1979): 53–69.

————. *Science, Community, and the Transformation of American Philosophy, 1860–1930*. Chicago: University of Chicago Press, 1990.

Wilson, Logan. *The Academic Man: A Study in the Sociology of a Profession*. New York: Octagon Press, [1942] 1964.

Winterer, Caroline. *The Culture of Classicism: Ancient Greece and Rome in American Intellectual Life, 1780–1910*. Baltimore: Johns Hopkins University Press, 2002.

Witherspoon, John. *Lectures on Moral Philosophy*, edited by Varnum Lansing Collins. Princeton, NJ: Princeton University Press, [1795] 1912.

Woodbridge, Frederick James Eugene. "Pragmatism and Education." *Educational Review* 34, no. 3 (October 1907): 227–40.

————. "The Problem of Metaphysics." *Philosophical Review* 12, no. 4 (July 1903): 367–85.

————. "The Promise of Pragmatism." *Journal of Philosophy* 26, no. 20 (26 September 1929): 541–52.

Woody, Thomas, *A History of Women's Education in the United States*. 2 vols. Lancaster, PA: Science Press, 1929.

Yerkes, Robert Mearns. "Psychology in Relation to the War." *Psychological Review* 25, no. 2 (March 1918): 85–115.

———, ed. *Psychological Examining in the United States Army, Memoirs of the National Academy of Sciences* 15. Washington, DC: Government Printing Office, 1921.

Yoakum, Clarence S., and Robert Mearnes Yerkes, eds. *Army Mental Tests.* New York: Henry Holt, 1920.

Index

AAUP. *See* American Association of
University Professors
ACLS. *See* American Council of
Learned Societies
Adams, George Plimpton, 93, 260,
265 n.17, 303
and *Contemporary American
Philosophy*, 261–63
Adler, Felix, 33, 208, 299
Aesthetics, 125–26, 143–45
Albee, Ernest
on idealism, 126
on Lovejoy, 173–74, 177
Alexander, Hartley Burr, 32, 159,
263, 268, 297, 299, 303
and APA unification, 248–56, 258
as president of all three divisions of
APA, 252 n.2
on Carus Committee, 258, 265
on professionalized philosophy,
285
on World War I, 199–201, 213,
234, 243
American Association of University
Professors (AAUP), 98
American Council of Learned
Societies (ACLS), 270
American Historical Association, 63
and World War I, 231–32
American Journal of Psychology, 36,
50

American Philosophical Association
(APA) (national), 277, 290
founding, 255–56, 263–65
American Philosophical Association
(APA) (regional), 298–99
early meetings, 78–80
employment service, 80 n.7
founding, 64–70, 75, 277
leadership, 86–88
membership, 89–91
memorials, 91–94
name change to 'Eastern Division,'
254–55
participation in Liberty Loan
program, 229
purposes, 70–74
teaching, 70–71, 83–86, 187,
193–95
unification with the WPA, 245–65
women members, 89–90
American Philosophical Society
(APS), 66–67, 79 n.4
American Psychological Association
(AΨA), 40, 50, 252, 277,
294–95
founding, 55–63
in World War I, 229–231
Ames, Edward Scribner, 95, 184,
297
APA. *See* American Philosophical
Association

327